HTML

FOR THE WORLD WIDE WEB

5th Edition
with XHTML and CSS

VISUAL QUICKSTART GUIDE

Jan. 19, 2004

 **Peachpit Press**

by Elizabeth Castro

**HTML for the World Wide Web, Fifth Edition, with XHTML and CSS:
Visual QuickStart Guide**
by Elizabeth Castro

Peachpit Press
1249 Eighth Street
Berkeley, CA 94710
(510) 524-2178
(510) 524-2221 (fax)

Find us on the World Wide Web at: *http://www.peachpit.com*
Or check out Liz's Web site at *http://www.cookwood.com/*

To report errors, send a note to *errata@peachpit.com*

Peachpit Press is a division of Pearson Education

Copyright © 2003 by Elizabeth Castro
All images are copyright © 1997–2003 by Elizabeth Castro

Cover design: The Visual Group

Notice of rights

All rights reserved. No part of this book may be reproduced or transmitted in any form by any means, electronic, mechanical, photocopying, recording, or otherwise, without the prior written permission of the publisher. For information on getting permission for reprints and excerpts, contact *permissions@peachpit.com*.

Notice of liability

The information in this book is distributed on an "As is" basis, without warranty. While every precaution has been taken in the preparation of the book, neither the author nor Peachpit Press, shall have any liability to any person or entity with respect to any loss or damage caused or alleged to be caused directly or indirectly by the instructions contained in this book or by the computer software and hardware products described in it.

Trademarks

Visual QuickStart Guide is a registered trademark of Peachpit Press, a division of Pearson Education. Openwave, the Openwave logo, Openwave SDK, Openwave SDK Universal Edition, Openwave SDK, WAP Edition are trademarks of Openwave Systems Inc. All other trademarks are the property of their respective owners. Many of the designations used by manufacturers and sellers to distinguish their products are claimed as trademarks. Where those designations appear in this book, and Peachpit Press was aware of a trademark claim, the designations appear as requested by the owner of the trademark. All other product names and services identified throughout this book are used in editorial fashion only and for the benefit of such companies with no intention of infringement of the trademark. No such use, or the use of any trade name, is intended to convey endorsement or other affiliation with this book.

ISBN: 0-321-13007-3

0 9 8 7 6 5

Printed in the United States of America

For my parents
(all four of them!)
who didn't always agree,
but who supported me anyway.

Special thanks to:

Nancy Davis, at Peachpit Press, who I'm happy to report is not only my awesome editor, but also my friend.

Kate Reber and *Nolan Hester*, both formerly of Peachpit Press, for their help with earlier editions of this book.

The dedicated betatesters who poured through the drafts of my book and diligently pointed out errors and suggested improvements. In particular, I'd like to thank *Jennifer Simmons Wheelock* (http://www.wheelockweb.com), *Randal Rust* (http://www.r2communications.com), *Marc Seyon* (http://www.delime.com/milsweb/), *Andrew Stevens* (http://4serendipity.com), *Jonathon Isaac Swiderski* (http://dangercat.net/), *Elaine Nelson*, and *Deepak Sharma* (http://www.webjives.com). Thanks also to *Bob Sawyer*, *Morten Reiersen*, *John Kenneth Fisher*, *Andy J. Williams Affleck*, *Nicole E.M. Ramsey*, *Hugh Blair*, and *Ward Conant*.

The Web is an incredible resource. Not only do people share their knowledge freely on their Web sites, but they are also incredibly generous with their time, answering my questions. In particular, I'd like to thank *Alan Wood*, whose Unicode Resources Web site (http://www.alanwood.net/unicode/) was a major source of information for the Symbols and Non-English Characters chapter, *Eric Costello* (http://www.glish.com), who designed the beautiful example I used in the Layout with Styles chapter, *Jeffrey Zeldman*, whose online magazine, *A List Apart (http://www.alistapart.com)*, is an essential resource for Web designers, and *Arun Ranganathan*, the Netscape engineer who helped me with the Multimedia chapter. I could not have written this book without the specifications published by The World Wide Web Consortium (http://www.w3.org).

Andreu, for his feedback, for his great Photoshop tips, and for sharing his life with me.

Llumi and *Xixo*, for chasing cherry tomatoes and each other around my office and for helping me think up examples of HTML documents.

And all the readers of earlier versions of this book, who took the time to write me with accolades, questions, and suggestions.

Table of Contents

Table of Contents

Table of Contents

Table of Contents

Table of Contents

INTRODUCTION

The World Wide Web is the Gutenberg press of our time. Just about anyone can create their own Web site and then present it to the Internet public. Some Web pages belong to businesses with services to sell, others to individuals with information to share. You get to decide what your page will be like.

All Web pages are written with some form of HTML. HTML lets you format text, add graphics, sound, and video, and save it all in a Text Only or ASCII file that any computer can read. (Of course, to project video or play sounds, the computer must have the necessary hardware.) The key to HTML is in the *tags*, keywords enclosed in less than (<) and greater than (>) signs, that indicate what kind of content is coming up.

While there are many software programs that will create HTML code for you *(see page 462)*, learning HTML yourself means you'll never be limited to a particular program's features. Instead you'll be able to add whatever you need without having to struggle with confusing software or wait for software updates.

In this book, you'll find clear, easy-to-follow instructions that will take you through the process of creating Web pages step-by-step. It is ideal for the beginner, with no knowledge of HTML, who wants to begin to create Web pages.

If you're already familiar with HTML, this book is a perfect reference guide. You can look up topics in the hefty index and consult just those subjects about which you need more information.

The Internet, the Web, and HTML

Sure, you've heard of the Internet, but what is it exactly? Simply put, the Internet is a collection of computers that are all connected to each other. Some people, typically at universities and large companies, have 24-hour connections, while others use a modem to link their home computers during a certain amount of time each day. Regardless of the type of connection, once you're on, you and your computer become a part of the Internet and are linked to every other computer that's also connected at that moment.

The World Wide Web, for its part, is much more ethereal. It is an ever-changing, kaleidoscopic collection of hundreds of millions of documents, all of which reside someplace on the Internet and are written in some form of HTML.

HTML, or *HyperText Markup Language*, has two essential features—hypertext and universality. Hypertext means you can create a link in a Web page that leads the visitor to any other Web page or to practically anything else on the Internet. It means that the information on the Web can be accessed from many different directions. Tim Berners-Lee, the creator of the Web, wanted it to work more like a person's brain and less like a static source of data, such as a book.

Universality means that because HTML documents are saved as Text Only files, virtually any computer can read a Web page. It doesn't matter if your visitors have Macintosh or Windows machines, or whether they're on a Unix box or even a hand-held device like a Palm. The Web is open to all.

Open but Not Equal

However, while HTML is available to all, that doesn't mean that everyone experiences it the same way. It's something like Central Park in New York City. You and I can both go take a walk there. However, if you live in a penthouse apartment on Fifth Avenue and I sleep on a bench, our view of the park will be quite different.

So it is with HTML. While practically any computer can display Web pages, what those pages actually look like depends on the type of computer, the monitor, the speed of the Internet connection, and lastly, the software used to view the page: the *browser.* The most popular browsers today are Internet Explorer, Netscape Communicator, and Opera, with handhelds and PDAs on the way. Unfortunately, none of these displays a Web page exactly like the next. So it turns out it's not enough to design a beautiful park, you've also got to worry about your visitor's accommodations.

But as you worry, remember that your control is limited. While the New York City Tourist Board would like to ensure that everyone has a good time in their town, they're not handing out free vouchers for rooms at the Park Plaza Hotel, and some people wouldn't accept them even if they did, preferring instead a bed and breakfast or their sister's house. You get the idea. The moral is this: People will be viewing your pages with vastly different setups. Create your pages accordingly—so that the largest number of visitors can view your page as close to the way you want them to as is possible. This book will show you how.

The Browser Wars

Now imagine what would happen if each hotel and apartment building on Fifth Avenue staked out a bit of Central Park and put a fence around it, limiting access to its own residents. It's bad enough that those of us on park benches can only glimpse in to "exclusive" areas. But, there's also the problem that folks from one hotel can't get to the piece of park that belongs to the other hotel. Instead of a rich, public resource, teeming with rollerbladers, hot dog carts, and strolling elders, the park is divided into small, sterile, isolated lots. This is what is happening on the Web.

In 1994, Netscape put up the first fences on the Web in the so-called *browser wars*. In order to attract users, they threw universality to the wind and created a set of extensions to HTML that only Netscape could handle. For example, Web surfers using Netscape could view pages with colored text, photographs, and other improvements. Surfers with any other browser would get errors and funny looking results. Or nothing at all.

But people liked those extensions so much that they flocked to Netscape's "hotel". By 1996, it had become the most popular computer program in the world. Microsoft started fencing in its own chunk of the Web. Again, to attract users they added non-standard extensions that only Internet Explorer, Microsoft's browser, could recognize.

According to The Web Standards Project *(www.webstandards.org)*, founded by a coalition of top-flight designers disgusted with the increasing fragmentation of the Web, Web designers wasted an incredible 25% of their time devising workarounds for proprietary tags, writing multiple versions of pages to satisfy each browser, and simply educating their clients about the impossibility of creating certain effects for all browsers. It was a mess.

The Push for Standards

The Web's United Nations is an organization called the World Wide Web Consortium *(www.w3.org)*, often abbreviated as W3C, and directed by the Web's inventor, Tim Berners-Lee. Its aim is to convince the Web community of the importance of universality while attempting to satisfy its thirst for beautiful looking pages. They want to take down the fences.

Both Netscape Communications (now a part of America Online) and Microsoft are members of the W3C, as are other important Web-related companies, including Adobe and Macromedia (makers of some of the more important Web tools), and many others. The idea is that these companies come together and agree on the standards and then try to differentiate their products with speed, ease of use, price, or other features that don't turn the Web back into the tower of Babel.

HTML 3.2: Standardization begins

The W3C's first answer to the Web's balkanization was to standardize the proprietary extensions, including some in the official specifications and removing others altogether. At the same time, they encouraged browser manufacturers to support the official HTML specifications as closely as possible, so that a Web page written to standards would behave the same way across browsers.

The Push for Standards

HTML 4 and CSS

The W3C's next move was much more bold. The old version of HTML joined content, structure, and formatting instructions in a single document, which was simple but not very powerful. The W3C envisioned a new system in which formatting instructions could be saved separately from the content and structure and thus could be applied not just to a single paragraph or Web page but to an entire site, if so desired. So, in the new HTML version 4, the W3C marked most of the formatting elements for future removal from the specifications. These elements would henceforth be *deprecated*, and their use discouraged. At the same time, they created the new system for formatting instructions—called *Cascading Style Sheets*, or *CSS*—to fill the gap.

The original specifications for Cascading Style Sheets mostly limited themselves to recreating HTML effects. CSS Level 2, published in 1998, however, brought new capabilities, in particular the ability to position elements on a Web page with great precision. CSS could now not only recreate HTML's formatting, it could make professional looking layouts.

However, between proprietary extensions and just plain sloppy code, HTML pages themselves were still a mess. Most browsers bent over backward to accommodate them, always in slightly different ways, which just made the whole situation worse. And there was still no standard system for adding new features. HTML was simply not a sturdy enough platform upon which to build. The W3C decided that we all needed a bit of structure. Their answer was XML, or *Extensible Markup Language*.

XML and XHTML

From the outside, XML looks a lot like HTML, complete with tags, attributes, and values. But rather than serving as a language just for creating Web pages, XML is a language for *creating other languages*. You can use XML to design your own custom markup language which you can then use to format your documents. Your custom markup language will contain tags that actually describe the data that they contain.

And herein lies XML's power: If a tag identifies data, that data becomes available for other tasks. A software program can be designed to extract just the information that it needs, perhaps join it with data from another source, and finally output the resulting combination in another form for another purpose. Instead of being lost on an HTML-based Web page, labeled information can be reused as often as necessary.

But, as always, power comes with a price. XML is not nearly as lenient as HTML. To make it easy for XML *parsers*—software that reads and interprets XML data—XML demands careful attention to upper- and lowercase letters, quotation marks, closing tags and other minutiae. In addition, there are billions of Web pages already written in HTML and millions of servers and browsers that already know how to read them.

The solution was quite clever. The W3C rewrote HTML *in* XML. This new language has all of the features of HTML and thus can be understood by every browser on the planet. And since its entire lexicon comes from HTML, people who already know HTML only have to learn a few basic syntax rules before they're off and running. And at the same time, since it uses XML's syntax, it gains all of XML's power and flexibility and is a perfect foundation for CSS. It is the best of both worlds. It's name? XHTML.

The Push for Standards

The Real World

While XHTML and CSS are a powerful combination, there is one small wrench in the works: browser support. While it didn't seem to be much of a problem to add extensions willy-nilly, when it came down to serious and full support of the specifications, no browser has yet been up to the task. At the same time, it's important to note that they've come a long way.

Netscape 6, completely reformed from its extension madness days, now boasts the most complete support for CSS. Opera 6, though lesser known, is a fast, lean browser with excellent CSS support. And the market front-runner, Internet Explorer 6, is not far behind, although it still has a number of glaring bugs.

However, while current browsers finally support most of CSS, not everyone uses a current browser. While estimates vary, perhaps 10% of the Web-surfing public still use a browser with marginal CSS support, which may not sound like a lot until you translate it to the 50 million people it represents.

At the same time, we can't wait forever. One option, espoused by the folks at *A List Apart*[1], a leading Web design online magazine, is to write XHTML/CSS based pages that look brilliant on standards-compliant browsers and reasonable, if a bit simpler, on older browsers. A note appears in the pared down version explaining the situation and suggesting an upgrade. Whether that solution works for you depends on your circumstances and perhaps your boss.

[1] *http://www.alistapart.com/stories/tohell/*

What Should You Use?

And now an admission. I liked HTML. I thought it was great that you didn't have to obsess over punctuation. Maybe I'm just lazy, but I honestly believe that the Web's popularity is due in part to the fact that browsers cut us all some slack. It made it easy to write Web pages, and so all of us did. Now, two billion pages later, perhaps it's time to change our ways. Or perhaps not.

There are a lot of people out there that will tell you that HTML is evil and XHTML is the *only* solution. I think that's silly. XHTML is a great improvement over HTML. It's stronger, more flexible, more powerful, more likely to be supported in the future, and can be expanded to fit any need. But I'll tell you something. Sometimes you don't need to fill every need. Sometimes, you just want to publish a simple page without stressing over every last quotation mark.

Luckily there is a lot of middle ground. There are actually three standard flavors of both HTML and XHTML. The first, called *transitional*, allows the use of the deprecated tags. The second, called *frameset*, allows both the use of deprecated tags and the use of frames, which we'll discuss later in this book. The third flavor, *strict*, prohibits the use of any of the deprecated tags. You can combine each of these flavors in varying degrees with CSS. Which combination you choose may depend on several factors. (Keep reading.)

Deciding between HTML, XHTML, and CSS:

While I don't recommend using proprietary extensions—since they leave out part of your audience—there are a lot of other options. Here are some guidelines.

■ The bigger the site, the more important it is that you use CSS and XHTML. The former makes it easy to apply, edit, and update formatting across the entire site; the latter gives your page the structure it needs to make sure it lasts into the future.

■ Many companies and government agencies, including the U.S. government, require that your Web page fulfill specific *accessibility* requirements in order to make their sites available to people with disabilities. In these cases, you should adhere as closely as possible to XHTML strict, with CSS for formatting. And be sure to check the company's or agency's pertinent guidelines for details in your particular case.

■ Large commercial sites that want to reach the widest audience may opt for transitional XHTML, taking advantage of some deprecated tags' practically universal support, while banking on XHTML's rock-solid stability. These kinds of sites will very likely shift to the more powerful CSS as support continues to increase.

■ Small or personal sites may want to take advantage of HTML's easy going syntax along with CSS's powerful formatting and an occasional deprecated tag where necessary.

■ My personal choice is to use XHTML and CSS and a bare minimum of deprecated tags.

How This Book Works

If you've ever been to a different part of your country than where you're from, you've probably noticed how the folks there talk, well, a little funny. They use different words or they say them with a different accent. And yet, you understand them just fine even if you chuckle about it in the car afterwards. That's the way it is with HTML and XHTML. In their case, they share *precisely* the same vocabulary (to the letter) but have a slightly different syntax.

Since they are so similar, I'll teach you HTML and XHTML at the same time. I'll start by explaining the syntax differences that distinguish them. And then throughout the book I will explain the vocabulary that they share. In those explanations, I use the stricter XHTML syntax. You can either use it as is (to write XHTML), or opt for the looser HTML syntax (to write HTML). The choice is yours.

It would be tiresome to have to refer to *HTML and XHTML* all the time, so I have chosen to use the abbreviated *(X)HTML* to refer to both at once. In the few instances I use one of the individual names, you'll know that the information pertains to that language only and not to the other.

CSS is incorporated into the descriptions of (X)HTML—again, that means, *both* HTML and XHTML—as a natural extension and yet a separate tool. While the information about CSS is concentrated in Chapters 8–11, you'll find bits and pieces throughout the book, next to the part of (X)HTML to which it is most applicable.

I have taken pains to offer illustrations from all of the major browsers, on both platforms. While you may stick with one browser on your computer, there's no telling what your visitors will use. It's a good idea to get used to how other browsers treat (X)HTML.

How This Book Works

The HTML VQS Web Site

With the Web constantly changing, it seemed most appropriate to add a dynamic element to this book: the HTML VQS 5th Edition Web site *(http://www.cookwood.com/html/)*.

On my site, you'll find the full source code for every one of the examples in this book, including the (X)HTML and the CSS *(http://www.cookwood.com/html5ed/examples/)*, a list of errata, updates, articles, reviews and comments, a complete discussion of the new features in this edition, and even the full table of contents and index.

There are also several resources available on my site that I hope you'll enjoy, including color tables, symbol and character tables, pixel shims, and complete lists of both (X)HTML elements and attributes and of CSS properties and values.

Next, as I was writing this book, I amassed a collection of lesser tips and tricks that simply didn't fit on the appropriate page. I've made them all available on the site.

Finally, you'll find a lively Question and Answer board *(www.cookwood.com/html/qanda)* where you can post your most vexing questions—and easy ones too. While I hang out there and will do my best to answer, there is a dedicated team of Web designers who usually beat me to the punch. If you're so inclined, feel free to step in and answer questions yourself. Your help will be greatly appreciated.

See you on the Web!

WEB PAGE BUILDING BLOCKS

While Web pages have become increasingly complex, their underlying structure remains remarkably simple. A Web page is made up of three principal components: *text content,* the actual headers and paragraphs that appear on the page; occasional *references* to more complex content like links, images, and even Flash animations; and *markup*—instructions that describe how the content and references should be displayed. It is important to note that each of these components is comprised exclusively of text. This essential feature means that Web pages can be saved in text-only format and viewed on practically any browser on any platform. It guarantees the universality of the Web.

Web pages also include information about the language or script in which the text was written *(the encoding)* as well as the kind of the markup that describes it *(doctype).*

I will devote this chapter to explaining each of these important concepts.

Note: As I mentioned in the introduction, I use *(X)HTML* to simultaneously refer to both HTML 4 and XHTML 1.0 in situations where they have identical properties, as in "*(X)HTML*'s `table` element". On the other hand, for those instances in which I'm highlighting special characteristics unique to one or the other, I will use their individual names: "*XHTML* requires quotation marks around attribute values." For more details, consult *How This Book Works* on page 23.

Markup: Elements, Attributes, and Values

(X)HTML is an ingenious system of including information about the content right in a text document. This information—called *markup*, accounting for the *m* in (X)HTML—can include formatting instructions as well as details about the relationships between parts of the document. However, because the markup itself is comprised chiefly of text, the document is practically universally accessible.

XHTML has three principal types of markup: *elements*, *attributes*, and *values*. Later on in the book we'll also talk about *declarations* (see page 38) and *entities* (see page 340).

Elements

Elements are like little labels that identify and structure the different parts of a Web page: "This is a *header*, that thing over there is a *paragraph*, and that is *important* information." Some elements have one or more attributes, which further describe the purpose and content, if any, of the element.

Elements can contain text and/or other elements, or they can be empty. A non-empty element consists of an opening tag (the element's name and attributes, if any, enclosed in less than or greater than signs), the content, and a closing tag (a forward slash followed by the element's name, again enclosed in greater than and less than signs) **(Figure 1.1)**.

An empty element looks like a combination opening and closing tag, with an initial less than sign, the element's name followed by any attributes it may have, a space, a forward slash, and the final greater than sign **(Figure 1.2)**.

In XHTML, the closing tag is *always required* In HTML, it is sometimes optional. The corresponding section in this book for each element will provide the pertinent details.

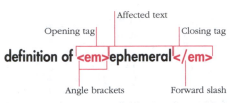

Figure 1.1 *Here is a typical (X)HTML element. The opening and closing tags surround the text that will be affected. In this case, the word "ephemeral" will be* emphasized, *which in most browsers means it will be set in italics.*

Figure 1.2 *Empty elements, like* img *shown here, do not surround any text content. They have a single tag which serves both to open and close the element. In HTML the final slash is optional. In XHTML it is required.*

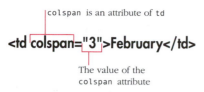

colspan is an attribute of td

The value of the colspan attribute

Figure 1.3 *Here is an element (for a table cell) with a simple attribute-value pair. Attributes are always located inside an element's opening tag. Their values should always be enclosed in quotation marks.*

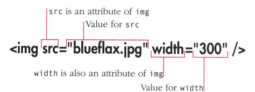

src is an attribute of img
Value for src
width is also an attribute of img
Value for width

Figure 1.4 *Some elements, like img shown here, can take one or more attributes, each with its own value. The order is not important. Separate each attribute-value pair from the next with a space.*

```
<link rel="stylesheet" type="text/css"
media="screen" href="blueflax.css" />
```

Predefined value

Figure 1.5 *Some attributes only accept specific values. For example, the media attribute in the link element can be set to screen, handheld, or print, among others, but you can't just make up a value for it. When an attribute is limited to a given list of values, XHTML requires that they always be written in lowercase letters.*

Attributes and Values

Attributes contain information *about* the data in the document, as opposed to being that data itself **(Figures 1.3 and 1.4)**. In XHTML, an attribute's value must always be enclosed in quotation marks. In HTML, quotes may sometimes be omitted (*see page 36*) though I recommend you always use them anyway.

While you'll find complete details about an attribute's acceptable values in the appropriate section of this book, let me give you an idea of the kinds of values you'll run into.

Some attributes can accept any value at all, others are more limited. Perhaps the most common are those that accept *enumerated* or predefined values. In other words, you must select a value from a standard list of choices **(Figure 1.5)**. In XHTML, enumerated values are always written in all lowercase letters. (In HTML, the case doesn't matter.)

Many attributes require a number or percentage for their value, particularly those describing size and length. A numeric value never includes units. Where units are applicable, as in the height of text or the width of an image, they are understood to be pixels.

The attributes controlling color can contain values that are either a color name or a hexadecimal representation of the red, green, and blue content of the color. You can find a list of the sixteen predefined color names as well as a selection of hex colors on the inside back cover of this book. You can find instructions for creating your own hex colors on page 46. Note that (X)HTML does not support numeric or percentage values for color.

Some attributes reference other files and thus must contain values in the form of a URL, or *Uniform Resource Locator*, a file's unique address on the Web. We'll talk more about URLs beginning on page 45.

Markup: Elements, Attributes, and Values

Block vs Inline

An element can be *block-level* or *inline*. If it is block-level, it will always be displayed on a new line, like a new paragraph in a book; if it is inline, it will be displayed in the current line, like the next word in a paragraph.

Block-level elements are considered the bigger structural pieces of your Web page, and as such can usually contain other block-level elements, inline elements, and text. Inline elements, in contrast, can generally only contain other inline elements and text.

(Elements can also be *list-items*, which is considered distinct from block-level or inline, but it seems such a small category as to hardly warrant discussion outside of Chapter 13, *Lists*.)

```
<div><img src="blueflax.jpg" alt="Blue Flax (Linum lewisii)" width="300" height="175" />

<p>I am continually amazed at the beautiful, delicate Blue Flax that somehow took hold in my garden.

They are awash in color every morning, yet not a single flower remains by the afternoon.

They are the very definition of <em>ephemeral</em>.</p>

<p>&copy; 2002 by Blue Flax Society.</p>

</div>
```

Figure 1.6 *The block-level elements, shown here highlighted in bold, are* div *and* p. *The inline elements, highlighted but without bold, are* img *and* em.

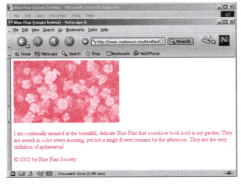

Figure 1.7 *Each block-level element starts on a new line. The inline elements (the image and the italic text) continue the line begun by the block-level element in which they're contained.*

```
<div>
    <img src="blueflax.jpg" ... />
    <p>... of
        <em>ephemeral</em>
    </p>
    <p>... by Blue Flax Society</p>
</div>
```

Figure 1.8 *The* div *element is parent to the* img *and both* p *elements. Conversely, the* img *and* p *elements are children (and descendants) of the* div*. The first* p *element is parent to the* em *tag. The* em *is a child of the first* p *and also a descendant (but not a child) of the* div*.*

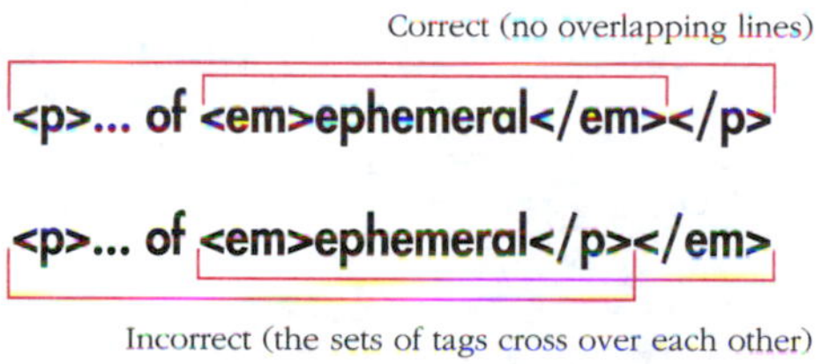

Correct (no overlapping lines)

`<p>... of <em>ephemeral</em></p>`

`<p>... of <em>ephemeral</p></em>`

Incorrect (the sets of tags cross over each other)

Figure 1.9 *Elements must be properly nested. If you open* p *and then* em*, you must close* em *before you close* p*.*

Parents and Children

If one element contains another, it is considered to be the *parent* of the enclosed, or *child* element. Any elements contained in the child element are considered *descendants* of the outer, parent element **(Figure 1.8)**. You can actually create a family tree of a Web page, that both shows the hierarchical relationships between each element on the page and uniquely identifies each element.

This structure is a key feature of (X)HTML code and facilitates adding style to the elements (which we'll introduce on page 41) and applying JavaScript effects to them (briefly discussed in Chapter 19, *JavaScript Essentials*).

It is important to note that when elements contain other elements, each element must be properly *nested*, that is fully contained within its parent. Whenever you use a closing tag, it should correspond to the last unclosed opening tag. In other words, first open A then open B, then close B, and then close A **(Figure 1.9)**.

Markup: Elements, Attributes, and Values

A Web Page's Text Content

The text contained within elements is perhaps a Web page's most basic ingredient. If you've ever used a word processor, you've typed some text. Text in an (X)HTML page, however, has some important differences.

First, (X)HTML compresses extra spaces or tabs into a single space and either converts returns and line feeds into a single space or ignores them altogether **(Figures 1.10 and 1.11)**.

Next, HTML used to be restricted to ASCII characters—basically the letters of the English language, numerals, and a few of the most common symbols. Accented characters (common to many languages of Western Europe) and many everyday symbols had to be created with special character references like **é** (for *é*) or **©** (for ©).

Nowadays, you have two options. You can still use character references for maximum compatibility or you can simply type most characters and then encode your (X)HTML files in *Unicode*, and particularly with UTF-8, which is explained on pages 334–335 **(Figure 1.12)**. Because Unicode is a superset of ASCII—that is, everything ASCII is, and a lot more—Unicode-encoded documents are compatible with existing browsers and editors. Browsers that don't understand Unicode will interpret the ASCII portion of the document properly, while browsers that do understand Unicode—Netscape and IE 4+—will display the non-ASCII portion as well. (See Chapter 20, *Symbols and Non-English Characters*.)

The only symbol that you *must* not type in directly is the **&**. Since it has special meaning in (X)HTML, namely to begin those character references, it *must always* be expressed as **&** when used as text, as in *AT&T*. For more details, consult *Adding Characters from Outside the Encoding* on page 340.

```
<div><img src="blueflax.jpg" alt="Blue Flax (Linum
lewisii)" width="300" height="175" />

<p>I am continually amazed at the beautiful,
delicate Blue Flax that somehow took hold in my
garden.

They are awash in color every morning, yet not a
single flower remains by the afternoon.

They are the very definition of
<em>ephemeral</em>.</p>

<p>&copy; 2002 by Blue Flax Society.</p>

</div>
```

Figure 1.10 *The text content is basically anything outside of the markup. Note that each line happens to be separated with a carriage return. Also, I've used a special character reference © for the copyright symbol to ensure that it is properly displayed no matter how I save this document.*

Figure 1.11 *Note how the extra returns are ignored when the document is viewed with a Web browser, the text appears otherwise as expected, and the character reference is replaced by the corresponding symbol (©).*

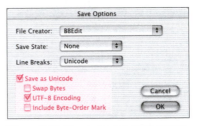

Figure 1.12 *If you save your Web page in Unicode with the UTF-8 encoding, you don't have to bother with character references as in Figure 1.10.*

```
<div><img src="blueflax.jpg" alt="Blue Flax (Linum
lewisii)" width="300" height="175" />

<p>I am continually amazed at the beautiful,
delicate Blue Flax that somehow took hold in my
garden.

They are awash in color every morning, yet not a
single flower remains by the afternoon.

They are the very definition of
<em>ephemeral</em>.</p>

<p>&copy; 2002 by Blue Flax Society.</p>

</div>
```

Figure 1.13 *In this (X)HTML document, there is a reference to a file called* blueflax.jpg, *which the browser will
access, open, and load when it loads the rest of the page.*

Figure 1.14 *Images, and other non-text content, are
referenced from a Web page and the browser displays
them together with the text.*

Links, Images, and Other Non-Text Content

Of course, what makes the Web so vibrant are the links from one page to another, the images, Flash animations, RealAudio trans-missions, QuickTime movies, and more. Instead of actually enclosing the external files in the (X)HTML file, these files are saved independently and are simply *referenced* from within the page. Since the reference is nothing more than text, the (X)HTML file remains universally accessible.

Most browsers can handle links and images without any trouble. They can't necessarily handle every other kind of file, however. If you reference a file that your visitor's browser doesn't understand, the browser will usually try to find a *plugin* or *helper application*—some appropriate program on the visitor's computer—that is capable of opening that kind of file. You can also give browsers extra information about how to download plugins for viewing particular files if the visitor doesn't already have one on their computer.

We'll cover images in Chapters 5 and 6 (*Creating Web Images* and *Using Images*, respectively), and plugins and helper applica-tions in Chapter 17, *Multimedia*.

File Names

Like any other text document, Web pages have a file name that identifies the documents to you, your visitors, and to your visitors' Web browser. There are a few tips to keep in mind when assigning file names to your Web pages that will help you organize your files, make it easier for your visitors to find and access your pages, and ensure that their browsers view the pages correctly.

Use lowercase file names

Since the file name you choose for your Web page determines what your visitors will have to type in order to get to your page, you can save your visitors from inadvertent typos (and headaches) by using only lowercase letters in your file names. It's also a big help when you go to create links between your pages yourself. If all your file names have only small letters, it's just one less thing you'll have to worry about.

Use the proper extension

The principal way a browser knows that it should read a text document as a Web page is by looking at its extension: .htm or .html. If the page has some other extension, like say ".txt", the browser will treat it as text, and show all your nice code to the visitor.

- Macintosh users—unless you're on a Mac server and *all* your visitors use Macs—this goes for you too.

- Windows folks, be aware that Windows doesn't always reveal a document's real extension. Change your Folder Options, if necessary, so you can see extensions.

- Only folks on Windows 3.1 are limited to .htm. Practically everyone else can use either .htm or .html without problem. Just be consistent to avoid having to remember which one you used.

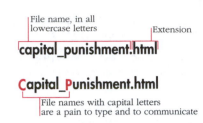

File name, in all lowercase letters | Extension

capital_punishment.html

Capital_Punishment.html
File names with capital letters are a pain to type and to communicate

Figure 1.15 *Remember to use all lowercase letters for your file names and to consistently add either the .htm or .html extension. Mixing upper and lowercase letters makes it harder for your visitors to type the proper address and find your page.*

http://www.yoursite.com/WebPages/ TORTURE/Capital_Punishment.html

Figure 1.16 *Use all lowercase letters for your directories and folders as well. The key is consistency. If you don't use uppercase letters, your visitors (and you) don't have to waste time wondering, "Now, was that a capital C or a small one?"*

Figure 1.17 *Your basic URL contains a scheme, server name, path, and file name.*

Figure 1.18 *A URL with a trailing forward slash and no file name points to the default file in the last directory named (in this case the* liz *directory). Some common default file names are* index.html *and* default.htm.

Figure 1.19 *When the user clicks this URL, the browser will begin an FTP transfer of the file* prog.exe.

Figure 1.20 *A URL for a newsgroup looks a bit different. There are no forward slashes after the scheme and colon, and generally, there is no file name. (Although you could add the message number or ID, a message's extremely short lifespan limits its usefulness as a link.)*

Figure 1.21 *A URL for an e-mail address is similar in design to a newsgroup URL (Figure 1.20); it includes the* mailto *scheme followed by a colon but no forward slashes, and then the e-mail address itself.*

Figure 1.22 *To reference a file on a local Windows machine, use the* file *scheme. For Macintosh, use* file:///Harddisk/path/filename. *No vertical bar is required. (This sometimes works for Windows as well.)*

URLs

Uniform resource locator, or URL, is a fancy name for *address*. It contains information about where a file is and what a browser should do with it. Each file on the Internet has a unique URL.

The first part of the URL is called the *scheme*. It tells the browser how to deal with the file that it is about to open. One of the most common schemes you will see is HTTP, or *Hypertext Transfer Protocol*. It is used to access Web pages **(Figure 1.17)**.

The second part of the URL is the name of the server where the file is located, followed by the path that leads to the file and the file's name itself. Sometimes, a URL ends in a trailing forward slash with no file name given **(Figure 1.18)**. In this case the URL refers to the default file in the last directory in the path (which generally corresponds to the home page), often called *index.html* or *default.htm*.

Other common schemes are HTTPS, for secure Web pages; FTP (File Transfer Protocol) for downloading files from the Net **(Figure 1.19)**; News, for sending and reading messages posted to a Usenet newsgroup **(Figure 1.20)**; Mailto, for sending electronic mail **(Figure 1.21)**; and File, for accessing files on a local hard disk **(Figure 1.22)**.

A scheme is generally followed by a colon and two forward slashes. Mailto and News are exceptions; these take only a colon.

Notice that the File scheme uses three slashes. That's because the host, which in other schemes goes between the second and third slashes, is assumed to be the local computer. Always type schemes in lowercase letters.

Absolute URLs

URLs can be either absolute or relative. An *absolute URL* shows the entire path to the file, including the scheme, server name, the complete path, and the file name itself. An absolute URL is analogous to a complete street address, including name, street and number, city, state, zip code, and country. No matter where a letter is sent from, the post office will be able to find the recipient. In terms of URLs, this means that the location of the absolute URL itself has no bearing on the location of the actual file referenced—whether it is in a Web page on your server or on mine, an absolute URL will look exactly the same.

When you're referencing a file from someone else's server, you'll always use an absolute URL. You'll also need to use absolute URLs for FTP sites, newsgroups, and e-mail addresses—in short, any kind of URL that doesn't use an HTTP protocol.

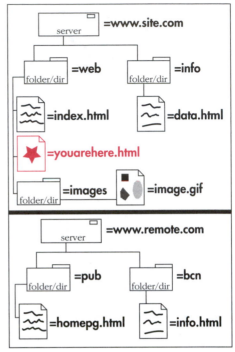

Figure 1.23 *The document that contains the URLs—* youarehere.html *in this case—is the reference point for relative URLs. In other words, relative URLs are relative to that file's location on the server. Absolute URLs don't care where they are located.*

File name	Absolute URL (can be used anywhere)	Relative URL (only works in *youarehere.html*)
index.html	www.site.com/web/index.html	index.html
image.gif	www.site.com/web/images/image.gif	images/image.gif
data.html	www.site.com/info/data.html	../info/data.html
homepg.html	www.remote.com/pub/homepg.html	*(none: use absolute)*
info.html	www.remote.com/bcn/info.html	*(none: use absolute)*

Absolute URLs vs. Relative URLs

Inside the current folder, there's a file called *index.html*

"index.html"

Figure 1.24 *The relative URL for a file in the same folder (see Figure 1.23) as the file that contains the link is just the file's name and extension.*

Inside the current folder there's a folder called "images"...

"images/image.gif"

...that contains... ...a file called *image.gif*

Figure 1.25 *For a file that is within a folder inside the current folder (see Figure 1.23), add the folder's name and a forward slash in front of the file name.*

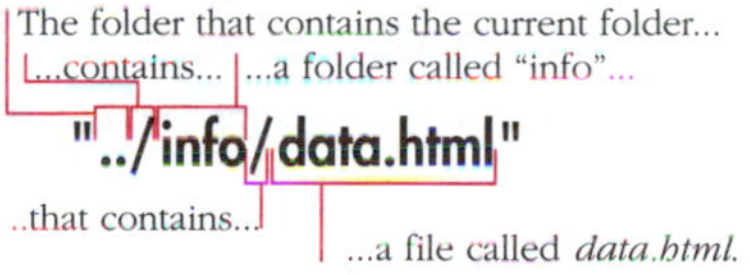

The folder that contains the current folder...
...contains... ...a folder called "info"...

"../info/data.html"

..that contains... ...a file called *data.html.*

Figure 1.26 *This file, as you can see in Figure 1.23, is in a folder that is inside the folder that contains the current folder (whew!). In that case, you use two periods and a slash to go up a level, and then note the subdirectory, followed by a forward slash, followed by the file name.*

Relative URLs

To give you directions to my neighbor's house, instead of giving her complete address, I might just say "it's three doors down on the right". This is a *relative* address—where it points to depends on where the information is given from. With the same information in a different city, you'd never find my neighbor.

In the same way, a *relative URL* describes the location of the desired file with reference to the location of the file that contains the URL itself. So, you might have the URL say something like "show the xyz image that's in the same directory as the current file".

Thus, the relative URL for a file that is in the same directory as the current file (that is, the one containing the URL in question) is simply the file name and extension **(Figure 1.24)**. You create the URL for a file in a subdirectory of the current directory with the name of the subdirectory followed by a forward slash and then the name and extension of the desired file **(Figure 1.25)**.

To reference a file in a directory at a *higher* level of the file hierarchy, use two periods and a forward slash **(Figure 1.26)**. You can combine and repeat the two periods and forward slash to reference any file on the same hard disk as the current file.

Generally, for files on the same server, you should always use relative URLs. They're much easier to type and they make it easy to move your pages from a local system to a server—as long as the relative position of each file remains constant, the links will work correctly.

One added advantage of relative URLs is that you don't have to type the scheme—as long as it's HTTP.

URLs

HTML vs XHTML

I like to imagine HTML as a laid-back don't-sweat-the-details kind of person. Perhaps not quite as hard-working as XHTML, but much happier and at ease with herself. XHTML, on the other hand is downright uptight. Always vigilant, never taking a rest. Sure, she gets more done, but what a price!

Before I go off the deep end with my personification of Web page code types, let me tell you the specifics. For starters, know that HTML 4 and XHTML 1.0 use *precisely the same* elements, attributes, and values. The difference is in the syntax.

- Where HTML doesn't care if you use the `html`, `head` and `body` elements and `DOCTYPE`, XHTML requires them.

- Where HTML lets you omit some closing tags, XHTML insists on them for every element, even empty ones. For the best compatibility with browsers, add a space and / to empty elements and include an independent closing tag for non-empty elements **(Figures 1.27–1.30)**. Note that the slash is not strictly valid in empty elements in HTML, though all browsers I've seen simply ignore it.

- Where HTML lets you omit quotes around attribute values that contain just letters, numbers and four simple symbols (-, ., _, and :), XHTML gets nightmares (and generates errors) if you leave quotes out **(Figures 1.31 and 1.32)**.

- Where HTML is flexible about case, XHTML is not, demanding that all elements, attributes, and predefined values be in lowercase **(Figures 1.33 and 1.34)**.

- Where HTML allows you to omit values that have the same name as the attribute, XHTML insists that all values be stated explicitly **(Figures 1.35 and 1.36)**.

Figure 1.27 *In HTML, some elements, like p, do not requiring a closing tag. Subsequent p tags implicitly close earlier ones.*

Figure 1.28 *In XHTML, all elements must have closing tags.*

Figure 1.29 *In HTML, empty elements do not have a final slash, though browsers won't complain if they do.*

Figure 1.30 *In XHTML, even empty elements must have a closing tag. While an independent closing tag for an empty element, like </img>, would be technically correct, adding a space and / to the single img tag ensures compatibility with non-XHTML-savvy browsers.*

```
<img src=blueflax.jpg alt="Blue Flax (Linum
lewisii)" width=300 height=175 align=left>
```

Figure 1.31 *In HTML, attribute values only need to be quoted when they contain spaces or other special characters (anything besides letters, numbers, hyphens, periods, underscores, or colons). So, in this example, only the* alt *attribute's value must be quoted (though it wouldn't hurt to quote all of them).*

```
<img src="blueflax.jpg" alt="Blue Flax (Linum
lewisii)" width="300" height="175" align="left" />
```

Figure 1.32 *In XHTML, all attribute values must always be enclosed in quotes.*

```
<IMG SRC=blueflax.jpg ALT="Blue Flax (Linum
lewisii)" width=300 height=175 align=LEFT>
```

Figure 1.33 *In HTML, it doesn't matter if you write element names, attribute names, or predefined values in upper or lowercase.*

```
<Img src="blueflax.jpg" alt="Blue Flax (Linum
lewisii)" width="300" height="175" align="left" />
```

Figure 1.34 *In XHTML, all element names, attribute names, and predefined values must be written in lowercase.*

```
<hr width=75% noshade>
```

Figure 1.35 *In HTML, some attributes, like* noshade *shown here, don't require any value.*

```
<hr width="75%" noshade="noshade" />
```

Figure 1.36 *In XHTML, attribute values must be stated explicitly. For those attributes that in HTML have no value, simply repeat the attribute's name as its value.*

What do you get for your troubles?

You might be wondering if it's worth it to worry about every last quotation mark. The answer is, it depends.

XHTML's rigidity affords a lot of advantages. Think of a clean workshop, with hammers and screwdrivers hanging in their places on the wall and all the nuts and bolts in labeled containers. It's so easy to find what you need that it makes projects a hundred times easier. Similarly, XHTML helps you keep your code consistent, well structured, and free of non-standard tags, which in turn makes it easier to update and edit, to format with CSS, to generate from or convert into a database, and to adapt for other systems, like handhelds and aural browsers.

In addition, XHTML is a logical step in the transition from HTML to XML, since it uses familiar HTML elements and attributes together with modern XML syntax. And since XHTML is the new standard, you can be sure that it will be used with other new and future technologies.

Perhaps one of XHTML's most important gifts is that its insistence on standards makes it more likely to be properly and consistently supported by current browsers, on all platforms—which makes good business sense. And since Web page accessibility is now required by U.S. law, and the laws of many other nations, it is something that should not be ignored. For more information on accessibility laws, visit the W3C Web Accessibility Initiative at *http://www.w3.org/WAI/*.

For more details about why standards matter, I recommend a trip to The Web Standards Project (*http://www.webstandards.org*), a consortium of designers turned diplomats determined to end the browser wars, and Jeffrey Zeldman's *A List Apart*, an excellent online magazine for Web designers (*http://www.alistapart.com*).

HTML vs XHTML

Versions, flavors, and DOCTYPE

There are three current flavors of both HTML 4 and XHTML 1.0: *strict, transitional,* and *frameset*. In an attempt to separate structure from formatting, the W3C has been earmarking some elements for eventual removal from the specifications. (X)HTML strict is characterized by its prohibition of these so-called *deprecated* tags. The only difference between transitional and frameset, both of which consider deprecated tags to be valid, is that the latter allows frames (which we discuss in Chapter 15, *Frames*).

Does it matter which version you use? The flip answer is "not to me". I think it's perfectly reasonable to use HTML and depend on its easy-going nature if you're writing a personal site. If you want your pages to follow strict standards, take advantage of XHTML's ability to connect to databases and the like, work well with styles *(see page 41)*, and be easily updated for future systems, use XHTML.

Likewise, if you use deprecated tags, you should use the transitional flavor of either HTML or XHTML. No deprecated tags? Use strict. If your site uses frames *(see page 241)*, use the frameset flavor. Note that there is no strict flavor that allows frames—which clues you in about what the W3C thinks of them.

You can state which version and flavor you're using in your document by using a DOCTYPE *declaration (see page 60)*. Once that information is part of your Web page, you can use a validator to determine if the code used in your page actually corresponds to the code allowed for that version and flavor. Validators are a great way to check for typos and in general, to make sure your code is correct. For more details, see page 394.

Note that there are earlier versions of HTML (3.2 and earlier), but they are outdated and not particularly useful.

```
<!DOCTYPE html

    PUBLIC "-//W3C//DTD XHTML 1.0
Transitional//EN"

    "http://www.w3.org/TR/xhtml1/DTD/xhtml1-
transitional.dtd">
```

Figure 1.37 *Here is the official* DOCTYPE *for XHTML transitional documents. You can find a list of* DOCTYPE *declarations on my Web site. (They're rather a drag to type in manually.)*

```
body {background:url(bg_flax.jpg) bottom right no-repeat}

p {font-family: "Trebuchet MS", "Helvetica", sans-serif; font-weight: bold; color:3366cc; }

img {float:left;margin-right:10px}
```

Figure 1.38 *Some browsers, notably Internet Explorer, do not care if you leave out the initial hash sign (#) for a hexadecimal color. While you may think that's nice of them, it encourages Web developers to write incorrect code which then breaks on other browsers.*

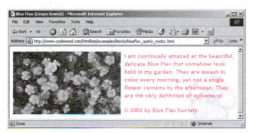

Figure 1.39 *If you omit the* DOCTYPE, *Explorer continues to act in its non-standard, quirky way, and views the text color correctly—as dark blue (shown here in red).*

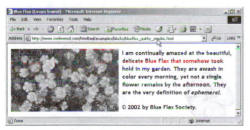

Figure 1.40 *If you use the* DOCTYPE, *IE assumes you want it to follow the standards, and so it ignores the faulty color value (and displays the text as black).*

Figure 1.41 *If you decide to clean up your faulty CSS, and add the missing # symbol, then you should use the* DOCTYPE *in the corresponding document since IE can view your document properly in standards mode.*

The DOCTYPE and Standards vs. Quirks mode

In the old days, when each browser had its own way of interpreting HTML and CSS, Web designers often used workarounds or *hacks* that depended on a browser's quirky behavior in order to create a desired effect on a Web page. Now that browsers for the most part support the (X)HTML and CSS standards, designers no longer need to rely on such hacks and can take advantage of the power of standards to control the display of their new pages.

What becomes, however, of the millions upon millions of existing pages designed for quirky browsers? Instead of displaying these pages according to standards, which might ruin their quirk-dependent designs, Explorer and Netscape 6 revert to their old quirky ways in order to display these pages "properly"—that is, how they were designed, but not according to standards. (Opera has no quirks mode.)

And how can a browser tell if a page might rely on quirks? It looks for the DOCTYPE declaration at the top of the page. If it finds a proper DOCTYPE declaration, it assumes the page has been designed using all the power of standards, and displays it accordingly. This is called *standards* mode (or sometimes *strict* mode, though this is more confusing since it has nothing to do with strict (X)HTML). If there is no proper DOCTYPE declaration (or if it is omitted entirely), the browser assumes the page is old-fashioned and relies on soon to be obsolete browser bugs, and displays it in that way. This is called *quirks* mode.

These two modes allow you to write standards-based pages for the future without losing your quirks-based pages of the past. I'll show you how to write appropriate DOCTYPE declarations on page 60.

Versions, flavors, and DOCTYPE

The Default Display of (X)HTML

Every Web browser has a default system for displaying each kind of (X)HTML element. While the system may vary from browser to browser, they all maintain the basic structure that you set forth in the Web page.

So, for example, a level one header (h1) will always be set larger than a level two header (h2), which will always be larger than a level three header (h3). Similarly, an em element will always be set off from the surrounding text in order to emphasize it.

That doesn't mean that the h1 element will always be in say, 24pt Times, or that emphasis will always be achieved with italics. While the default display systems are very similar on all personal computer-based browsers—including Explorer, Netscape, and Opera on both Macs and PCs **(Figure 1.42)**, they are quite different on PDAs, cell phones, and of course, on aural browsers. And that's a good thing. The structure of the Web page is maintained but its display is adapted to fit the browser on which it appears. And that means your Web page is universally accessible and intelligible.

It doesn't mean, however, that your Web page is a work of art. A browser's default display system is typically quite generic. Luckily you can override that system by applying *styles* to your elements. We'll get to them next.

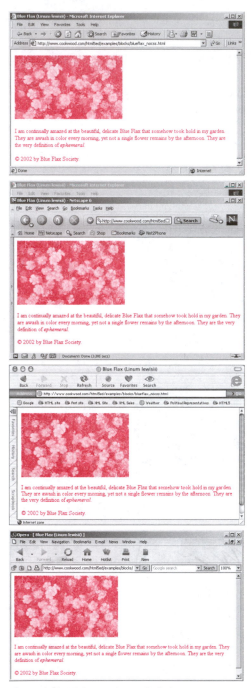

Figure 1.42 *With no styles applied, the text appears after the image, in its default font and color. Most current versions of major browsers have identical defaults.*

The selector determines which elements the rule is applied to.

This rule has three declarations.

```
p {
    font-family: "Trebuchet MS",
      "Helvetica", sans-serif;
    font-weight: bold;
    color: #3366cc;
}
```

Each declaration has a property name, a colon, one or more values, and a final semicolon.

The opening and closing curly brackets enclose the declarations.

Figure 1.43 *Here is a typical CSS rule. This one has a simple selector (that indicates the rule will be applied to all* p *elements), and three associated declarations.*

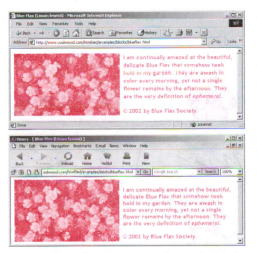

Figure 1.44 *With styles, the image floats to the left, the text is displayed in a different font and weight, and there is a background image in the bottom-right corner. Styles are well supported by current versions of major browsers, including IE5 and Opera 6 (shown) and Netscape 6, on both platforms.*

Adding Style to Your Web Pages

While (X)HTML gives your Web pages their basic structure, CSS (Cascading Style Sheets) defines their appearance.

A CSS style sheet is made up of one or more *rules*. Each rule is comprised of a *selector*, which identifies the parts of the Web page that should be affected, and one or more *declarations*, which specify the formatting which should be applied. For example, a style sheet might be comprised of two rules, one that says all level one headers should be big and blue and another that says all paragraphs should be in a sans serif font.

The simplest kind of selector is just the name of an (X)HTML element, like h1 or p. More complex selectors might specify that a rule be applied to an entire class of elements, to the children of a particular element, or even to all the descendants of an element. You'll learn how to define all sorts of selectors in Chapter 8, *Creating Styles*.

A rule's declaration lists the *property* that is being defined followed by a colon and then the desired *value* for that property. For example, to make the text blue, I've used the color property with a value of #3366cc **(Figure 1.43)**.

A rule can have as many declarations as you need. Simply separate multiple declarations with a semicolon. You may omit the semicolon from the last declaration in a rule, though some people prefer to leave it for consistency's sake.

Note: CSS prefers one aspect of XHTML over HTML: the use of closing tags. If you want to use CSS with HTML, be sure to close all your non-empty elements, even when it's not required (like p and li). CSS doesn't care if you add the / to empty tags like img.

The Cascade: When Rules Collide

There are many ways to apply styles. As we've already seen, every browser has its own default system *(see page 40)*. Next, you can write style rules and apply them to a specific (X)HTML element right in the code, insert them at the top of an (X)HTML document, and import one or more from an external file *(see page 147)*. And some browsers let your visitors create and apply their own style sheets to any pages they visit—including yours. Finally, some styles are inherited from parent element to child.

What happens, you might ask, when there is more than one style rule that applies to a given element? CSS uses the principle of the *cascade*, from which it gets its first initial, to take into account such important characteristics as *inheritance*, *specificity*, and *location* in order to determine which of a group of conflicting rules should win out.

Let's start with inheritance. Many CSS properties affect not only the elements defined by the selector but are also *inherited* by the descendants of those elements. For example, suppose you make all your `h1` elements blue with a red border. Since the `color` property is inherited, but the border property is not, any elements contained within the `h1` elements will also be blue, but will *not* have their own red border. You'll learn which properties are inherited in the individual section describing each property (and in Appendix B, *CSS Properties and Values*). You can also use a value of `inherit` with most properties to force inheritance.

While inheritance determines what happens if no style rule is applied to an element, *specificity* is the key when more than one rule is applied. The law of specificity states that the more specific the selector, the stronger the

```
body {background:url(bg_flax.jpg) bottom right no-repeat}

p {font-family: "Trebuchet MS", "Helvetica", sans-serif; font-weight: bold; color:#3366cc; }

img {float:left;margin-right:10px}
```

Figure 1.45 *Here is the style sheet for this document. Don't worry too much about the details right now, but do notice that there is a rule for* p *elements, but not for* em *elements.*

```
<p>I am continually amazed at the beautiful, delicate Blue Flax that somehow took hold in my garden.

They are awash in color every morning, yet not a single flower remains by the afternoon.

They are the very definition of <em>ephemeral</em>.</p>

<p>&copy; 2002 by Blue Flax Society.</p>
```

Figure 1.46 *The* em *element is contained within the* p *element, and thus is a child of* p*.*

Figure 1.47 *In the absence of a rule specified explicitly for the* em *element in Figure 1.45, it inherits the font, weight, and color from its parent, the* p *element.*

```
p {color:red}

p.group {color:blue}

p#one {color:green}

p#one {color:magenta}
```

Figure 1.48 *Here are four rules of varying specificity. The first affects any old p element, the second affects only those p elements with a class equal to* group, *and the third and fourth affect only the single p element with an id equal to* one. *Since the third and fourth rules have the same specificity, their position becomes a factor— and thus the fourth rule wins out since it appears last. Don't worry about the specifics yet. We'll discuss classes and ids and how to apply styles to them later, in detail.*

```
<p>Here's a generic p element. It will be red.</p>

<p class="group">Here's a group-class p element.
There are two rules that apply, but since the p.group
rule is more specific, this paragraph will be
blue.</p>

<p class="group" id="one">Here's a p element
with an id of one. There are four rules that could
apply to this paragraph. The first two are overruled
by the more specific last two. The position breaks
the tie between the last two: the one that appears
later wins, and thus this paragraph will be
magenta.

</p>
```

Figure 1.49 *Here are three paragraphs, one generic one, one with just a class, and one with a class and an id.*

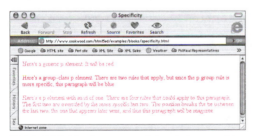

Figure 1.50 *The first paragraph is red, the second is blue, and the third one is magenta. (You can see for yourself on my Web site—see page 24.)*

rule. So if one rule states that all `h1` elements should be blue but a second rule states that all `h1` elements with a `class` of *Spanish* be red, the second rule will override the first for all those `h1` elements whose `class` is *Spanish*.

Note that `id` attributes are considered the most specific (since they must be unique in a document), while the presence of a `class` attribute makes a selector more specific than a simple selector that has none. (You'll learn all about classes and ids in Chapter 3, *Basic (X)HTML Structure*.) Inherited rules are considered to be the most general of all, and are overruled by *any* other rule.

Sometimes, specificity is not enough to determine a winner among competing rules. In that case, the *location* of the rule breaks the tie: Rules that appear later have more weight. For example, rules that are applied locally right in the (X)HTML element *(see page 153)* are considered to appear after (and thus have more weight than) equally specific rules applied internally at the top of the (X)HTML document *(see page 151)*. For details, consult *The Importance of Location* on page 154.

If that isn't enough, you can override the whole system by declaring that a particular rule should be more *important* than the others by adding `!important` at the end of the rule. However, this feature is not well supported, and in my opinion, creates more problems than it solves.

In summary, in the absence of a rule, many styles are inherited from parent element to child. With two competing rules, the more specific the rule, the more weight or importance it has—regardless of its location. With two rules of equal specificity, the one that appears later wins.

The Cascade: When Rules Collide

A Property's Value

Each CSS property has different rules about what values it can accept. Some properties only accept one of a list of predefined values. Others accept numbers, integers, relative values, percentages, URLs, or colors. Some can accept more than one type of value. While the acceptable values for each property are listed in the section describing that property (mostly in Chapters 10 and 11), I'll discuss the basic systems here.

Predefined Values

Most CSS properties have a few predefined values that can be used. For example, the `display` property can be set to **block**, **inline**, **list-item**, or **none**. In contrast with (X)HTML, you don't need to and indeed *must not* enclose predefined values in quotation marks **(Figure 1.51)**.

Lengths and Percentages

Many CSS properties take a *length* for their value. All length values must contain a quantity and a unit, with no spaces between them, for example, **3em** or **10px (Figure 1.52)**. The only exception is **0**, which may be used with or without units.

There are length types that are *relative* to other values. An *em* is usually equal to the element's font-size, so **2em** would mean "twice the font-size". (When the em is used to set the element's `font-size` property itself, its value is derived from the font size of the element's *parent*.) The *ex* should be equal to the font's x-height, that is, the height of a letter *x* in the font, but is not well supported.

Pixels (px) are relative to the resolution of the monitor—though not to other style rules. Most monitors these days display about 80 pixels to the inch (though they range from 72 to 96 pixels to the inch), so 16 pixels is about 1/5 of an inch high (or 0.5cm).

Figure 1.51 *Many CSS properties will only accept values from a predefined list. Type them exactly and do not enclose them in quotation marks.*

Figure 1.52 *Lengths must always explicitly state the unit. There should be no space between the unit and the measurement.*

Figure 1.53 *Percentages are generally relative to the parent element. So, in this example, the font would be set to 80% of the parent's font-size.*

A number

line-height: 1.5;

Figure 1.54 *Don't confuse numbers and integers with length. A number or integer has no unit (like px). In this case, the value shown here is a factor that will be multiplied by the font-size to get the line-height.*

A URL

background: url(bg_flax.jpg);

Figure 1.55 *URLs in CSS properties do not need to be enclosed in quotation marks.*

There are also the largely self-explanatory *absolute* units—inches (in), centimeters (cm), millimeters (mm), points (pt), and picas (pc). In general, you should only use absolute lengths when the size of the output is known (as with the printed page—see Chapter 12).

Percentage values, **65%**, for example—work much like ems, in that they are relative to some other value **(Figure 1.53)**.

Bare Numbers

A very few CSS properties accept a value in the form of a number, without a unit, like **3**. The most common are `line-height` **(Figure 1.54)** and `z-index`. (The others are mostly for print and aural style sheets and are not yet well supported.)

URLs

Some CSS properties allow you to specify the URL of another file. In that case, use **url(file.ext)**, where *file.ext* is the path and file name of the desired document **(Figure 1.55)**. Note that the specifications state that relative URLs should be relative to the style sheet and not the (X)HTML document. Unfortunately, Netscape 4 got that one wrong, so to be compatible with that browser, you have to use absolute URLs.

While you may use quotations around the file name, they're not required. On the other hand, there should be no space between the word **url** and the opening parentheses.

For more information on writing the URLs themselves, consult *URLs* on page 33.

A Property's Value

CSS Colors

There are several ways to specify colors for CSS properties. First, and easiest, the value can be one of 16 predefined color names **(Figure 1.56)**. Of course, 16 colors get pretty boring pretty quickly.

Instead of limiting yourself to those colors, you can construct your own by specifying the amount of red, green, and blue in the desired color. You can give the values of each of these contributing colors as a percentage, a number from 0–255, or a hexadecimal representation of the number. For example, if you wanted to create a dark purple, you might use 35% red with 50% blue. That color could be written **rgb(%35, 0%, 50%)** as shown in Figure 1.57. If you use numerical values, you could write the same color as **rgb(89, 0, 127)**, since 89 is 35% of 255 and 127 is 50% of 255.

I've saved the most common though most convoluted method for last **(Figure 1.58)**: convert those numerical values to hexadecimals, join them together, and add an initial #: **#59007F**. (59 is the hexadecimal equivalent of 89, 00 is the hexadecimal equivalent of 0, and 7F is the hex equivalent of 127.)

And if that weren't enough, when a hexadecimal color is comprised of three pairs of repeating digits, as in **#ff3344**, you may abbreviate the color to **#f34**.

While most current image editors, including Photoshop and Photoshop Elements, include tools for choosing colors and displaying their hex values, I've also included a do-it-yourself table in Appendix E, along with some esoteric details about hexadecimal conversions.

Perhaps more useful is the inside back cover of this book, in which you'll find a selection of colors, together with their hex values, that you can use on your Web pages. I'd also recommending taking a look at *Color* on page 84.

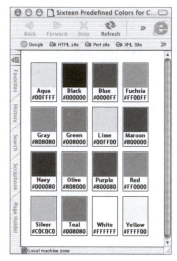

Figure 1.56 *Here are the sixteen predefined color names together with their equivalent hexadecimal codes. You can find these colors—in color!—on the inside back flap of this book and on my Web site (see page 24).*

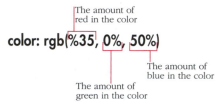

Figure 1.57 *You can express the amount of each of the three contributing colors with a percentage (shown here), or with a number ranging from 0-255. Define the red first, followed by green, and then blue.*

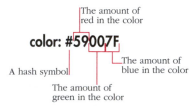

Figure 1.58 *The most common way to define a color is by specifying, with hexadecimal numbers, the amounts of red, green, and blue that it contains. Notice the initial hash symbol and note that hex numbers are case insensitive, that is, it doesn't matter if you write #ffffff or #FFFFFF or indeed #ffFFfF.*

A Property's Value

WORKING WITH WEB PAGE FILES

2

Before you start writing (X)HTML elements and attributes, it's important to know how to create the files in which you'll use such code. In this chapter, you'll learn how to create, edit, and save Web page files. I'll also touch on some design and organizational considerations.

If you can't stand waiting any longer, and already know how to create the actual files, skip on ahead to Chapter 3, *Basic (X)HTML Structure*, where I begin to explain the (X)HTML code itself.

Designing Your Site

Although you can just jump in and start writing Web pages right away, it's a good idea to first think about and design your site. That way, you'll give yourself direction and save reorganizing later.

To design your site:

1. Figure out why you're creating this site. What do you want to convey?

2. Think about your audience. How can you tailor your content to appeal to this audience? For example, should you add lots of graphics or is it more important that your page download quickly?

3. How many pages will you need? What sort of structure would you like it to have? Do you want visitors to go through your site in a particular direction, or do you want to make it easy for them to explore in any direction?

4. Sketch out your site on paper.

5. Devise a simple, consistent naming system for your pages, images, and other external files *(see page 32)*.

✔ Tips

■ Don't overdo the design phase of your site. At some point, you've got to dig in and start writing.

■ If you're not very familiar with the Web, do some surfing first to get an idea of the possibilities. You might start with Yahoo *(http://www.yahoo.com)* or Google *(http://www.google.com/dirhp)* or even your competitors.

■ There are lots of good books on Web design. You might ask people for recommendations on my Question and Answer board *(see page 24)*.

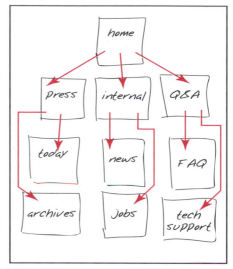

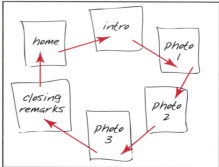

Figure 2.1 *Sketching out your site and thinking about what it might contain can help you decide what sort of structure it needs: a centralized, hierarchical model (top), a circular model that leads the visitor from one page to the next (above), or some other system.*

Figure 2.2 *Open your text editor or word processor and choose File > New. (Shown are Simple-Text for Macintosh at far left and WordPad for Windows.)*

Figure 2.3 *This is SimpleText's document window where you'll write the (X)HTML code for your Web page.*

Figure 2.4 *This is WordPad's document window where Windows users can create (X)HTML pages.*

Creating a New Web Page

You don't need any special tools to create a Web page. You can use *any* word processor, even WordPad or SimpleText, which are included with the basic Windows and Macintosh system software.

To create a new Web page:

1. Open any text editor or word processor.

2. Choose File > New to create a new, blank document **(Figure 2.2)**.

3. Create the (X)HTML content as explained in the rest of this book, starting on page 59.

4. Be sure to save your file as directed on page 50.

✔ Tips

- If you like Microsoft Word, you can use it for writing (X)HTML too. Just be sure to save the file correctly (as Text Only and with the .htm or .html extension). For more details, see pages 50–52.

- If you use FrontPage, Dreamweaver, or some other Web page editor to start your pages, you can still tweak the (X)HTML code by hand. Just choose File > Open from your text editor of choice and open the file. Then use the rest of this book to add your own (X)HTML tags and create the (X)HTML page *you* want.

- You *can* use SimpleText or WordPad, but if you want to get fancy, try BBEdit for Mac or HomeSite for Windows. Both display (X)HTML tags in color, and have powerful search and replace functions, syntax checkers for debugging problematic pages, and assorted other helpful features. For more details, consult *(X)HTML Editors* on page 462.

Creating a New Web Page

Saving Your Web Page

Web pages are created with a text editor or word processor but are meant to be viewed with multiple browsers on multiple platforms. To be accessible to all of these different programs, Web pages are saved in a universal "text only" format—without any proprietary formatting that a word processor might otherwise apply.

So that browsers (and servers) recognize Web pages and know to interpret the markup they contain, as well as distinguish them from plain text files that are not Web pages, Web page files also have the .htm or .html extension.

Because of that extension, a Web page's icon matches the system's default browser and not the word processor with which the file was written. Indeed, when you double-click a Web page file, it is opened in a browser, not a word processor. This is great for Web surfers, but it adds an extra step to editing Web pages *(see page 54)*.

To resume, when you save your Web page, you must save it in text only format with either the .htm or .html extension.

To save your Web page:

1. Once you've created your Web page, choose File > Save As from your word processor **(Figure 2.6)**.

2. In the dialog box that appears, choose Text Only or Text Document (or however your program words it) for the format.

3. Give the document the .htm or .html extension. (This is very important!)

4. Choose the folder in which to save the Web page.

5. Click Save.

Accounts.xls   webpage.html

Figure 2.5 *An Excel file has the .xls extension and is identified with the Excel icon (left). If you double-click it, it is displayed with Excel. A Web page file, created with any word processor, has the .htm or .html extension but is identified with the default browser's icon. If you double-click it, it is displayed with the browser (not the word processor).*

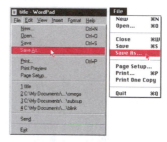

Figure 2.6 *Choose File > Save As from your word processor or text editor. (WordPad is on the left, SimpleText on the right.)*

Figure 2.7 *In SimpleText, give the file the .htm or .html extension, choose the desired location, and then click Save. (Since SimpleText only saves in Text Only format, you don't have to specify the format.)*

Figure 2.8 *In WordPad, choose Text Document under Save as type, give the file the .htm or .html extension, choose the desired location, and then click Save.*

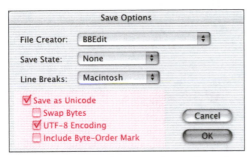

Figure 2.9 *Many word processors let you choose the encoding for your file, so that you can save characters from different languages in the same document. This illustration is from BBEdit 6.5.2. (Click the Options button in the Save box to get here.)*

✔ Tips

■ Only Windows 3.1 users are limited to the three letter extension, .htm. Practically everyone else—Windows 95/98, Unix, and Macintosh—can choose what they like best. Just be consistent.

■ Some word processors (like Microsoft Word and Corel WordPerfect to name a few) offer a "Save as HTML" or "Save as Web page" option. *Don't touch it!* That option is for folks who want to create a Web page from a word processing document without learning HTML and it completely messes up hand-written code *(see page 52).*

■ Some text editors on Windows have the annoying habit of adding their default extension to your file name, even if you've already specified .htm or .html. Your file, now named *webpage.html.txt* cannot be properly viewed in a browser. To make matters worse, Windows often hides extensions on the Desktop so that the problem is not completely obvious, especially to the uninitiated. There are two solutions. The first is to enclose your file name in double quotes when you save your document. This should keep the extra extension from being added. Next, you can display the extensions on the Desktop and then select the offending extension and eliminate it. For details, see my Web site *(see page 24).*

■ When you choose Text Only (or similar), your file is saved with your system's default character encoding. If you want to create Web pages in another encoding (perhaps to include special symbols or text in other languages), you'll have to use a word processor that lets you choose the encoding **(Figure 2.9)**. For more details, see Chapter 20, *Symbols and Non-English Characters.*

Saving Your Web Page

About Microsoft Word and Web Pages

Word can automatically create Web pages from existing documents, often whether you want it to or not. Its commands are particularly confusing to Web page designers who create their own markup code—which is probably you if you're reading this book.

Word's "Save as Web Page" command (available both from the File menu **(Figure 2.10)** and as a format in the Save dialog box) means "convert the present document into HTML, adding markup where there is formatting, and saving as text-only with the .htm extension". There are two problems with this command. First, it converts any markup that you've entered manually into plain text, using special symbols. Second, Microsoft adds an incredible amount of proprietary code. If you're writing your own markup with this book, you don't want to use this option.

Instead, choose File > Save As **(Figure 2.11)**, choose Text Only from the Save as type box, and then change the default .txt extension to .htm or .html **(Figure 2.12)**.

✔ Tips

■ Text Only saves files with the ANSI encoding. If you'd prefer some other encoding (perhaps a more standard or a non-Western European encoding), Word 2000 offers Encoded Text in the Save as type box. Once you click Save, you'll have to confirm that you really want to save as Encoded Text and will be able to choose the desired Encoding. For more details, consult *Saving Your Page with the Proper Encoding* on page 336.

■ These instructions cover Word 2000 for Windows. Other versions may have slightly different wording or dialog boxes.

Figure 2.10
Don't use Word's Save as Web Page option. It's for converting regular Word documents into Web pages and will mess up hand-coded markup.

Figure 2.11
Instead, choose Save As and then choose the proper type and extension as shown in Figure 2.12.

Figure 2.12 *In the Save As dialog box, first choose Text Only in the Save as type box. Then add the .htm or .html extension. (If you do it in the reverse order, the Text Only option will change your extension back to .txt.)*

About Microsoft Word and Web Pages

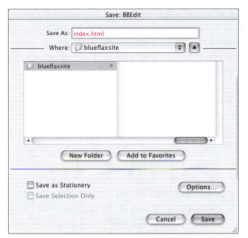

Figure 2.13 *Save the file with the special default name: either* index.html *or* default.htm, *depending on your server. Note that this is BBEdit's Save box (on Mac OS X), but it doesn't matter which program you use to save the files.*

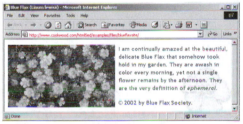

Figure 2.14 *When the visitor types the path to the directory, but omits the file name itself, the file with the default name is used.*

Specifying a Default or "Home" Page

Most servers have a system for recognizing a default page in each folder, based on the name of the file. So, when your visitors type a URL with a directory but no specific file, the default file is used.

To specify a default or "home" page:

1. First, ask your ISP how such a default page should be named. On most servers, use *index.html*. (Microsoft servers generally use *default.htm*.)

2. Next, when you save your file *(see page 50)*, use the proper name.

✔ Tips

■ You can create a default page for any and every directory on your site.

■ The default page that you create at the top level of your Web directory is your site's *home page*, the one that will appear when your visitors type your domain with no additional path information: *http://www.yourdomain.com*

■ If you don't have such a default page in each directory, most servers will show a list of the directory's contents (which you may or may not want to reveal to your visitors). To keep those prying eyes out, create a default page for every directory on your site.

Editing Web Pages

Because Web pages are most often viewed with a Web browser, when you double-click them on the Desktop, the default browser cheerily opens up and displays them. If you want to edit the Web page, you'll have to manually open them in your word processor.

To edit Web pages:

1. Open your word processor.

2. Choose File > Open.

3. Navigate to the directory that contains the desired file.

4. If you don't see your file listed, choose the All Documents option in the Files of type box **(Figures 2.15 and 2.16)**. The name and location may vary slightly from program to program and platform to platform.

5. Then click Open. Your file is ready to edit.

✔ Tips

■ Usually, once you've made changes to an already saved document, you can simply choose File > Save to save the changes, without having to worry about the format as described on page 50.

■ Right-click the Web page's icon in Windows and then choose Edit to open the Web page in the default HTML editor **(Figure 2.17)**. You can specify the word processor that should appear in this menu, but it's a bit involved to go into right here. Check my Web site for the details *(see page 24)*.

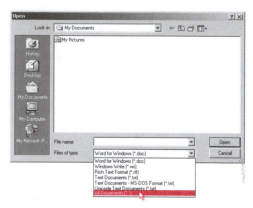

Figure 2.15 *Many word processors in Windows can't automatically see (X)HTML files. Choose All Documents if necessary to view files with any extension.*

Figure 2.16 *Once files with any extension are displayed, you can choose the appropriate file and click Open.*

Figure 2.17 *In Windows, you can also right-click the document's icon and then choose Edit in the pop-up menu that appears. (Note that the default browser here appears to be Netscape, given the Web page's icon.)*

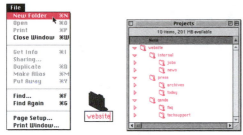

Figure 2.18 *On a Mac, choose New Folder, and then give the folder a name. Then create a separate folder for each section of your site.*

Figure 2.19
In Windows, from the desktop or the Windows Explorer, choose File > New > Folder.

Figure 2.20 *Give the folder a name. Then divide it into additional folders if needed. You can use the Windows Explorer (as shown here) to display the complete hierarchy of your site.*

Organizing Files

Before you have too many files, it's a good idea to figure out where you're going to put them.

To organize your files:

1. Create a central folder or directory to hold all the material that will be available at your Web site. On the Mac, choose File > New Folder in the Finder (**Figure 2.18**). In Windows, from the Desktop, choose File > New > Folder (**Figure 2.19**).

2. Give the folder a name and divide it in a way that reflects the organization of your Web site (**Figure 2.20**).

3. You may decide to create a separate folder for each section of your site, along with individual subfolders for images and other external files.

4. You can create a top-level *images* folder for images that are common to all areas of your Web site.

✔ Tip

■ Use simple, one-word names without symbols or punctuation for your files *and* folders. Use all lowercase letters so that your URLs are easier to type and thus your pages are easier to reach. For more details on how to create good file names, consult *File Names* on page 32.

Organizing Files

Viewing Your Page in a Browser

Once you've created a page, you'll want to see what it looks like in a browser. In fact, since you don't know which browser your visitors will be using, it's a good idea to look at the page in *several* browsers.

To look at your page in a browser:

1. Open a browser.

2. Choose File > Open, Open File, or Open Page (just *not* Open Location), depending on the browser **(Figure 2.21)**.

3. In the dialog box that appears, either type the location of the page on your hard disk, or click Browse (IE) or Choose File (Netscape) to find it **(Figure 2.22)**.

4. If you've clicked Browse or Choose File in step 3, in the new dialog box that appears, navigate to the folder on your hard disk that contains the desired Web page and click Open **(Figure 2.23)**.

5. Back in the Open Page dialog box, click Open. The page is displayed in the browser just as it will appear when you actually publish it on the server *(see page 405)*.

✔ Tips

- You can (usually) also double-click a Web page's icon to view it in a browser.

- If your Web page does not appear in the Open dialog box, make sure that you have saved it as Text Only and given it the .htm or .html extension *(see page 50)*.

- You don't have to close the document in the text editor before you view it with a browser, though you do have to save it.

- It is generally not necessary to publish your pages on the server before you view them.

Figure 2.21 *From the desired browser (this is Netscape for Windows), choose File > Open Page. In Explorer for Windows, it's called File > Open. In Explorer for Mac, it's File > Open File.*

Figure 2.22 *On Windows machines, you'll get an intermediary box asking if you want to type the path in by hand. If you don't (!), click the Choose File button (in IE, it's Browse). You'll get the dialog box shown in Figure 2.23.*

Figure 2.23 *Choose the file that you want to open and click the Open button.*

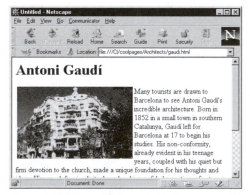

Figure 2.24 *The page appears in the browser. Check it over well to see if it's coming out the way you planned.*

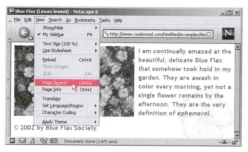

Figure 2.25 *All browsers have a menu command that lets you view a page's (X)HTML code. The name varies from Page Source (in Netscape, shown) to View Source, to just Source.*

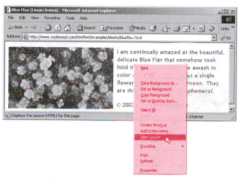

Figure 2.26 *Most browsers will also let you right-click (click and hold on a Mac) and choose the Source command (however it's called) from the pop-up menu that appears.*

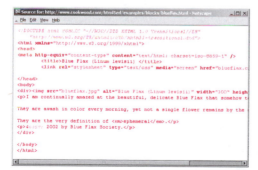

Figure 2.27 *Some browsers display the code in the specified text editor. Others, like Netscape, let you choose between the default window right inside the browser or your preferred text editor.*

The Inspiration of Others

One of the easiest ways to expand your (X)HTML fluency is by looking at how other page designers have created *their* pages. Luckily, (X)HTML code is easy to view and learn from. However, text content, graphics, sounds, video, and other external files may be copyrighted. As a general rule, use other designers' pages for inspiration with your (X)HTML, and then create your own contents.

To view other designers' (X)HTML code:

1. Open a Web page with any browser.

2. Choose View > Source in Opera or Internet Explorer, or View > Page Source in Netscape **(Figure 2.25)**. The (X)HTML code will be displayed **(Figure 2.27)**.

3. If desired, save the file for further study.

✔ Tips

■ You can also save the source code by selecting File > Save As and then HTML Source in the Format pop-up menu in the dialog box that appears.

■ Most browsers also let you right-click (or click and hold on a Mac) and then choose a source command (of varying wording) from the pop-up menu **(Figure 2.26)**. This is also a good way to look at the code for a frame (which you'll learn about in Chapter 15, *Frames*).

■ Although there are JavaScript scripts that can make it more difficult (for Windows folks, but not for Mac users), there's no real way to keep people from looking at a Web page's source code. Instead, you might want to add a copyright notice, encourage people to link instead of stealing, and do periodical searches of key phrases in your documents.

The Inspiration of Others

BASIC (X)HTML STRUCTURE

This chapter covers the most basic (X)HTML elements—the ones you need to create the structure of your document. You'll learn how to create new paragraphs, headers, page breaks, comments, and more.

Creating a clear and consistent structure makes it that much easier to apply styles to your document.

Starting Your Web Page

Begin your page by using a DOCTYPE *(see page 38)* to declare what type of HTML or XHTML you're using. The DOCTYPE lets browsers know what to expect and tells validators how to judge your code in order to check its syntax. Then, signal the beginning of the actual code with the opening html tag.

To start a transitional HTML 4 page:

1. Type **<!DOCTYPE HTML PUBLIC "-//W3C //DTD HTML 4.01 Transitional//EN" "http://www.w3.org/TR/html4/ loose.dtd">** to declare that you're using transitional HTML 4.01 in your Web page.

2. Type **<html>** to begin the actual HTML portion of your document.

3. Leave a few spaces for creating the rest of your page (using the rest of this book).

4. Type **</html>**.

To begin a transitional XHTML page:

1. If desired, type **<?xml version="1.0" encoding="UTF-8"?>** to declare that your document is an XML document and that its encoding is *UTF-8*.

2. Type **<!DOCTYPE html PUBLIC "-//W3C //DTD XHTML 1.0 Transitional//EN" "http://www.w3.org/TR/xhtml1/DTD/ xhtml1-transitional.dtd">** to declare that you're using transitional XHTML in your Web page.

3. Type **<html xmlns="http://www.w3.org/ 1999/xhtml">** to begin the XHTML portion of your page and declare its namespace.

4. Leave a few spaces for creating the rest of your page (using the rest of this book).

5. Type **</html>**.

```
<!DOCTYPE HTML PUBLIC
"-//W3C//DTD HTML 4.01 Transitional//EN"
"http://www.w3.org/TR/html4/loose.dtd">
<html>



</html>
```

Figure 3.1 *Here's the DOCTYPE for a transitional HTML document as well as the opening and closing* html *tags. It's a gruesome bit of text. I recommend just copying it from one document to the next instead of trying to type all that gobbledy-gook.*

```
<!DOCTYPE html PUBLIC "-//W3C//DTD XHTML
1.0 Transitional//EN"

"http://www.w3.org/TR/xhtml1/DTD/xhtml1-
transitional.dtd">

<html xmlns="http://www.w3.org/1999/xhtml">




</html>
```

Figure 3.2 *Here's the* DOCTYPE *for a transitional XHTML document, the opening* html *tag and required namespace declaration, and the closing* html *tag. Ugh!*

✔ **Tips**

- Both the DOCTYPE and the html element are optional in HTML (even strict HTML). XHTML requires both (with the namespace declaration in the opening html tag). Note that there is no xhtml element.

- I've only shown how to write the DOCTYPE for transitional HTML and XHTML. You can find a list of common DOCTYPE declarations on my Web site *(see page 24)* or at *http://www.w3.org*. For help choosing an appropriate DOCTYPE, see page 38.

- Create a template with the appropriate DOCTYPE declaration and html tag as a starting point for all your pages.

- Declaring a DOCTYPE with a URL at the top of your Web page generally puts current browsers in *standards* mode— letting you use standards-compliant code in order to have more control over the display of your Web page *(see page 39)*.

- If you start an XHTML page with the xml declaration, IE 6 for Windows goes into *quirks* mode. That's a huge bug. The workaround? Skip the (optional) declaration and declare the encoding with the meta tag instead *(see page 63)* .

- If you use non-standard HTML tags, there's no point in specifying a DOCTYPE. Just enclose your page in opening and closing html tags. Current browsers will use *quirks* mode when displaying your pages, letting you take advantage of old, soon-to-be-obsolete bugs *(see page 39)*.

- Declaring the appropriate DOCTYPE tells validators which specifications to compare your code against *(see page 394)*.

- Note that the word DOCTYPE (since it actually originated from *another* language called SGML) is typed in all uppercase letters, both in HTML and in XHTML.

Starting Your Web Page

Creating the Foundation

Most Web pages are divided into two sections: the *head* and the *body*. The head section is where you define the title of your page, include information about your page for search engines like Google, set the location of your page, add style sheets, and write scripts. Except for the title *(see page 64)*, the content of the head section is not readily visible to the visitor.

To create the head section:

1. Directly after the opening html tag *(see page 60)*, type **<head>**.

2. Leave a few spaces for the contents of the head section.

3. Type **</head>**.

The *body* of your (X)HTML document encloses the content of your Web page, that is, the part that your visitors will see, including the text and graphics.

To create the body:

1. After the final </head> tag, type **<body>**.

2. Leave a few spaces for the contents of your Web page (which you'll create with the help of the rest of this book).

3. Type **</body>**.

✔ Tips

■ The head and body tags are required in XHTML. They're optional in HTML but even if you don't physically type them, the browser acts as if they are there and even lets you assign styles to them.

■ Another reason to use head and body tags is for controlling when a particular script will run *(see page 314)*.

```
<!DOCTYPE html PUBLIC "-//W3C//DTD XHTML
1.0 Transitional//EN"
"http://www.w3.org/TR/xhtml1/DTD/xhtml1-
transitional.dtd">
<html xmlns="http://www.w3.org/1999/xhtml">

<head>

</head>
<body>

</body>
</html>
```

Figure 3.3 *The* head *and* body *elements help you structure your (X)HTML documents.*

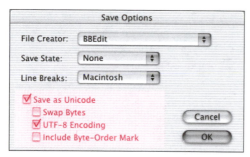

Figure 3.4 *I've saved my files in Unicode, with the UTF-8 encoding. (This is BBEdit. For more details about saving files with encodings other than the default for your system, consult Chapter 20, Symbols and Non-English Characters.)*

```
<!DOCTYPE html PUBLIC "-//W3C//DTD XHTML
1.0 Transitional//EN"

"http://www.w3.org/TR/xhtml1/DTD/xhtml1-
transitional.dtd">

<html xmlns="http://www.w3.org/1999/xhtml">
<head>
<meta http-equiv="content-type"
content="text/html; charset=utf-8" />

</head>
<body>



</body>
</html>
```

Figure 3.5 *When the visitor's browser sees this* meta *tag, it will know that the page was encoded with UTF-8, and will display it properly. The key is that the encoding that you declare in the* meta *tag match the one with which you actually saved the file.*

Declaring the Encoding

All text documents, (X)HTML files included, are saved with a character *encoding* . Since there are many encodings in use in the world, it's a good idea to declare which encoding your page was saved in right in the (X)HTML code. This makes it easier for browsers on systems with different default encodings to view the characters in your pages correctly.

To declare the character encoding:

In the head section of your page, type **<meta http-equiv="content-type" content="text/html; charset=encoding" />**, where *encoding* is the character encoding with which you saved the file.

✔ Tips

■ Your Web page's character encoding depends on the way you saved it. If you saved it as Text Only—that is, you didn't choose a special encoding—it's a safe bet that your document was saved with the default encoding for your language. For example, the default encoding for English Windows is windows-1252 and for English Macintosh is x-mac-roman.

■ If you chose a particular encoding upon saving the file, that's the encoding you should use in the meta tag.

■ You can find a list of common character set codes at *http:// www.w3.org/ International/O-charset-lang.html.*

■ XHTML requires that you declare the encoding if it is anything other than the default UTF-8 or UTF-16. You can use either the xml declaration *(see page 60)* or the meta tag described above.

■ For more about encodings, see Chapter 20, *Symbols and Non-English Characters.*

Declaring the Encoding

Creating a Title

Each (X)HTML page must have a `title` element. A title should be short and descriptive. In most browsers, the title appears in the title bar of the window **(Figure 3.7)**. Perhaps even more importantly, the title is used by search indexes like Yahoo and Google as well as in your visitors' browsers' history lists and bookmarks.

To create a title:

1. Place the cursor between the opening and closing `head` tags *(see page 62)*.

2. Type **`<title>`**.

3. Enter the title of your web page.

4. Type **`</title>`**.

✔ Tips

■ The `title` element is required.

■ A title cannot contain any formatting, images, or links to other pages.

■ A page's title directly affects its ranking in many search engines. The closer a title is to the exact words that a potential visitor types—without any extra words—the higher up it will appear in the listings. It is also used to identify your page in the results **(Figure 3.8)**.

■ The title is also used in History lists, Favorites lists, and Bookmarks menus to identify your page **(Figure 3.9)**.

■ If your title contains special characters like accents or some symbols, they'll either have to be part of your encoding *(see page 63)* or you'll have to write them with references *(see page 340)*.

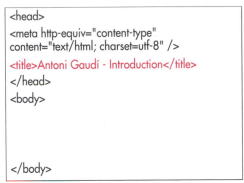

```
<head>
<meta http-equiv="content-type"
content="text/html; charset=utf-8" />
<title>Antoni Gaudí - Introduction</title>
</head>
<body>




</body>
```

Figure 3.6 *The* `title` *element should be placed in the head section. It is required.*

Figure 3.7 *The title of a Web page is shown in the title bar of the window.*

Figure 3.8 *Perhaps most importantly, the title is used to describe your page in search results from Google and others. In addition, it's purportedly one of the more important factors for determining a page's relevance and rank in search results.*

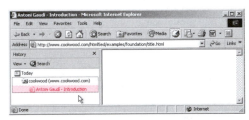

Figure 3.9 *The title also appears in your visitor's History pane (shown), Favorites list, and Bookmarks list.*

```
<head>
<meta http-equiv="content-type"
content="text/html; charset=utf-8" />
<title>Antoni Gaudí - Introduction</title>
</head>
<body>

<h1>Antoni Gaudí</h1>

<h2>La Casa Milà</h2>

<h2>La Sagrada Família</h2>


</body>
```

Figure 3.10 *You can use headers to give your document structure, like an outline.*

Figure 3.11 *The most common default display for first level headers is 24 pixels, Times New Roman, in boldface.*

Creating Section Headers

(X)HTML provides for up to six levels of headers in your Web page for separating your page into manageable chunks.

To organize your Web page with headers:

1. In the body section of your (X)HTML document, type **<hn>**, where *n* is a number from 1 to 6, depending on the level of header that you want to create.

2. Type the contents of the header.

3. Type **</hn>** where *n* is the same number used in step 1.

✔ Tips

■ Think of your headers as hierarchical dividers. Use them consistently.

■ The only official rule about headers is that the higher the level (the smaller the number), the more prominently they should be displayed. Nevertheless, the major browsers currently display them all the same: in Times New Roman, boldface, at 24, 18, 14, 12, 10 and 8 pixels (9 pixels on the Mac), respectively.

■ You can use styles to format headers with a particular font, size, or color (and more). For details, consult Chapter 10, *Formatting with Styles.*

■ Add a named anchor (or id) to your headers so that you can create links directly to that header *(see page 120).*

■ If desired, you can align the text in the header by typing **align="direction"** in the opening tag, where *direction* is left, right, or center. But note that the align attribute has been deprecated in favor of style sheets *(see page 171).*

Creating Section Headers

Starting a New Paragraph

(X)HTML does not recognize the returns or other extra white space that you enter in your text editor. To start a new paragraph in your Web page, you use the p tag.

To begin a new paragraph:

1. Type **<p>**.

2. Type the contents of the new paragraph.

3. Type **</p>** to end the paragraph.

✔ Tips

■ In HTML, the closing </p> tag is optional. However, it is required both in XHTML and when applying styles to a paragraph. Therefore, I recommend always ending a paragraph with </p>.

■ You can use styles to format paragraphs with a particular font, size, or color (and more). For details, consult Chapter 10, *Formatting with Styles*.

■ To control the amount of space between lines, consult *Setting the Line Height* on page 164. To control the amount of space after a paragraph, consult *Adding Padding around an Element* on page 188 or *Setting the Margins around an Element* on page 189.

■ One quick and dirty (and valid) trick for adding extra space between paragraphs is to type ** ** (a non-breaking space) between each additional p element. Better yet, use CSS *(see pages 188–189)*.

■ You can align the text in the paragraph by typing **align="direction"** in the opening p tag, where *direction* is left, right, center, or justify. But note that the align attribute has been deprecated in favor of style sheets *(see page 171)*.

```
</head>
<body>
<h1>Antoni Gaudí</h1>
<p>Many tourists are drawn to Barcelona to see Antoni Gaudí's incredible architecture. </p>
<p>Barcelona celebrates the 150th anniversary of Gaudí's birth in 2002.</p>
<h2>La Casa Milà</h2>
<p>Gaudí's work was essentially useful. La Casa Milà is an apartment building and real people live there.</p>
<h2>La Sagrada Família</h2>
<p>The complicatedly named and curiously unfinished Expiatory Temple of the Sacred Family is the most visited building in Barcelona. </p>
</body>
```

Figure 3.12 *Enclose each paragraph in opening and closing p tags. If you don't close them (which is perfectly legal in HTML but not XHTML), styles won't be applied properly.*

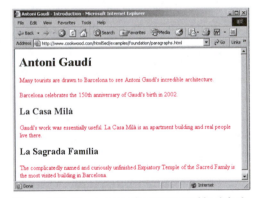

Figure 3.13 *The amount of space inserted by default with a p tag depends on the size of the text surrounding it.*

Naming Elements

You can give your HTML elements either a unique name or one that identifies them as belonging to a particular class. You can then apply styles to all elements with a given name.

To name unique elements:

Within the opening tag of the element, type **id="name"**, where *name* uniquely identifies the element.

To name groups of elements:

Within the opening tag of the element, type **class="name"**, where *name* is the identifying name of the class.

✔ Tips

■ Each id in an (X)HTML document must be unique. In other words, no two elements can be named with the same id.

■ More than one element may belong to, and thus be marked with, the same class.

■ For information about applying styles to an element with a particular id or class, consult *Selecting Elements by Class or ID* on page 137.

■ The `class` and `id` attributes may be added to most (X)HTML elements but are particularly useful with the `div` and `span` elements *(see pages 68–69)*.

■ The `id` attribute automatically turns the element into an anchor, to which you can direct a link. For more details, consult *Creating Anchors* on page 120.

■ Finally, the `id` attribute can also be used to identify elements that will be affected by a scripting language, such as JavaScript.

Naming Elements

Breaking up a Page into Divisions

Breaking up your page into divisions allows you to apply styles to an entire chunk of your page at once. This is particularly useful for designing layouts with CSS *(see page 175)*.

To break up a page into divisions:

1. At the beginning of the division, type **<div**.

2. If desired, type **id="name"**, where *name* uniquely identifies the division.

3. If desired, type **class="name"**, where *name* is the identifying name of the class that the division belongs to.

4. Type **>** to complete the opening `div` tag.

5. Create the contents of the division.

6. At the end of the division, type **</div>**.

✔ Tips

■ A division is a block-level element. That means that its contents automatically start on a new line.

■ In fact, the line breaks are the only formatting inherent to a division. Apply additional formatting by assigning styles to the division's class or id.

■ You're not required to label each division with a class or id, though they're much more powerful if you do.

■ You may apply both a `class` and `id` attribute to the same `div` element, although it's probably more usual to apply one or the other. The principal difference is that `class` is for a group of elements while `id` is for identifying individual, unique elements.

```
</head><body>
<div id="gaudi">
<h1>Antoni Gaudí</h1>
<p>Many tourists are drawn to Barcelona to see Antoni Gaudí's incredible architecture. </p>
<p>Barcelona celebrates the 150th anniversary of Gaudí's birth in 2002.</p>

<div class="works">
<h2>La Casa Milà</h2>
<p>Gaudí's work was essentially useful. La Casa Milà is an apartment building and real people live there.</p>
</div>

<div class="works">
<h2>La Sagrada Família</h2>
<p>The complicatedly named and curiously unfinished Expiatory Temple of the Sacred Family is the most visited building in Barcelona. </p>
</div>

</div>
</body></html>
```

Figure 3.14 *There is one large enclosing division (that begins with the level one header and goes to just before the closing body tag) and two inner divisions (that include the level two headers and corresponding paragraphs).*

Figure 3.15 *You generally can't see the effect of divisions until you add styles (see page 147). Then they really shine. You can see this page with styles on my Web site (see page 24).*

```
<body>
<div id="gaudi">
<h1>Antoni Gaudí</h1>

<p>Many tourists are drawn to Barcelona to see
Antoni Gaudí's incredible architecture. </p>

<p>Barcelona celebrates the 150th anniversary of
Gaudí's birth in 2002.</p>


<div class="works">
<h2>La Casa Milà</h2>

<p>Gaudí's work was essentially useful. La Casa
Milà is an apartment building and <span
class="emph">real people</span> live there.</p>
</div>


<div class="works">
<h2>La Sagrada Família</h2>

<p>The complicatedly named and curiously
unfinished Expiatory Temple of the Sacred Family is
the <span class="emph">most visited</span>
building in Barcelona. </p>
</div>


</div>
</body></html>
```

Figure 3.16 *The* span *tag is used to mark a bunch of inline content, usually, but not always, text. You can then format the marked text however you like (which we'll do in Chapters 10 and 11).*

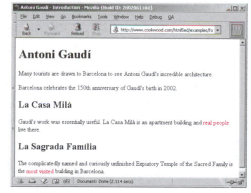

Figure 3.17 *Again, the* span *element gives your document underlying structure. You can't see its effect until you apply styles (see page 147). You can see this page with styles on my Web site (see page 24).*

Creating Inline Spans

While you can organize big chunks of your Web page into head and body sections, into divisions, or even with headers (h1, h2, etc.), you can name smaller chunks or *spans* of text or other inline elements in order to identify them and apply styles to them.

To name inline spans:

1. At the beginning of the inline content, type **<span**.

2. If desired, type **id="name"**, where *name* uniquely identifies the spanned content.

3. If desired, type **class="name"**, where *name* is the identifying name of the class that the spanned content belongs to.

4. Type **>** to complete the opening span tag.

5. Create the inline contents you wish to name.

6. At the end of the span, type **</span>**.

✔ Tips

- For more details on the difference between block-level and inline content, consult *Block vs Inline* on page 28.

- A span has no inherent formatting. It becomes useful when you apply styles to it (generally through its class or id).

- You may apply both a class and id attribute to the same span element, although it's probably more usual to apply one or the other. The principal difference is that class is for a group of elements while id is for identifying individual, unique elements.

Creating a Line Break

Browsers automatically wrap text according to the width of the block or window, creating new lines as necessary. While you can start a new paragraph with the p tag *(see page 66)*, you can also create manual line breaks anywhere you like.

The br tag is perfect for poems or other short lines of text that should appear one after another without a lot of space in between.

To insert a line break:

Type **
** where the line break should occur. There is no separate closing br tag.

✔ Tips

■ The closing slash (/) is only required in XHTML documents to satisfy the rule that all elements be properly closed *(see page 36)*. Make sure there is a space between *br* and the slash. You may omit the slash entirely in HTML documents, though it does no harm to include it.

■ You can use multiple br tags to create extra space between lines or paragraphs.

■ Styles can help you control the space between lines in a paragraph *(see page 164)* and between the paragraphs themselves *(see pages 188 and 189)*. There are also a slew of non-standard and deprecated methods.

■ The br tag used to be used with the deprecated clear attribute to control text that is wrapped around images *(see page 112)*. Its function has been replaced by the CSS clear property *(see page 195)*.

■ The CSS white-space property is great for maintaining original page breaks *(see page 170)*. Also see page 358 for details on the non-standard nobr element.

```
<body>
<div id="toc">Antoni Gaudí<br />La Casa
Milà<br />La Sagrada Família</div>
<div id="gaudi">
<h1>Antoni Gaudí</h1>
<p>Many tourists are drawn to Barcelona to see
Antoni Gaudí's incredible architecture. </p>
<p>Barcelona celebrates the 150th anniversary of
Gaudí's birth in 2002.</p>

<div class="works">
<h2>La Casa Milà</h2>
<p>Gaudí's work was essentially useful. La Casa
Milà is an apartment building and <span
class="emph">real people</span> live there.</p>
</div>
```

Figure 3.18 *I've created a new division at the top of the page that can serve as a table of contents. There will be three lines (thanks to the* br *tag) with the minimum of space between each one.*

```
<body>
<div id="toc">Antoni Gaudí
<br />La Casa Milà
<br />La Sagrada Família</div>
```

Figure 3.19 *Remember that the returns in your code are always ignored. This code is equivalent to that shown above in Figure 3.18.*

Figure 3.20 *The* br *element starts the subsequent elements on a new line.*

Creating a Line Break

```
<body>
<!--Here is the table of contents, which in a real
document might be a good deal longer.-->
<div id="toc">Antoni Gaudí<br />La Casa
Milà<br />La Sagrada Família</div>
<div id="gaudi">
<h1>Antoni Gaudí</h1>
<p>Many tourists are drawn to Barcelona to see
Antoni Gaudí's incredible architecture. </p>
<p>Barcelona celebrates the 150th anniversary of
Gaudí's birth in 2002.</p>

<div class="works">
<h2>La Casa Milà</h2>
<p>Gaudí's work was essentially useful. La Casa
Milà is an apartment building and <span
class="emph">real people</span> live there.</p>
</div>

<div class="works">
<h2>La Sagrada Família</h2>
<p>The complicatedly named and curiously
unfinished Expiatory Temple of the Sacred Family is
the <span class="emph">most visited</span>
building in Barcelona. </p>
</div>
</div>
</body></html>
```

Figure 3.21 *Comments are a great way to add reminders to your text. You can also use them to keep track of revisions.*

Figure 3.22 *Comments are invisible (though they readily appear when the source code is displayed—see page 57).*

Adding Comments

You can add comments to your (X)HTML documents in order to remind yourself (or future editors) what you were trying to achieve with your (X)HTML tags. These comments only appear when the document is opened with a text editor. They are invisible to visitors in the browser.

To add comments to your HTML page:

1. In your (X)HTML document, where you wish to insert comments, type **<!--**.

2. Type the comments.

3. Type **-->** to complete the commented text.

✔ Tips

- Comments are particularly useful for describing why you used a particular tag and what effect you were hoping to achieve.

- Another good use for comments is to remind yourself (or future editors) to include, remove, or update certain sections.

- You should view your commented page with a browser before publishing to avoid sharing your (possibly) private comments with your public.

- Beware, however, of comments that are *too* private. While invisible in the browser, they cheerfully reappear when the user saves the page as (X)HTML code (source). For more information on viewing a page's code, consult *The Inspiration of Others* on page 57.

- Comments may not be nested within other comments.

Labeling Elements in a Web Page

You can use the `title` attribute to add a tool tip label to practically every part of your Web site. It's particularly helpful for giving your visitors clues about what's needed in form elements, but you can use it to label just about anything.

To label elements in a Web page:

In the (X)HTML tag for the item you want to label, add **title="label"**, where *label* is the text that should appear in the tool tip when a visitor points at the element.

✔ Tip

■ Explorer for Windows also makes pop-up labels or tool tips out of the `alt` attribute used in image tags (*see page 105*). However, if both the `title` and `alt` attributes are present in an image tag, the tool tip is set to the contents of the `title` tag, not the `alt` tag. So, if you don't want Explorer for Windows to use your `alt` tag as a tool tip, use an empty `title`: **title=""**.

```
<body>
<!--Here is the table of contents, which in a real
document might be a good deal longer.-->
<div id="toc" title="Table of Contents">Antoni
Gaudí<br />La Casa Milà<br />La Sagrada
Família</div>
<div id="gaudi">
<h1>Antoni Gaudí</h1>
<p>Many tourists are drawn to Barcelona to see
Antoni Gaudí's incredible architecture. </p>
<p>Barcelona celebrates the 150th anniversary of
Gaudí's birth in 2002.</p>

<div class="works">
<h2>La Casa Milà</h2>
<p>Gaudí's work was essentially useful. La Casa
Milà is an apartment building and <span
class="emph">real people</span> live there.</p>
</div>

<div class="works">
<h2>La Sagrada Família</h2>
<p>The complicatedly named and curiously
unfinished Expiatory Temple of the Sacred Family is
the <span class="emph">most visited</span>
building in Barcelona. </p>
```

Figure 3.23 *You can add a title to any element you wish.*

Figure 3.24 *When your visitors point at the labeled element, the title will appear.*

BASIC (X)HTML FORMATTING

While it's a good idea to try to separate formatting from content and to use style sheets for controlling the appearance of your page, there are a few simple (and still legal) ways to format text in (X)HTML that I will discuss in this chapter.

Why should you use basic (X)HTML formatting instead of CSS? There are two main reasons. First, most of the elements discussed in this chapter are *logical* elements, that is, they give structure to your document by describing what they contain. For example, the code element is specifically designed for formatting lines of code from a script or program. While it formats such content in a monospace font, it also more importantly identifies the text as code.

The second reason to use the basic formatting elements in this chapter is because CSS is sometimes too big a bazooka for the job. If you want to highlight a word or phrase on your page, instead of enclosing it in a span element with a particular class and then creating a style sheet for that class, you can just wrap it in a simple formatting element and be done with it.

There are a number of formatting elements—for changing the font, size, and color, for example—that, while still legal and supported, are being phased out of (X)HTML in favor of style sheets. I discuss these (and the pros and cons of using them) in Chapter 21, *Formatting: The Old Way.*

Making Text Bold or Italic

One way to make text stand out is to format it in bold face or italics.

To make text bold:

1. Type **<b>**.

2. Type the text that you want to make bold.

3. Type **</b>**.

To make text italic:

1. Type **<i>**.

2. Type the text that you want to make italic.

3. Type **</i>**.

✔ Tips

■ You can also use the less common em and strong tags to format text **(Figures 4.3 and 4.4)**. These are *logical* formatting tags for "emphasizing" text or marking it as "strong". In most browsers, em is displayed in italics and strong in bold. Both require opening (<em>, <strong>) and closing tags (</em>, </strong>).

■ You may use cite (for citations), dfn (for definitions), and var (for variables) to make text italic, although they are less widely used than the i tag.

■ The address tag—old-fashioned but still valid—is another logical tag for making text italic. It's usually only used to format the Web page designer's e-mail address.

■ For more control over bold and italics, try style sheets. For details, consult *Creating Italics* on page 160 and *Applying Bold Formatting* on page 161.

<h1>Barcelona Night Life</h1>

<p>Barcelona is such a great place to live. People there really put a premium on <b>socializing</b>. Imagine it being more important to go out with your friends than to get that big promotion. Even when you're, gasp, <i>pushing 30</i>. They say there are more bars in Barcelona than in the rest of the European community <i>combined</i>.</p>

Figure 4.1 *You may use bold or italic formatting anywhere in your HTML document, except in the* title.

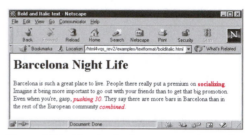

Figure 4.2 *Bold and italic formatting are the simplest and most effective ways to make your text stand out.*

<h1>Barcelona Night Life</h1>

<p>Barcelona is such a great place to live. People there really put a premium on <strong>socializing</strong>. Imagine it being more important to go out with your friends than to get that big promotion. Even when you're, gasp, <em>pushing 30</em>. They say there are more bars in Barcelona than in the rest of the European community <em>combined</em>.</p>

Figure 4.3 *If you prefer, you can use the* em *and* strong *tags for emphasizing text.*

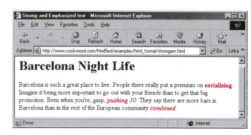

Figure 4.4 *Most browsers display* em *with italics and* strong *with bold.*

```
<h1>Barcelona Night Life</h1>

<p>Barcelona is such a great place to live. People
there really put a premium on <strong>socializing
</strong>. Imagine it being more important to go
out with your friends than to get that big promotion.
Even when you're, gasp, <em>pushing 30</em>.
They say there are more bars in Barcelona than in
the rest of the European community
<em>combined</em>.</p>

<p><big>Don't get me wrong,</big> I don't mean
that everyone gets drunk all the time--bars are for
hanging out and talking or for having a cup of
coffee (espresso, of course).</p>

<p><small>The opinions expressed on this page
are mine and mine alone. </small></p>
```

Figure 4.5 *The* big *and* small *tags are a fast and easy way to make text stand out.*

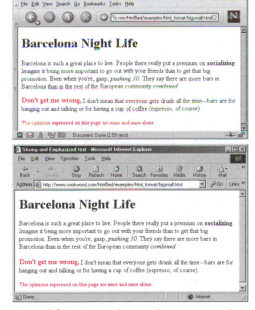

Figure 4.6 *The* big *and* small *elements enjoy wide support. They have identical effects in most browsers (Netscape above, Explorer below).*

Changing the Size of Text

The big and small tags change the relative size of a given word or phrase with respect to the surrounding text.

To make the text bigger or smaller than the surrounding text:

1. Type **<big>** or **<small>** before the text that you wish to make bigger or smaller, respectively.

2. Type the text that should be bigger or smaller.

3. Type **</big>** or **</small>** according to the tag used in step 1.

✔ Tips

- Of course, big and small are relative, and the specifications do not dictate just how much bigger or smaller browsers are supposed to make the text. In general, they stick to typical font sizes, like 8, 9, 10, 12, 14, 16, 18, 24, 36, and 48, moving one step up or down the ladder depending on the element used. The default size for most browsers is 16px.

- Although the big and small tags have not been deprecated in (X)HTML, you may still want to use style sheets in order to have more control over the size of the text. For more information, consult *Setting the Font Size* on page 162.

- Both the big and small tags have a cumulative effect if used more than once. So **<small><small>teensy text</small></small>** would be *two* sizes smaller than surrounding text.

Changing the Size of Text

Using a Monospaced Font

Every visitor to your page has two fonts specified in their browser's preferences: one regular, proportionally spaced one, and the other monospaced, like a typewriter's text. These are usually Times and Courier, respectively. If you are displaying computer codes, URLs, or other information that you wish to offset from the main text, you might want to format the text with the monospaced font.

The `tt` element (it stands for *typewriter text*) is the most common monospaced font tag. Use `code` for formatting computer *code* in languages like C or Perl. Use `kbd` for formatting *keyboard* instructions. And `samp` is for displaying *sample* text. None of these tags is used very often. The truth is that monospaced text is kind of ugly.

To format text with a monospaced font:

1. Type **<tt>**, **<code>**, **<kbd>**, or **<samp>**.

2. Type the text that you want to display in a monospaced font.

3. Type **</tt>**, **</code>**, **</kbd>**, or **</samp>**. Use the tag that matches the code you chose in step 1.

✔ Tips

■ Remember that the monospaced font tags will not have a very dramatic effect in browsers that display all their text in monospaced fonts (like Lynx: *http://www.delorie.com/web/lynxview.html*).

■ You can also format several lines of monospaced text with the `pre` tag *(see page 77)*.

■ You can apply *any* font (that your visitor has installed) to your text with styles *(see page 158)*.

```
<body>

<h2>Perl Tutorial, Lesson 1</h2>

<p>If you're on a UNIX server, every Perl script should start with a shebang line that describes the path to the Perl interpreter on your server. The shebang line might look like this:</p>

<p><code>#!/usr/local/bin/perl</code></p>
```

Figure 4.7 *The* `code` *element not only formats its contents with a monospaced font but also indicates that the contents are computer code. It's a* logical *tag.*

Figure 4.8 *Monospaced text is perfect for URLs and computer code and anything else that should look kind of geeky.*

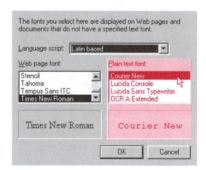

Figure 4.9 *Any text tagged with* `code`, `kbd`, `samp`, *or* `tt` *will be displayed in the font that your visitors have chosen for monospaced text for their browser. The dialog box shown here is the Windows Fonts box. It appears when you choose Tools > Internet Options from Explorer and then click the Fonts button in the General tab.*

```
<body>

<p>Here's the first part of the Cat and Otter Bistro
script (see the WAP/WML chapter), where the
variables are declared, and the $number variable
is screened to make sure it's actually a number:

<pre>my $number = param('number');

my $smoke = param('smoke');

my $dinner_index = param('dinner_index');


$number =~ /([0-9]*)/ ;

$number = $1;

</pre>
```

Figure 4.10 *The* pre *element is ideal for text that contains important spaces and line breaks, like the chunk of Perl CGI code shown above.*

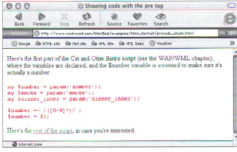

Figure 4.11 *Notice how the line breaks, including the extra return between the third and fourth lines of code, are maintained.*

Using Preformatted Text

Usually, browsers eliminate all extra returns and spaces and automatically create line breaks according to the size of the window. Preformatted text lets you maintain the original line breaks and spacing that you've inserted in the text. It is ideal for code, poetry, homemade tables, and ASCII art.

To use preformatted text:

1. Type **<pre>**.

2. Type or copy the text that you wish to display as is, with all the necessary spaces, returns, and line breaks.

3. Type **</pre>**.

✔ Tips

■ Preformatted text is generally displayed with a monospaced font like Courier. You can use styles to change the font, if you like *(see page 158)*.

■ You can insert additional formatting within preformatted text. However, you should do it *after* you set up your preformatted text, since the tags take up space in the (X)HTML document, but not in the page.

■ If what you want to display contains (X)HTML elements, you'll have to substitute the appropriate character entities for the greater than and less than signs (namely **>** and **<**, respectively). Otherwise the browser will try to display those elements; the pre tag works no magic on them. For more information, consult *Adding Characters from Outside the Encoding* on page 340.

■ You can also use styles to maintain line breaks and spaces *(see page 170)*.

■ Note that pre is block-level while the tags on page 76 are all inline.

Using Preformatted Text

Quoting Text

There are two special tags for marking quoted text so that you can identify its author, origin, and language. Block-level quotes are generally indented by browsers. Inline quotes are supposed to be automatically enclosed in quotation marks and thus, you should not include them in the text.

To quote block-level text:

1. Type **<blockquote** to begin a block-level quote.

2. If desired, type **cite="url"**, where *url* is the address of the source of the quote.

3. Type **>** to complete the opening tag.

4. Type the text that you wish to appear set off from the preceding and following text, including any necessary HTML tags.

5. Type **</blockquote>** to complete the element.

To quote inline text:

1. Type **<q** to begin.

2. If desired, type **xml:lang="xx" lang="xx"**, where *xx* is the two-letter code for the language the quote will be in. This code is supposed to determine the type of quote marks that will be used ("" for English, « for many European languages, etc.).

3. Type **>** to complete the opening tag.

4. Type the text that should be quoted.

5. Type **</q>**.

6. If desired, in the `html` tag, add **xml:lang="xx" lang="xx"**, where *xx* is the two-letter code for the language that most of your Web page is in.

<p>Sometimes I get to the point where I'm not sure anything matters at all. Then I read something like this and I am inspired: </p>

<blockquote cite="http://www.kingsolver.com">

<p>It's not hard to figure out what's good for kids, but amid the noise of an increasingly antichild political climate, it can be hard to remember just to go ahead and do it: for example, to vote to raise your school district's budget, even though you'll pay higher taxes. (If you're earning enough to pay taxes at all, I promise, the school needs those few bucks more than you do.) To support legislators who care more about afterschool programs, affordable health care, and libraries than about military budgets and the Dow Jones industrial average. To volunteer time and skills at your neighborhood school and also the school across town. To decide to notice, rather than ignore it, when a neighbor is losing it with her kids, and offer to babysit twice a week. This is not interference. Getting between a ball player and a ball is interference. The ball is inanimate.</p>

</blockquote>

<p>This is from Barbara Kingsolver's brilliant collection of essays, <cite>High Tide in Tucson</cite> (1995, HarperCollins)</p>.

Figure 4.12 *A block quote can be as short or as long as you need. You can even divide it into various paragraphs by adding* p *tags as necessary.*

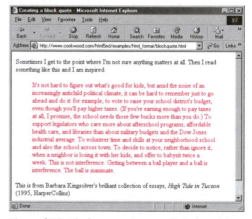

Figure 4.13 *Block quotes are generally indented from both sides. The* cite *attribute is not yet supported by any browser I've seen.*

```
<html xmlns="http://www.w3.org/1999/xhtml"
lang="en">

[snip]

<p>And then she said <q>Have you read
Kingsolver's <q>High Tide in Tucson</q>? It's
inspiring.</q></p>

<p>She tried again, this time in French: <q
lang="fr">Avez-vous lu le livre <q lang="fr">High
Tide in Tucson</q> de Kingsolver? C'est
inspirational.</q></p>
```

Figure 4.14 *The* lang *attribute in the* html *tag is supposed to be a default for the other tags. In my tests, it does serve as a default, but can't quite be overridden.*

Figure 4.15 *If you specify "en" for the* lang *attribute in the* html *element, Explorer for Mac uses curly quotes. Note how the inner quotes are single in the English quote, but all of the quotes are double in the French quote.*

```
<html xmlns="http://www.w3.org/1999/xhtml"
lang="fr">

[snip]

<p>And then she said <q lang="en">Have you
read Kingsolver's <q lang="en">High Tide in
Tucson</q>? It's inspiring.</q></p>

<p>Grasping at straws, she gave it one last shot,
this time in French: <q>Avez-vous lu le livre
<q>High Tide in Tucson</q> de Kingsolver? C'est
inspirational.</q></p>
```

Figure 4.16 *This time, we use "fr" for the* lang *attribute in the* html *tag. (And please, pardon my French!)*

Figure 4.17 *Now we've got those cute guillemet quotes around everything except nested quotes—which might be OK if the document is all French.*

✔ **Tips**

- Text and inline elements should not be placed directly between the opening and closing blockquote tags. Instead, enclose the text and inline elements in a block-level tag—like p, for example—*within* the blockquote tags.

- You can nest both blockquote and q elements. Nested q elements should automatically have the appropriate quotation marks—in English the outer quotes should be double and the inner ones should be single.

- Proper support for q varies widely from one browser to the next. Explorer 5 for Mac is best, using curly quotes and nesting them properly, and even using guillemets (») for French (as long as you set the lang attribute in the html tag). Netscape 6 Mac/Win uses straight double quotes for everything except nested q elements, where it uses single straight quotes. Opera 5 Mac/Win uses straight double quotes for everything, including nested q elements. Explorer for Windows (up to and including version 6) ignores the q element completely.

- The cite attribute may also be used with the q element, although it makes less sense. I haven't seen a browser that does anything with it in either element.

- For more details on the xml:lang and lang attributes, consult *Specifying Your Page's Language* on page 342.

- You can find a complete list of language codes at *http://www.w3.org/WAI/ER/ IG/ert/iso639.htm.*

Quoting Text

Creating Superscripts and Subscripts

Letters or numbers that are raised or lowered slightly relative to the main body text are called superscripts and subscripts, respectively. (X)HTML includes tags for defining both kinds of offset text.

To create superscripts or subscripts:

1. Type **<sub>** to create a subscript or **<sup>** to create a superscript.

2. Type the characters or symbols that you wish to offset relative to the main text.

3. Type **</sub>** or **</sup>**, depending on what you used in step 1, to complete the offset text.

✔ Tips

- Most browsers automatically reduce the font size of a sub- or superscripted character by a few points.

- Superscripts are the ideal way to format certain foreign language abbreviations like M[lle] for *Mademoiselle* in French or 3[a] for *Tercera* in Spanish.

- Subscripts are perfect for writing out chemical molecules like H_2O.

- Superscripts are also handy for creating footnotes. You can combine superscripts and links to make active footnotes (the visitor jumps to the footnote when they click the number or asterisk). For more information, see Chapter 7, *Links*.

- Super- and subscripted characters gently spoil the even spacing between lines. You can remedy this by changing the size of the sub or sup text *(see pages 75 and 162)* and adjusting its line height *(see page 164)*.

```
<body>

<h1>Famous Catalans</h1>

<p>When I was in the sixth grade, I played the
cello. There was a teacher at school who always
used to ask me if I knew who "Pablo Casals" was. I
didn't at the time (although I had met Rostropovich
once at a concert). Actually, Pablo Casals' real
name was <i>Pau</i> Casals, Pau being the
Catalan equivalent of Pablo<sup>1</sup>.</p>

<p>In addition to being an amazing cellist, Pau
Casals is remembered in this country for his
empassioned speech against nuclear proliferation
at the United Nations<sup>2</sup> which he
began by saying "I am a Catalan. Catalonia is an
oppressed nation."</p>

<p><sup>1</sup>It means Paul in English.<br />

<sup>2</sup>In 1963, I believe.</p>

</body>
```

Figure 4.18 *The opening* sup *or* sub *tag precedes the text to be affected.*

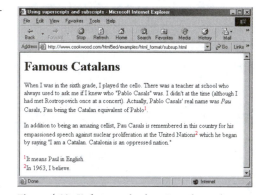

Figure 4.19 *Unfortunately, the* sub *and* sup *elements spoil the line spacing. Notice that there is more space between lines 3 and 4 of the first paragraph and lines 1 and 2 of the second than between the other lines.*

Figure 4.20 *You can use styles to adjust the size and leading so that the lines are properly spaced.*

```
<body>

<p><big>I promise to do all of my homework, <ins>
all of my chores,</ins> clean the cat litter, and not
watch more than <del>six</del> a half
hour<del>s</del> of tv.</big></p>


<p>signed</p>
```

Figure 4.21 *You have to be a little bit careful to include the associated punctuation with the* ins *and* del *elements.*

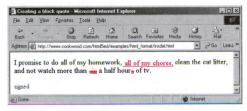

Figure 4.22 *The changes become quite apparent.*

Marking Changed Text

Another set of logical tags that you might find useful are for marking text that has changed from one version to the next. Lawyers and writers do this all the time.

To mark newly inserted text:

1. Type **<ins>**.

2. Type the new text.

3. Type **</ins>**.

To mark deleted text:

1. Place the cursor before the text you wish to mark as deleted.

2. Type **<del>**.

3. Place the cursor after the text you wish to mark as deleted.

4. Type **</del>**.

✔ Tips

■ Text marked with the ins tag is generally underlined. Since links are often underlined as well (if not in your site, in many others), this may be confusing to visitors. You may want to add an explanation at the beginning of your page and/or use styles to change how inserted passages (or links) are displayed *(see page 157)*.

■ Text marked with the del element is generally stricken out. Why not just erase it and be done with it? Striking it out makes it easy for others to see what has changed.

■ You can also use styles to underline and strike out text *(see page 174)*. The advantage of the ins and del elements is that they identify the text as being *inserted* or *deleted*, and not just underlined or stricken.

Explaining Abbreviations

Abbreviations and acronyms (an abbreviation that can be pronounced as a word) abound. Unfortunately, people use them so often that they sometimes forget that not everyone knows what they mean. You can use the `abbr` and `acronym` elements to add meaning to the abbreviation or acronym in question without breaking the flow of your Web page or distracting your readers with extra links.

To explain abbreviations:

1. Type **<abbr**.

Or type **<acronym** if the abbreviation can be pronounced as a word.

2. Next type **title="explanation"**, where *explanation* gives more details about the abbreviation.

3. Type **>**.

4. Then type the abbreviation itself.

5. Finally, finish up with **</abbr>** or **</acronym>** depending on what you used in step 1.

✔ Tips

- Netscape 6 (on both platforms) supports both `abbr` and `acronym`, highlighting both elements with a dotted underline and providing the `title` attribute's contents as a tool tip **(Figure 4.24)**.

- Explorer for Mac supports just the `acronym` tag, displaying its contents in small caps and the `title` attribute as a tool tip **(Figure 4.25)**, though you have to point at just the right place. It completely ignores the `abbr` element.

- Explorer for Windows (up to version 6) supports neither `abbr` nor `acronym` (though it still shows titles as tool tips).

```
<p><abbr title="Lyndon Baynes Johnson">LBJ
</abbr> took the <abbr title="Interborough Rapid
Transit">IRT</abbr> down to 4th Street <abbr
title="United States of America">USA</abbr>.

<br />When he got there, what did he see?

<br />The youth of America on <abbr title="d-
Lysergic Acid Diethylamide">LSD</abbr>.</p>

<p>--Hair, the Musical, 1967</p>

<p>Or perhaps you'd rather talk about something
slightly less political, like <acronym title="Light
Amplification By Stimulated Emission of Radiation">
laser</acronym>, or <acronym title="Radio
Detection And Ranging">radar</acronym>, or
<acronym title="Self-Contained Underwater
Breathing Apparatus">scuba</acronym>? </p>
```

Figure 4.23 *It seems an awful lot of code for just a few words. Still, it can be very helpful to get immediate information about an abbreviation, at least the first time it is used.*

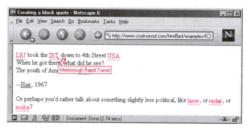

Figure 4.24 *Netscape 6 Mac/Win highlight abbreviations and acronyms with a dotted underline and when your visitors hover, they get a question mark pointer, and then the contents of the element's* `title` *attribute.*

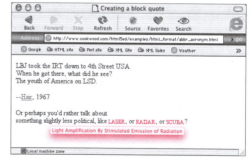

Figure 4.25 *Explorer 5 for Mac displays acronyms in small caps, and if the visitor hovers over them in just the right place, produces the contents of the element's* `title` *attribute. It completely ignores the* `abbr` *elements.*

CREATING WEB IMAGES

5

What Program to Use?

There are many, many different tools that you can use to create and save images for the Web. It was hard deciding whether to try to give general instructions that really wouldn't fit any actual piece of software, or focus on one program that most but probably not all of my readers would have. In the end, I opted for two related programs: the industry standard, Adobe Photoshop ($600), and its less expensive cousin, Photoshop Elements ($100). Most of the techniques in this chapter can be executed with either program; a very few noted exceptions work only in Photoshop. Both are available for Macintosh and Windows.

There are many other alternatives, including Paint Shop Pro for Windows by Jasc Software and GraphicConverter for Macintosh. Feel free to use whatever program you're most comfortable with.

Let me stress, in addition, that the basic techniques for optimizing images for the Web are the same regardless of the software you choose. The command names may be slightly different and there may be more or fewer steps, but the ideas remain the same. In short, my hope is that this chapter will be useful even if you don't use the same software that I do.

Creating images for the Web is a bit different from creating images for output on paper. Although the basic characteristics of Web images and printable images are the same, six main factors distinguish them: format, color, size/resolution, speed, transparency, and animation. This chapter will explain the important aspects of each of these six factors and how to use that knowledge to create the most effective images for your Web site.

Please note, however, that this chapter is no substitute for your image editing program's documentation. Nor is it meant to be a manual for learning about design. Instead, use this chapter to learn about the particular *components and features* that distinguish Web images. Then combine that knowledge with your computing and design expertise to create awesome images for your page.

About Images for the Web

Now let's look at those six factors that you should keep in mind as you create Web images.

Format

People who print images on paper don't have to worry about what their readers will use to look at the images. You do. The Web is accessed every day by millions of Macs, Windows-based PCs, Unix machines, and other kinds of computers. The graphics you use in your Web page should be in a format that each of these operating systems can recognize. Presently, the two most widely used formats on the Web are GIF and JPEG, with PNG gaining in popularity. Current versions of Explorer and Netscape can view all three image formats.

Color

Currently (mid 2002), 50% of the Web surfing public use 24-bit monitors, 40% use 16-bit monitors, and fewer than 10% (which is still a lot of people) use 8-bit monitors. My guess is that the first number will continue to rise, while the second two will fall, although probably never all the way to zero.

What's the difference? 24-bit, or "True Color" monitors can show any one of 16,777,216 colors. In fact, if the monitor was big enough, you could show every one of those colors on the same 24-bit monitor. In contrast, while an 8-bit monitor can show the same variety of colors, it can only display 256 of them at any one time. 16-bit monitors, for their part can display some 65,536 colors. (The details are a bear; it's all about the amount of memory devoted to each pixel.) To make matters worse, browsers, in order to run faster, take a little shortcut. Instead of showing *any* 256 colors, on 8-bit monitors they will only display a *specific set* of 256 colors.

Figure 5.1 *Logotypes and other computer-generated images or images with few colors are compressed efficiently with LZW and thus could be saved in GIF format. Even better at compressing images of this type is PNG format, but not everyone supports it.*

Figure 5.2 *Full-color photographs and other naturally created images, or images with more than 256 colors, should be saved in JPEG format.*

About Images for the Web

Figure 5.3 *Both of these images have exactly 18 colors and look about the same on high-end monitors. But notice how the* dither *image is full of noise and patterning (called dithering) while the* safe *image is clean and sharp. That's because this page was viewed on an old 8-bit monitor and the* safe *image uses browser-safe colors while the* dither *image doesn't.*

If a browser is called upon to show a color that's out of its range, it has two options: it can mix two colors to produce the missing one (this is called *dithering*), or it can *shift* the missing color to one in the current set. Sometimes you hardly notice; sometimes it's a disaster.

So, if you don't want your colors to dither or shift on an 8-bit monitor, you have to use one of the colors in the browser's particular set. However, since browsers reserve a bunch of colors for the browser window itself, and because the sets for Windows and Mac are slightly different, there are actually only 216 colors that won't ever dither on browsers on 8-bit monitors on either platform. These colors are called *Web-safe* or *browser-safe*. On the down side, this set of colors, or *palette*, offers a very limited choice of colors. (And if that weren't enough, version 4 browsers and earlier shift them around on 16-bit monitors.)

But since there are fewer and fewer 8-bit monitors, it's seeming less and less important to completely limit color choice because of them—especially when you may exacerbate a problem with 16-bit monitors.

My recommendation is to first analyze your Web logs (if you have access to them—ask your ISP) to gauge your public. What monitors do the people who surf your site use? Then, base your use of colors on that data. If your numbers match the averages, try to limit dithering and shifts—particularly in large areas of color—but feel free to take advantage of the other sixteen million colors!

Check the inside back cover of this book for a handy table for choosing colors. If you'd rather stick to browser-safe colors, you can find a complete table on my Web site. (Since browser-safe colors don't print well, it doesn't make sense to include them on the cover.)

Size and Resolution

Computer images are measured in pixels. Your digital camera, for example, may take pictures that are 640 pixels wide by 480 pixels high. But how big is that? The answer is, it depends. If you're printing the image to a printer at 200 ppi (pixels per inch), that image will measure a rather petite 3.2 by 2.4 inches. But if you're using that page on the Web, the image will depend on your visitor's monitor's resolution, which is more likely to be around 86 ppi (and might be as low as 72 or as high as 100 or so), and thus will display at a heftier 7.5 x 5.5 inches (about 19 x 14 cm) on screen.

Perhaps a better way to think of image size is with respect to the browser window. Since monitors with a resolution of 640 pixels wide by 480 pixels high were the standard for so long, browser manufacturers, and indeed Web page designers, tend to keep their pages under 600 pixels wide, so that viewers can see the entire contents of the page without scrolling horizontally. So, if you can envision the width of a basic browser window (say, just to the end of the navigation bar), then you know approximately how big 640 pixels is and can plan your images accordingly.

Don't forget of course, that plenty of people have bigger monitors (1024 x 768 is not unusual) and more than a few have smaller. Still, just because someone has a bigger monitor doesn't mean they're going to fill it with a single browser window containing your Web page.

Note that *resolution* can mean one of two quite distinct concepts: the actual number of pixels on a monitor or in an image, say 640 x 480, *or* the number of pixels in an inch of that monitor or image, say 72 or 86 ppi. Regardless, the higher the resolution, the more pixels. On paper, pixels can add details or size. On screen, more pixels *always* translate to a bigger size image.

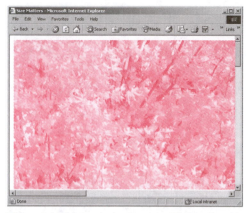

Figure 5.4 *This particular image is 1704 pixels wide and in Photoshop has an output resolution of 284 ppi and only measures 6 x 8 inches. Here in Explorer on this monitor, however, its output resolution is determined by the visitor's monitor—about 86ppi—which means that the picture is about 20 inches wide!*

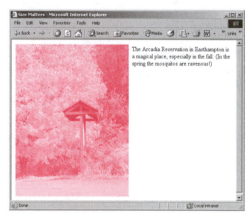

Figure 5.5 *This image also measures 6 x 8 inches in Photoshop, though it has an output resolution of 50ppi. Again, however, these relative measurements are irrelevant. What counts is that it measures 300 pixels wide, which is about half the width of an average browser window.*

Speed

The next principal difference between Web images and printed images is that your visitors have to wait for Web images to download. (Imagine waiting for pictures to appear in your morning paper!)

How can you keep download time to a minimum? The easiest way is to use small images. The larger an image's file size, the longer it takes to appear before your visitors' eyes.

The second way to speed up download time is by compressing the image. There are three popular compression methods (that correspond to the three major formats): LZW (for GIF images), JPEG, and PNG. LZW is particularly effective for computer-generated art like logos, rendered text, and other images that have large areas of a single color. In fact, if you can reduce the number of colors in an image, LZW can often (but not always) compress the image even more.

JPEG, on the other hand, is better at compressing photographs and other images that have many different colors. In fact, if you blur an image, thereby creating even more colors, JPEG compression is often more effective *(see page 100)*.

Each method has its drawbacks. Because LZW is patented (at least until 2003), developers have to pay royalties on software that uses it. (This is one of the principal reasons that PNG was developed.) And GIF images are limited to 256 colors. JPEG has two main disadvantages. First, its compression information takes up a lot of space and is simply not worth it for very small images. Second, it is *lossy* compression—permanently eliminating details in order to save space. Uncompressing the image will not restore the lost data. If you plan on editing an image in the future you should save a copy in an uncompressed format (e.g., PSD or TIFF) and only save it as a JPEG after you have made your final edits.

About Images for the Web

PNG compresses better than LZW without losing information like JPEG. Its chief weakness is its limited support in older browsers, though current browsers display PNG images just fine.

Another way to keep your visitors happy while they're waiting is to offer a sneak preview of what the image will look like. All three major formats offer some form of progressive display, often called *interlacing*. For details on progressively rendering images, consult page 99.

Transparency

Transparency is important for two reasons. First, you can use it to create complex layouts by making one image move behind another. Second, you can take advantage of transparency to give an image a non-rectangular outline, adding visual interest to your pages **(Figure 5.6)**. Both GIF and PNG allow transparency; JPEG does not.

Animation

One thing you won't be seeing on paper anytime soon are moving images. On the Web, they're everywhere. For information on creating animated images, see page 101. Animated images can be saved in GIF format, but not JPEG. You can also create animation with Flash *(see page 464)*.

Figure 5.6 *The courthouse image's transparent background helps the image blend into the page, no matter what background color the visitor has chosen to view Web pages against. Real transparency is only available for GIF and PNG images.*

About Images for the Web

Getting Images

So how do you get an image that you can use for your Web page? There are several ways. You can buy or download ready-made images, digitize photographs or handdrawn images with a scanner, use a digital camera, or draw images from scratch in an image editing program like Photoshop. Once you've got them in your computer, you can adapt them to the Web, if necessary, with the rest of the techniques in this chapter.

To get images:

■ Although you can use Google to find images on the Web (clicking the Images button and entering criteria as usual), the results are not necessarily images you can use on your site. Instead, do a regular search for "free images".

■ Generally, even free images found on the Web are for personal use only and cannot be modified. Images you buy can usually be used for any purpose (except for reselling the images themselves). Read any disclaimers or licenses carefully.

■ Many companies sell stock photography and images on CD. Such disks often have several versions of each image for different purposes. Look for the Web or Multimedia version.

■ Many photo processing outfits will develop a roll of film directly onto a CD.

■ Scanners and digital cameras have grown in quality as they've plummeted in price. They are an ideal way to convert print photographs into digital ones, or to create digital ones from scratch.

■ If you create your own images, save them as GIF, JPEG, or PNG. Don't save them as BMP—only Explorer for Windows users will be able to see them.

Getting Images

The Save for Web Command

Both Adobe Photoshop and Adobe Photoshop Elements offer the awesome Save for Web command. It lets you visually compare the original image with up to three versions that you can optimize while keeping an eye on any resulting savings in file size and download time.

To use Adobe's Save for Web command:

1. Create your image.

2. Choose File > Save for Web. The Save For Web window appears **(Figure 5.8)**.

3. In Photoshop, click the 2-up tab to see one optimized version or the 4-up tab to see three. Photoshop Elements always shows a single alternative.

4. Click an optimized version, if necessary.

5. Choose the desired format.

   In general, images that have been created on a computer, including logos, banners, line art, text, and any graphic with large areas of a single color and sharp detail should be saved in GIF or PNG-8 format **(Figure 5.7)**.

   Images with continuous tones, like photographs, should be saved in either JPEG or PNG-24 format **(Figure 5.8)**.

6. Adjust the additional settings that appear until you get the smallest file possible with an acceptable quality. (These settings are discussed throughout the rest of this chapter.)

7. Click OK in Photoshop Elements or Save in Photoshop. Choose a directory and name the new file. It will automatically carry the extension of the selected format (and thus normally will not replace the original image).

Figure 5.7 *In this example, the image has a lot of flat color, as well as text, which should be kept sharp. Both are good reasons to choose GIF format (lower right), which you can see compresses the image the best, to just over 2K. JPEG, even at very low quality, doesn't do nearly as well.*

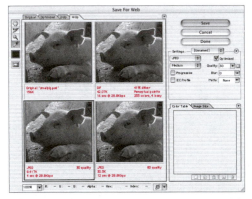

Figure 5.8 *The original image is shown in the top left. Since this is a photograph, the GIF compression is pretty useless (top right). I can choose between the bottom two JPEG options depending on my bandwidth and quality constraints.*

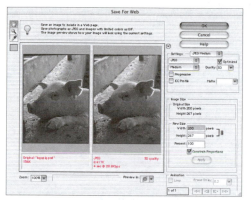

Figure 5.9 *The Save For Web window in Photoshop Elements, Adobe's consumer-end digital-imaging program, is slightly simpler than Photoshop's—for example, only allowing for one optimized version to be shown at a time—but still contains the most important features. Perhaps the most important difference is the absence of the Color Table. However, with the dwindling base of 8-bit monitors, exerting precise control over which colors appear in an image begins to look a lot like overkill (see page 96).*

✔ Tips

■ Remember that your main objective is to get the smallest file size possible while still maintaining acceptable image quality.

■ Images should be created in RGB mode, not CMYK (which is for print).

■ If you're not sure which format to choose, compare two optimizations and see which format compresses better while leaving the image at the best quality.

■ PNG is a powerful lossless format that can be used for both computer-generated and "natural" color images. It is often better than GIF but not quite as good as JPEG. Unfortunately, Photoshop is probably not the best tool for creating PNG images, as its compression algorithms aren't as tight as they might be. PNG's other disadvantage is that older browsers don't support it, although frankly, older browsers don't support much of anything, so it hardly seems a deciding factor.

■ If you have an image with both types of content, you can either slice it into distinct chunks and compress them separately (and then reassemble them with a borderless table—see page 215) or you can just use a single format and let it do its best.

■ The Save for Web command creates a new, independent image and leaves the original image intact. The exception, of course, is if you save the new image with the same name and extension as the old.

■ Only an image's visible layers are saved in the optimized version.

■ The Save For Web window varies a bit between Photoshop and Photoshop Elements (and between versions of these) but the key commands stay the same **(Figure 5.9)**.

The Save for Web Command

Making Images Smaller

Most images are simply too big for a Web page. While an image destined for print might measure 1800 pixels across (in order to print at 300 dpi and be six inches wide), images for Web pages should rarely be wider than 600 pixels, and often more like 200, depending, of course, on what you're doing.

To make images smaller:

1. In the lower right portion of the Save For Web window, click the Image Size tab.

2. Enter a new width or height in pixels, or a percentage, and then click Apply.

✔ Tips

■ You can continue to adjust the size up or down until you're satisfied. The image is not actually resampled until you press OK or Save.

■ Don't use this technique to make an image *bigger* than its original. Adding pixels with Photoshop increases the file size but doesn't add any image data. If you must increase the image's size, use (X)HTML *(see page 108)* or better yet, rescan or redigitize your image.

■ You can also use the Image Size command to change the size of an image. Remember that the Resolution box is irrelevant (it refers to the *output resolution*, which is determined on the Web not by you or Photoshop, but rather by the visitor's monitor). Instead, base the size on the number of pixels in the image. You will have to check the Resample Image box to get it to change the image's size (as opposed to its output resolution).

■ Before you make images proportionally smaller, be sure to crop them to eliminate any unwanted areas.

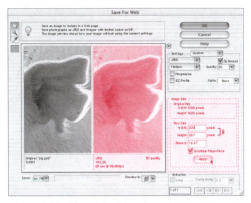

Figure 5.10 *The original image, snapped with my digital camera's default values measured 1600 by 1200 pixels, which besides being big enough for almost three browsers, weighed in at a whopping 192.2K, even when compressed as a medium quality JPEG. Instead, type the desired new width of 200 pixels in the Width box and click Apply.*

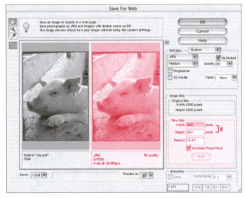

Figure 5.11 *The reduced-size image will fit properly on my page and will take only 4 seconds to download at 28.8Kbps (less with a faster connection).*

Figure 5.12 *Choose File > New to create a new image being sure to check the Transparent box at the bottom of the New dialog box to start with a transparent background.*

Figure 5.13 *Select the desired portion of an existing image (left) and then choose Edit > Copy.*

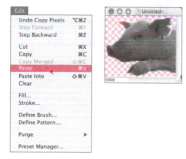

Figure 5.14 *Choose Edit > Paste to create a new layer with the copied image. Notice how the background around the pig's head at right is transparent (shown with checkered pattern).*

Creating Transparency

Transparency allows the background to shine through the affected areas often creating a more interesting layout. Images with transparent areas can be saved either in GIF or PNG format, but not JPEG.

In Photoshop and Photoshop Elements, you create transparency in an image and then you indicate that you want that area to be transparent in the Save For Web window. In addition, if you know what color will be showing through the transparent areas, you can have Photoshop create a smooth transition from the image to the transparent areas, using the background color. This is called a *matte*.

To create transparency:

1. Choose File > New to create a new document and click the Transparent button at the bottom of the New dialog box to start with a transparent background **(Figure 5.12)**. Then click OK.

2. Create the image in the normal way, leaving part of the background transparent.

Or...

1. Copy part of an existing image **(Figure 5.13)**.

2. Paste it to a new layer. New layers by default have a transparent background **(Figure 5.14)**.

3. Hide or eliminate any non-transparent layers, if necessary.

Or...

You may have to combine the two techniques, for example, pasting a new layer into a new document with a transparent background.

Creating Transparency

Saving Images with Transparency

Once you've created transparency in an image, you can save the image as either a GIF or PNG to preserve the transparency in the Web page.

To save images with transparency:

1. In the Save For Web window, choose the GIF or PNG-8 format.

2. Click Transparency **(Figure 5.15)**.

3. If you know the color of the background upon which the image will be placed (that will shine through the transparent areas), choose that color in the Matte menu **(Figure 5.16)**. The pixels that are partially transparent will be blended with the Matte color to make a smooth transition from the image to the background.

   If you don't know the background color, choose None in the Matte pop-up menu. This creates a hard border, converting pixels that are 50% or more transparent to fully transparent and pixels that are less than 50% transparent to fully opaque.

4. Click OK and give the file a name.

✔ Tips

■ In Photoshop, but not Photoshop Elements, you can select individual colors from the Color Table and convert them to transparency.

■ While creating titles out of GIF images lets you use fancy fonts, it has a number of disadvantages: namely, that search engines can't read them (*see page 416*) and they're a bit of a hassle to update. If you insist, at least be sure to set the Matte to the background color of your page, otherwise the text will look jagged and any benefit from the nice font is lost.

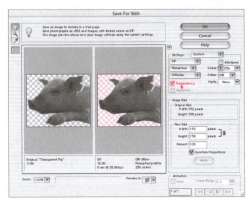

Figure 5.15 *Once you're satisfied with the image that contains transparent areas, choose File > Save for Web, choose a format that supports transparency (GIF or PNG) and then click the Transparency box.*

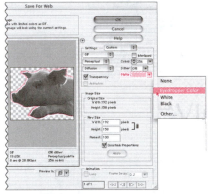

Figure 5.16 *If you know the color of the background upon which the image will go, select it in the Matte menu. This will create a smooth transition between the image and the background color.*

Figure 5.17 *Here's the result. Both the title and the left pig were created with a matte set to the background color of this Web page and thus have smooth borders. The right pig was created with no matte and thus has a hard, sometimes jagged border.*

Saving Images with Transparency

Figure 5.18 *One way to select the background is to first select the foreground and then choose Select > Inverse.*

Figure 5.19 *Once the background is selected, choose the desired color in the foreground color box (the upper of the two boxes at the bottom of the toolbar) and then press Option-Delete (or Alt-Delete if you're on Windows). The background is changed to the desired color.*

Figure 5.20 *This time the pig looks like it's on a transparent background, but it's actually not. It's on a background that matches the Web page's background.*

Simulating Transparency

Simulating transparency means making the image's background the same color as the background of your page so that the image blends in as if the background were transparent. It's useful in JPEG images which don't allow real transparency.

To simulate transparency by making the background a solid color:

1. Select the background **(Figure 5.18)**.

2. Click the foreground color control box to set it to the desired color.

3. Press Option-Delete (Alt-Delete on Windows) to change the color of the selected area (the background) to the selected color **(Figure 5.19)**.

4. Use the Save For Web window to save the image as usual (without choosing the Transparency option, since there are no real transparent areas).

✔ Tips

■ It's probably a good idea to choose a browser safe color for the background (though I didn't in this example). Otherwise, it will dither on 256-color monitors. For more details, consult *Using (Mostly) Browser Safe Colors* on page 96.

■ Since JPEG compresses photographs much better than GIFs, this is a way to simulate transparency on files that have too many colors to be effectively compressed as GIFs.

■ Of course, if your visitors override the background color, the effect is lost.

Simulating Transparency

Using (Mostly) Browser Safe Colors

As I discussed earlier *(see page 84)*, if you want to avoid dithering on 8-bit monitors, you should restrict the colors in GIF or PNG-8 images to the Web-safe palette. However, if you limit yourself to those 216 colors, it's hard to create the soft, anti-aliased edges which make text look half decent. A compromise is in order: get rid of dither in big areas of flat color areas, while being less strict with edges.

Before getting rid of dither, it's helpful to know if it's a problem. Photoshop has a helpful, if rather hidden option to preview dither.

To preview dither:

1. If necessary, select the desired optimized GIF image in the Save For Web window.

2. Choose Browser Dither—in the pop-up menu that descends from the triangle in the top-right corner of the image area **(Figure 5.21)**—to preview how the selected optimized image will appear on an 8-bit monitor **(Figure 5.22)**.

To convert *all* colors to Web-safe:

In the Save For Web window, choose Web in the Dither pattern menu **(Figure 5.23)**. All colors in the image are converted to Web-safe colors, which may or may not be close substitutes.

To convert selected colors to Web-safe colors (Photoshop only):

1. Deselect the Browser Dither option.

2. Click the Color Table tab to make it visible, if necessary.

3. Select the eyedropper and click in an area that is being dithered. The corresponding color will be selected in the Color Table tab **(Figure 5.24)**.

Figure 5.21 *In order to see what your image will look like on an 8-bit monitor, choose Browser Dither from the pop-up menu that descends from the little arrow at the top-right corner of the image area.*

Figure 5.22 *The background color is not Web-safe and so it dithers on an 8-bit monitor.*

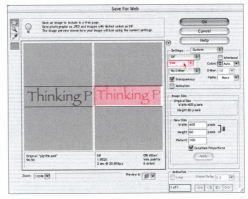

Figure 5.23 *In Photoshop Elements, your only recourse is to change all of the colors in the image to Web-safe colors by choosing Web in the Dither pattern menu in the top right area of the Save For Web window. And in this example, the result is a non-dithered image. Remember that most monitors are 16 and 24-bit which never dither images. (The Web option for Dither is available in Photoshop as well.)*

Figure 5.24 *In Photoshop only, select the eyedropper (from the top left) and then click in the color that's getting dithered. Notice how the color is selected in the Color Table at right.*

Figure 5.25 *Then click the little cube at the bottom of the Color Table (second icon from the left) to shift the selected color to its nearest Web-safe substitute.*

Figure 5.26 *Instead of changing all the colors, we change only the color that was dithering badly.*

4. Click the color cube icon at the bottom of the Color Table tab (the second icon from the left) to shift the dithering color to a Web-safe color **(Figure 5.25)**.

5. Go through steps 1–5 for each color that is noticeably dithering.

✔ Tips

■ Since there are only 216 Web-safe colors, a suitable substitute for your color may not be available. You have to decide whether it's worth it to switch to a Web-safe color in order to avoid dithering (which is not always the end of the world and which only occurs on 8-bit monitors).

■ The Browser Dither option actually shows you the colors you would see if you were viewing the image in a Web browser. Therefore, in Photoshop, if you try to select a dithering color with the Browser Dither option on, you'll end up selecting the Web-safe color, if it's available in the Color Table. Instead, turn off the Browser Dither option so that you can select the real culprit.

■ In Photoshop (but not Photoshop Elements) you can unshift colors by selecting them and choosing Shift/Unshift Selected Colors to/from Web Palette in the document panel menu.

■ You can also let Photoshop decide which colors to shift by setting a tolerance level in the Web Snap box at the bottom right of the Save For Web window's options area. Personally, I like manually choosing just the colors that are causing a problem.

■ Since JPEG images generally have many more than 256 colors, there's no way to keep them from dithering. Only worry about Web-safe colors with GIF or PNG-8 images.

Using (Mostly) Browser Safe Colors

Reducing the Number of Colors

You can make compression more efficient in GIF and PNG-8 files by reducing the number of colors in the image.

To reduce the number of colors:

1. In the Save For Web window, choose GIF or PNG-8 in the Format menu **(Figure 5.27)**.

2. Click in the Colors pop-up menu and reduce the number of colors **(Figure 5.28)**.

3. Check the quality and file size of the resulting image.

✔ Tip

■ In my tests, it seems that in general, if reducing colors helps GIF or PNG compression, switching to JPEG format does even better. The rub is that JPEG doesn't support transparency. So, if you must have transparency, reducing colors can be a fruitful exercise, since this will effectively reduce the size of a transparent GIF.

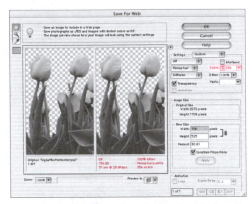

Figure 5.27 *Before we adjust the number of colors, the image is compressed to 156.8K and will take 57 seconds to download (at 28.8Kbps).*

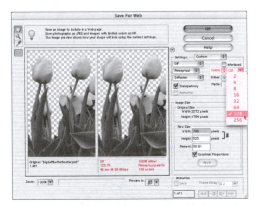

Figure 5.28 *Select a reduced number of colors in the Colors pop-up menu in the top-right part of the window. Reducing the colors in this admittedly large image saved an impressive 31.1K and 11 seconds of download time.*

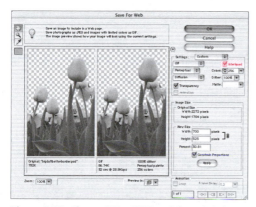

Figure 5.29 *Choose GIF or PNG and then click the Interlaced box. Or choose JPEG and then click Progressive.*

Showing Images Progressively

You can save an image in such a way that a browser can show it at gradually increasing resolutions. Although the initial image is blurry, the visitor immediately gets an idea of what the image will (eventually) look like.

To show images progressively:

In the Save For Web window, check the Interlaced box for GIF or PNG formats **(Figure 5.29)** or the Progressive box for JPEG.

✔ Tips

- Displaying images progressively is probably most useful with large images.

- Interlacing has the biggest impact on slow computers with slow connections. On faster computers, it's often hard to notice any effect at all.

- If you readjust any of the other settings in the Save For Web window or scroll the preview around with the Hand tool, the Interlaced option goes back to being unchecked. Be sure to recheck it before you click OK.

Blurring Images to Aid JPEG Compression

Because of the way JPEG works, the softer the transition from color to color, the more efficiently the image can be compressed. So, if you blur the image slightly, you may be able to reduce the file size—and thus the load time—even further.

To blur images to aid JPEG compression:

Choose Filter > Blur > Gaussian Blur **(Figure 5.30)**.

Or...

(Photoshop Only) In the Save For Web window, adjust the Blur slider. Keep an eye on the ratio of quality vs. file size **(Figures 5.31 and 5.32)**.

✔ Tips

- This is one of those cases in which a little goes a long way. You don't need to blur the image beyond recognition to get file size savings.

- You have to decide if the loss of detail is worth faster download times and less waiting for your visitors. If all your visitors use 14K modems on 256-bit monitors, this technique may be very useful. Visitors with T1 lines on high-end systems, on the other hand, may not benefit enough from the speed improvement to make sacrificing image sharpness worthwhile.

- You can make a selection before applying the Gaussian Blur filter in order to limit and control what gets blurred. You needn't blur the entire image. (Photoshop's Blur slider does nothing more than apply a Gaussian Blur to the entire image.)

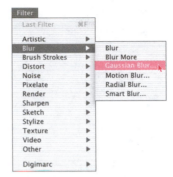

Figure 5.30 *In both Photoshop and Photoshop Elements, you can select part of your image and then choose Filter > Blur > Gaussian Blur.*

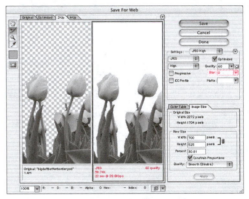

Figure 5.31 *By default, no Blur is applied. This image will occupy 58.74K and take 22 seconds to download. Note that we've lost the transparency since we're saving in JPEG.*

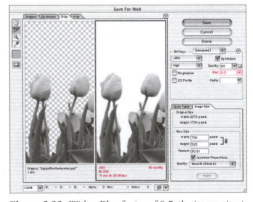

Figure 5.32 *With a Blur factor of 0.5, the image size is reduced to 50.74K and the download time goes to 19 seconds. Also notice, however, that the image is noticeably, if subtly, blurred.*

Figure 5.33 *Every layer that will be a frame in the animated GIF should be visible. Here we see the last frame (the top layer) of our soon-to-be animated GIF and the Layers palette.*

Figure 5.34 *In the Save For Web window, choose the GIF format, click Animation and then choose the desired options in the lower part of the window.*

Creating Animated GIFs

An animated GIF is a single file that contains a collection of images that are shown in sequence, one after another. They're often used for advertising banners.

To create an animated GIF:

1. In Photoshop Elements, create each frame of the animated GIF on a separate layer. The bottom layer corresponds to the first frame, the second to bottom is the second frame, and so on **(Figure 5.33)**.

2. Choose File > Save for Web.

3. In the Save For Web window, choose GIF Format and check the Animation box. The controls become active in the bottom part of the window **(Figure 5.34)**.

4. Set the number of seconds that should elapse between each frame in the Frame Delay box.

5. Check the Loop box if you'd like the animation to begin again each time it reaches the end.

6. Click the arrows at the bottom of the Animation area to preview the different frames of the animation in the optimization window.

✔ Tips

■ You insert an animated GIF on your page just like any other image *(see page 104)*.

■ I set a frame delay of about one second if the animation's frames contain text. If you want to animate an actual graphic, you'd probably want to use less.

■ Animated GIFs are created essentially the same way in Photoshop, but it relies on ImageReady (which is included with Photoshop) for saving them.

Creating Animated GIFs

USING IMAGES

Once you've created the fastest-loading, hottest-looking images you can—perhaps with the techniques in the previous chapter—you're ready to get back to (X)HTML and get those images on your page.

Inserting Images on a Page

You can place all kinds of images on your Web page, from logos to photographs. Images placed as described here appear automatically when the visitor jumps to your page, as long as the browser is set up to view them.

To insert an image on a page:

1. Place the cursor where you want the image to appear.

2. Type **<img src="image.url"** where *image.url* indicates the location of the image file on the server *(see page 33)*.

3. Type a space and then the final **/>**.

✔ Tips

■ Add a p or br tag before an image to start it on its own line.

■ For information on creating images especially for Web pages, consult Chapter 5, *Creating Web Images*.

■ Use this technique to place GIF, JPEG, PNG, or any other kind of images that the browser recognizes.

■ Don't expect your visitors to wait more than 10 seconds to load and view your entire page (about 50K total with a 56 Kbps modem connection). One alternative is to create miniatures *(see page 92)* of large images and let visitors *choose* to view the larger images *(see page 109)*.

■ There is a deprecated border attribute (border="n", where *n* is the width in pixels) that adds or eliminates a border around images, especially the automatic border that appears around images used in links *(see page 128)*. Better yet, you can use styles to control this and all other aspects of images *(see page 186)*.

<h1>Barcelona's Market</h1>

<img src="outsidemarket.jpg" />

<p>This first picture shows the entranceway to the Mercat de la Boquería, the central market that is just off the Rambles. It's an incredible place, full of every kind of fruit, meat, fish, or whatever you might happen to need. It took me a long time to get up the nerve to actually take a picture there. You might say I'm kind of a chicken, but since I lived there, it was just sort of strange. Do you take pictures of your supermarket?</p>

Figure 6.1 *The URL for this image, since it contains only the file name and no path, indicates that the image is located in the same folder as this Web page.*

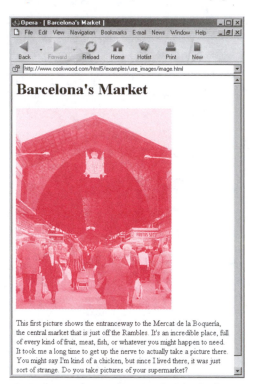

Figure 6.2 *Images are aligned to the left side of the page, by default. You can change the alignment or wrap text around an image. See page 171 and page 194 for details.*

```
<h1>Barcelona's Market</h1>

<img src="outsidemarket.jpg" alt="Entranceway to
Mercat de la Boquería" />

<p>This first picture shows the entranceway to the
Mercat de la Boquería, the central market that is just
off the Rambles. It's an incredible place, full of every
kind of fruit, meat, fish, or whatever you might
```

Figure 6.3 *While the alternate text can theoretically be as long as you like, most browsers don't automatically wrap long lines. Therefore, it's a good idea to keep it under 50 characters.*

Figure 6.4 *The alternate text appears if the image can't be found, if the visitor has deselected Autoload images, or if the browser doesn't support images.*

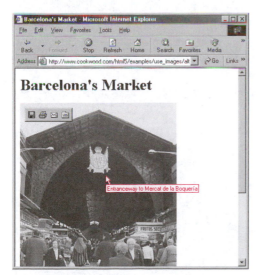

Figure 6.5 *On Explorer for Windows, when the visitor points at an image with alternate text, the alternate text appears in a tool tip. You can create tool tips for all current browsers by using the* title *tag (see page 72).*

Offering Alternate Text

While images are wonderful on a big screen with a fast connection, they're not nearly so useful on handhelds, mobile phones, slow connections, or for the blind. You can add descriptive text that will appear if the image, for whatever reason, does not.

To offer alternate text when images don't appear:

1. Within the img tag, after the src attribute and value, type **alt="**.

2. Type the text that should appear if, for some reason, the image itself does not.

3. Type **"**.

✔ Tips

- The alt attribute is required for *all* img tags in both XHTML and HTML.

- On IE Win 5+ and Netscape 4.x, the alt tag text is automatically used as a *tool tip* (**Figure 6.5**), similar to the effect of the title tag in *all* current browsers (*see page 72*). If you'd like tool tips on images in all browsers, use the title tag in addition to alt (which will still appear when the image does not). If you don't want tool tips at all, set **title=""**.

- If the image is just for formatting, like a horizontal line or a bullet image, the W3C suggests you use **alt=""**.

- Some browsers, like Lynx, that do not support images, are used by the blind because they can read the contents of the alt tag out loud. This is just one more reason to add alternate text to your images.

- You can actually format the alternate text with different fonts and sizes by applying styles to the img tag. For details on styles, see Chapter 10, *Formatting with Styles*.

Specifying Size for Speedier Viewing

When a browser gets to the (X)HTML code for an image, it must load the image to see how big it is and how much space must be reserved for it. If you specify the image's dimensions, the browser can fill in the text around the image as the image loads, so that your visitors have something to read while waiting for the images.

You can either use your browser or your image editing program to get the exact dimensions of your image.

To find the size of your image with your browser:

1. Right-click (in Windows) or Control-click (in Macintosh) the image. A contextual pop-up menu appears **(Figure 6.6)**.

2. Choose Properties or Get Image Info (depending on your browser). A box appears that shows the dimensions of your image, in pixels **(Figure 6.7)**.

To figure out the size of your image with Photoshop or Photoshop Elements:

1. Open the image in Photoshop or Photoshop Elements.

2. Choose Window > Info to display the Info palette, if it's not already visible.

3. Choose Select All (Command-A on a Mac, Control-A on Windows). The image's dimensions will be displayed in the bottom-right corner of the Info palette **(Figure 6.9)**. You may have to choose Palette Options in the Info palette's menu to display the dimensions in pixels.

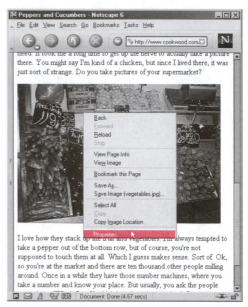

Figure 6.6 *Right-click or Control-click the image to make the contextual pop-up menu appear. Then choose Properties (or Get Image Info).*

Figure 6.7 *A box appears (its appearance varies depending on the browser you're using) that shows the dimensions of the image in pixels.*

Figure 6.8 *If you open an image directly in a browser (this is Explorer 5 for Mac), its dimensions are displayed in the title bar.*

Specifying Size for Speedier Viewing

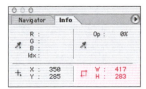

Figure 6.9 *The Info palette in both Photoshop and Photoshop Elements displays the size of a selection. Choose the units by selecting Palette Options in the pop-up menu.*

[snip] just sort of strange. Do you take pictures of your supermarket?</p>

<img src="vegetables.jpg" width="417" height="283" alt="Peppers and Cucumbers" />

<p>I love how they stack up the fruit and vegetables. I'm always tempted to take a pepper out of the bottom row, but of course, you're not supposed to touch them at all. Which I guess makes sense. Sort of. Ok, so you're at the market and there are ten thousand other people milling around.

Figure 6.10 *If you specify the exact height and width values in pixels, the browser won't have to spend time doing it and will display the image more quickly.*

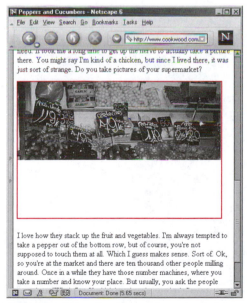

Figure 6.11 *Notice that the second paragraph of text is displayed even though the image has not finished loading. This means your visitors will have something to do while they're waiting.*

To specify the size of your image for speedier viewing:

1. Figure out the size of your image using one of the techniques described on page 106.

2. Within the `img` tag, after the `src` attribute, type **width="x" height="y"**, using the values you jotted down in step 1 to specify the values for *x* and *y* (the width and height of your image) in pixels.

✔ Tips

■ The `width` and `height` attributes don't necessarily have to reflect the actual size of the image. For more details, consult *Scaling an Image* on page 108.

■ If you have several images that are all the same size, you can set their height and width all at the same time with styles *(see page 190)*.

■ You can also find the size of an image in a browser by opening the image in its own window. The size is shown in the title bar **(Figure 6.8)**. (This is the only way to get the size with Explorer for Mac.)

■ In Photoshop or Photoshop Elements, if you Option-click (Alt-click on Windows) the "Doc" bar in the lower-left corner of the image's window, a small box appears with information about the image, including its size. If you can't see the "Doc" bar, make the window larger until it appears.

Scaling an Image

You can change the size of an image just by specifying a new height and width in pixels. This is an easy way to have large images on your page without long loading times. Beware, though, if you enlarge your pictures too much, they'll be grainy and ugly.

To scale an image:

1. Type **<img src="image.url"**, where *image.url* is the location on the server of the image *(see page 33)*.

2. Type **width="x" height="y"** where *x* and *y* are the desired width and height, respectively, in pixels, of your image.

3. Add any other image attributes as desired and then type the final **/>**.

✔ Tips

- You can also use a percentage value in step 2, with respect to the browser window (not the original image size).

- Using the width and height attributes is a quick and dirty way to change how the image is displayed on a Web page, especially if you don't have an image editor (or don't have the time or inclination to use it). However, since the file itself is not changed, the visitor always gets cheated. Reduced images take longer to view than images that are really that size; enlarged images appear grainy. A better solution is to use your image editor to change the size of the image *(see page 92)*.

- You can set just the width or just the height and have the browser adjust the other value proportionally.

- You can also use styles to control the width and height of elements. For more information, consult *Setting the Height or Width for an Element* on page 190.

Figure 6.12 *At its original size of 396 by 439 pixels, the image is way too big on the page.*

```
<h1>Fish Ladies</h1>

<img src="fishlady.jpg" width="198"
height="219" alt="One of the fish ladies" />

<p>The fish ladies hold a special place in the
market's heart, where the floors are wet and kind of
slimy, the pervasive smell of fish floats in the air, and
the cold chill from the ice makes you forget the
sunny day you left outside. Unless they're helping
```

Figure 6.13 *Since the width and height always reflect the dimensions in pixels, you never explicitly specify the units in (X)HTML.*

Figure 6.14 *The image appears at half its original size. It's important to note, however, that it takes the same time to load as before. After all, it's the same file.*

```
<h1>More Market Pictures</h1>

<p><a href="flowers.jpg"><img
src="flowers_little.jpg" alt="Flowers on the
Rambles" width="83" height="125" /></a> <a
href="fruitstand.jpg"><img
src="fruitstand_little.jpg" alt="Fruit stand"
width="103" height="67" /></a> <a
href="ham.jpg"><img src="ham_little.jpg"
alt="Charcuterie" width="123" height="85"
/></a> <a href="cannedgoods.jpg"><img
src="cannedgoods_little.jpg" alt="Canned goods,
hams, wine, oil, olives!" width="84" height="123"
/></a></p>
```

Figure 6.15 *Remember to use the full size image in the link and the thumbnail in the image definition.*

Figure 6.16 *In this example, the thumbnails are about 4K and take a few seconds to load. The visitor can choose to view the larger image (by clicking the icon) or to continue reading the page.*

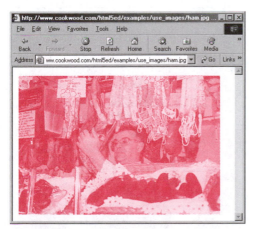

Figure 6.17 *If the visitor clicks the icon, the browser opens a new window with the full size image.*

Linking Thumbnails to Images

If you have a particularly large image, you can create a miniature version or *thumbnail* of it *(see page 92)* that displays quickly on the page and then add a link that leads the visitor to the full size image. (We'll cover links in full starting on page 117.)

To link a thumbnail to a larger image:

1. Place the cursor in your (X)HTML page where you wish the icon to be placed.

2. Type **<a href="image.jpg">**, where *image.jpg* is the location of the full-sized image on your server *(see page 33)*.

3. Type **<img src="mini.jpg"**, where *mini.jpg* is the location of the thumbnail version on the server.

4. If desired, type **alt="alternate text"**, where *alternate text* is the text that should appear if, for some reason, the thumbnail does not.

5. Type the final **/>** of the thumbnail definition.

6. If desired, type the label text that should accompany the thumbnail. It's a good idea to include the actual file size of the full-sized image so the visitor knows what they're getting into by clicking it.

7. Type **</a>** to complete the link to the full sized image.

✔ Tip

■ Using miniatures or thumbnails is an ideal way to get a lot of graphic information on a page without making your visitors wait too long to see it. Then they can view the images that they are most interested in at their leisure.

Linking Thumbnails to Images

Making Images Float

You can use the `align` attribute (with the *left* and *right* values only) to make images float along one side of your page, with text and other elements wrapping around the other.

To make images float:

1. Type **<img src="image.jpg"** where *image.jpg* indicates the location of the image on the server.

2. *Either* type **align="left"** to float the image on the left of the screen while the text flows to the right, *or* type **align="right"** to float the image on the right edge of the screen while the text flows on the left side of the image.

3. Add other image attributes, as described in other parts of this chapter, if desired.

4. Type the final **/>**.

5. Create the elements that should flow next to the image.

✔ Tips

- Don't get confused about right and left. When you choose **align="right"**, it's the *image* that goes to the right (while the text goes to the left). When you choose **align="left"**, again, the image will be on the left side with the text flowing around the right side.

- The `align` attribute is deprecated. Nevertheless, since the CSS `float` property *(see page 194)* is still not fully supported by all current browsers, I think it's important to know how the `align` attribute works.

- Why use *align* for floating images? I don't know. Personally, I'd prefer a `float` attribute, but it doesn't exist. For more details about what you can do with `align`, see page 114.

```
<body>

<img src="house.jpg" align="right" alt="house" width="237" height="225" />

<h1>The Pioneer Valley: Northampton</h1>

This triplex on South Street is a good [snip]
</body>
```

Figure 6.18 *When you align an image to the right, you are actually wrapping text to its left.*

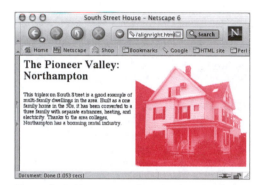

Figure 6.19 *The image is aligned to the right and the text wraps around it.*

```
<body>

<img src="house.jpg" align="left" alt="house" width="237" height="225" />

<h1>The Pioneer Valley: Northampton</h1>

This triplex on South Street is a good [snip]
</body>
```

Figure 6.20 *To make the image appear on the left with the text wrapped around the right side, use* `align="left"`.

Figure 6.21 *With the image floated on the left, the text wraps around on the right side.*

```
<body>

<img src="courthouse.jpg" alt="courthouse"
align="right" width="256" height="229" />

<h1>The Pioneer Valley: Northampton</h1>

<p>This building, that some might say looks like a
church, is actually the Hampshire County
Courthouse. If you ever get called to be [snip] </p>

<img src="house.jpg" alt="house" align="left"
width="237" height="225" />

<p>This triplex on South Street is a good example
of multi-family dwellings in the area. Built as a one
family home in the 30s, it has been [snip].</p>

</body>
```

Figure 6.22 *The image always precedes the text that should flow around it.*

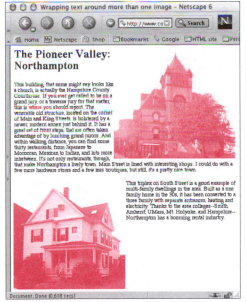

Figure 6.23 *The first image is floated to the right and the text flows to its left. The next image appears after the last line of text in the preceding paragraph and pushes the following paragraph to the right.*

To float images on both sides:

1. Type **<img src="right.image" align="right">** where *right.image* indicates the location on the server of the image that should appear on the right side of the screen.

2. Type the text that should flow around the first image.

3. Type **<img src="left.image" align="left">** where *left.image* indicates the location on the server of the image that should appear on the left side of the screen.

4. If desired, type **<p>** to begin a new paragraph, that will be aligned with the image placed in step 3.

5. Type the text that should flow around the second image. Type **</p>** to complete that paragraph, if necessary.

✔ Tips

- The key is to place each image *directly before* the text it should "disrupt."

- Each image will continue to push the text to one side until it either encounters a break *(see page 112)* or until there is no more text.

- The `align` attribute is deprecated. Nevertheless, since the CSS `float` property *(see page 194)* is still not fully supported by all current browsers, I think it's important to know how the `align` attribute works.

Making Images Float

Stopping Elements from Wrapping

A floated image affects all the elements that follow it, unless you insert a special line break. The clear attribute added to the regular br tag indicates that the text should not begin until the specified margin is clear (that is, at the end of the image or images).

To stop elements from wrapping:

1. Create your image and the text or other elements *(see pages 110 and 111)*.

2. Place the cursor where you want to stop wrapping text and elements to the side of the image.

3. *Either* type **<br clear="left" />** to stop flowing content until there are no more floating objects aligned to the left margin.

   Or type **<br clear="right" />** to stop flowing content until there are no more floating objects aligned to the right margin.

   Or type **<br clear="all" />** to stop flowing content until there are no more floating objects on either margin.

✔ Tips

- The clear attribute is deprecated in favor of style sheets. However, the CSS float and clear properties are still not fully supported in all current browsers, and thus, I think it's important to know about the clear attribute. For information on using styles to control the text flow, consult *Controlling Where Elements Float* on page 195.

- Note that the clear attribute affects the elements that follow a floated image, while the CSS clear property described on page 195 more directly affects the floated element itself. It's just a slightly different perspective.

```
<img src="house.jpg" align="right" height="200" alt="house" />

<h1>The Pioneer Valley: Northampton</h1>

<img src="flower.gif" align="left" alt="flower" width="43" height="43" />

<br clear="left" />

This triplex on South Street is a good example of
```

Figure 6.24 *Notice the order: first comes the house, then the header, then the flower logo, then the text.*

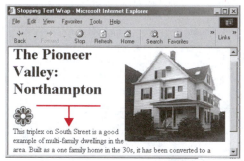

Figure 6.25 *The* clear="left" *attribute makes the text stop flowing until it reaches an empty left margin (that is, below the bottom of the left-aligned flower).*

```
<img src="house.jpg" align="right" width="237" height="225" alt="house" />

<h1>The Pioneer Valley: Northampton</h1>

<img src="flower.gif" align="left" alt="flower" width="43" height="43" />

<br clear="all" />

This triplex on South Street is a good example of
```

Figure 6.26 *The order is the same as in the last example; only the* clear *attribute has changed.*

Figure 6.27 *The* clear="all" *code stops the flow of text until all images have been passed.*

Figure 6.28 *No space is left, by default, between floating images and the elements they float next to.*

```
<p><img src="house.jpg" align="right"
height="200" alt="house" vspace="15" /></p>

<h1>The Pioneer Valley: Northampton</h1>

<p><br clear="right" />

<img src="flower.gif" align="left" width="43"
height="43" hspace="6" alt="flower" /> This
triplex on South Street is a good example of [snip]
```

Figure 6.29 *You can add horizontal space or vertical space, or both, to your images.*

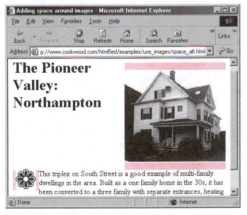

Figure 6.30 *One of the limitations of* hspace *and* vspace *is that they add space to both sides of an image. Note, for example, that the words* The Pioneer *are no longer aligned with the top of the image.*

Adding Space around an Image

Look carefully at the image in Figure 6.28. If you don't want your text butting right up to the image, you can use the deprecated vspace and hspace attributes to add a buffer around your image.

To add space around an image:

1. Type **<img src="image.location"** where *image.location* indicates the location on the server of your image.

2. Type **hspace="x"** where *x* is the number of pixels of space to add on *both* the right and left sides of the image.

3. Type **vspace="x"** where *x* is the number of pixels of space to add on *both* the top and bottom of the image.

4. Add other image attributes as desired and type the final **/>**.

✔ Tips

- You don't have to add both hspace and vspace at the same time.

- Both hspace and vspace are deprecated in favor of style sheets. For information about using styles to control the space around your images, consult *Adding Padding around an Element* on page 188 and *Setting the Margins around an Element* on page 189.

- The worst part about hspace and vspace is that you can't add space to just one side. This is a perfect example where styles are really worth the extra trouble.

- If you just want to add space to one side of the image, you could use Photoshop to add blank space to that side, and skip hspace and vspace altogether. Then, make the blank space transparent *(see page 93)*.

Aligning Images

Perhaps the more expected use of the `align` attribute is for aligning images with text. You can align an image in various ways to a single line in a paragraph. However, be careful with multiple images on the same line—different `align` options have different effects depending on which image is taller and which appears first.

To align an image with text:

1. Type **<img src="image.location"** where *image.location* indicates the location on the server of the image.

2. Type **align="direction"** where *direction* is `texttop`, `top`, `middle`, `absmiddle`, `bottom`, or `absbottom` **(Figure 6.32)**.

3. Add other attributes as desired and then type the final **/>**.

4. Type the text with which you wish to align the image. (This text may also precede the image.)

✔ Tips

■ The `absmiddle`, `absbottom`, and `texttop` values are proprietary extensions developed by Netscape, but current browsers of both versions support them. Earlier versions of Explorer treated `texttop` as `top`, `absmiddle` as `middle` and `absbottom` as `bottom`. IE also understands `center`, for `middle`.

■ The `align` attribute is deprecated. That means the W3C recommends you start using style sheets to control how elements are aligned on your page (*see page 196*).

```
<img src="castle.jpg" alt="castellers" /> default
<img src="star.gif" align="texttop" alt="star" />
texttop

<p><img src="castle.jpg" alt="castellers" />
default <img src="star.gif" align="top" /> top</p>

<p><img src="castle.jpg" alt="castellers" />
default <img src="star.gif" align="middle" />
middle</p>

<p><img src="castle.jpg" alt="castellers"  />
default <img src="star.gif" align="absmiddle" />
absmiddle</p>

<p><img src="castle.jpg" alt="castellers"
align="texttop"/> texttop <img src="star.gif"
align="bottom" /> bottom</p>

<p><img src="castle.jpg" alt="castellers"
align="texttop"/> texttop <img src="star.gif"
align="absbottom" /> absbottom</p>
```

Figure 6.31 *Each image can be aligned in its own way with respect to the line. For example, in the last example, the first image is aligned to the top of the text while the second is aligned to the bottom of the entire line.*

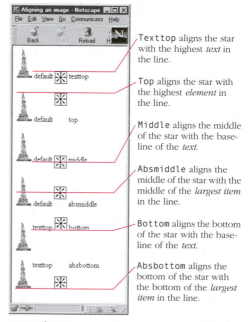

Texttop aligns the star with the highest *text* in the line.

Top aligns the star with the highest *element* in the line.

Middle aligns the middle of the star with the baseline of the *text*.

Absmiddle aligns the middle of the star with the middle of the *largest item* in the line.

Bottom aligns the bottom of the star with the baseline of the *text*.

Absbottom aligns the bottom of the star with the bottom of the *largest item* in the line.

Figure 6.32 *There are four elements on each line: a castle, some text, a star, and some more text. The first word indicates the castle's alignment, the second word describes the star's alignment.*

```
<body>
<img src="banner.gif" alt="SE banner" />
<h1>New products</h1>
<p>AstroFinder 3
<br />Pleiades Expander
<br />Southern Cross</p>
<hr size="10" width="80%" align="center"
noshade="noshade" />
</body>
```

Figure 6.33 *The* hr *tag includes an automatic line break both before and after the rule.*

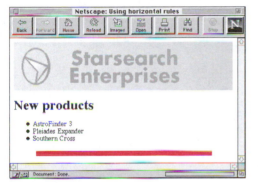

Figure 6.34 *Horizontal rules are helpful for dividing sections on your page.*

Adding Horizontal Rules

One graphic element that is completely supported by the majority of the browsers is the horizontal rule. There are several attributes you can use to jazz up horizontal rules, although they've all been deprecated in favor of styles.

To insert a horizontal rule:

1. Type **<hr** where you want the rule to appear. The text that follows will appear in a new paragraph below the new rule.

2. If desired, type **size="n"**, where *n* is the rule's height in pixels.

3. If desired, type **width="w"**, where *w* is the width of the rule in pixels, or as a percentage of the document's width.

4. If desired, type **align="direction"**, where *direction* refers to the way a rule should be aligned on the page; either left, right, or center. The align attribute is only effective if you have made the rule narrower than the browser window.

5. If desired, type **noshade** to create a solid bar, with no shading. Add **="noshade"** in XHTML.

6. Type the final **/>** to complete the horizontal rule definition.

✔ Tips

■ All of the attributes for hr (but not hr itself) are deprecated. The W3C recommends using styles to format your horizontal rules *(see page 175)*.

■ There is no CSS equivalent to noshade. One solution is to omit rules and just apply borders *(see page 186)*.

■ IE supports a color attribute, which automatically sets the noshade attribute.

LINKS

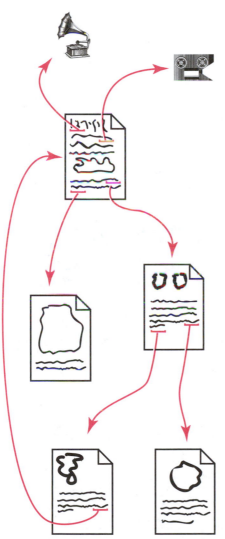

Figure 7.1 *Some of your pages may have links to many other pages. Other pages may have only one link. And still others may have no links at all.*

Links are the distinguishing feature of the World Wide Web. They let you skip from one page to another, call up a movie or a recording of The Nields (or *your* favorite band), and download files with FTP.

A link has three parts: a destination, a label, and a target. The first part, the *destination*, is arguably the most important. You use it to specify what will happen when the visitor clicks the link. You can create links that show an image, play a sound or movie, download files, open a newsgroup, send an e-mail message, run a CGI program, and more. The most common links, however, connect to other Web pages, and sometimes to specific locations on other Web pages called *anchors*. All destinations are defined by writing a URL *(see page 33)* and are generally only visible to the visitor in the status area of the browser.

The second part of the link is the *label*, the part the visitor sees and clicks on to reach the destination. It can be text, an image, or both. Label text is often, but not always, shown underlined. The more appealing, enticing, and attractive the label, the more likely a visitor will click on it. In fact, eliciting Web visitors' clicks is an art.

The last part of the link, the *target*, is often ignored or left up to the browser. The target determines where the destination will be displayed. The target might be a particular named window or frame, or a *new* window or frame.

Creating a Link to Another Web Page

If you have more than one Web page, you will probably want to create links from one page to the next (and back again). You can also create connections to Web pages designed by other people on other servers.

To create a link to another Web page:

1. Type **<a href="page.html">** where *page.html* is the URL of the destination Web page.

2. Type the label text, that is, the text that is highlighted (usually blue and underlined), and that when clicked upon will take the user to the page referenced in step 1.

3. Type **</a>** to complete the definition of the link.

✔ Tips

■ As a general rule, use relative URLs for links to Web pages on your site and absolute URLs for links to Web pages on other sites. For more details, consult *URLs* on page 33.

■ So, a link to a page at another site might look like: **<a href="http://www.site.com/directory/page.html"> Label text</a>** (**Figures 7.5, 7.6, and 7.7**).

■ Specify the path but omit the file name to link to the default file for a directory, usually one of *index.html* or *default.htm*: **http://www.site.com/directory/**. Omit the path as well to link to a *site's* default (home) page: **http://www.site.com/**.

■ It's a good idea to use all lowercase letters for your URLs to avoid problems on the many servers that are case sensitive.

■ href stands for *hypertext reference*.

```
<body>

<h1>Cookie and Woody</h1>

<img src="woodygran.jpg" alt="Woody"
width="202" height="131" /> <img src=
"cookiefora.jpg" width="143" height="131" />

<p>Generally considered the sweetest and yet most
independent cats in the <a href="pioneerval.html">
Pioneer Valley,</a> Cookie and Woody are
consistently underestimated by their humble
humans.</p>
```

Figure 7.2 *Since there is only a file name (and no path) referenced in the* href *attribute, the file* pioneerval.html *must be in the same directory as this Web page that contains the link.*

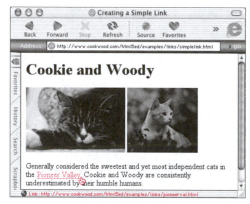

Figure 7.3 *When a visitor points at a link (displayed in blue underlined text, by default), the destination URL is shown in the status area. If they actually click on a link…*

Figure 7.4 *…the page associated with that destination URL is displayed in their browser.*

```
<body>

<h1>Pixel</h1>

<p>If you'd like to meet a JavaCat, check out <a
href="http://www.pixel.mu/">Pixel</a> at Tom
Negrino and Dori Smith's great site about their <a
href="http://www.javascriptworld.com/">
<em>JavaScript for the World Wide Web: Visual
QuickStart Guide</em></a>.</p>

</body>
```

Figure 7.5 *If you're creating links to someone else's Web site, you'll have to use an absolute URL, with the http://, server, full path, and file name.*

Figure 7.6 *When a visitor points at a link (displayed in blue underlined text, by default), the destination URL is shown in the status area. If they click on a link…*

Figure 7.7 *…the page associated with that destination URL is displayed in their browser.*

- There seems to be some question in the Web community about whether it's OK to link to any page on a site besides the home page. A direct "deep" link, as they're sometimes called, helps your visitor arrive promptly at their destination. However, they may miss important information or advertising that the site's creators left on the home page. One possible compromise is to give the direct connection *as well as* a connection to the site's home page. You may want to create a link to your home page from every other page on your site in case other sites create deep links to your inner pages.

- Don't make the link's label too long. If the label is part of a sentence, keep only the key words within the link definition, with the rest of the sentence before and after the less than and greater than signs.

- Try not to use "Click here" for a label. Instead use the key words that already exist in your text to identify the link.

- You may apply styles *(see page 157)* or (X)HTML basic text formatting *(see page 73)* to the label or even use an image as a label *(see page 128)*.

- To create a link to a particular place on a page, use an anchor *(see pages 120–121)*.

- To make the link appear in a given window or frame, use a target *(see page 122)*.

- You can create keyboard shortcuts for links. For more details, see page 126.

- You can determine the tab order for visitors who use their keyboards to navigate your page. For more details, consult *Setting the Tab Order for Links* on page 127.

- An a element may contain any kind of inline tag except another a element. It may not contain a block-level element like p.

Creating Anchors

Generally, a click on a link brings the user to the *top* of the corresponding Web page. If you want to have the user jump to a specific section of the Web page, you have to create an *anchor* and then reference that anchor in the link.

To create an anchor:

1. Place the cursor in the part of the Web page that you wish the user to jump to.

2. Type **<a name="anchor name">**, where *anchor name* is the text you will use internally to identify that section of the Web page.

3. Add the words or images that you wish to be referenced.

4. Type **</a>** to complete the definition of the anchor.

✔ Tips

- You can also create an anchor by adding an id attribute to the desired element *(see page 67)*.

- Quotes are *always* required around the anchor name in XHTML. While they're sometimes optional in HTML *(see page 36)*, I highly recommend them.

- In a long document, create an anchor for each section and link it to the corresponding item in the table of contents.

- The W3C, Netscape, and others are not at all consistent with the terminology. Some folks call links anchors—a is for anchor, after all—others call targets anchors. In this book, the word *anchor* refers to a specific location in a document that you link to. (A *target* is the window or frame where a link will appear. See page page 122.)

```
<body>
<div class="toc">
<h2>Table of Contents</h2>
<a href="#intro">Introduction</a><br />
<a href="#descrip">Description of the Main
Characters</a><br />
<a href="#rising">Rising Action</a><br />
<a href="#climax">Climax</a><br />
<a href="#denoue">Denouement</a>
</div>

<h2><a name="intro">Introduction</a></h2>

<p>This is the intro. If I could think of enough things
to write about, it could span a few pages, giving all
the introductory information that an introduction
should introduce. </p>

<h2><a name="descrip">Description of the Main
Characters</a></h2>

<p>Frankie and Johnny are the main characters.
She's jealous, and seems to have a reason to be.
He's a sleaze, and will pay the price. </p>

<h2><a name="rising">Rising Action</a></h2>

<p>This is where everything starts happening.
Johnny goes out, without Frankie, without even tellin'
her where he's going. She's not crazy about it, but
she lets him go. A while later, she gets thirsty and
decides to go down to the corner bar for some beer.
Chatting with the bartender, she learns that Johnny
has been there with no other than Nellie Bly. Furious,
she catches the cross town bus to find him.</p>

<h2><a name="climax">Climax</a></h2>

<p>When Frankie gets to Nellie's house, she looks
up and sees them kissing on the balcony. With tears
in her eyes, she picks up her shotgun and kills her
Johnny. He falls to the ground.</p>

<h2 id="denoue">Denouement</h2>

<p>Frankie feels bad but it's kind of late now, and
Johnny <em>was</em> a lech. But the police come
and cart her off anyway.</p></body>
```

Figure 7.8 *Notice that most of the anchors are created with the* a *element and* name *attribute, while the last is created by simply adding an* id *attribute to the existing* h2 *element (see first tip). The* id *attribute does double duty as an anchor in all but the oldest browsers.*

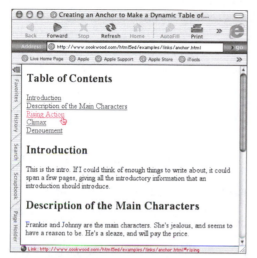

Figure 7.9 *When the visitor points at a link with an anchor, the URL and the anchor name appear in the status bar (in the lower-left corner of the window).*

Figure 7.10 *Once the visitor clicks the link, the particular part of the page that the anchor references is displayed at the top of the browser window.*

Linking to a Specific Anchor

Once you have created an anchor you can define a link so that a user's click will bring them directly to the section of the document that contains the anchor, not just the top of that document.

To create a link to an anchor:

1. Type **<a href="#anchor name">**, where *anchor name* is the value of the name attribute in the destination's a tag *(step 2 on page 120)* or the value of the destination's id attribute *(see first tip on page 120)*.

2. Type the label text, that is, the text that is highlighted (usually blue and underlined), and that when clicked upon will take the user to the section referenced in step 1.

3. Type **</a>** to complete the definition of the link.

✔ Tips

■ If the anchor is in a separate document, use **<a href="page.html#anchorname">** to reference the section. (There should be no space between the URL and the #.) If the anchor is on a page on a different server, you'll have to type **<a href= "http://www.site.com/path/page.html #anchorname">** (with no spaces).

■ While you obviously can't add anchors to other people's pages, you can take advantage of the ones that they have already created. View the source code of their documents to see which anchor names correspond to which sections. (For help viewing source code, consult *The Inspiration of Others* on page 57.)

■ If the anchor is at the bottom of the page, it may not display at the top of the window, but rather towards the middle.

Targeting Links to Specific Windows

Targets let you open a link in a particular window, or even in a new window created especially for that link. This way, the page that contains the link stays open, enabling the user to go back and forth between the page of links and the information from each of those links.

To target links:

Within the link definition, type **target= "window"**, where *window* is the name of the window where the corresponding page should be displayed.

✔ Tips

■ Target names are case sensitive! In addition, you should always enclose them in quotation marks.

■ Open a link in a completely new window by using **target="_blank"**.

■ If you target several links to the same window (e.g., using the same name), the links will all open in that same window.

■ If a named window is not already open, the browser opens a new window and uses it for all future links to that window.

■ Targets are most effective for opening Web pages (or even FTP links) in particular windows or frames *(see page 255)*. They don't make sense for e-mail or news links which open in different kinds of windows.

■ The W3C has removed the `target` attribute from (X)HTML strict to promote accessibility. Instead, they suggest using JavaScript or the yet-to-be-finalized XLink. I say, use `target`. (It *is* part of both (X)HTML transitional and frameset.)

```
<!DOCTYPE html PUBLIC "-//W3C//DTD XHTML
1.0 Transitional//EN"

"http://www.w3.org/TR/2000/REC-xhtml1-
20000126/DTD/xhtml1-transitional.dtd">

[snip]<h1>Nathaniel Hawthorne</h1>

<p>Nathaniel Hawthorne was one of the most
important writers of 19th century America. His most
famous character is <a href="hester.html" target=
"characters">Hester Prynne</a>, a woman living
in Puritan New England. [snip]</p>

<p>Besides <a href="scarlet.html" target=
"books"><em>The Scarlet Letter</em></a>,
Hawthorne wrote <a href="gables.html" target=
"books"><em>The House of Seven Gables</em>
```

Figure 7.11 *In this example, some links will appear in the* characters *window and others will appear in the* books *window. (Note that this document is XHTML transitional, not strict.)*

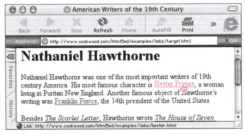

Figure 7.12 *When the visitor clicks a link with a target...*

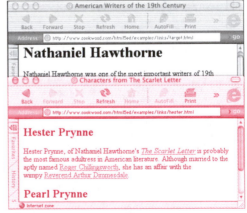

Figure 7.13 *...the corresponding page is shown in the targeted window. In this example, it's the* characters *window.*

```
<!DOCTYPE html PUBLIC "-//W3C//DTD XHTML
1.0 Transitional//EN"

"http://www.w3.org/TR/2000/REC-xhtml1-
20000126/DTD/xhtml1-transitional.dtd">

<html xmlns="http://www.w3.org/1999/xhtml">

<head>

<meta http-equiv="content-type"
content="text/html; charset=iso-8859-1" />

<title>American Writers of the 19th Century</title>

<base target="characters" />

</head>

<body>

<h1>Nathaniel Hawthorne</h1>

<p>Nathaniel Hawthorne was one of the most
important writers of 19th century America. His most
famous character is <a href="hester.html">Hester
Prynne</a>, a woman living in Puritan New
England. Another famous object of Hawthorne's
writing was <a href="http://www.ripon.edu/
dept/pogo/presidency/Pierce/">Franklin Pierce
</a>, the 14th president of the United States.</p>

<p>Besides <a href="scarlet.html" target="books">
<em>The Scarlet Letter</em></a>, Hawthorne
wrote <a href="gables.html" target="books">
<em>The House of Seven Gables</em></a>, <a
```

Figure 7.14 *Use the* base *tag to set the default target (in this case the* characters *window) in order to save typing. Notice that I no longer have to specify the target for the links in the first paragraph. This document is equivalent to the one shown in Figure 7.11.*

Setting the Default Target

A link, by default, opens in the same window or frame that contains the link. You can choose another target for each link individually, as described on page 122, or specify a default target for all the links on a page.

To set a default target for a page:

1. In the head section of your Web page, type **<base**.

2. Type **target="title"**, where *title* is the name of the window or frame in which all the links on the page should open, by default.

3. Type **/>** to complete the base tag.

✔ Tips

■ Target names are case sensitive! In addition, you should always enclose them in quotation marks.

■ You can override the default target specified in the base tag by adding a target attribute to an individual link *(see page 122)*.

■ While the base tag is part of (X)HTML strict, the target attribute is not. I use it anyway (see the last tip on page 122).

■ You can also use the base tag to set the base URL for constructing relative URLs. This can be particularly useful when a Perl CGI script, located off in the cgi-bin directory, is generating the (X)HTML page, and you want to reference a bunch of images or links in the main part of your server. Use **<base href="base.url" />** where *base.url* is the URL that all relative links should be constructed from. Put another way, the URL reflects the *virtual* location of the generated (X)HTML page.

Setting the Default Target

Creating Other Kinds of Links

You are not limited to creating links to other Web pages. You can create a link to any URL—FTP sites, files that you want visitors to be able to download, newsgroups, and messages. You can even create a link to an e-mail address.

To create other kinds of links:

1. Type **<a href="**.

2. Type the URL:

- For a link to any file on the Web, including movies, sounds, programs, Excel spreadsheets, or whatever, type **http://www.site.com/path/file.ext**, where *www.site.com* is the name of the server and *path/file.ext* is the path to the desired file, including its extension.

- For a link to an FTP site, type **ftp://ftp.site.com/path**, where *ftp.site.com* is the server and *path* is the path to the desired directory or file.

- For a newsgroup, type **news:newsgroup**, where *newsgroup* is the name of the desired newsgroup. For a particular message, type **news:article**, where *article* is the number (as shown in the header) of the individual article.

- For a link to an e-mail address, type **mailto:name@site.com**, where *name@site.com* is the e-mail address.

- For a link to a telnet site (like a library catalog), type **telnet://site**, where *site* is the name of the server you want to open the telnet connection to.

3. Type **">**.

```
<h1>Getaway Destinations</h1>

<p>There are lots of different kinds of links that you can create on a Web page.</p>

<p>You might want to create a link to a directory on <a href="ftp://www.joy.ne.jp/welcome/igs/Go/">the IGS Go site</a> to help visitors download articles or problems about Go (a Japanese strategy game). Or point them to a specific file like the <a href="ftp://www.joy.ne.jp/welcome/igs/Go/FAQ">Go FAQ</a> so they don't have to navigate the FTP site.</p>

<p>To allow access to a <a href="ftp://name:password@ftp.site.com/directory">private FTP site</a>, you have to preface the server name with the user name and password.</p>

<p>A link to an e-mail address is a great way to elicit comments about your Web page. Unfortunately, spammers are great at snatching up e-mail addresses from Web pages and filling your mailbox with unsolicited junk. Don't think so? <a href="mailto:html5ed@cookwood.com">Tell me</a> about it.</p>

<p>Links to newsgroups help visitors find other people interested in the same topic. For example, check out the <a href="news:rec.pets.cats">newsgroup for cat lovers</a>. Can you believe there's no special section for Llumi and Xixo? </p>

<p>Some libraries let you <a href="telnet://melvyl.ucop.edu:23/">log into their system</a> from home with telnet to see if a particular book is available or checked out. Most browsers don't view telnet connections inline, but instead open a helper application like Nifty Telnet.</p>

<p>Hey, what if you just want to let your visitors download a file that's on your server in the same directory as your Web pages? No problem. The link will look like any other Web link. Here, download the Windows version of the <a href="http://www.cookwood.com/html5ed/examples/html5ed_examples.zip"> examples</a> from this book.</p>

</body>
```

Figure 7.15 *You can create a link to all different kinds of URLs.*

Figure 7.16 *No matter where a link goes, it looks pretty much the same in the browser window. Notice that I've tried to create labels that flow with the body of the text—instead of a lot of "click me's". These are all real links (OK, except the private FTP site). You can see where they lead by opening this page in your own browser—http://www.cookwood.com/html5ed/examples/links/links_other.html*

4. Type the label for the link, that is, the text that will be underlined or highlighted, and that when clicked upon will take the visitor to the URL referenced in step 2.

5. Type **</a>**.

✔ Tips

- If you create a link to a file that a browser doesn't know how to handle (an Excel file, for example), the browser will either try to open a helper program to view the file or will try to download it to the visitor's hard disk. For more information, consult *Of Plugins and Players* on page 294.

- It's a good idea to compress files that you want visitors to download. This makes them faster to download and it also protects them from being corrupted as they go from one system to another. Aladdin Systems *(www.aladdinsys.com)* has some good compression tools for both Macs and Windows machines.

- You can also create links to less common destinations (like Gopher and WAIS servers). Just enter the URL in step 2.

- You can preface an FTP URL with **name:password@** to access a private FTP site. Beware that browsers keep track of where you've been, however, including your password. (For example, in Netscape, type **about:global**.)

- If you want to create an FTP link to a particular directory on the FTP site (as opposed to an individual file), simply use *ftp://ftp.site.com/directory*. You don't need to use the trailing forward slash. When you don't specify a specific file to download, the browser automatically displays the contents of the last directory in the path.

Creating Other Kinds of Links

Creating Keyboard Shortcuts for Links

Keyboard shortcuts let your visitors select and activate links without using a mouse.

To add a keyboard shortcut to a link:

1. Inside the link's tag, type **accesskey="**.

2. Type the keyboard shortcut (any letter or number).

3. Type the final **"**.

4. If desired, add information about the keyboard shortcut to the text so that the visitor knows it exists.

✔ Tips

■ On Netscape (Mac/Win) and Explorer for Mac, typing a keyboard shortcut activates the link, but on Explorer for Windows, it merely gives focus to the link and the visitor must still press Return to actually follow it.

■ On Windows systems, to invoke the keyboard shortcut, visitors use the Alt key plus the letter you've assigned. On Macintosh, visitors use the Control key, plus the letter.

■ Keyboard shortcuts don't work at all in Opera and are unreliable with frames, unless the visitor selects the frame—which kind of defeats the purpose.

■ Keyboard shortcuts that you choose can (annoyingly) override the browser's shortcuts. For example, in most Windows programs, Alt-F is for accessing the File menu. If you use Alt-F for a keyboard shortcut, your visitors won't be able to use the keyboard to access their browser's File menu.

```
<h1>Our Cats</h1>

<p>Each of our cats has their own home page.
Click on the corresponding link or use the keyboard
shortcut to see each one.

<br /><a href="gatetseng.html#woody"
accesskey="w">Woody</a> (Alt-W, Ctrl-W)

<br /><a href="gatetseng.html#cookie"
accesskey="c">Cookie</a> (Alt-C, Ctrl-C)

<br /><a href="gatetseng.html#xixona"
accesskey="x">Xixona</a> (Alt-X, Ctrl-X)

<br /><a href="gatetseng.html#llumeta"
accesskey="l">Llumeta</a> (Alt-L, Ctrl-L)</p>

</body>
```

Figure 7.17 *Create a keyboard shortcut for a link by adding the* accesskey *attribute to its tag. The explanatory text (Alt-W, etc.) is optional but helpful.*

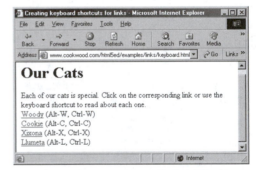

Figure 7.18 *There's no way to tell a link has a keyboard shortcut unless you've labeled it as such.*

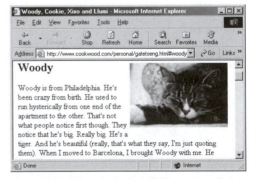

Figure 7.19 *When the keyboard shortcut is used, the link is immediately accessed (and the corresponding page is shown).*

```
<div id="toc"><a href="toc.html" tabindex="2">
Contents</a> <a href="search.html" tabindex
="2">Search</a> <a href="company.html"
tabindex="2">About Us</a></div>

<h1>Our Cats</h1>

<p>Each of our cats is special. Click on the
corresponding link or use the keyboard shortcut to
read about each one.</p>

<p><a href="gatetseng.html#woody"
accesskey="w" tabindex="1">Woody</a> (Alt-
W, Ctrl-W)

<br /><a href="gatetseng.html#cookie"
accesskey="c" tabindex="1">Cookie</a> (Alt-C,
Ctrl-C)

<br /><a href="gatetseng.html#xixona"
accesskey="x" tabindex="1">Xixona</a> (Alt-X,
Ctrl-X)

<br /><a href="gatetseng.html#llumeta"
accesskey="l" tabindex="1">Llumeta</a> (Alt-L,
Ctrl-L)</p>

</body>
```

Figure 7.20 *This page begins with a set of links, which, while useful, don't have anything to do with this particular page. So that the first tab selects the first "real" link, I've assigned it the lowest tab index.*

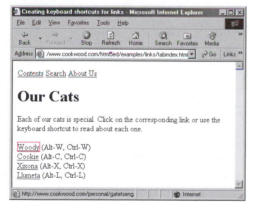

Figure 7.21 *When the visitor hits Tab the first time (OK, the second time, see the second to last tip), the Woody link is selected. If they hit Tab again, Cookie will be selected, and so on until Llumeta. At that point, a tab will bring them up to the Contents link.*

Setting the Tab Order for Links

Many browsers let users navigate through the links, image maps, and form elements with the Tab key. You can determine a custom tab order, to emphasize certain elements.

To set the tab order:

In the link's tag, type **tabindex="n"**, where *n* is the number that sets the tab order.

✔ Tips

- To *activate* a link the visitor must tab to it and then press Enter.

- The value for `tabindex` can be any number between 0 and 32767. Use a negative value to take a link out of the tab sequence altogether.

- By default, the tab order depends on the order of the elements in the (X)HTML code. When you change the tab order, the lower-numbered elements are activated first, followed by higher numbered ones.

- Elements with the same tab index value are accessed in the order in which they appear in the (X)HTML document.

- You can also assign tab order to client-side image maps and form elements. For more information, consult *Creating a Client-Side Image Map* on page 130 or *Setting the Tab Order in a Form* on page 289, respectively.

- Actually, when the visitor hits Tab for the first time, the page's URL is selected (in the Address/Location bar, even if it's hidden). The *second* time they hit Tab, the link with the lowest tab index on the page will be selected.

- In a page with frames, the visitor has to select the frame before they can tab through the links it contains.

Using Images to Label Links

In this age of graphical interfaces, people are used to clicking on images and icons to make things happen. Adding an image to a link creates a navigational button that the visitor can click to access the referenced URL. (For more information about images, see Chapter 5, *Creating Web Images*, and Chapter 6, *Using Images*.)

To use images to label links:

1. Type **<a href="destination.html">**, where *destination.html* is the URL of the page that the user will jump to when they click the button.

2. Type **<img src="image.jpg"** where *image.jpg* gives the location of the image file on the server.

3. If desired, type **border="n"**, where *n* is the width in pixels of the border. Use a value of 0 to omit the border.

4. Add other image attributes as desired and then type the final **/>**.

5. If desired, type the label text, that is, the text that will be underlined or highlighted in blue, that when clicked upon will take the user to the URL referenced in step 1.

6. Type **</a>** to complete the link.

✔ Tips

■ If you invert steps 5 and 6, only a click on the *image* will produce the desired jump. A click on the text has no effect. (You can also leave the text out altogether.)

■ Most browsers surround clickable images with a border of the same color as the links (generally blue). For no border, use a value of 0 in step 3. Note that the border attribute is deprecated for images. You can use CSS instead *(see page 186)*.

```
<body>

<h1>Cookie and Woody</h1>

<p>Generally considered the sweetest and yet most independent cats in the <a href="pioneerval.html">Pioneer Valley,</a> Cookie and Woody are consistently underestimated by their humble humans.</p>

<p>

<a href="prevpage.html"><img src="pointleft.gif" alt="Previous page" /></a>

<a href="nextpage.html"><img src="pointright.gif" alt="Next page" /></a></p>

<p><a href="mailto:lcastro@crocker.com"><img src="writeletter.gif" alt="Send mail" />Send me comments</a> on this page!</p>

</body>
```

Figure 7.22 *There is no text in the first two button links. The final </a> comes right after the image tag.*

Figure 7.23 *If you do add text to the link, make sure you insert a space between the text and the image (or use* hspace *or styles to space the text, see pages 188–190).*

Figure 7.24 *This is the original* pointright.gif *image. It does not have a border. In most browsers (not Opera), borders are automatically added to all images used to label links. You can adjust the border with the deprecated* border *attribute in the* img *tag, or with styles (see page 186).*

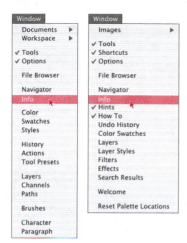

Figure 7.25 *In either Photoshop (left) or Photoshop Elements, choose Window > Info to show the Info palette.*

Figure 7.26 *Place the cursor in the upper-left corner of the rectangle and jot down the x and y coordinates shown in Photoshop's Info palette. (In this example, x=395 and y=18.) Then do the same with the lower-right corner.*

Dividing an Image into Clickable Regions

A clickable image is like a collection of buttons combined together in one image. A click in one part of the image brings the user to one destination. A click in another area brings the user to a different destination.

There are two important steps to implementing a clickable image: First you must map out the different regions of your image, and second you must define which destinations correspond to which areas of the image.

To divide an image into clickable regions:

1. Create an image, consulting Chapter 5, *Creating Web Images*, as necessary.

2. Open the image in Photoshop or other image editing program.

3. Choose Window > Palettes > Show Info **(Figure 7.25)**.

4. Make sure that the units are pixels (by clicking the tiny arrow next to the cross hairs at the bottom of the Info window).

5. Point the cursor over the upper-left corner of the region you wish to define.

6. Using the Info window, jot down the *x* and *y* coordinates for that corner **(Figure 7.26)**.

7. Repeat steps 5–6 for the rectangle's lower-right corner, for each point of a polygon, or for a circle's center and radius.

Creating a Client-Side Image Map

Image maps link the areas of an image with a series of URLs so that a click in a particular area brings the user to the corresponding page. There are two kinds of image maps, *client-side* and *server-side (see page 132)*. Client-side image maps run more quickly because they are interpreted in your visitors' browsers and don't have to consult the server for each click. In addition, since they do not require a CGI script, they are simpler to create, and you don't need to get permission (or help) from your Internet service provider. Only very old browsers may not understand them.

To create a client-side image map:

1. In the (X)HTML document that contains the image, type **<map**.

2. Type **name="label" id="label">**, where *label* is the name of the map.

3. Type **<area** to define the first clickable area.

4. Type **alt="info"**, where *info* describes what will happen when the visitor clicks.

5. Type **shape="type"**, where *type* represents the area's shape. Use *rect* for a rectangle, *circle* for a circle, and *poly* for an irregular shape.

6. For a rectangle, type **coords="x1, y1, x2, y2"**, where *x1*, *y1*, *x2*, and *y2* represent the upper-left and lower-right corners of the rectangle, as obtained on page 129, and shown in Figure 7.26.

    For a circle, type **coords="x, y, r"** where *x* and *y* represent the center of the circle and *r* is the radius.

    For a polygon, type **coords="x1, y1, x2, y2"** (and so on), giving the *x* and *y* coordinates of each point on the polygon.

```
<body><p>

<map name="banner" id="banner">

<area alt="new information" shape="rect"
coords="395, 18, 445, 35" href="newinfo.html" />

<area alt="press releases" shape="rect"
coords="395, 38, 445, 55"
href="pressrelease.html" />

<area alt="events" shape="rect" coords="395, 58,
445, 75" href="events.html" />

</map>

<img src="clickimage.gif" alt="SE banner"
usemap="#banner" width="450" height="100" />

</p>

<div id="content">

<h1>Starsearch Enterprises</h1>

<a href="newinfo.html">New programs</a>
<br />

<a href="pressrelease.html">Press
releases</a><br />

<a href="events.html">Upcoming events</a>
<br />

<a href="infoSE.html">About Starsearch
Enterprises</a><br />

</div>

</body>
```

Figure 7.27 *You can put the* map *anywhere you like in your (X)HTML document. Each clickable area is defined by its own set of coordinates, and has its own corresponding URL. Then, don't forget to add the* usemap *attribute to the image that will serve as the map.*

Figure 7.28 *When your users point at one of the defined areas, the destination URL appears in the status bar at the bottom of the window.*

Figure 7.29 *And if a user clicks the link, the browser will immediately display the corresponding page.*

7. Type **href="url.html"**, where *url.html* is the address of the page that should appear when the user clicks in this area.

 Or type **nohref** if a click in this area should have no result. For XHTML add **="nohref"** immediately thereafter.

8. If desired, type **target="name"**, where *name* is the name of the window where the page should appear *(see page 122)*.

9. If desired, add a keyboard shortcut by typing **accesskey="x"** *(see page 126)*.

10. Type **/>** to complete the clickable area.

11. Repeat steps 3–10 for each area.

12. Type **</map>** to complete the map.

13. Type **<img src="image.gif"**, where *image.gif* is the name of the image to be used as an image map.

14. Add image attributes, including `alt`.

15. Type **usemap="#label"**, where *label* is the map name defined in step 2.

16. Type the final **/>** for the image.

✔ Tips

- Usually, maps are in the same (X)HTML document as the image that uses them. Internet Explorer, however, can use maps that are in an external (X)HTML file. Just add the full URL of that file in front of the label name: **usemap="map.html#label"**.

- With overlapping areas, most browsers use the URL of the first area defined.

- The `target` attribute is only allowed in (X)HTML transitional and frameset.

- The `id` attribute in `map` is required in XHTML strict, but most browsers need the `name` for it to work. So use both.

Creating a Client-Side Image Map

Using a Server-Side Image Map

To use a server-side image map, you have to have the *imagemap* program on your NCSA HTTPd server or *htimage* on your CERN server. The program should be located in the cgi-bin directory. Ask your server administrator for help, if necessary.

To use a server-side image map:

1. In your (X)HTML document, type **<a href="http://www.yoursite.com/cgi-bin/imagemap**, where *imagemap* is the name of the program that interprets your set of coordinates.

2. Type **/path/coords"** (adding no spaces after step 1) indicating the path to the text file that contains the coordinates (the map) for the image.

3. Type the final **>** of the link definition.

4. Type **<img src="clickimage.gif"** where *clickimage.gif* is the image that you want your readers to click.

5. Type **ismap** to indicate a clickable image for a server-side map. In XHTML, add **="ismap"** directly thereafter.

6. Add any other image attributes as desired and then type the final **/>**.

7. Type the clickable text that should appear next to the image, if any.

8. Type **</a>** to complete the link.

✔ Tip

■ For information on creating sets of coordinates for server-side image maps, consult your Internet service provider. They'll be able to tell you what kind of server they have and in what format the coordinates should be.

```
<body>

<p><a href="http://www.cookwood.com/cgi-bin/imagemap/banner.map">

<img src="clickimage.gif" alt="SE banner" ismap="ismap" />

</a></p>

<h1>Starsearch Enterprises</h1>

<p><a href="newinfo.html">New programs</a>
<br />

<a href="pressrelease.html">Press releases</a>
<br />

<a href="events.html">Upcoming events</a>
<br />

<a href="infoSE.html">About Starsearch Enterprises</a></p>

</body>
```

Figure 7.30 *The text-based alternate links below the image point to the same URLs as the buttons in the clickable image. This gives equal access to your users who can't see the images.*

Figure 7.31 *When your user points at a part of a clickable image, the cursor changes into a hand and the corresponding URL shows in the status area at the bottom of the window.*

CREATING STYLES

Once you have the basic structure of your page laid out you can begin to format that content by applying styles. While you can theoretically use different kinds of style sheets, CSS is the current standard. This chapter explains how to create CSS style rules and how to apply them to selected elements.

In Chapter 9, *Applying Styles*, you'll learn how to organize a collection of style rules in a style sheet and then associate them with one or more (X)HTML pages.

You'll learn about the actual properties and values used in style rules principally in Chapter 10, *Formatting with Styles* and in Chapter 11, *Layout with Styles*. Some more specialized style properties are discussed throughout the rest of this book. Until then, we'll use the very simple and relatively obvious `{color:red;}` in our examples.

Constructing a Style Rule

Each style rule in a style sheet has two main parts: the *selector*, which determines which elements are affected and the *declaration*, made up of one or more property/value pairs, which specifies just what should be done **(Figures 8.1 and 8.2)**.

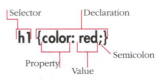

Figure 8.1 *A style rule is made up of a selector (which indicates which elements will be formatted), and a declaration (which describes the formatting that should be executed).*

Figure 8.2 *Multiple property/value pairs in the declaration must be separated by a semicolon. Some folks simply end every property/value pair with a semicolon—including the last pair in a list—so that they never forget to add it. That's fine, as shown here, but not required. Note the extra spacing and indenting to keep everything readable.*

To construct a style rule:

1. Type **selector**, where *selector* identifies the elements you wish to format. You'll learn how to create all sorts of selectors throughout the rest of this chapter.

2. Type **{** (an opening curly bracket) to begin the declaration.

3. Type **property: value;**, where *property* is the name of the CSS property that describes the sort of formatting you'd like to apply and *value* is one of a list of allowable options for that property. CSS properties and their values are described in detail in Chapters 10 and 11.

4. Repeat step 3 as needed.

5. Type **}** to complete the declaration and the style rule.

✔ Tips

- You may add extra spaces between the steps above as desired to keep the style sheet readable **(Figure 8.2)**.

- While each property/value pair should be separated from the next by a semicolon, you may omit the semicolon that follows the *last* pair in the list. Still, it's easier to always use it than to remember when it's possible to omit it.

- Missing (or duplicate) semicolons can make the browser completely ignore the style rule.

Constructing a Style Rule

Name of desired element

Figure 8.3 *The simplest kind of selector is simply the name of the type of element that should be formatted, in this case,* h1 *elements.*

Name of desired element

Context

Figure 8.4 *This selector uses context. The style will only be applied to the* em *elements within* h1 *elements. The* em *elements found elsewhere are not affected.*

Name of desired element
Class

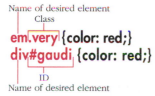

ID
Name of desired element

Figure 8.5 *The first selector chooses all the* em *elements that belong to the* very *class. The second selector chooses the one* div *element with an id of* gaudi.

Name

Pseudo-class

Figure 8.6 *In this example, the selector chooses* a *elements that belong to the* link *pseudoclass (in English this means the* a *elements that haven't yet been visited).*

Name
Attribute

Figure 8.7 *You can use the square brackets to add information to a selector about the desired element's attributes and/or values.*

Constructing Selectors

The selector determines which elements a style rule is applied to. For example, if you want to format all p elements with the Times font, 12 pixels high, you'd need to create a selector that identifies just the p elements while leaving the other elements in your code alone. If you want to format the first p in each division with a special indent, you'll need to create a slightly more complicated selector that identifies only those p elements that are the first element in their division.

A selector can define up to five different criteria for choosing the elements that should be formatted:

- the type or name of the element **(Figure 8.3)**,

- the context in which the element is found **(Figure 8.4)**,

- the class or id of an element **(Figure 8.5)**,

- the pseudo-class of an element or a pseudo-element itself **(Figure 8.6)**. (I'll explain that awful sounding *pseudo-class*, I promise.)

- and whether or not an element has certain attributes and values **(Figure 8.7)**.

Selectors can include any combination of these five criteria in order to pinpoint the desired elements. Mostly, you use one or two. In addition, you can apply the same declarations to several selectors at once if you need to apply the same style rules to different groups of elements *(see page 145)*.

The rest of this chapter will explain exactly how to define selectors and will give information about which selectors are best supported by current browsers.

Selecting Elements by Name

Perhaps the most common criteria for choosing which elements to format is the element's name or *type*. For example, you might want to make all of the h1 elements big and bold and format all of the p elements with a sans-serif font.

To select elements to format based on their type:

1. Type **selector**, where *selector* is the name of the desired type of element, without any attributes.

2. Create the rest of the style rule as usual For more details, consult *Constructing a Style Rule* on page 134.

✔ Tips

■ Unless you specify otherwise (using the techniques in the rest of this chapter) all the elements of the specified type should be formatted, no matter where they appear in your document. (Older browsers don't always follow this imperative, especially with elements in tables.)

■ Not all selectors need to specify an element's name. If you want to apply formatting to an entire class of elements, regardless of which elements have been identified with that class, you'd want to leave the name out of the selector.

■ The wild card, * (asterisk), matches any element name in your code.

■ You can choose a group of element names for a selector by using the comma to separate them. For more details, consult *Specifying Groups of Elements* on page 145.

■ Name or type selectors are well supported by current browsers.

```
<h1>Antoni Gaudí</h1>
<div id="gaudi">
<p>Many tourists are drawn to Barcelona to see Antoni Gaudí's incredible architecture. </p>
<p>Barcelona <a href="http://www.gaudi2002.bcn.es/english/flash/home/GO.htm">celebrates </a> the 150th anniversary of Gaudí's birth in 2002.</p>
<div class="works"><h2>La Casa Milà</h2>
<p>Gaudí's work was essentially useful. La Casa Milà is an apartment building and <em>real people</em> live there.</p>
</div>
<div class="works"><h2>La Sagrada Família</h2>
<p>The complicatedly named and curiously unfinished Expiatory Temple of the Sacred Family is the <em>most visited</em> building in Barcelona.</p>
</div>
</div>
```

Figure 8.8 *Our (X)HTML code has two* h2 *elements.*

```
h2 {color:red;}
```

Figure 8.9 *This selector will choose all of the* h2 *elements in the document.*

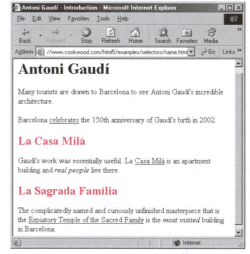

Figure 8.10 *All the* h2 *elements are colored red.*

```
<h1>Antoni Gaudí</h1>
<div id="gaudi">
<p>Many tourists are drawn to Barcelona to see
Antoni Gaudí's incredible architecture. </p>
<p>Barcelona <a href="http://www.gaudi2002.
bcn.es/english/flash/home/GO.htm">celebrates
</a> the 150th anniversary of Gaudí's birth in
2002.</p>
<div class="works"><h2>La Casa Milà</h2>
<p>Gaudí's work was essentially useful. La Casa
Milà is an apartment building and <em>real
people</em> live there.</p>
</div>
<div class="works"><h2>La Sagrada
Família</h2>
<p>The complicatedly named and curiously
unfinished Expiatory Temple of the Sacred Family is
the <em>most visited</em> building in Barcelona.
</p>
</div>
</div>
```

Figure 8.11 *The division with an* id *of* gaudi *encloses almost the entire page (everything but the initial* h1*).*

```
div#gaudi {color:red;}
```

Figure 8.12 *This selector will choose the* div *element with an* id *equal to "gaudi".*

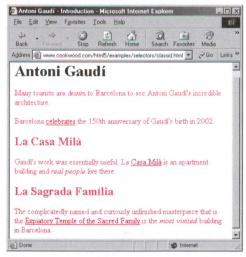

Figure 8.13 *The gaudi* div*, but not the* h1 *element, is displayed in red.*

Selecting Elements by Class or ID

If you've labeled elements with a class or id *(see page 67)*, you can use that criteria in a selector to apply formatting to only those elements that are so labeled.

To select elements to format based on their class:

1. Type **.** (a period).

2. With no intervening space, immediately type **label**, where *label* identifies the class to which you'd like to apply the styles.

3. Create the rest of the style rule as usual *(see page 134)*.

To select elements to format based on their id:

1. Type **#** (a hash or pound sign).

2. With no intervening space, immediately type **id**, where *id* uniquely identifies the element to which you'd like to apply the styles.

3. Create the rest of the style rule as usual *(see page 134)*.

✔ Tips

■ You can use class and id selectors alone or together with other selector criteria. For example, **.news {color: red;}** would affect all elements with the news class, while **h1.news {color: red;}** would affect only the h1 elements of the news class.

■ For more information on assigning classes to elements in the (X)HTML code, consult *Naming Elements* on page 67.

■ Class and id selectors are well supported by current browsers.

Selecting Elements by Context

In CSS you can pinpoint elements depending on their ancestors, their parent, or their siblings *(see page 29)*.

An *ancestor* is any element that contains the desired element (the *descendant*), regardless of the number of generations that separate them.

To select elements to format based on their ancestor:

1. Type **ancestor**, where *ancestor* is the name of the element that contains the element you wish to format.

2. Type a space **(Figure 8.15)**.

3. If necessary, repeat steps 1–2 for each successive generation of ancestors.

4. Type **descendant**, where *descendant* is the name of the element you wish to format.

5. Create the rest of the style rule as usual *(see page 134)*.

✔ Tips

■ A selector based on an element's ancestor is called a *descendant selector*.

■ Descendant selectors are well supported by current browsers.

■ Don't be thrown off by the **div#gaudi** portion of the example (even though it's ugly). Remember that it simply means "the div whose id is equal to *gaudi*" *(see page 137)*. So **div#gaudi p** means "any p element that is contained in the div whose id is equal to *gaudi*".

```
<h1>Antoni Gaudí</h1>
<div id="gaudi">
    <p>Many tourists ... </p>
    <p>Barcelona ...</p>
    <div class="works"><h2>La Casa Milà</h2>
        <p>Gaudí's work ...</p>
    </div>
    <div class="works"><h2>La Sagrada
        Família</h2>
        <p>The complicatedly named ... </p>
    </div>
</div>
```

Figure 8.14 *I've snipped the text to make the relationships between elements easier to see. Each indentation represents a generation. Note that there are two second generation p elements, directly within the gaudi div, and two third generation p elements, within the works divs (within the gaudi div).*

```
div#gaudi p {color:red;}
```

Figure 8.15 *The space between div#gaudi and p means that this selector will find any p element that is a descendant of the gaudi div, regardless of its generation.*

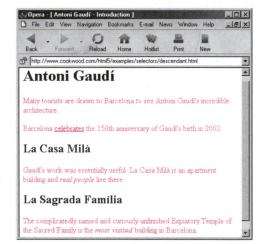

Figure 8.16 *All of the p elements that are contained within the gaudi div are red, even if they're also within other elements within that gaudi div.*

```
div#gaudi > p {color:red;}
```

Figure 8.17 *This selector will only choose those* p *elements that are children of the* gaudi *div. They may not be contained within any other element in order to qualify.*

Figure 8.18 *Only the first two* p *elements are children of the* gaudi *div. The two other* p *elements are children of the* works *div. For the (X)HTML code used in this example, see Figure 8.14 on page 138.*

A *parent* is the element that directly contains the desired element (the *child*) with no intermediary containing elements.

To select elements to format based on their parent:

1. Type **parent**, where *parent* is the name of the element that directly contains the element you wish to format.

2. Type **>** (the greater than sign) **(Fig. 8.17)**.

3. If necessary, repeat steps 1–2 for each successive generation of parents.

4. Type **child**, where *child* is the name of the element you wish to format.

5. Create the rest of the style rule as usual (*see page 134*).

✔ Tips

■ A selector based on an element's parent is called a *child selector*.

■ Among current browsers, only IE 5.5 and IE 6 for Windows fail to support the child selector.

(continued)

Selecting Elements by Context

It's sometimes useful to be able to select only the *first* child of an element, as opposed to all of the children of an element.

To select elements to format that are the *first* child of their parent:

1. Type **parent**, where *parent* is the name of the desired element's parent.
2. Type **:first-child** (just like that) **(Figure 8.19)**.

An adjacent sibling is the element that directly precedes the desired element within the same parent element.

To select elements to format based on an adjacent sibling:

1. Type **sibling**, where *sibling* is the element that directly precedes the desired element within the same parent element.
2. Type **+** (a plus sign).
3. If necessary, repeat steps 1–2 for each successive sibling.
4. Type **tag**, where *tag* is the name of the element you wish to format.
5. Create the rest of the style rule as usual *(see page 134)*.

✔ Tips

- Also see *Parents and Children* on page 29.
- The `:first-child` part of the selector is called a *pseudo-class*, because it identifies a group of elements without you, the designer, having to mark them in the (X)HTML code. Unfortunately, it is not yet supported by Internet Explorer for Windows (as of version 6).
- Adjacent sibling selectors are currently supported only by Netscape 6.

```
div#gaudi p:first-child {color:red}
```

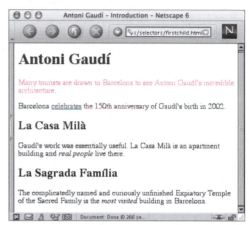

Figure 8.19 *This selector chooses only those* p *elements that are the first child of the* gaudi *div.*

Figure 8.20 *The first* p *element contained in the* gaudi *div is colored red. Only Netscape 6 properly deals with the first-child pseudo-element. For the (X)HTML code, see Figure 8.14 on page 138.*

```
div#gaudi p+p {color:red}
```

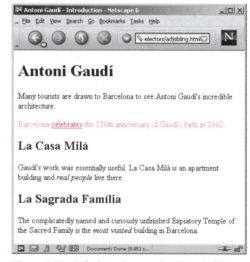

Figure 8.21 *This selector chooses only those* p *elements which directly follow a sibling* p *element.*

Figure 8.22 *Only the* p *elements that directly follow a sibling* p *element are red. (Currently, only Netscape 6 supports this rather useful selector. Think indented paragraphs with the first paragraph flush.)*

```
<h1>Antoni Gaudí</h1>
<div id="gaudi">
<p>Many tourists are drawn to Barcelona to see
Antoni Gaudí's incredible architecture. </p>
<p>Barcelona <a href="http://www.gaudi2002.
bcn.es/english/flash/home/GO.htm">celebrates
</a> the 150th anniversary of Gaudí's birth in
2002.</p>
<div class="works"><h2>La Casa Milà</h2>
<p>Gaudí's work was essentially useful. La Casa
Milà is an apartment building and <em>real
people</em> live there.</p>
</div>
<div class="works"><h2>La Sagrada
Família</h2>
<p>The complicatedly named and curiously
unfinished Expiatory Temple of the Sacred Family is
the <em>most visited</em> building in Barcelona.
</p>
</div></div>
```

Figure 8.23 *You can't specify in the code what state a link will have. It's controlled by your visitors.*

```
a:link {color:red;}
a:visited {color:yellow;}
a:focus {color: olive;}
a:hover {color:green;}
a:active {color:blue;}
```

Figure 8.24 *Styles for links should always be defined in this order, to avoid overriding properties when a link is in more than one state (say, visited and hovered).*

Figure 8.25 *The a element (the link) is red when it's new and unvisited, yellow after the visitor clicks it, olive when it has the focus, green when pointed at, and blue when clicked on.*

Selecting Link Elements Based on Their State

CSS lets you apply formatting to links based on their current *state*, that is whether they've been visited, whether the visitor is hovering their cursor on top of them, or whatever.

To select link elements to format based on their state:

1. Type **a** (since *a* is the name of the link tag).

2. Type **:** (the colon).

3. Type **link** to change the appearance of links that haven't yet been or currently aren't being clicked or pointed at.

   Or type **visited** to change the appearance of links that the visitor has already clicked.

   Or type **focus** if the link is selected via the keyboard and is ready to be activated.

   Or type **hover** to change the appearance of links when pointed to.

   Or type **active** to change the appearance of links when clicked.

4. Create the rest of the style rule as usual *(see page 134)*.

✔ Tips

- These *pseudo-classes* (classes for intangible characteristics you can't mark manually) are supposed to work with all kinds of elements, but current browsers only support them for the link (a) tag.

- Since a link can be in more than one state at a time (say, simultaneously active *and* hovered above), it's important to define the rules in the following order: link, visited, focus, hover, active (LVFHA).

Selecting Part of an Element

You can also select just the first letter or first line of an element and then apply formatting to that.

To select the first line of an element:

1. Type **tag**, where `tag` is the name of the element whose first line you'd like to format.

2. Type **:** (the colon).

3. Type **first-line** to select the entire first line of the element referenced in step 1.

4. Create the rest of the style rule as usual *(see page 134)*.

To select the first letter of an element:

1. Type **tag**, where `tag` is the name of the element whose first line you'd like to format.

2. Type **:** (the colon).

3. Type **first-letter** to select the first letter of the element referenced in step 1.

4. Create the rest of the style rule as usual *(see page 134)*.

```
<h1>Antoni Gaudí</h1>
<div id="gaudi">
<p>Many tourists are drawn to Barcelona to see Antoni Gaudí's incredible architecture. </p>
<p>Barcelona <a href="http://www.gaudi2002.bcn.es/english/flash/home/GO.htm">celebrates </a> the 150th anniversary of Gaudí's birth in 2002.</p>
<div class="works"><h2>La Casa Milà</h2>
<p>Gaudí's work was essentially useful. La Casa Milà is an apartment building and <em>real people</em> live there.</p>
</div>
<div class="works"><h2>La Sagrada Família</h2>
<p>The complicatedly named and curiously unfinished Expiatory Temple of the Sacred Family is the <em>most visited</em> building in Barcelona. </p>
</div></div>
```

Figure 8.26 *There is nothing highlighted here because you can't identify the first line until the page is displayed in the browser.*

```
p:first-line {color:red;}
```

Figure 8.27 *Here the selector will choose the first line of each p element.*

Figure 8.28 *Adjusting the width of the window changes the content of the first line (and thus, what is formatted).*

```
p:first-letter {color:red;}
```

Figure 8.29 *Here the selector will choose just first letter of each* p *element. For the corresponding (X)HTML code, see Figure 8.26 on page 142.*

Figure 8.30 *Netscape 6 continues its good record of support by displaying just the first letter of each* p *element in red.*

✔ **Tips**

■ The first-letter and first-line selectors are called *pseudo-elements*, since they refer to actual content that can't be manually marked as an independent element. OK, you could conceivably mark each first letter of the paragraph with a special span tag (though it would be cumbersome), but the content of the first line depends on a myriad of factors, including such uncontrollable issues as the size of the visitor's window and the visitor's monitor resolution.

■ If the paragraph begins with a quotation mark, the first-letter selector may include an opening quotation mark together with the first letter.

■ Netscape 6, Internet Explorer 6, and Opera 6 all support both the first-line and first-letter pseudo-elements.

■ You may combine the first-letter or first-line pseudo-elements with more complicated selectors than that which I've used in this example. For example, if you wanted just the first-letter of the p elements in the *works* divs, your selector would be **div.works p:first-letter**.

Selecting Elements Based on Attributes

You can also apply formatting to those elements that have a given attribute or attribute value.

To select elements to format based on their attributes:

1. If desired, type **element**, where *element* is the name of the element whose attributes are in question.

2. Type **[attribute**, where *attribute* is the name of the attribute that an element must have to be selected.

3. If desired, type **="value"** if you want to specify the *value* that the attribute must have for its element to be selected.

    Or, if desired, type **~="value"**, to specify a *value* that the attribute can contain (along with other content) for its element to be selected.

    Or, if desired, type **|="value"** to specify that the attribute's value begin with *value-* (that is, what you typed followed by a hyphen) in order for its element to be selected. (This is most common when searching for elements in a particular language.)

4. Type **] (Figure 8.32)**.

5. Create the rest of the style rule as usual (*see page 134*).

✔ Tip

■ Selecting elements based on the attributes (and values) they contain is not supported by current versions of Internet Explorer (for either Windows or Macintosh).

```
<h1>Antoni Gaudí</h1>
<div id="gaudi">
<p>Many tourists are drawn to Barcelona to see Antoni Gaudí's incredible architecture. </p>
<p>Barcelona <a href="http://www.gaudi2002.bcn.es/english/flash/home/GO.htm">celebrates </a> the 150th anniversary of Gaudí's birth in 2002.</p>
<div class="works"><h2>La Casa Milà</h2>
<p>Gaudí's work was essentially useful. La Casa Milà is an apartment building and <em>real people</em> live there.</p>
</div>
<div class="works"><h2>La Sagrada Família</h2>
<p>The complicatedly named and curiously unfinished Expiatory Temple of the Sacred Family is the <em>most visited</em> building in Barcelona. </p>
</div>
</div>
```

Figure 8.31 *In this code, only the two inner* div *elements have* class *attributes.*

```
div[class] {color:red;}
```

Figure 8.32 *The square brackets enclose the desired attribute and any desired value.*

Figure 8.33 *Every* div *element that contains a* class *attribute, regardless of the class's value, is red.*

Selecting Elements Based on Attributes

```
<h1>Antoni Gaudí</h1>

<div id="gaudi">

<p>Many tourists are drawn to Barcelona to see
Antoni Gaudí's incredible architecture. </p>

<p>Barcelona <a href="http://www.gaudi2002.
bcn.es/english/flash/home/GO.htm">celebrates
</a> the 150th anniversary of Gaudí's birth in
2002.</p>

<div class="works"><h2>La Casa Milà</h2>

<p>Gaudí's work was essentially useful. La Casa
Milà is an apartment building and <em>real
people</em> live there.</p>

</div>

<div class="works"><h2>La Sagrada
Família</h2>

<p>The complicatedly named and curiously
unfinished Expiatory Temple of the Sacred Family is
the <em>most visited</em> building in Barcelona.
</p>

</div>

</div>
```

Figure 8.34 *There is one* h1 *and two* h2 *elements.*

```
h1, h2 {color:red;}
```

Figure 8.35 *You can list any number of individual selectors, as long as you separate each with a comma.*

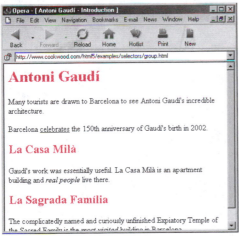

Figure 8.36 *Now both the* h1 *and the* h2 *elements will be colored red.*

Specifying Groups of Elements

It's often necessary to apply the same style rules to more than one element. You can either reiterate the rules for each element, or you can combine selectors and apply the rules in one fell swoop.

To apply styles to groups of elements:

1. Type **selector1**, where *selector1* is the name of the first element that should be affected by the style rule.

2. Type **,** (a comma).

3. Type **selector2**, where *selector2* is the next tag that should be affected by the style rule.

4. Repeat steps 2–3 for each additional element.

5. Create the rest of the style rule as usual *(see page 134).*

✔ Tips

■ This is nothing more than a handy shortcut. The rule **h1, h2 {color: red}** is precisely the same as the two rules **h1 {color: red}** and **h2 {color: red}**.

■ You can group any kind of selector, from the simplest (as shown in the example) to the most complex. For example, you could use **h1, div.works p:first-letter** to choose the level one headers *and* the first letter of the p elements in divs whose class is equal to *works* (!).

■ It is sometimes useful to create a single style rule with the common styles that apply to several selectors and then create individual style rules with the styles they do not share. Just be careful about the cascade *(see page 42).*

Combining Selectors

You can combine any of the techniques that I've explained in the last few pages in order to pinpoint the elements that you're interested in formatting.

To combine selectors:

1. Define the context of the desired element. For more details, consult *Selecting Elements by Context* on page 138.

2. Next, either spell out the element's name *(see page 136)* or use the wild card character *(see page 136)*.

3. Then, specify the class or id of the desired element(s). For more details, consult *Selecting Elements by Class or ID* on page 137.

4. Next, specify the pseudo-class or pseudo-element. For more details, consult *Selecting Link Elements Based on Their State* on page 141 and *Selecting Part of an Element* on page 142.

5. Finally, specify which attributes and values must be present for the element to be selected. For more details, consult *Selecting Elements Based on Attributes* on page 144.

6. And then, create the rest of the style rule as usual *(see page 134)*.

✔ Tip

- You may leave out any of the steps that you don't need. This page is designed to show you the *order* in which the different criteria should be listed.

Figure 8.37 *Here's a doozy for you. It says "choose only the first letter of the em elements that are found within p elements that are in the div elements whose class is equal to* works.*

Combining Selectors

APPLYING STYLES

In the previous chapter you learned how to construct individual style rules. In this chapter, you'll learn how to combine those style rules into a style sheet and then apply that style sheet to an individual element, a whole Web page, or an entire Web site.

We start working on the actual properties and allowed values in Chapters 10, *Formatting with Styles*, and 11, *Layout with Styles*.

Creating an External Style Sheet

External style sheets are ideal for giving all the pages on your Web site a common look. You can define all your styles in an external style sheet and then tell each page on your site to consult the external sheet, thus ensuring that each will have the same settings.

To create an external style sheet:

1. Create a new text document in your text editor of choice.

2. Define as many style rules as desired *(see page 134)* **(Figure 9.1)**.

3. Save the document in Text Only format in the desired directory **(Figure 9.2)**. Give the document the extension .css to designate the document as a Cascading Style Sheet.

✔ Tips

■ Make sure you save the style sheet as Text Only (sometimes called Text Document or ASCII) and give it the .css extension. When you upload it to the server (which we'll get to in Chapter 25), be sure to choose ASCII mode—not Binary—just the same as for (X)HTML files. This goes for Mac folks too!

■ External style sheets must be either linked to *(see page 149)* or imported *(see page 152)*.

■ XSL is an up and coming style sheet language for XHTML documents. Since it is not as well supported as CSS, I do not cover it in this book. Note that XSL style sheets are also saved as text only but with the .xsl extension. For more information, see *http://www.w3.org/Style/XSL/,* the W3C's XSL site.

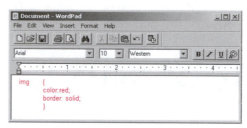

Figure 9.1 *Use any text editor you like to write CSS documents. This is WordPad.*

Figure 9.2 *Be sure to save the CSS file with the .css extension and as a Text Document (or Text Only, or in ASCII, or however your text editor calls it).*

Creating an External Style Sheet

```
img {color:red; border: solid}
```

Figure 9.3 *Here's the external style sheet that we cre-ated on page 148 (called* base.css*). Don't worry about the properties and values just yet. (It just means create a solid red border around all the* img *elements.)*

```
<head>
    <meta http-equiv="content-type"
content="text/html; charset=utf-8" />
    <title>La Casa Mil&agrave;</title>
    <link rel="stylesheet" type="text/css"
href="base.css" />
</head>
<body>
<img src="palau_corner.jpg" alt="Palau de La
M&uacute;sica, from the corner" width="63"
height="163" align="left"/>
<img src="palau250.jpg" alt="El Palau de la
M&uacute;sica" width="250" height="163"
```

Figure 9.4 *The* link *tag goes inside the* head *section of your (X)HTML document.*

Figure 9.5 *The styles (a red, solid border) are applied to each* img *element.*

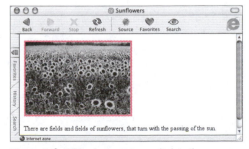

Figure 9.6 *Other documents can link to the very same external style sheet.*

Linking External Style Sheets

The easiest, best supported and most common way to apply the rules in a style sheet to a Web page is to *link* to the style sheet.

To link an external style sheet:

1. In the head section of each (X)HTML page in which you wish to use the style sheet, type **<link rel="stylesheet" type="text/css"**, where *text/css* indicates that the style sheet is written in CSS.

2. Type **href="url.css"**, where *url.css* is the name of your CSS style sheet *(see step 3 on page 148)*.

3. Type the final **/>**.

✔ Tips

- When you make a change to an external style sheet, all the pages that reference it are automatically updated as well.

- URLs in an external style sheet are relative to the location of the style sheet file on the server, not to the (X)HTML page's location. Note that Netscape 4.x gets this wrong, considering relative URLs with respect to the (X)HTML file. One solution is to use absolute URLs *(see page 33)*. For more details about dealing with Netscape 4.x's bugs, consult *Importing External Style Sheets* on page 152.

- The relative influence of styles applied in different ways is summarized on page page 154.

- You can link to several style sheets at a time. The later ones take precedence over the earlier ones.

- You can offer alternate versions of linked style sheets and let your visitors choose among them *(see page 150)*.

Offering Alternate Style Sheets

You can link to more than one style sheet and let visitors choose the styles they like best. The specifications allow for a base set of *persistent* styles that are applied regardless of the visitor's preference, a default or *preferred* set of styles that are applied if the visitor makes no choice, and one or more *alternate* style sheets that the visitor can choose, at which point the preferred set (though not the persistent one) is deactivated and ignored.

To offer alternate style sheets:

1. To designate the style sheet that should be used as a base, regardless of the visitor's preferences, use the simple syntax described on page 149.

2. To designate the style sheet that should be offered as a first choice, but that can be deactivated by another choice, add **title="label"** to the link element, where *label* identifies the preferred style sheet.

3. To designate a style sheet that should be offered as an alternate choice, use **rel="alternate stylesheet" title="label"** in the link element, where *label* identifies the alternate style sheet.

✔ Tips

■ Currently, only Netscape 6 (on both Mac and Windows) offers a way to switch from one style sheet to another. However, there are JavaScript solutions for other browsers. For one such solution, check out *http://www.alistapart.com/stories/alternate/*.

■ You can also create style sheets that are used just for printing your Web page (or just for viewing it on screen). For more details, consult Chapter 12, *Style Sheets for Printing*.

```
img {color:red; border: solid}
```

Figure 9.7 *This CSS file* (base.css) *will be our persistent style sheet, and will be applied no matter what the visitor does.*

```
img {border: dashed}
```

Figure 9.8 *This style sheet* (preferred.css) *is the one that I want to be loaded by default, when the visitor jumps to my page.*

```
img {border: dotted}
```

Figure 9.9 *The visitor will be able to load this alternate style sheet if they want. Its file name is* alternate.css.

```
<head>
    <meta http-equiv="content-type"
content="text/html; charset=utf-8" />
    <title>La Casa Mil&agrave;</title>
    <link rel="stylesheet" type="text/css"
href="base.css" />
    <link rel="stylesheet" type="text/css"
href="preferred.css" title="Dashed" />
    <link rel="alternate stylesheet" type="text/css"
href="alternate.css" title="Dotted" />
</head>
```

Figure 9.10 *In order, I've defined the base or persistent style sheet, the preferred or automatic style sheet, and an alternate style sheet. Each style sheet needs its own* link *element.*

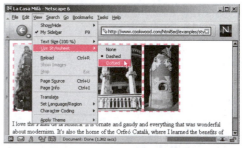

Figure 9.11 *When the page is loaded, it has a dashed border (the preferred value overrides the base value of solid, but the base color is maintained). If the visitor chooses Dotted, the alternate style sheet will be used instead of the Dashed one. Currently, only Netscape (versions 6.x+) makes it easy for visitors to choose among alternate style sheets.*

```
<head>
    <meta http-equiv="content-type"
content="text/html; charset=utf-8" />
    <title>La Casa Mil&agrave;</title>
    <style type="text/css">
    img { color: red;
        border: solid;
        }
    </style>
    </head>
<body>
<img src="palau250.jpg" alt="El Palau de la
M&uacute;sica" width="250" height="163" />
<p>I love the Palau de la Música. It is ornate and
```

Figure 9.12 *The* style *element and its enclosed style rules go in the* head *section of your document. Don't forget the closing* </style> *tag, as for some reason I am wont to do.*

Figure 9.13 *The result is exactly the same as if you linked to the styles in an external style sheet. However, no other Web page can take advantage of the styles used on this page.*

Creating an Internal Style Sheet

Internal style sheets let you set the styles at the top of the (X)HTML document to which they should be applied. If you plan to apply the style sheet to more than one page, you're better off using external style sheets *(see page 148)*.

To create an internal style sheet:

1. In the head section of your (X)HTML document, type **<style type="text/css">**.

2. Define as many style rules as desired *(see page 134)*.

3. Type **</style>** to complete the internal style sheet.

✔ Tips

■ Add (X)HTML comment tags (**<!--**) after the initial <style> tag and before (**-->**) the final </style> tag to hide styles from very old browsers *(see page 71)*. In XHTML, you can enclose an internal style sheet in **<![CDATA[...]]>** to hide it from XML parsers *(see page 321)*.

■ You can also apply styles to individual (X)HTML tags. For more details, consult *Applying Styles Locally* on page 153.

■ If you want to apply your styles to more than one Web page, you should use an external style sheet. For more information, consult *Creating an External Style Sheet* on page 148 and *Linking External Style Sheets* on page 149.

■ The relative influence of styles applied in different ways is discussed on page 154.

■ If you use a different style sheet language (like XSL), you'll have to adjust the type attribute accordingly, e.g., *text/xsl*.

Creating an Internal Style Sheet

Importing External Style Sheets

Early on, importing style sheets was simply an alternative to linking to them. Now, it's used as a way to save buggy browsers— Netscape 4 in particular—from themselves.

To import an external style sheet:

Within the `style` element *(see page 151)*, but before any individual style rules, type **@import "external.css";**, where *external.css* is the name of your CSS style sheet *(see step 3 on page 148)*.

✔ Tips

■ Netscape 4 doesn't support the `@import` rule. However, because its support of CSS in general is pretty abysmal, many Web page coders use this limitation to their advantage. For example, you could *link* to style sheets with rules that Netscape 4 deals with properly and then *import* style sheets with advanced techniques it can't handle. Netscape 4 will then have at least some of the style information while browsers who support `@import` will have it all. For more on hiding CSS from buggy browsers, see Johannes Koch's helpful *http://pixels.pixelpark.com/~koch/ hide_css_from_browsers/*

■ The `@import` rule can also be written as **@import url(external.css);** or **@import url("external.css");**. Regardless, always put it before any other style rules in the `style` element and don't forget the semicolon.

■ Style rules in an imported style sheet take precedence over any rules that come before the `@import` rule (for example, rules in earlier `@import` rules or in external sheets placed before the `style` element).

■ You may use the `@import` rule in an external style sheet (as always, before any other style rules).

Figure 9.14 *Some browsers not only don't support particular CSS features but create something hideous instead. Such is the case of Netscape 4.x and borders. Look how it creates those charming little boxes instead of the borders we asked for (see Figure 9.5 on page 149). Yuck!*

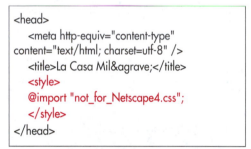

Figure 9.15 *The `@import` rule must be placed before any individual style rules in the `style` element. (It may come after other `@import` rules.)*

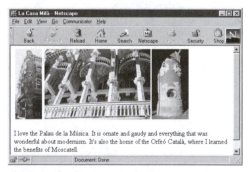

Figure 9.16 *Since Netscape 4.x doesn't understand the `@import` rule, it won't import the style rules in not_for_Netscape4.css, and won't display the border incorrectly—or at all for that matter. (It can still link to external style sheets with rules that it does understand.) Other browsers that do support `@import`, including IE5+, Netscape 6+, and Opera 3+ will continue to display the border correctly.*

```
<head>
    <meta http-equiv="content-type"
content="text/html; charset=utf-8" />
    <title>La Casa Mil&agrave;</title>
    </head>
<body>
<img src="palau_corner.jpg" alt="Palau de La
M&uacute;sica, from the corner" width="63"
height="163" align="left"/>
<img src="palau250.jpg" alt="El Palau de la
M&uacute;sica" width="250" height="163"
style="color: red; border: solid" align="left" />
<img src="tickets.jpg" alt="The Ticket Window"
width="87" height="163"/>
<br clear="all" />
<p>I love the Palau de la Música. It is ornate and
```

Figure 9.17 *Rules applied locally affect only a single element, in this case, the middle* img *tag.*

Figure 9.18 *Only the middle image has a border. To repeat the effect shown in the rest of this chapter, you'd have to add* `style="color:red;border:solid"` *to every single* img *tag individually.*

Applying Styles Locally

If you are new to style sheets and would like to experiment a bit before taking the plunge, applying styles locally is an easy, small-scale, and rather safe way to begin. Although it doesn't centralize all your formatting information for easy editing and global updating, it does open the door to the additional formatting that is impossible to create with conventional (X)HTML tags.

To apply styles locally:

1. Within the (X)HTML tag that you want to format, type **style="**.

2. Create a style rule without curly brackets or a selector. The selector isn't necessary since you're placing it directly inside the desired element.

3. To create additional style definitions, type a semicolon **;** and repeat step 2.

4. Type the final quote mark **"**.

✔ Tips

- Be careful not to confuse the equals signs with the colon. Since they both assign values it's easy to interchange them without thinking.

- Don't forget to separate multiple property definitions with a semicolon.

- Don't forget to enclose your style definitions in straight quote marks.

- Styles applied locally take precedence over all other styles *(see page 154)*.

- If you specify the font family in a local style declaration, you'll have to enclose multi-word font names with *single* quotes in order to avoid conflict with the `style` element's double quotes. Actually, the reverse is also fine. You just can't use the same type of quotes in both places.

Applying Styles Locally

The Importance of Location

With so many ways to apply styles, it's not unusual for more than one style rule to apply to the same element. As we discussed in Chapter 1, *Web Page Building Blocks*, and specifically on pages 42–43, a style's *location* can break ties in inheritance and specificity. The basic rule is, with all else equal, the later the style appears, the more precedence or importance it has.

So, locally applied styles *(see page 153)* have the most precedence and will override any conflicting styles applied earlier.

In a `style` element, any `@import` rules present will lose out to any individual style rules that also appear in the `style` element (since these must follow the `@import` rules, by definition).

The relationship between the `style` element and any linked external style sheets depends on their relative positions. If the `link` element comes later in the (X)HTML code, it overrides the `style` element. If it comes earlier, the `style` element (and any imported style sheets it contains) overrides the rules in the linked style sheet.

External style sheets can also contain `@import` rules. In that case, the imported rules are overridden by the other rules contained in the external style sheet (since, by definition, they must follow the `@import` rule). Their relationship with the document's other style sheets is determined by the position of the link to the external style sheet, as usual.

```
<head>
    <title>La Casa Mil&agrave;</title>
    <link rel="stylesheet" type="text/css"
href="base.css" />
    <style> img {border: dashed} </style>
</head>
```

Figure 9.19 *In this example, the* `style` *element comes last. Therefore, the rules it contains will have precedence over rules in the* base.css *style sheet (as long as the conflicting rules have the same inheritance and specificity factors).*

Figure 9.20 *The* `style` *element's dashed border wins out over the linked solid border.*

```
<head>
    <title>La Casa Mil&agrave;</title>
    <style> img {border: dashed} </style>
    <link rel="stylesheet" type="text/css"
href="base.css" />
</head>
```

Figure 9.21 *Here, the linked style sheet comes last and has precedence over rules in the style element (all else being equal).*

Figure 9.22 *The solid border from the* base.css *style sheet wins out over the internal* `style` *element's dashed border.*

```
/* Images will have a solid red border */
img {color:red; border: solid}
```

Figure 9.23 *Comments can be used to describe style rules so that they are easier to edit and update later on. (OK, this one isn't very complicated, but yours might be.)*

```
img {color:red; border: solid} /* Images will have a
solid red border */
```

Figure 9.24 *If you prefer, you can insert comments after a style rule.*

Adding Comments to Style Rules

It's a good idea to add comments to your style sheets so that you can remember what particularly complicated style rules are supposed to do. When you come back later, you'll be happy you left yourself these reminders.

To add comments to style rules:

1. In your style sheet, be it internal or external, type **/*** to begin your comments.

2. Type the comments.

3. Type ***/** to signal the end of the comments.

✔ Tips

■ Comments may include returns, and thus span several lines.

■ You can put comments around style rules effectively hiding them from the browser. This is a good way to test style sheets without permanently removing problematic portions.

■ You may not put comments inside other comments. In other words, comments may not include */.

■ You may start comments on their own line, or at the end of a style rule.

FORMATTING WITH STYLES

```
<body>

<div id="toc">

<a href="#gaudi">Antoni Gaudí</a> -
<a href="#mila">La Casa Milà</a> -
<a href="#sagrada">La Sagrada Família</a>

</div>

<div id="gaudi">

<h1><a name="gaudi">Antoni Gaudí</a></h1>

<p>Many tourists ... </p>

<p>Gaudí's ... the <a href="#mila">Casa
Milà</a> and its undulating balconies, to the
Church of the <a href="#sagrada">Sacred
Family</a> and its organic, bulbous towers.</p>

<p>Barcelona <a href="...G0.htm">celebrates
</a> the 150th anniversary ... There has <span
class="emph">never</span> been a better time to
visit this incredible city.</p>

<div class="work">

<h2><a name="mila">La Casa Milà</a></h2>

<p>If you walk down ... Domènec i Muntaner's
<a href="lleomorera.html">Casa Lleó i Morera</a>
to Puig i Cadalfach's <a href="amatller.html">Casa
Amatller</a>. But there is ...</p>

<p>One of the things ... real people live there. (OK,
<span class="emph">rich</span> people live
there.) Originally built ...</p>
```

Figure 10.1 *Here is an abbreviated version of the (X)HTML code that is formatted throughout this chapter. You can find the full file in the Examples section of my site: http://www.cookwood.com/html5ed/examples/*

In the old days, there were special HTML tags for making text bold or italic, bigger or smaller, or even for changing its font or color. As Web pages become larger and more sophisticated, formatting a page by using these individual tags gets more and more cumbersome, as you have to wade through piles of code to edit individual formatting instructions.

The push has been to separate formatting instructions from the actual content of the page in order to make it easier to control, update, and edit the formatting. With this in mind, the W3C decided to gradually remove almost all of the formatting tags from (X)HTML in favor of style sheets. While these formatting tags are still legal in the transitional and frameset flavors of (X)HTML, they are not permitted in documents written in strict (X)HTML. They remain popular, however, so I'll explain all about them in Chapter Chapter 21, *Formatting: The Old Way*.

It should be noted that (X)HTML still permits a very few formatting tags: tt, i, b, big, and small. You saw those already in Chapter 4, *Basic (X)HTML Formatting*.

Thankfully, styles offer many more possibilities than HTML tags and extensions ever did. Now you can change the size, weight, slant, line height, foreground and background color, spacing, and alignment of text, decide whether it should be underlined, overlined, struck through, or blinking, and convert it to all uppercase, all lowercase, or small-caps. You'll learn it all in this chapter!

Choosing a Font Family

Because not everyone has the same set of fonts, the font-family property has a special characteristic: you can specify more than one font, in case the first is not available in your visitor's system. You can also have a last ditch attempt at controlling the display in the visitor's system by specifying a generic font style like serif or monospace.

To set the font family:

1. After the desired selector in your style sheet, type **font-family: name**, where *name* is your first choice of font.

2. If desired, type **, name2**, where *name2* is your second font choice. Separate each choice with a comma and a space.

3. Repeat step 2 as desired.

✔ Tips

■ Surround multi-word font names with quotes (single or double).

■ You can specify fonts for different alphabets in the same font-family rule (say, Japanese and English) to format a chunk of text that contains different languages *and* writing systems.

■ Common fonts on Windows systems are Times New Roman and Arial. Most Macs have Times and Helvetica available.

■ You can use the following generic font names—**serif**, **sans-serif**, **cursive**, **fantasy**, and **monospace**—as a last ditch attempt to influence which font is used for display.

■ You can set the font family, font size, and line height all at once, using the general font property *(see page 165)*.

■ The font-family property is inherited.

```
h1, h2 {font-family: "Arial Black", "Helvetica Bold",
sans-serif}

p {font-family: "Verdana", "Helvetica", sans-serif}
```

Figure 10.2 *You can specify as many choices as you like. The browser will use the first one that it finds installed on the visitor's system.*

Figure 10.3 *On this system, both first choices, Arial Black and Verdana, were available.*

Choosing a Font Family

```
@font-face {font-family: "Sunnyside";

        src: url(SUNNYSI0.eot)}

h1, h2 {font-family: "Sunnyside", "Helvetica Bold"}

p {font-family: "Verdana", "Helvetica", sans-serif}
```

Figure 10.4 *To embed a font for Internet Explorer users, use* @font-face. *The* src *URL points to a special version of the font that can be downloaded to your visitor's system.*

Figure 10.5 *The headers are set in an unusual font, probably not found on many systems. Nevertheless, it will display properly because it is embedded in the style sheet.*

Embedding Fonts on a Page

You can choose whatever font you want, but if your visitors don't have it installed on their computers, they won't be able to view it. One solution is to embed a font in a page.

To embed fonts on a page:

1. Type **@font-face {**

2. Type **font-family: "name";** where *name* is the full name of the font that you wish to embed.

3. Next, indicate where the embedded font can be found by typing **src: url(font.eot)**, where *font.eot* is the location of the embedded font on the server

4. Type **}** to complete the @font-face rule.

5. Use the font name from step 2 in other style rules, as desired.

✔ Tips

■ You can't just choose any font file as the source for an embedded font (in step 3). You have to use a special format of the font. Internet Explorer requires fonts to be in the .eot format. You can convert your installed fonts into .eot with a program called WEFT. For more information, see *www.microsoft.com/typography/web/embedding/weft3/*. Unfortunately, only Explorer supports .eot fonts.

■ Bitstream has a technology called True-Doc that allows you to embed fonts in Web pages for viewing in Netscape 4 (but not 6) and Internet Explorer 4+ for Windows. However, in my tests, it didn't look so great, and the limited compatibility is a huge drawback. You can check out *www.truedoc.com* for more details.

■ In short, there is still no cross-platform, cross-browser format for embedded fonts.

Embedding Fonts on a Page

Creating Italics

Italics are often used to set off quotations, emphasized text, foreign words, magazine names and much more.

To create italics:

1. Type **font-style:**.

2. Type **oblique** for oblique text, or **italic** for italic text.

To remove italics:

1. Type **font-style:**.

2. Type **normal**.

✔ Tips

■ It used to be that the italic version of a font was created by a font designer from scratch, while the oblique version was created by the computer, on the fly. This distinction has blurred somewhat, but generally holds.

■ If you set the font style as italic and there is no italic style available, the browser should try to display the text as oblique.

■ One reason you might want to remove italics is to emphasize some text in a paragraph that has inherited italic formatting from a parent tag. For more details about inheritance, consult *The Cascade: When Rules Collide* on page 42.

■ You can also use the i or em tags in the (X)HTML code to create italics. For details, see page 74.

■ The font-style property is inherited.

h1, h2 {font-family: "Arial Black", "Helvetica Bold", sans-serif}

p {font-family: "Verdana", "Helvetica", sans-serif}

.emph {font-style: italic}

Figure 10.6 *In this example, I've made the* .emph *class display in italics.*

Figure 10.7 *Any elements in the* emph *class (like the word* never *in the third full paragraph above) will be displayed in italics.*

Creating Italics

```
h1, h2 {font-family: "Arial Black", "Helvetica Bold",
sans-serif;font-weight: normal}

p {font-family: "Verdana", "Helvetica", sans-serif}

.emph {font-style: italic; font-weight:bold}

a:link, a:hover {font-weight:bold}
```

Figure 10.8 *Browsers add bold formatting to headers (like* h1 *and* h2*) automatically. I can apply a normal font weight to remove it (since it's a bit much on this page). I've also added bold formatting to the* emph *class and to new and hovered links.*

Figure 10.9 *The headers are not so overbearing with the extra bold formatting removed. New links stand out (while visited ones are less obtrusive). And the emphasized text (the word* never *in the third full paragraph) is not only italic (from the preceding page) but also bold.*

Applying Bold Formatting

Bold formatting is probably the most common and effective way to make text stand out. Using style sheets gives you much more flexibility with bold text, providing relative values or allowing you to get rid of it altogether.

To apply bold formatting:

1. Type **font-weight:**.

2. Type **bold** to give an average bold weight to the text.

3. Or type **bolder** or **lighter** to use a value relative to the current weight.

4. Or type a multiple of **100** between 100 and 900, where 400 represents normal or book weight and 700 represents bold.

To remove bold formatting:

1. Type **font-weight:**.

2. Type **normal**.

✔ Tips

- Since the way weights are defined varies from font to font, the predefined values may not be relative from font to font. They are designed to be relative *within* a given font family.

- If the font family has fewer than nine weights, or if they are concentrated on one end of the scale, it is possible that some numeric values will correspond to the same font weight.

- What can you remove bold formatting from? Any tag where it's been applied automatically (b and h1 come to mind) and where it's been inherited from a parent tag (see page 42).

- The font-weight property is inherited.

Applying Bold Formatting

Setting the Font Size

There are two basic ways to set the font size for the text in your Web page. You can mandate that a specific size be used or you can have the size depend on the element's parent.

To mandate a specific font size:

1. Type **font-size:**.

2. Type an exact size: say, **16px** or **1em**.

   Or use a keyword to specify the size: **xx-small**, **x-small**, **small**, **medium**, **large**, **x-large**, or **xx-large**.

✔ Tips

- See page 44 for details about units.

- There shouldn't be any spaces between the number and the unit.

- The average pixel is about 1/80th of an inch high (1/32 cm), though it depends on the screen resolution. Imagine a 17" monitor, whose screen is roughly 12.5" wide, with a resolution of 1024 x 768. At that resolution, text at 16 pixels would be about 1/5 of an inch high (about 1/2cm).

- Pixels are probably the most popular sizing unit. They give the designer control over the text size and, except in Internet Explorer for Windows, the visitor can resize the text when needed with their browser's Text Size (or Zoom) option.

- Only use points, cm, mm, or picas in style sheets that format printed output (*see page 197*).

- Different browsers interpret the keywords in different ways. Explorer 5.x uses `small` as its base size while IE 6, Opera, and Netscape use `medium`. It's not worth the hassle to me.

- The `font-size` property is inherited.

```
h1, h2 {font-family: "Arial Black", "Helvetica Bold",
sans-serif;font-weight: normal}

h1 {font-size: 20px}

h2 {font-size: 14px}

p {font-family: "Verdana", "Helvetica", sans-serif;
font-size:12px}

.emph {font-style: italic; font-weight:bold}

a:link, a:visited, a:hover {font-weight:bold}

#toc {font-size:12px}
```

Figure 10.10 *Here I use pixel values to have control over the initial size of the text (which I've decreased in size throughout, compared with most browsers' defaults).*

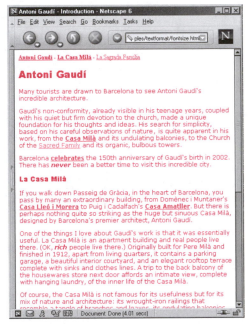

Figure 10.11 *The sizes I've specified are displayed in the browser, regardless of the default size that the visitor may have chosen in their browser's Preferences box.*

```
h1, h2 {font-family: "Arial Black", "Helvetica Bold",
sans-serif;font-weight: normal}

h1 {font-size: 1.25em}

h2 {font-size: .875em}

p {font-family: "Verdana", "Helvetica", sans-serif;
font-size:75%}

.emph {font-style: italic; font-weight:bold}

a:link, a:hover {font-weight:bold}

#toc {font-size:75%}
```

Figure 10.12 *Assuming a default text size of 16 pixels, this style sheet will be equivalent to the one shown in Figure 10.10 on page 162, but will maintain the relative sizes even when the visitor chooses some other default size.*

Figure 10.13 *Some visitors might set their default text size a bit larger (here it is 20 pixels), which, with sizes defined with ems and percentages, will make everything grow proportionally.*

To set a size that depends on the parent element's size:

1. Type **font-size:**.

2. Type the relative value, say **1.5em** or **150%**.

   Or use a relative keyword: **larger** or **smaller**.

✔ Tips

- There should not be any spaces between the number and the unit.

- How do you know what the parent element's size is? One way is to set it yourself as discussed on page 162. The other way is to rely on the visitor's browser's defaults (which the visitor may adjust however they like best).

- On most current browsers, the default size for the body element (which may be your element's parent) is 16 pixels.

- An em is equal to the size of the font. So 1 em equals 100%.

- There's also an ex unit, which refers to the x-height of the parent element, but it is not widely supported.

- Ems and percentages are well supported in current browsers, and quite badly supported by earlier browsers.

- You can set font size together with other font values (*see page 165*).

- Use the em and percentage values when you want to give the visitor more control over how your page looks to them, while still controlling the relative size of the elements on your page.

- If you use a percentage or em value, it is the resulting size (not the factor) that is inherited.

Setting the Font Size

Setting the Line Height

Line height refers to a paragraph's leading, that is, the amount of space between each line in a paragraph. Using a large line height can sometimes make your body text easier to read. A small line height for headers (with more than one line) often makes them look classier.

To set the line height:

1. Type **line-height:**.

2. Type **n**, where *n* is a number that will be multiplied by the element's font-size *(see page 162)* to obtain the desired line height.

   Or type **p%**, where *p%* is a percentage of the font size.

   Or type **a**, where *a* is an absolute value in pixels, points, or whatever.

✔ Tips

- You can specify the line height together with the font family, size, weight, style, and variant, as described on page 165.

- If you use a number to determine the line height, this factor is inherited by all child items. So if a parent's font-size is 16 pixels and the line-height is 1.5, the parent's line height will be 24 (16 x 1.5). If the child's font-size is 10, its line height will be 15 (10 x 1.5).

- If you use a percentage or em value, only the resulting size (or "computed value") is inherited. So, given a parent at 16 pixels with a line height of 150%, the parent's line height will still be 24 pixels. However, all child elements will also inherit a line height of 24 pixels, regardless of their font size.

h1, h2 {font-family: "Arial Black", "Helvetica Bold", sans-serif;font-weight: normal}

h1 {font-size: 20px}

h2 {font-size: 14px}

p {font-family: "Verdana", "Helvetica", sans-serif; font-size:12px; line-height:150%}

.emph {font-style: italic; font-weight:bold}

a:link, a:hover {font-weight:bold}

#toc {font-size:12px}

Figure 10.14 *The line-height of the text in* p *elements will be 150% of 12 pixels, or 18 pixels.*

Figure 10.15 *Spacing out the lines makes them easier to read.*

```
h1, h2 {font: 20px "Arial Black", "Helvetica Bold",
sans-serif}

h2 {font-size:14 px}

p {font: 12px/150% "Verdana", "Helvetica", sans-
serif}

.emph {font-style: italic; font-weight:bold}


a:link, a:hover {font-weight:bold}


#toc {font-size:12px}
```

Figure 10.16 *This style sheet is equivalent to the one shown in Figure 10.14 on page 164. I've simply consolidated the* font *properties for the* h1, h2 *and* p *rules. Note that I don't have to specify that the* font-weight *be* normal *for* h1, h2, *since* normal *is the default for the* font *property.*

Figure 10.17 *This page is identical to the one shown in Figure 10.15 on page 164 (though I've displayed it in Netscape 6 for Windows instead of Explorer 6 for Windows).*

Setting All Font Values at Once

You can set the font style, weight, variant, size, line height, and family all at once.

To set all font values at once:

1. Type **font:**.

2. If desired, type **normal**, **oblique**, or **italic** to set the font style *(see page 160)*.

3. If desired, type **normal**, **bold**, **bolder**, **lighter**, or a multiple of **100** (up to 900) to set the font weight *(see page 160)*.

4. If desired, type **normal** or **small-caps** to remove or set small caps *(see page 173)*.

5. Type the desired font size *(see pages 162–163)*.

6. If desired, type **/line-height**, where *line-height* is the amount of space there should be between lines *(see page 162)*.

7. Type a space followed by the desired font family or families, in order of preference, separated by commas, as described on page 158.

✔ Tips

- You can also set each property separately. See the page referenced with the desired step.

- The first three properties may be specified in any order or omitted. If you omit them, they are set to `normal`—which may not be what you expected.

- The size and family properties must always be explicitly specified, first the size, then the family.

- The line height, which is optional, must come directly after the size and the slash.

- The `font` property is inherited.

Setting the Text Color

You can change the color of any amount of text on your Web page.

To set the text color:

1. Type **color:**.

2. Type **colorname**, where *colorname* is one of the 16 predefined colors *(see page 46 and the inside back cover)*.

   Or type **#rrggbb**, where *rrggbb* is the color's hexadecimal representation.

   Or type **rgb(r, g, b)** where *r*, *g*, and *b* are integers from 0–255 that specify the amount of red, green, or blue, respectively, in the desired color.

   Or type **rgb(r%, g%, b%)** where *r*, *g*, and *b* give the percentage of red, green, and blue, respectively, in the desired color.

✔ Tips

- If you type a value for r, g, or b higher than 255 it will be replaced with 255. Similarly a percentage higher than 100% will be replaced with 100%.

- You can use the color property to change the color of *any* (X)HTML element. For more information, consult *Changing the Foreground Color* on page 184.

- You can also use **#rgb** to set the color where the hex values are repeated digits. So you could write **#FF0099** as **#F09**. (Don't do this in (X)HTML.)

- The hex number should *not* be enclosed in double quotes (as it is when used in an (X)HTML tag as described on page 344.)

- The color property is inherited.

- The inside back cover of this book offers sample colors and their hex values.

h1, h2 {font: 20px "Arial Black", "Helvetica Bold", sans-serif; color:navy}

h2 {font-size: 14px}

p {font: 12px/150% "Verdana", "Helvetica", sans-serif; color:#909}

.emph {font-style: italic; font-weight:bold}

a:link {font-weight:bold; color:#cc00ff}

a:visited {font-weight:normal}

a:hover {font-weight:bold; color: #0000ff}

#toc {font-size:12px; color:#cc00ff}

Figure 10.18 *You can use color names, hexadecimals, or even rgb values to define your colors. I've separated the link rules in order to keep them in their proper order so that they don't override each other (see page 141). Note that the second color (#909) uses the abbreviation discussed in the third tip.*

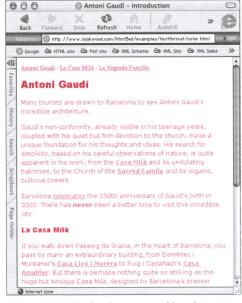

Figure 10.19 *The headers are navy blue, the text is light purple, and the links are pink, but turn blue when hovered on.*

```
body {background:#9cf}

h1, h2 {font: 20px "Arial Black", "Helvetica Bold",
sans-serif; color:navy}

h2 {font-size: 14px}

p {font: 12px/150% "Verdana", "Helvetica", sans-
serif; color:#909}

.emph {font-style: italic; font-weight:bold}

a:link {font-weight:bold; color:#cc00ff}

a:visited {font-weight:normal}

a:hover {font-weight:bold; color: #0000ff}

#toc {font-size:12px; color:#cc00ff;
background:#ccc}
```

Figure 10.20 *It's a good idea to set the background color for every element that you've set a foreground color for. Setting the background color of the* body *element, covers the background of all of its child elements.*

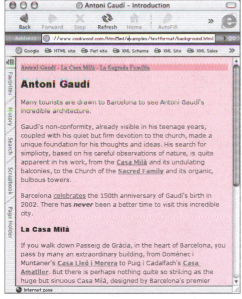

Figure 10.21 *The background of the* body *element is light blue. The background of the table of contents is gray.*

Changing the Text's Background

The background refers not to the background of the entire page, but to the background of the specified element. In other words, you can change the background of just a few paragraphs or words, by setting the background of those words to a different color.

To change the text's background:

1. Type **background:**.

2. Type **transparent** or **color**, where *color* is a color name or hex color *(see page 166)*.

3. If desired, type **url(image.gif)**, to use an image for the background.

    If desired, type **repeat** to tile the image both horizontally and vertically, **repeat-x** to tile the image only horizontally, **repeat-y** to tile the image only vertically, and **no-repeat** to not tile the image.

    If desired, type **fixed** or **scroll** to determine whether the background should scroll along with the canvas.

    If desired, type **x y** to set the position of the background image, where *x* and *y* can be expressed as a percentage or an absolute distance from the top-left corner. Or use values of top, center, or bottom for *x* and left, center, and right for *y*.

✔ Tips

■ You can specify both a color and an image's URL for the background. The color will be used until the image is loaded—or if it can't be loaded for any reason—and will be seen through any transparent portions of the image.

■ Create enough contrast between the background and the foreground so that your visitors can actually read the text.

■ The background property is not inherited.

Changing the Text's Background

Controlling Spacing

You can add or reduce space between words (tracking) or between letters (kerning).

To specify tracking:

1. Type **word-spacing:**.

2. Type **length**, where *length* is a number with units, as in **0.4em** or **5px**.

To specify kerning:

1. Type **letter-spacing:**.

2. Type **length**, where *length* is a number with units, as in **0.4em** or **5px**.

✔ Tips

■ You may use negative values for word and letter spacing, although the actual display always depends on the browser's capabilities.

■ Word and letter spacing values may also be affected by your choice of alignment.

■ Use a value of **normal** or **0** to set the letter and word spacing to their defaults (that is, to add no extra space).

■ If you use an em value, only the resulting size (or "computed value") is inherited. So, a parent at 16 pixels with .1em of extra word-spacing, will have 1.6 pixels of extra space between each word. And all child elements will also have 1.6 pixels of extra space between words, regardless of their font size. Set the extra spacing explicitly for the child elements if you need to override such a value.

■ Both the `word-spacing` and `letter-spacing` properties are inherited.

```
body {background:#9cf}

h1, h2 {font: 20px "Arial Black", "Helvetica Bold",
sans-serif; color:navy; letter-spacing:0.4em}

h2 {font-size: 14px}

p {font: 12px/150% "Verdana", "Helvetica", sans-
serif; color:#909}

.emph {font-style: italic; font-weight:bold}

a:link {font-weight:bold; color:#cc00ff}

a:visited {font-weight:normal}

a:hover {font-weight:bold; color: #0000ff}

#toc {font-size:12px; color:#cc00ff;
background:#ccc}
```

Figure 10.22 *Here I've added .4em of extra space between letters (which at a font-size of 20px will mean an additional 5 pixels between each letter).*

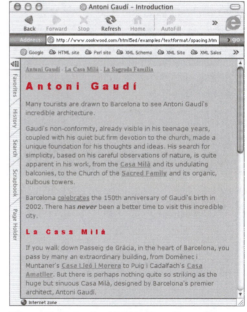

Figure 10.23 *I rather like the effect of spaced out headers.*

```
body {background:#9cf}

h1, h2 {font: 20px "Arial Black", "Helvetica Bold",
sans-serif; color:navy; letter-spacing:.4em}

h2 {font-size: 14px}

p {font: 12px/150% "Verdana", "Helvetica", sans-
serif; color:#909; text-indent:1.5em}

.emph {font-style: italic; font-weight:bold}

a:link {font-weight:bold; color:#cc00ff}

a:visited {font-weight:normal}

a:hover {font-weight:bold; color: #0000ff}

#toc {font-size:12px; color:#cc00ff;
background:#ccc}
```

Figure 10.24 *I added a 1.5 em indent to the* p *ele-ments (which, since their font-size is 12 pixels, will be an indent of 18 pixels).*

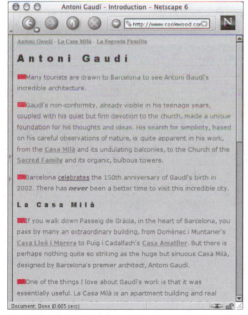

Figure 10.25 *Each paragraph is indented 18 pixels.*

Adding Indents

You can determine how much space should precede the first line of a paragraph.

To add indents:

1. Type **text-indent:**.

2. Type **length**, where *length* is a number with units, as in **1.5em** or **18px**.

✔ Tips

■ A positive value creates a typical para-graph indent and serves as a visual clue as to where new paragraphs begin.

■ A negative value creates a hanging indent. You may need to increase the padding *(see page 188)* or margins *(see page 189)* around a text box with a hang-ing indent in order to accommodate the overhanging text.

■ Em values, as usual, are calculated with respect to the element's font-size. Per-centages are calculated with respect to the width of the *parent* element.

■ The `text-indent` property is inherited.

■ If you use a percentage or an em value, only the resulting size (or "computed value") is inherited. So, if the parent is 300 pixels wide, a text-indent of 10% will be 30 pixels. And all child elements will also have their first lines indented 30 pix-els, regardless of the width of their respective parents.

■ Use a value of 0 to remove an inherited indent. For example, you might want to create a special class for the first para-graph in each section and set its text indent to 0.

Setting White Space Properties

By default, multiple spaces and returns in an (X)HTML document are either displayed as a single space or ignored outright. If you want the browser to display those extra spaces, use the `white-space` property.

To set white space properties:

1. Type **white-space:**.

2. Type **pre** to have browsers display all the spaces and returns in the original text.

   Or type **nowrap** to treat all spaces as non-breaking.

   Or type **normal** to treat white space as usual (*see page 30*).

✔ Tips

- The value of `pre` for the `white-space` property gets its name from the `pre` tag, which is an old-fashioned HTML tag that displays text in a monospace font while maintaining all of its spaces and returns. The `pre` tag, in turn, got its name from the word "pre-formatted". You can find more information about the `pre` tag on page 77.

- Note that the `pre` value for the `white-space` property has no effect on an element's font (in contrast with the `pre` tag, which changes the display to a monospace font).

- You may use the `br` tag to manually create line breaks in an element styled with `white-space:nowrap`. For details about the `br` tag, consult *Creating a Line Break* on page 70.

- IE versions earlier than 6 don't support the `pre` value for `white-space`.

```
body {background:#9cf}

h1, h2 {font: 20px "Arial Black", "Helvetica Bold",
sans-serif; color:navy; letter-spacing:.4em}

h2 {font-size: 14px}

p {font: 12px/150% "Verdana", "Helvetica", sans-
serif; color:#909;text-indent:1.5em}

.emph {font-style: italic; font-weight:bold}

a:link {font-weight:bold; color:#cc00ff}

a:visited {font-weight:normal}

a:hover {font-weight:bold; color: #0000ff}

#toc {font-size:12px; color:#cc00ff;
background:#ccc; white-space: nowrap}
```

Figure 10.26 *The* `nowrap` *value for* `white-space` *treats spaces as non-breaking.*

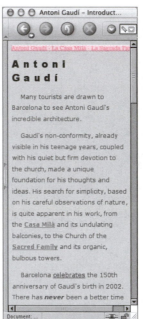

Figure 10.27
The table of contents line won't wrap, even when the browser window is too narrow to display the entire line.

```
body {background:#9cf}

h1, h2 {font: 20px "Arial Black", "Helvetica Bold",
sans-serif; color:navy; letter-spacing:.4em;
text-align: center}

h2 {font-size: 14px}

p {font: 12px/150% "Verdana", "Helvetica", sans-
serif; color:#909;text-indent:1.5em;
text-align: justify}

.emph {font-style: italic; font-weight:bold}

a:link {font-weight:bold; color:#cc00ff}

a:visited {font-weight:normal}

a:hover {font-weight:bold; color: #0000ff}

#toc {font-size:12px; color:#cc00ff; background:
#ccc; white-space:nowrap; text-align: center}
```

Figure 10.28 *Don't forget the hyphen in* `text-align`.

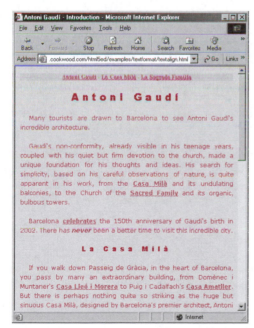

Figure 10.29 *The table of contents and headers are centered while the paragraph text is justified.*

Aligning Text

You can set up certain (X)HTML elements to always be aligned to the right, left, center, or justified, as desired.

To align text:

1. Type **text-align:**.

2. Type **left** to align the text to the left.

   Or type **right** to align the text to the right.

   Or type **center** to center the text in the middle of the screen.

   Or type **justify** to align the text on both the right and left.

✔ Tips

- If you choose to justify the text, be aware that the word spacing and letter spacing may be adversely affected. For more information, consult *Controlling Spacing* on page 168.

- Note that the `text-align` property can only be applied to block-level elements. If you want to align inline content, you must place that inline content within a block-level element like p or div to which you've applied the `text-align` property. Also see pages 190–191.

- The `text-align` property is inherited. Its default value is supposed to depend on the document's language and writing system, but in most cases it's indiscriminately set to `left`.

Changing the Text Case

You can define the text case for your style by using the `text-transform` property. In this way, you can display the text either with initial capital letters, in all capital letters, in all small letters, or as it was typed.

To change the text case:

1. Type **text-transform:**.

2. Type **capitalize** to put the first character of each word in uppercase.

   Or type **uppercase** to change all the letters to uppercase.

   Or type **lowercase** to change all the letters to lowercase.

   Or type **none** to leave the text as is (possibly canceling out an inherited value).

✔ Tips

- I'm unimpressed with the `capitalize` value. While I sometimes need to capitalize all the important words in a sentence, or even just the first word in a sentence, I am hard pressed to think of an example where I'd need to capitalize everything. Now, a true headline-style capitalization property would be welcome. Of course it would have to be language dependent.

- The `lowercase` value can be useful for creating stylish headers (or if you're e.e. cummings).

- The `text-transform` property is inherited.

```
body {background:#9cf}

h1, h2 {font: 20px "Arial Black", "Helvetica Bold",
sans-serif; color:navy; letter-spacing:.4em; text-
align:center}

h1 {text-transform:uppercase}

h2 {font-size: 14px}

p {font: 12px/150% "Verdana", "Helvetica", sans-
serif; color:#909;text-indent:1.5em; text-
align:justify}

.emph {font-style: italic; font-weight:bold}
```

Figure 10.30 *I've decided to display the level 1 header in all uppercase letters for emphasis.*

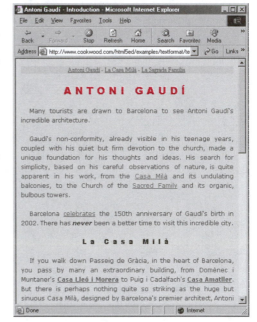

Figure 10.31 *Now the header really stands out.*

```
body {background:#9cf}

h1, h2 {font: 20px "Arial Black", "Helvetica Bold",
sans-serif; color:navy; letter-spacing:.4em; text-
align:center}

h1 {text-transform:uppercase}

h2 {font-size: 14px; font-variant:small-caps}

p {font: 12px/150% "Verdana", "Helvetica", sans-
serif; color:#909;text-indent:1.5em; text-
align:justify}

.emph {font-style: italic; font-weight:bold}
```

Figure 10.32 *Don't forget the hyphen in* small-caps!

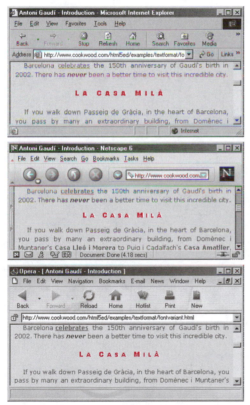

Figure 10.33 *Notice how different these three versions of small caps are, even on the same computer with the same fonts installed. On top you see Explorer 6 for Windows, which I believe reduces the uppercase letters for a fake small caps effect. The two bottom browsers, Netscape and Opera, show true, or at least more attractive, small caps.*

Using Small Caps

Many fonts have a corresponding small caps variant that includes uppercase versions of the letters proportionately reduced to small caps size. You can call up the small caps variant with the `font-variant` property.

To use a small caps font:

1. Type **font-variant:**.

2. Type **small-caps**.

To remove small caps:

1. Type **font-variant:**.

2. Type **none**.

✔ Tips

- Small caps are not quite as heavy as uppercase letters that have been simply reduced in size.

- Not all fonts have a corresponding small caps design. If the browser can't find such a design, it has a few choices. It can fake small caps by simply reducing the size of uppercase letters (which tends to make them look a bit squat), it can forget about small caps altogether and display the text in all uppercase (similar to `text-transform: uppercase` as described on page 172), or, theoretically, it can choose the next font in the list to see if it has a small caps design (though I've never seen this happen).

- IE 6 for Windows has a rather strange small-caps style **(Figure 10.33)**. IE5.5 for Windows and earlier didn't even do that well and used uppercase letters instead.

- The `font-variant` property is inherited.

Using Small Caps

Decorating Text

Style sheets let you adorn your text with underlines, overlining, lines through the text (perhaps to indicate changes), and even blinking text.

To decorate text:

1. Type **text-decoration:**.

2. To underline text, type **underline**.

   Or, for a line above the text, type **overline**.

   Or, to strike out the text, type **line-through**.

   Or to make the text appear and disappear intermittently, type **blink**.

To get rid of decorations:

1. Type **text-decoration:**.

2. Type **none**.

✔ Tips

■ You can eliminate decorations from elements that normally have them (like a, strike, or ins) or from elements that inherit decorations from their parents.

■ Many graphic designers hate underlining and consider it a relic from the typewriter age. While it's perfectly fine to remove underlining from link elements, you'll have to identify the links some other way or nobody will know to click on them.

■ The blink value has a troubled past. Originally designed by Netscape to add pizzazz to Web pages and get an edge over its competition, it was soon scorned by both graphic designers and Internet Explorer, which never deigned to support it. Netscape 6 no longer supports it either (Opera 6 for Windows does).

[snip]

a:link {font-weight:bold; color:#cc00ff; text-decoration:none}

a:visited {font-weight:normal; color:#cc00ff; text-decoration:none}

a:hover {font-weight:bold; color: #0000ff; text-decoration:underline}

#toc {font-size:12px; color:#cc00ff; background:#ccc; white-space:nowrap; text-align:center}

Figure 10.34 *You don't have to restrict underlining, or other text decorations to link elements, as I have done here. They can be applied to any element.*

Figure 10.35 *I've removed the underlining from both new and visited links. (Visited links—like the word cele-brates in the third full paragraph—lose the bold formatting so as to not call so much attention to themselves as the unvisited ones do.) Finally, I added underlining to links that are being hovered over to help visitors know that they are links.*

174

LAYOUT WITH STYLES

Figure 11.1 *This page was laid out with CSS. It is explained step-by-step throughout this chapter.*

Using CSS for layout has several advantages over using other methods, like tables (which we'll discuss in Chapter 14). First, CSS is good for creating *liquid layouts*, that expand or contract depending on the size of your visitor's monitor. In addition, keeping content separate from layout instructions means you can easily apply the same layout to an entire Web site all at once. You can then change the layout of the whole site simply by modifying the CSS file. The CSS + (X)HTML combination also tends to produce smaller file sizes, which means your visitors don't have to wait as long to see your site. Finally, since CSS and XHTML are the current standards, pages that adhere to their rules are guaranteed to be supported in future browsers (and required of professional Web designers).

The principal disadvantage of CSS, especially for layout, is that older browsers either don't understand it or understand it badly. Netscape 4.x, in particular, has notoriously bad CSS layout support. And even current browsers get some things wrong or have different opinions about what is right. There are strategies you can use to provide styled content to users of older browsers and to accommodate buggy current browsers, as we saw in Chapter 9, *Applying Styles*.

The example used in this chapter—beautifully designed by Eric Costello *(www.glish.com)*—works great in current browsers and degrades gracefully in older ones **(Figure 11.1)**.

Structuring Your Pages

The whole point of using CSS is to separate the formatting and styling rules from the content of your page. This frees your page from rigid appearance directives and gives it the flexibility to work well in different browsers, platforms, media, and even print. Perhaps the most important aspect of a page to be styled with CSS is its structure. A reasonable, logical structure can be easily adapted for more than one kind of output device.

To structure your page:

1. Divide logical sections of your document into `div` elements. In our example, we have a *navigation* division, that will hold the links to other pages on the site, a *bg* division that will contain a background image for the navigational area, and a *content* division that will contain the principal text and images. There is also a *calendar* division that will serve as a floating sidebar of upcoming events.

2. Put your `div` elements in an order that would make sense even if the CSS was not used, for example, a title at the top, followed by a table of contents, followed by the main content. While you can change the position of each element with CSS, the content will always be intelligible, regardless of the CSS. (The order depends on the situation, audience, and other factors. Think about how to keep the page useful even if the CSS layout is not used.)

3. Use header elements (`h1`, `h2`, etc.) consistently to identify and prioritize information on your page.

4. Use comments to identify different areas of your page and what they should contain.

```
<body>
<div id="navigation">
    <h1>Catalonia</h1>
    <a href="index.html">Home</a>
    <a href="barcelona.html">Barcelona</a>
    <a href="buildings.html">Famous
Buildings</a>
    <a href="language.html">Language</a>
    <a href="festivals.html">Festivals</a>
    <a href="castle.html" class="current">Castle
Makers</a>
</div>

<div id="bg">
    <img alt="" src="img/nearthetop_b.jpg"
width="100" />
</div>

<div id="content">
<h2>Castle Makers</h2>
<p>If you've ever marveled at the amazing
```

Figure 11.2 *This is the document I use throughout this chapter. Notice that there are three main divisions: navigation, bg, and content. You can find the complete file on my Web site (see page 24).*

Figure 11.3 *Here's what our example looks like with no styles at all (in Netscape 4 for Windows). Thanks to its decent structure, it is perfectly intelligible in older browsers like this one, if perhaps a bit spartan.*

The *margin* is the invisible space beyond the border. (Here there's a top margin of 10px.)

The outside edge is the *border*. (This box has none.)

The default size of the *content area* is determined by its contents (including line height).

The space between the content area and the border is the *padding*. (Here there is left and right padding of 10px.)

Figure 11.4 *Each element's box has four important properties that determine its size: in order from the center to the outside, they are the content area, the padding, the border, and the margin. You can control each property (and even parts of each of these properties) individually.*

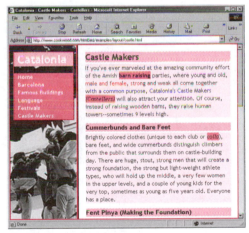

Figure 11.5 *Each element has its own box. In this example, the block-level elements are the divisions (outlined), and there are various headers (medium shading) and paragraphs (light shading) as well as the navigational links ("Home", "Barcelona", etc.), which, while normally inline, have been set to block-level here. Notice the inline a element ("barn raising"), and em elements ("Castellers" and "colla") that do not generate new paragraphs.*

The Box Model

CSS treats your Web page as if every element it contains is enclosed in an invisible box. The box is comprised of a content area, the space surrounding that area (padding), the outside edge of the padding (border), and the invisible space around the border (margin).

You can use CSS to determine both the appearance and the position of each element's box, and in so doing, have considerable control over the layout of your Web page.

As we discussed earlier *(see page 28)*, an element's box may be *block-level* (thereby generating a new paragraph) or *inline* (not generating a new paragraph). This trait governs the initial layout of the Web page: by default, elements are displayed in the order that the (X)HTML *flows* from top to bottom, with line breaks at the beginning and end of each block-level element's box.

There are four principal ways to position an element box: you can leave the box in the flow (the default, also called *static*), you can remove the box from the flow and specify its exact coordinates with respect to either its parent element (*absolute*) or the browser window (*fixed*), or you can move the box with respect to its default position in the flow (*relative*). In addition, if boxes overlap one another, you can specify the order in which they should do so (*z-index*).

Once you've determined where the box should go, you can control its appearance, including its padding, border, margins, size, alignment, color, and more. We'll discuss all of these properties in this chapter.

Note that some layout properties, particularly em and percentage values, depend on an element's parent. Remember that a *parent* is the element that contains the current element *(see page 28)*.

The Box Model

Displaying and Hiding Elements

The `display` property is useful for hiding or revealing particular elements depending on the visitor's browser, language preference, or other criteria. You can also override an element's natural display type (from block-level to inline, or vice-versa). Or you can display an element as a list item—even without the `li` tag (which we get to on page 203).

To specify how elements should be displayed:

1. Type **display:**.

2. Type **none** to hide the given element.

   Or type **block** to display the element as block-level (thus starting a new paragraph).

   Or type **inline** to display the element as inline (not starting a new paragraph).

   Or type **list-item** to display the element as if you had used the `li` tag *(see pages 203–212)*.

✔ Tips

■ Netscape 6 is so scrupulous with standards that it adds a bit of space under inline images in table cells—for descenders, one must presume. As long as you only have one image per cell, you can get rid of the space by making the images block level.

■ If you use **display: none**, no trace remains of the hidden element in the browser window. There is no empty space.

■ The `display` property is not inherited.

■ You can use `visibility:hidden` to hide elements without taking them out of the flow. In other words, the space they would have occupied remains behind.

```
#navigation a {display: block}
```

Figure 11.6 *We'll use the* `display` *property to change the navigation division's* a *elements to* `block-level` *so that each is displayed on its own line. Notice that I'm only changing the* `display` *property of the* a *elements found in the* navigation *division. The* a *elements in other divisions will not be affected.*

Figure 11.7 *The* a *elements are now displayed on individual lines. Notice that the* a *element on the first line of the last paragraph shown ("barn raising'), is still displayed inline (as it should be).*

```
#bg  {position: absolute; top: 250px; left: 2%;}

#content {position: absolute; top: 0px; left: 30%;}

#navigation {position: absolute; top: 10px; left: 2%;}
#navigation a {display: block}
```

Figure 11.8 *While you must say—with offsets—exactly where you want an absolutely positioned element to appear (with respect to the parent element) you can use percentages in order to keep the design flexible for different size monitors.*

Figure 11.9 *The page quickly snaps into shape. The content division (starting with "Castle Makers'" begins at a distance of 30% of the browser window from the left side, no matter how wide the window becomes. The navigation area, meanwhile, starts 10 pixels from the top and only 2% from the left. The bg area is temporarily placed below the navigation area.*

Positioning Elements Absolutely

The elements in your Web page generally flow in the order in which they appear. That is, if the img tag comes before the p, the image appears before the paragraph. This is called the normal flow. You can take elements out of the normal flow—and position them *absolutely*—by specifying their precise position with respect to their parent element.

To absolutely position elements:

1. Type **position: absolute;** (don't forget the semicolon; the space is optional).

2. Type **top**, **right**, **bottom**, or **left**.

3. Type **:v**, where *v* is the desired distance that you want to offset the element from its parent element, either expressed as an absolute or relative value (10px, or 2em, for example), or as a percentage of the parent element.

4. If desired, repeat steps 2 and 3 for additional directions separating each property/value pair with a semicolon as usual.

✔ Tips

- Remember that an element is positioned with respect to its parent element. For more information on parent elements, see page 28.

- Use percentages for liquid designs that adapt to your visitors' monitor size.

- Because absolutely positioned elements are taken out of the flow of the document, they can overlap each other. (This is not always bad.)

- If you don't specify an offset for an absolutely positioned item, the item appears in its natural position, but does not affect the flow of subsequent items.

- Positioning is not inherited.

Positioning Elements Absolutely

Affixing an Element to the Browser Window

When a visitor scrolls in the browser window, the contents of the window usually move up or down while the Back and Forward buttons, for example, stay stationary or *fixed*. CSS allows you to affix elements to the browser window so that they don't move when the visitor scrolls up or down.

To affix an element to the browser window:

1. Type **position: fixed;** (don't forget the semicolon).

2. Type **top**, **right**, **bottom**, or **left**.

3. Type **:v**, where *v* is the desired distance that you want to offset the element from the edges of the browser window, either expressed as an absolute or relative value (10px, or 2em, for example), or as a percentage of the browser window.

4. If desired, repeat steps 2 and 3 for additional directions, separating each property/value pair with a semicolon as usual.

✔ Tips

■ Remember that the offsets of a fixed element are relative to the browser window, while the offsets of an element positioned absolutely are relative to that element's parent.

■ If fixed positioning were more universally supported, it would be an ideal substitute for frames.

■ Unfortunately, Explorer for Windows (up to and including version 6) does not support fixed positioning.

■ Positioning is not inherited.

```
#bg  {position: fixed; top: 250px; left: 2%;}

#content {position:absolute; top: 0px; left: 30%;}

#navigation {position: fixed; top: 10px; left: 2%;}
#navigation a {display: block}
```

Figure 11.10 *The only difference between these style rules and the ones shown in Figure 11.8 on page 179 is the* fixed *value for* position *in the* bg *and* navigation *areas.*

Figure 11.11 *At first glance, this page looks identical to the one shown in Figure 11.9 on page 179.*

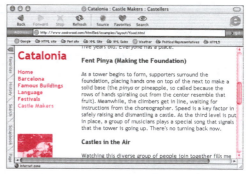

Figure 11.12 *When the visitor scrolls down, however, notice that the navigation area (Catalonia, Home, Barcelona, etc.) and the background image remain stationary.*

```
#bg  {position: absolute; top: 250px; left: 2%;}

#content {position:absolute; top: 0px; left: 30%;}

#navigation {position: absolute; top: 10px; left: 2%}
#navigation a {display: block}


h2, h3 {position:relative; left:-25px}
```

Figure 11.13 *This bit of code positions the* h2 *and* h3 *elements 25 pixels to the left of where they would have been without this rule.*

Figure 11.14 *The* h2 *and* h3 *headers actually stick out beyond the left edge of their containing division. That doesn't matter—they're offset with respect to their original position, no matter where they end up.*

Offsetting Elements In the Natural Flow

Each element has a natural location in a page's flow. Moving the element with respect to this original location is called *relative positioning*. The surrounding elements are not affected—at all.

To offset elements within the natural flow:

1. Type **position: relative;** (don't forget the semicolon).

2. Type **top**, **right**, **bottom**, or **left**.

3. Type **:v**, where *v* is the desired distance that you want to offset the element from its natural location, either as an absolute or relative value (10pt, or 2em, for example).

4. If desired, repeat steps 2 and 3 for additional directions, separating each property/value pair with a semicolon as usual.

✔ Tips

■ The "relative" in *relative positioning* refers to the element's original position, not the surrounding elements. You can't move an element with respect to other elements. Instead, you move it with respect to where it used to be. Yes, this is important!

■ The other elements are not affected by the offsets—they flow with respect to the *original* containing box of the element, and may even be overlapped.

■ Offsets don't work unless you're also using the `position` property.

■ Positioning is not inherited.

Changing the Background

The background refers not to the background of the entire page, but to the background of a particular element. In other words, you can change the background of any element—including images, form elements, and tables.

To change the background color:

1. Type **background-color:**

2. Type **transparent** (to let the parent element's background show through) or **color**, where *color* is a color name or rgb color *(see page 46 and the inside back cover)*.

To use a background image:

1. Type **background-image:**

2. Then type **url(image.gif)**, where *image.gif* is the name of the image that should be used for the background, or **none** to use no image at all **(Figures 11.17 and 11.18)**.

To repeat a background image:

Type **background-repeat: direction**, where *direction* is either `repeat` (to tile the image both horizontally and vertically), `repeat-x` (to tile the image only horizontally), `repeat-y` (to tile the image only vertically), or `no-repeat` (to not tile the image at all).

To control whether the background image is attached or not:

1. Type **background-attachment:**.

2. Then type **fixed** to stick the background image to the browser window or **scroll** to let it move when the visitor scrolls.

To specify the position of an element's background image:

Type **background-position: x y**, where *x* and *y* can be expressed as a percentage or as an absolute distance. Or use values of `top`, `center`, or `bottom` for *x* and `left`, `center`, or `right` for *y*.

```
body {background-color:#fff;}
#bg  {position: absolute; top: 250px; left: 2%;
background-color:black}


#content {position:absolute; top: 0px; left: 30%;
background-color:#fff}


#navigation {position: absolute; top: 10px; left: 2%}
#navigation a {display: block}
#navigation a:hover {background-color:#fff;}


#navigation a:hover.current {background-
color:transparent}


h1 {background-color: #339}
```

Figure 11.15 *We make the background of the body, the* content *division and hovered navigational links white. We set the background of the* bg *division to black (in anticipation of the changes on pages 190–192). We set the hover color for the current page's link to* `trans-parent` *since we don't want it to look like a link.*

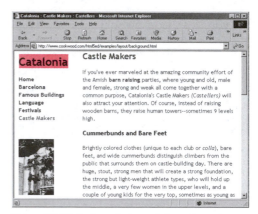

Figure 11.16 *Perhaps the least obvious of our changes is setting the background of the* content *area to white. Nevertheless, it is a crucial step for our layout (as we'll see later on pages 190–192).*

```
body {background:white url(img/castle_bg.jpg)
repeat-x bottom left}

#bg  {position: absolute; top: 250px; left: 2%;
background-color:black}

#content {position:absolute; top: 0px; left: 30%;
background-color:#fff}

#navigation {position: absolute; top: 10px; left: 2%}
#navigation a {display: block}
#navigation a:hover {background-color:#fff;}

#navigation a:hover.current {background-
color:transparent}

h1 {background-color: #339}
```

Figure 11.17 *We'll make a momentary digression to show background images, which are difficult to use effectively.*

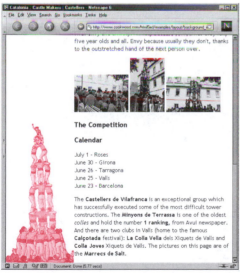

Figure 11.18 *Despite being repeated horizontally, the white background of the* content *area (which has higher specificity because it's an* id*) covers the body's background image. Note that the image starts in the bottom-left corner of the entire page, not just the screen (as IE 5 for Macintosh erroneously does).*

To change all the background properties at once:

1. Type **background:**

2. Specify any of the accepted background property values (as described on the preceding page), in any order.

✔ Tips

■ The default for `background-color` is `transparent`. The default for `background-image` is `none`. The default for `background-repeat` is `repeat`. The default for `background-attachment` is `scroll`. The default for `background-position` is `top left`.

■ When using the `background` shortcut property (above), you needn't specify all of the properties. But beware that any non-specified properties are set to their defaults (and thus may override earlier style rules).

■ The `background` properties are not inherited. You only need to explicitly set default values like `transparent` or `scroll` when you want to override another style rule.

■ If you use the `background-position` property with a repeat, the position specifies where the first image in the repeat starts, e.g., from the `top right`.

■ Set the `background` property for the body element to create a background for the entire page. (It's the only way Netscape 4 will apply a `background` property.)

■ If you specify both a color and a URL for the background, the color will be used until the URL is loaded, and will be seen through any transparent portions of the background image. (If you don't specify a color, Netscape 4 will use black.)

Changing the Foreground Color

You can change the color of any element, including text, horizontal lines, and form elements.

To change the foreground color:

1. Type **color:**.

2. Type **colorname**, where *colorname* is one of the 16 predefined colors (*see page 46 and the inside back cover*).

   Or type **#rrggbb**, where *rrggbb* is the hexadecimal representation of the desired color (*see page 46 and the inside back cover*).

   Or type **rgb(r, g, b)**, where *r*, *g*, and *b* are integers from 0–255 that specify the amount of red, green, or blue, respectively, in the desired color.

   Or type **rgb(r%, g%, b%)**, where *r*, *g*, and *b* specify the percentage of red, green, and blue, respectively, in the desired color.

✔ Tips

■ If you type a value for r, g, or b higher than 255 it will be replaced with 255. Similarly a percentage higher than 100% will be replaced with 100%.

■ The `color` property is most often used to affect text. For more information, consult *Setting the Text Color* on page 166.

■ Changing the foreground color of an image doesn't have any effect. (You'll have to do that in an image editing program.) You can, however, change the background color (that is, what will appear through transparent areas). For more information, consult *Changing the Background* on page 182.

```
body {background-color:#fff; color:#000}
#bg  {position: absolute; top: 250px; left: 2%;
background-color:black}

#content {position: absolute; top: 0px; left: 30%;
background-color:#fff}

#navigation {position: absolute; top: 10px; left: 2%;
color:white}
#navigation a {display: block}

#navigation a:link.current, #navigation
a:visited.current,  {color:#ff9;}
#navigation a:hover {background-color:#fff;
color:#339}

#navigation a:hover.current {background-color:
transparent; color:#ff9}

h1 {background-color: #339; color: #fff}
```

Figure 11.19 *We change the default color for all text to black (in the body element). Text in the navigation box, however, will be white (to offset it from the upcoming background that we'll adjust on pages 190–192). The current page's link in the navigation area (so that it doesn't look like a link), should always stay the same pale yellow (#339). The other links, however, should turn blue when hovered over (against the white background we set on page 182).*

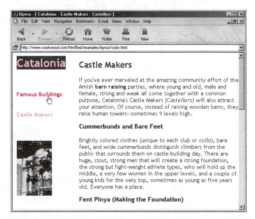

Figure 11.20 *Now that the navigation links are white, we can't see them unless we hover over them (or place the background on pages 190–192).*

```
body {background-color:#fff; color:#000}
#bg  {position: absolute; top: 250px; left: 2%;
background-color:black}

#content {position: absolute; top: 0px; left: 30%;
background-color:#fff}

#navigation {position: absolute; top: 10px; left: 2%;
color:white}
#navigation a {display: block}

#navigation a:link.current, #navigation
a:visited.current,  {color:#ff9;}
#navigation a:hover {background-color:#fff;
color:#339}

#navigation a:hover.current {background-color:
transparent; color:#ff9; cursor: default}

h1 {background-color: #339; color: #fff}
```

Figure 11.21 *I add the* cursor *property to the selector that chooses only those links in the* current *class that belong to the element whose id is* navigation, *and who are being hovered over. Quite a selector, no?*

Figure 11.22 *Now, when someone points to the link to the current page, it doesn't look like a link (although the status bar still shows the destination and the link still works).*

Changing the Cursor

Normally, the browser takes care of the cursor shape for you, using an arrow most of the time, and a pointing finger to highlight links. CSS lets you take the reigns.

To change the cursor:

1. Type **cursor:**.

2. Type **pointer** for the cursor that usually appears over links (🖑), **default** for an arrow (🖗), **crosshair** (+), **move** (✛), **wait** (⌛), **help** (🖗?), or **text** (I).

   Or type **auto** to get whatever cursor usually appears in that situation.

   Or type **x-resize** to get a double-sided arrow, where *x* is the cardinal direction one of the arrows should point—that is, n (north), nw (northwest), e (east), etc. For example, the e-resize cursor might look like this: ↔.

✔ Tips

- IE 5.x for Windows recognizes the hand value, but not the standard pointer value (for 🖑). To please do-it-their-own-way Microsoft as well as standards-supporting browsers like Netscape and IE 6, use *both*: cursor:pointer;cursor:hand;. The order is significant since IE 5.x for Windows will choke on pointer if it's last. (Thanks to Eric Meyer for this tip.)

- The illustrations shown above are from IE 6 on Windows 98. The cursors vary slightly from browser to browser and system to system. For example, the wait cursor on a Mac is the familiar watch: ⌚.

- I find the names confusing. The default isn't the default, but instead is an arrow, which I would call a pointer, but pointer means a hand, while hand is a non-standard value created by Microsoft. Ugh.

Setting the Border

You can create a border around an element and then set its thickness, style, and color. If you've specified any padding *(see page 189)* the border encloses both the padding and the contents of the element.

To define the border-style:

Type **border-style: type**, where *type* is none, dotted, dashed, solid, double, groove, ridge, inset, or outset.

To set the width of the border:

Type **border-width: n**, where *n* is the desired width, including abbreviated units (for example *4px*).

To set the color of the border:

Type **border-color: color**, where *color* is a color name or rgb color *(see page 46 and the inside back cover)*.

To set one or more border properties at once with a shortcut:

1. Type **border**.

2. If desired, type **-top**, **-right**, **-bottom**, or **-left** to limit the affect to a single side.

3. If desired, type **-property**, where *property* is one of style, width, or color, to limit the affect to a single property.

4. Type **:**.

5. Type the appropriate values (as described in the first three techniques above). If you've skipped step 3, you can specify any or all of the three types of border properties (e.g., border:1px solid or border-right:2px dashed green). If you have specified a property type in step 3, use an accepted value for just that property (e.g., border-right-style:dotted).

```
body {background-color:#fff; color:#000}
#bg  {position: absolute; top: 250px; left: 2%;
background-color:black}


#content {position:absolute; top: 0px; left: 30%;
background-color:#fff; border-left: 1px solid black}


#navigation {position: absolute; top: 10px; left: 2%;
color:white}
#navigation a {display: block}


#navigation a:link.current, #navigation
a:visited.current,  {color:#ff9;}
#navigation a:hover {background-color:#fff;
color:#339}


#navigation a:hover.current {background-color:
transparent; color:#ff9; cursor: default}


h1 {background-color: #339; color: #fff}
```

Figure 11.23 *You can set all three border properties to just the left side of the element with the* border-left *shortcut.*

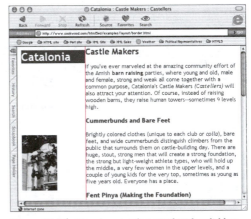

Figure 11.24 *Here is a simple 1 pixel-wide solid border. Notice that the text needs some space between it and the border. We'll get to that shortly (see page 188).*

```
div {height: 70px; width: 200px; margin-bottom:
10px; background: #ffc; border-color: #c06;
border-width: 2px 5px 10px 15px}

.dotted {border-style: dotted}
.dashed {border-style: dashed none}
.double {border-style: none double}
.groove {border-top-style: groove}
.ridge {border-right-style: ridge}
.inset {border-bottom-style: inset}
.outset {border-left-style: outset}
```

Figure 11.25 *I set the color for all four sides of the border with the single* `border-color` *property. Then I set individual widths for each side with* `border-width`, *starting with the top (2px) and moving clockwise around the box. Finally, I create classes for each style, and apply the style to one or more sides of the division.*

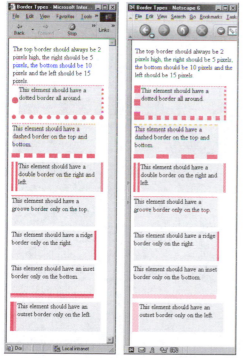

Figure 11.26 *Notice how the different shortcuts work. For example,* `border-style:dotted` *(the first example) creates a dotted border on all four sides, while* `border-style:dashed none` *creates a dashed border on the top and bottom and no border on the right and left sides. Browsers (IE 6 on left, Netscape 6 on right) interpret border styles slightly differently.*

✔ Tips

- Borders are not inherited.

- The individual border properties (`border-width`, `border-style`, and `border-color`) can have from one to four values. If you use one value, it is applied to all four sides. If you use two, the first is used for the top and bottom, and the second for the right and left. If you use three, the first is used for the top, the second for the right and left, and the third is used for the bottom. And if you use four, they are applied to the top, right, bottom, and left, in clockwise order.

- You must define at least the style for a border to display. If there's no style, there will be no border. The default is `none`.

- If you use a shortcut, like `border` or `border-left` (etc.), the properties you don't give values for are set to their defaults. So `border: 1px black` means `border: 1 px black none`, which means you won't get a border (even if you specified a style earlier with `border-style`).

- The default color is the value of the element's `color` property *(see page 166)*.

- The width can also be expressed in generic terms: `thin`, `medium`, and `thick`. The default is `medium`, which for IE is 4 pixels and for Netscape is 3.

- Older browsers (before IE 5.5 and Netscape 6) don't support every single border style.

- The `border` property can be used for tables and their cells. For more details, consult *Adding a Border* on page 218.

- Frankly, I think someone went a bit over the top in thinking up different ways of setting the border properties.

Setting the Border

Adding Padding around an Element

Padding is just what it sounds like: extra space around the contents of an element but inside the border. Think of Santa Claus' belly—nicely padded, while being held in by his belt (the border). You can change the padding's thickness, but not its color or texture.

To add padding around an element:

Type **padding:.x**, where *x* is the amount of desired space to be added, expressed in units *(10px)* or as a percentage of the width of the parent element *(20%)*.

✔ Tips

■ If you use one value in step , the specified padding is applied to all four sides equally. If you use two values, the first value applies to the top and bottom and the second value applies to the right and left. If you use three values, the first applies to the top, the second to the right and left, and the third to the bottom. If you use four values, they are applied to the top, right, bottom, and left, in clockwise order.

■ You can also add one of the following suffixes to the `padding` property to apply padding to a single side: `-top`, `-bottom`, `-left`, or `-right`. There should be no space between the word `padding` and the suffix.

■ Padding is not inherited.

■ Use percentages or ems to create liquid layouts that expand or contract depending on the visitor's monitor.

body {background-color:#fff; color:#000; padding:0;}
#bg {position: absolute; top: 250px; left: 2%; background-color:black}

#content {position:absolute; top: 0px; left: 30%; background-color:#fff;border-left: 1px solid black; padding: 20px; }

#navigation {position: absolute; top: 10px; left: 2%; color:white}
#navigation a {display: block;color:#fff; padding-left: 10px; padding-right: 10px;}

#navigation a:link.current, [snip]

h1 {background-color: #339; color: #fff; padding: 0 10px}

Figure 11.27 *It's not a bad idea to set the body padding to 0 since browsers have varying defaults for padding for different elements. Note that the last two padding styles (for* #navigation a *and* h1 *respectively) are equivalent.*

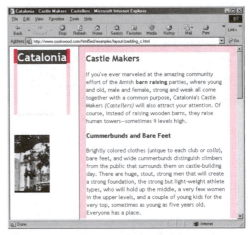

Figure 11.28 *The content looks much better when there is some empty space between it and the border. Notice that the background of the header ("Catalonia") is enlarged when padding is added.*

```
body {background-color:#fff;
color:#000;padding:0 0 0 0;margin:0 0 0 0}
#bg  {position: absolute; top: 250px; left: 2%;
background-color:black}

#content {position:absolute; top: 0px; left: 30%;
background-color:#fff;border-left: 1px solid black;
padding: 20px}

#navigation [snip]

h1 {background-color: #339; color: #fff;
padding: 0 10px; margin-top:10px}
h2 {margin:0}
h3 {margin: 15px 0 0}
p {margin: 5px 0}
```

Figure 11.29 *We could also have written the margin for the* h3 *element as* margin-top:15px.

Figure 11.30 *The text in the* content *area looks much better with less space between headers and paragraphs. Remember that the margin is the space between element boxes, which themselves are determined by such varied factors as content, line-height, the* height *property, and more. Finally, note that the margin between the* h3 *and* p *elements is 15 pixels (the greater of the touching margins) and not 20 pixels (the sum of the touching margins).*

Setting the Margins around an Element

The margin is the amount of transparent space between one element and the next, in addition to and outside of any padding (*see page 188*) or border (*see page 186*) around the element. (It's Santa's personal space.)

To set an element's margins:

Type **margin: x**, where *x* is the amount of desired space to be added, expressed as a length, a percentage of the width of the parent element, or auto.

✔ Tips

- You can use from one to four values for margin. See the first tip in the padding section for details (*see page 188*).

- You can also add one of the following suffixes to the margin property to apply a margin to a single side: -top, -bottom, -left, or -right. There shouldn't be any space after margin (e.g., margin-top: 10px).

- The margin property's auto value depends on the value of the width property (*see page 190*). Given a width of auto, if you set one margin to auto, it is set to the highest value possible. If you set both the right and left margins to auto, they are set to the highest possible *equal* values. You can use this fact to center an element.

- If one element is placed above another, only the greater of the two touching margins is used. The other one is said to *collapse*. Left and right margins don't collapse.

- Margins are not inherited.

Setting the Height or Width for an Element

You can set the height and width for most elements, including images, form elements, and even blocks of text.

To set the height or width for an element:

- Type **width: w**, where *w* is the width of the element's content area, and can be expressed either as a length (with units) or as a percentage of the parent element. Or use `auto` to let the browser calculate the width.

- Type **height: h**, where *h* is the height of the element, and can be expressed only as a length (with units). Or use `auto` to let the browser calculate the height.

✔ Tips

- If you don't explicitly set the `width`, `auto` is used *(see page 191)*.

- Remember that the percentage value is relative to the width *of the parent element—* not the original width of the element itself.

- The padding, borders, and margin are not included in the value of `width` (except in IE 5.x for Windows, which quite erroneously considers the `width` to be the sum of the content area, borders, and padding—see next page).

- Widths and heights are not inherited.

- There are also `min-width`, `min-height`, `max-width` and `max-height` properties but they are currently supported rather erratically.

```
<div id="bg">
    <img alt="" src="img/nearthetop_b.jpg"
width="100" />
</div>
```

Figure 11.31 *Remember that in the (X)HTML code, we set the width of the image in the* bg *area to 100 pixels.*

```
body {background-color:#fff;
color:#000;padding:0 0 0 0;margin:0 0 0 0}
#bg  {position: absolute; top: 250px; left: 2%;
background-color:black; top:0; left:10%; margin-
left:-200px;}

#bg img {width:538px; height:850px;}

#content {position:absolute; top: 0px; left: 30%;
background-color:#fff;border-left: 1px solid black;
padding: 20px; }

#navigation {position: absolute; top: 10px; left: 2%;
color:white; width: 26%}
#navigation a {display: block;color:#fff;padding-
left: 10px; padding-right: 10px;}
```

Figure 11.32 *I set the desired size of the image for the* bg *division with the* `width` *property (and override the (X)HTML attribute in Figure 11.31 above). Note I've also adjusted the top and left offsets of the* bg *div, and used a negative left margin to center on the parts of the photo I'm interested in.*

Figure 11.33 *Note that the* content *area overlaps the* bg *division, starting at 30% from the left side. Since the* content *area is white, the part of the image that extends behind it is hidden. Notice, as well, that our* navigation *area is also hidden. We'll fix that shortly.*

```
div {width:300px; height: 500px;
background: yellow}
    p.auto {width:auto; margin: 10px; padding:
5px; border: 5px solid blue; background: white;}
    p {width: 200px; margin: 10px; padding: 5px;
border: 5px solid purple; background: white;}
```

Figure 11.34 *I've set the width of the parent div to 300 pixels. This will be our containing block. Then, both paragraphs have 10 pixel margins, 5 pixel padding and 5 pixel borders on all sides. The first paragraph has the width set automatically, the second is set at 200 px.*

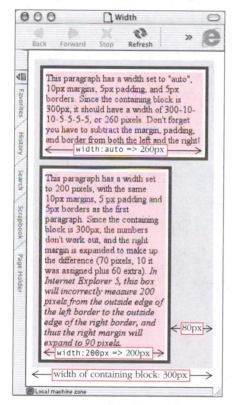

Figure 11.35 *If the width (pink shaded background) is auto, as in the top paragraph, its value is derived from the width of the containing block (the gray shaded background) minus the margins, padding, and border. If the width is set manually (as in the bottom paragraph), the right margin is usually adjusted to pick up the slack.*

Width, margins, and auto

For most block-level elements, the `auto` value for `width` is set to the width of the containing block minus the padding, borders, and margins. The *containing block* is the width that the element gets from its parent and is sometimes confusingly called the *inherited width*, even though it has nothing to do with normal CSS inheritance.

Elements with images and objects *(replaced elements)* have an `auto` width equal to their intrinsic value, that is, the actual dimensions of the external file. Floated elements have an `auto` width of 0. Non-floated inline elements ignore the `width` property altogether.

If you manually set the `width`, `margin-left`, and `margin-right` values, but together with the border and padding they don't equal the size of the containing block, something's got to give. And indeed, the browser will override you and set `margin-right` to `auto` **(Figures 11.34 and 11.35)**. If you manually set the `width` but set one of the margins to `auto`, then that margin will stretch or shrink to make up the difference. If you manually set the `width` but leave both margins set to `auto`, *both* margins will be set to the *same* maximum value (resulting in your element being centered).

Note that browsers never adjust the width of the borders or the padding.

Now those are the rules, for what they're worth. Unfortunately, IE 5 (and IE 6 in Quirks mode) thinks that when you set the width, you're setting the sum of the content area, the borders, and the padding, instead of just the content area as it should be. And IE 6 lets the margins and replaced elements of a child element affect the width of the containing block while asserting in their documentation that this should not be allowed. As if this weren't all complex enough!

Positioning Elements in 3D

Once you start using relative and absolute positioning, it's quite possible to find that your elements have overlapped. You can choose which element should be on top.

To position elements in 3D:

1. Type **z-index:**.

2. Type **n**, where *n* is a number that indicates the element's level in the stack of objects.

✔ Tips

■ The higher the value of the `z-index` property, the higher up the element will be in the stack. You can think of the `z-index` property as a measure of elevation, with the visitors in an airplane looking down, seeing the elements on the tops of mountains first.

■ You can use both positive and negative values for `z-index`.

■ If you have nested items within an element that has a certain `z-index`, all those nested items are first ordered according to their own individual z-indexes, and then, as a group, ordered in the larger context. So imagine A has a z-index of 10, and B has a z-index of 20, and C has a z-index of 30. B contains two children: bb, with a z-index of 35 and bbb with a z-index of 5. The four items will be displayed in the following order, from top to bottom: C (with the highest z-index of its level), B (with the 2nd highest z-index of its level), followed by its children, bb and bbb, in that order), and then finally A, whose z-index was lower than B's.

■ The `z-index` property is not inherited.

```
body {background-color:#fff;
color:#000;padding:0 0 0 0;margin:0 0 0 0}

#bg  {position: absolute; top: 250px; left: 2%;
background-color:black; top:0; left:10%; margin-
left:-200px; z-index: 1;}

#bg img {width:538px; height:850px;}

#content {position:absolute; top: 0px; left: 30%;
background-color:#fff;border-left: 1px solid black;
padding: 20px; z-index: 2;}

#navigation {position: absolute; top: 10px; left: 2%;
color:white; width: 26%;z-index: 3;}
#navigation a {display: block;color:#fff;padding-
left: 10px; padding-right: 10px;}
```

Figure 11.36 *The* content *and* navigation z-index *values could conceivably be interchanged as long as both remain higher than the* bg*'s* z-index *of 1. (The* content *area must have a higher z-index than* bg *because its white background conceals the extended parts of the image in the* bg *area.)*

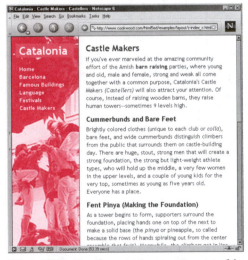

Figure 11.37 *Now the* navigation *area is on top of the* bg *division, and you can finally see why we made the links white!*

Positioning Elements in 3D

```
#calendar {background:#339; color:white;
padding:5px; margin-left:5px; margin-top:7px;
font-size:.8em; width:150px;}

#calendar h3 {margin:0;color:white}
```

Figure 11.38 *First, I format the* calendar *div so that it looks pretty.*

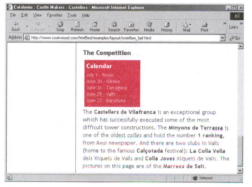

Figure 11.39 *The calendar looks nice down here at the end of our Web page, but it's too long, in my opinion.*

```
.dates {width:150px;height:2.5em; overflow:auto}
```

Figure 11.40 *I set the* width *and* height *of the* dates *paragraph within the calendar explicitly so I know just how big the resulting paragraph will be. Then I add the* overflow *property to deal with the parts that don't fit in the resulting size paragraph.*

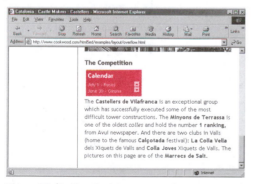

Figure 11.41 *Now the* dates *paragraph measures precisely 150 pixels wide by 2.5 ems tall, and scroll bars appear so that visitors can reach the rest of the data.*

Determining Where Overflow Should Go

Elements are not always contained in their boxes. Sometimes the box is simply not big enough. Or perhaps you've positioned the content outside of the box, either with negative margins or absolute positioning. Regardless of the cause, you can control the area outside of the element's box with the overflow property.

To determine where overflow should go:

1. Type **overflow:**.

2. Type **visible** to expand the element box so that its contents fit. This is the default option.

   Or type **hidden** to hide any contents that don't fit in the element box.

   Or type **scroll** to always add scroll bars to the element so that the visitor can access the overflow if they so desire.

   Or type **auto**, to have scroll bars appear only when necessary.

✔ Tips

- Note that IE 6 doesn't think you know what you're doing when you make a child bigger than its parent and will incorrectly extend the parent to be as big as the child. The only exception is if you set the overflow property to any value except visible (the default), in which case the parent will shrink down to its normal size and let the overflow property do its job.

- The default value for overflow is visible. The overflow property is not inherited.

Making Elements Float

You can make elements float in a sea of text (or other elements). Unfortunately, browsers tend to be a bit buggy with the float property.

To wrap text around elements:

1. Type **float:**.

2. Type **left** if you want the element on the left and the rest of the content to flow to its right.

   Or type **right** if you want the element on the right and the rest of the content to flow to its left.

3. Use the width property *(see page 190)* to explicitly set the width of the element.

✔ Tips

- Remember, the direction you choose applies to the element you're floating, not to the elements that flow around it. When you **float: left**, the rest of the page flows to the right, and vice-versa.

- The trick to making content flow between elements is to always put the image *directly before* the content that should flow next to it.

- For an old-fashioned, deprecated, and yet universally supported way of flowing text between images, consult *Making Images Float* on page 110.

- If you float more than one element in the same direction, the first element floated is placed farthest in that direction, the second element is the second farthest, and so on **(Figures 11.44 and 11.45)**.

- Non-replaced elements without an explicit width will not float properly.

- The float property is not inherited.

```
#content {position:absolute; top: 0px; left: 30%;
background-color:#fff;border-left: 1px solid black;
padding: 20px; z-index: 2;}

#calendar {background:#339; color:white;
padding:5px; margin-left:5px; margin-top:7px;
font-size:.8em; width:150px; float: right}
```

Figure 11.42 *We want the entire* calendar *division to float to the right of the paragraph.*

Figure 11.43 *The text that follows the* calendar *division flows around the calendar to the left.*

```
<h3>The Competition</h3>
<img src="img/anxaneta.jpg" alt="Anxaneta"
width="39" height="72" class="icon" />
<div id="calendar">
```

Figure 11.44 *Now imagine we had another image before the* calendar *div and float it to the right as well.*

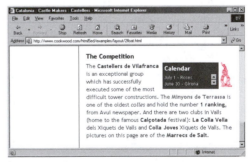

Figure 11.45 *Since the little image comes first in the (X)HTML, it gets floated farthest to the right.*

```
#content {position:absolute; top: 0px; left: 30%;
background-color:#fff;border-left: 1px solid black;
padding: 20px; z-index: 2;}

#calendar {background:#339; color:white;
padding:5px; margin-left:5px; margin-top:15px;
font-size:.8em; width:150px; float: right;
clear:right}

#calendar h3 {margin:0;color:white}

.dates {width:150px;height:2.5em;overflow:auto}

.icon {margin-top:7px;float:right}
```

Figure 11.46 *You add the* clear *property to the element whose sides should be free of floating elements. In this case, we want the right side of the* calendar *division to be clear so we apply the* clear:right *property to it.*

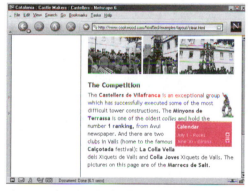

Figure 11.47 *The* calendar *division won't display until the right side is completely clear (that is, until below the little floating image).*

Controlling Where Elements Float

You can control which elements an element can float next to and which it cannot. To keep an element from floating next to something it shouldn't, use the clear property.

To control where elements float:

1. Type **clear:**.

2. Type **left** to keep elements from floating to the left of the element you're styling.

   Or type **right** to keep elements from floating to the right of the element you're styling.

   Or type **both** to keep elements from floating to either side of the element you're styling.

   Or type **none** to let elements flow to either side of the element you're styling.

✔ Tips

- The clear property stops the affected element (the one to which the clear property is applied) from displaying until the designated side is free of floating elements.

- You add the clear property to the element whose sides you want to be clear of floating objects. So, if you want an element not to be displayed until the right side is clear of floating elements, add clear:right to *it* (and *not* to the floating elements).

- The use of the clear property is similar to the br tag with the (alas, deprecated) clear attribute *(see page 112).*

Controlling Where Elements Float

Aligning Elements Vertically

You can align elements in many different ways to make them look neater on the page.

To position elements vertically:

1. Type **vertical-align:**

2. Type **baseline** to align the element's baseline with the parent's baseline.

   Or type **middle** to align the middle of the element with the middle of the parent.

   Or type **sub** to position the element as a subscript of the parent.

   Or type **super** to position the element as a superscript of the parent.

   Or type **text-top** to align the top of the element with the top of the parent.

   Or type **text-bottom** to align the bottom of the element with the bottom of the parent.

   Or type **top** to align the top of the element with the top of the tallest element on the line.

   Or type **bottom** to align the bottom of the element to the bottom of the lowest element on the line.

   Or type a percentage of the line height of the element, which may be positive or negative.

```
body {background-color:#fff;
color:#000;padding:0 0 0 0;margin:0 0 0 0}
#bg  {position: absolute; top: 250px; left: 2%;
background-color:black; top:0; left:10%; margin-
left:-200px; z-index: 1;}

#bg img {width:538px; height:850px}

#content {position:absolute; top: 0px; left: 30%;
background-color:#fff;border-left: 1px solid black;
padding: 20px; z-index: 2;}

img.line {vertical-align: top;}
```

Figure 11.48 *We apply the top vertical alignment only to the images that have the* line *class.*

Figure 11.49 *The top edges of the three* line *class images are aligned.*

STYLE SHEETS FOR PRINTING

CSS lets you create specialized style sheets that control how Web pages are printed. These need not be anything like the screen version of the style sheets for that page. For example, you might want to remove extraneous sidebars or advertisements from a print version.

Using Media-Specific Style Sheets

You can designate a style sheet to be used only when printing, only on screen, or for both print and screen. For example, you might create one general style sheet with features common to both the print and screen versions, and then individual print and screen style sheets with properties to be used only for print and screen, respectively.

To designate media-specific style sheets:

Add **media="output"** to the opening link or style tags, where *output* is one or more of the following: all, print, or screen **(Figure 12.1)**. Separate multiple values with commas.

Or, in an @import rule, add **output**, where *output* has the same values as above, after the URL but before the semicolon **(Figure 12.2)**. Again, separate multiple values with commas.

✔ Tips

■ There are actually ten possible output types: all, aural, braille, embossed, handheld, print, projection, screen, tty, and tv. Current desktop computer browsers will (properly) ignore style sheets designated as anything but screen, print, or all.

■ The default value for the media attribute is all.

■ There is also an @media rule, though it is less well supported than the options described above.

■ For more information on linking and importing style sheets, Chapter 9, *Applying Styles*.

```
<head>

<meta http-equiv="content-type"
content="text/html; charset=utf-8" />

<title>Red and Louis</title>

<link rel="stylesheet" media="screen"
type="text/css" href="screen.css" />

<link rel="stylesheet" media="print"
type="text/css" href="print.css" />

</head>

<body>

<div id="story">

<h1>Red and Louis</h1>
```

Figure 12.1 *In this (X)HTML document I've linked to the* screen.css *style sheet for the styles that will be used when displaying the page onscreen and the* print.css *style sheet for the styles that should be used when printing.*

```
<head>

<meta http-equiv="content-type"
content="text/html; charset=utf-8" />

<title>Red and Louis</title>

<link rel="stylesheet" media="screen"
type="text/css" href="screen.css" />

<style type="text/css">

@import "print.css" print;

</style>

</head>

<body>

<div id="story">

<h1>Red and Louis</h1>
```

Figure 12.2 *In this example, which should have the same effect in current browsers, I've linked to the* screen.css *style sheet but imported the* print.css *style sheet.*

Figure 12.3 *In a screen version, you might have a table of contents sidebar, some ads, and sans-serif fonts (which tend to be easier to read on screen).*

Figure 12.4 *When the document is printed, you can get rid of the sidebar and the ads, and use a serif font for added legibility. Note that the exact same (X)HTML code was used in both cases. The browser automatically selects the appropriate style sheet.*

How Print Style Sheets Differ

Depending on the complexity of your page, the print version might be very similar or indeed very different than the screen version.

Suggestions for print style sheets:

■ Use appropriate fonts and font sizes, using points rather than pixels, since the former work best for printing. For more details, consult *A Property's Value* on page 44 as well as pages 158–165.

■ Hide sections like sidebars or ads that need not be printed (using the display property described on page 178).

■ Remove background colors and images and use colors that print reasonably in black and white *(see pages 182–184)*.

■ Adjust margins, if necessary *(see page 189)*.

■ Control page breaks and other print-specific properties *(see pages 200–202)*.

■ Explain to your visitors how and why the print version will be different from what they see on screen.

✔ Tips

■ The page break and other print-specific CSS properties suffer from average to middling support. However, there are still many things that are worth changing that all browsers will understand.

■ As you test style sheets for printed output, be sure to take advantage of your browser or system's Print Preview option, if it has one. Print Preview (typically in the File menu and sometimes in the Print dialog box itself) lets you see how the page will be printed without having to waste paper.

Controlling Page Breaks

Browsers can show very long pages in a single window thanks to the scroll bar. When visitors go to print a page, the contents of particularly long pages must be divided to fit on a given paper size. CSS lets you control where those page breaks should occur.

To control page breaks before elements:

In the style rule, type **page-break-before: when** or **page-break-after:when**, where *when* is one of `always` (so that page breaks always occur before/after the selected elements), `avoid` (so that page breaks only occur before/after the selected elements when absolutely necessary), or `auto` (to let the browser decide).

To keep elements from being divided between two pages:

In the style rule, type **page-break-inside: avoid**.

✔ Tips

- The `page-break-before` and `page-break-after` properties theoretically accept values of `left` and `right` (to make pages start on the left or right side, respectively), but those values are currently not supported on any browser.

- The default value for all of the page-break properties is `auto`. Only `page-break-inside` is inherited.

- Currently, page breaks before and after elements are supported by Internet Explorer and Opera, though Explorer does not seem to understand the `avoid` value. Mozilla is rumored to have some support but Netscape 6 does not. Only Opera understands `page-break-inside`.

```
#toc {display:none}

p {font: 12pt serif; page-break-inside:avoid}

h2 {page-break-before:always}
```

Figure 12.5 *I don't want paragraphs to be divided between pages so I use* `page-break-inside:avoid`. *So that each second level header starts on its own page, I add* `page-break-before:always` *to the* h2 *tags.*

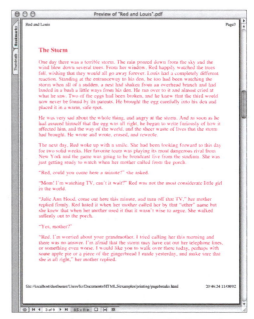

Figure 12.6 *By putting a page break before each* h2 *element (like* The Storm*), I ensure that they start on a a fresh page. Notice also the extra space at the bottom of the page since the paragraph that followed was too big to fit in its entirety (and "page breaks inside" were to be avoided). Instead the entire next paragraph will be printed in full on the following page.*

```
@page :left {size: 8in 10in; margin: 1in 1in .5in
.5in; marks: crop cross}

@page :right {size: 8in 10in; margin: .1in .5in .5in
1in; marks: crop cross}

@page toc {size: 8in 10in; margin:3in .5in .5in 1in;
marks: none}
```

Figure 12.7 *Here I've defined three types of pages. For left pages, there will be a slightly larger right margin (to allow for binding). For the same reason, right pages will have a slightly larger left margin. The named toc page will have a hefty top margin of 3 inches to set its contents in the middle of the page.*

Other Print Specific CSS Properties

CSS offers a number of other features that help control how Web pages are printed. Unfortunately, only widows and orphans are supported, and only by Opera. I'll give you a quick synopsis, nonetheless.

To describe the pages for printed output:

1. Within a style sheet, type **@page**.

2. If desired, type **name**, where *name* identifies the page being defined so that you can later make specific elements print on this kind of page *(see page 202)*.

3. If desired, type **:first**, **:right**, or **:left** to designate this page definition to be used for the first page, for all right pages, or for all left pages, respectively.

4. Type **{** to define the rules associated with this page.

5. If desired, type **size: w h;**, where *w* and *h* are the width and height, including units, of the desired print area. If you use just a single measurement, it is used for both width and height. Or use landscape or portrait to set the browser's page setup preferences accordingly.

6. If desired, type **margin: x;**, where *x* is as described in detail on page 189.

7. If desired, type **marks: kind;**, where *kind* is either crop (for marks that show where the page is to be cut) or cross (for marks that help align different color plates) or both. You can also use a value of none to keep marks from being printed, though in that case, you might as well skip the marks property altogether.

8. Type **}** to complete the @page rule.

continued

Other Print Specific CSS Properties

If you've named your page definition (as described in step 2 on page 201), you can then request that certain elements be printed only on that particular kind of page.

To print certain elements on specific kinds of pages:

In the style rule for the desired element, type **page: name;**, where *name* is the identifying label you used in step 2 on page 201.

One or two lines of a longer paragraph look unsightly when displayed alone at the beginning or end of a page. These stranded lines of text are called widows and orphans, respectively. CSS lets you specify the minimum number of lines of an element that can appear alone.

To control widows and orphans:

- ■ If desired, in the style rule, type **orphans: n;**, where *n* is the minimum number of lines that should appear at the *bottom* of a page.

- ■ If desired, in the style rule, type **widows: n;**, where *n* is the minimum number of lines in the element that should appear at the top of a page.

✔ Tips

- ■ Only Opera supports the `orphans` and `widows` properties.

- ■ It's a shame that these features are not better supported by other browsers. However, things move so quickly that perhaps by the time you read this, things will have improved.

- ■ Note that the better-supported `page-break-inside` property can also help avoid stranded lines. See page 200.

```
#toc {page: toc; font: bold 14pt sans-serif}
```

Figure 12.8 *The* toc *division will be printed on* toc *type pages (that is, the one I defined in Figure 12.7 on page 201).*

```
p {font: 12pt serif; orphans: 4; widows: 4; }
```

Figure 12.9 *The* p *elements will be allowed to split across pages, but at least four lines should appear at the bottom of the page and four lines must appear at the top of the page.*

Other Print Specific CSS Properties

LISTS

The (X)HTML specifications contain special codes for creating lists of items. You can create plain, numbered, or bulleted lists, as well as lists of definitions. You can also nest one kind of list inside another. In the sometimes sketchy shorthand of the Internet, lists come in very handy.

All lists are formed by a principal code to specify what sort of list you want to create (ol for ordered list, dl for definition list, etc.) and a secondary code to specify what sort of items you want to create (li for list item, dt for definition term, etc.).

Although the W3C does not recommend the use of list elements for simply indenting paragraphs, they *are* rather handy in this regard. You can find more information about that in Chapter 22, *Layout: The Old Way*, under *Creating Indents (with Lists)* on page 362.

Creating Ordered and Unordered Lists

The ordered list is perfect for explaining step-by-step instructions for how to complete a particular task or for creating an outline (complete with links to corresponding sections, if desired) of a larger document. You may create an ordered list anywhere in the body section of your HTML document.

Unordered lists are probably the most widely used lists on the Web. Use them to list any series of items that have no particular order, such as hot Web sites or names.

To create ordered lists:

1. Type **\<ol>** for an ordered list or **\<ul>** to begin an unordered list.

2. Type **\<li>** (that's the first two letters of the word *list*) to begin the first list item.

3. Type the text to be included in the list item.

4. Type **\</li>** to complete each list item.

5. Repeat steps 2–4 for each new list item.

6. Type **\</ol>** or **\</ul>**, to match the opening tag (from step 1) to complete the list.

```
<body>

<p>Ordered lists are the most common kinds of
lists, perfect for explaining step by step instructions
or for giving an outline (complete with links to the
corresponding sections, if desired) for a larger
document.

<h1>Changing a light bulb</h1>

<ol>

<li>Make sure you have unplugged the lamp from
the wall socket.</li>

<li>Unscrew the old bulb.</li>

<li>Get the new bulb out of the package.</li>

<li>Check the wattage to make sure it's
correct.</li>

<li>Screw in the new bulb.</li>

<li>Plug in the lamp and turn it on!</li>

</ol>

</body>
```

Figure 13.1 *There is no official way to format a list's title. You can use a regular header (see page 65).*

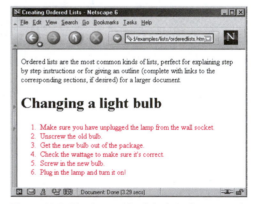

Figure 13.2 *This list uses the default Arabic numerals to create a numbered list.*

```
<body>

Unordered lists are probably the most widely used
lists on the Web. Use them to list any series of items
that have no particular order, such as hot web sites
or names.

<h1>PageWhacker, version 12.0--Features</h1>

<ul>

<li>New or improved features marked with a solid
bullet.</li>

<li>One click page layout</li>

<li>Spell checker for 327 major languages</li>

<li>Image retouching plug-in</li>

<li>Special HTML filters</li>

<li>Unlimited Undo's and Redo's</li>

<li>Automatic book writing</li>

</ul>
```

Figure 13.3 *The list items of unordered lists are identical to those for ordered lists. Only the* ul *tag is different.*

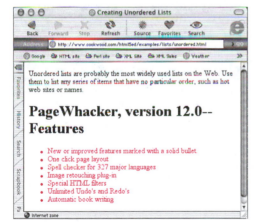

Figure 13.4 *Unordered lists have round, solid bullets by default.*

✔ Tips

- Unless you specify otherwise *(see page 206)*, items in ordered lists will be numbered with Arabic numerals (1, 2, 3, etc.) **(Figure 13.2)**.

- Items in unordered lists have solid round bullets by default **(Figure 13.4)**. You can choose different bullets *(see page 206)* or even create your own *(see page 208)*.

- Keep the text in your list items short. If you have more than a few lines of text in each item, you may have better luck using headers (h1, h2, etc.) and paragraphs (p).

- Inserting a line break (br) in a list item breaks the text to the next line, but maintains the same indenting.

- No text is permitted between the opening ol or ul tag and the first li tag. Nevertheless, browsers will display such text with the same indentation as the first item in the list, but without a bullet.

- The ul tag is often used for indentation, though this is considered a hack from the pre-standards era.

- You may create one list inside another, even mixing and matching ordered and unordered lists. Be sure to nest each list properly, using all the required opening and closing tags.

- Lists are automatically indented from the left margin (40 pixels is typical for the default 16 pixel size text). If you use CSS to style your lists, changing or reducing the left margin may make your bullets disappear beyond the left edge of the window.

Choosing Your Markers (Bullets)

When you create a list, be it ordered or unordered, you can also choose what sort of markers (bullets or numbers) should appear to the left of each list item.

To choose your markers:

In the style sheet rule, type **list-style-type: marker**, where *marker* is one of the following values: disc (●), circle (○), square(■), decimal (1,2,3, ...), upper-alpha (A, B, C, ...), lower-alpha (a, b, c, ...), upper-roman (I, II, III, IV, ...), or lower-roman (i, ii, iii, iv, ...).

To display lists without markers:

In the style sheet rule, type **list-style-type: none**.

✔ Tips

- You can also use the deprecated type attribute in the ul or ol tag and in individual li items to specify a marker style for the entire list or for individual list items, respectively. In unordered lists, the acceptable values are disc (for a solid round bullet), circle (for an empty round bullet), or square. In ordered lists, the acceptable values are A, a, I, i, and 1, which indicate the kind of numeration to be used.

- A type attribute in an li tag overrides one in a ol or ul tag.

- By default, unordered lists use discs for the first level, circles for the first nested level, and squares for the third and subsequent level lists.

- The disc, circle, and square bullets vary slightly in size and appearance from one browser to another.

```
<body>
<h1>The Great American Novel</h1>
<ol>
<li>Introduction</li>
<li>Development</li>
<li>Climax</li>
<li>Denouement</li>
<li>Epilogue</li>
</ol>
</body>
```

Figure 13.5 *Here is our simple ordered list, to which we will apply capital Roman numerals (upper-roman).*

```
li {list-style-type:upper-roman}
```

Figure 13.6 *You can apply the list-style-type property to any list item. If you had two lists on this page, one of which was unordered, you could apply capital Roman letters to just the ordered one by changing the selector in this example to ol li.*

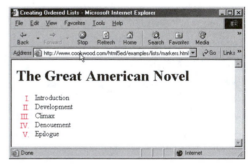

Figure 13.7 *Now the ordered list has capital Roman numerals. Note that most browsers align numeric markers to the right.*

```
<body>

<h1>Changing a light bulb</h1>

<ol start="2">

<li>Unscrew the old bulb.

<p>some omitted steps here</p></li>

<li value="5">Screw in the new bulb.</li>

<li>Plug in the lamp and turn it on!</li>

</ol>

</body>
```

Figure 13.8 *In this example, I've omitted some steps but want to maintain the original numbering. So I start the whole list at 2 (with* start="2"*) and then set the value of the third item to 5 (with* value="5"*).*

Figure 13.9 *Notice that not only are the first and third items numbered as we've specified, but the third item ("Plug in the lamp") is also affected.*

Choosing Where to Start List Numbering

You might want to start a particular ordered list's numbering somewhere other than 1 (which is the default).

To determine the initial value of an entire list's numbering scheme:

Within the ol tag, type **start="n"**, where *n* represents the initial value for the list.

To change the numbering of a given list item:

In the desired li item, type **value="n"**, where *n* represents the value for this list item. The value is always specified numerically and is converted automatically by the browser to the type of marker specified with CSS or with the type attribute *(see page 206).*

✔ Tips

■ By default, all lists start at 1.

■ The value attribute overrides the start value.

■ When you change a given list item's number with the value attribute, the subsequent list items are also renumbered accordingly.

■ Unfortunately, the W3C has deprecated both the start and value attributes without offering a CSS alternative. If you need them, just be sure to use the proper (transitional) DOCTYPE *(see pages 38 and 60).*

■ The start value is always numeric regardless of the numbering scheme. For more on choosing number styles for markers, see page 206.

Using Custom Markers

If you get tired of circles, squares and discs, or even Roman numerals, you can create your own custom marker with an image.

To use custom markers:

1. In the style sheet rule for the desired list or list item, type **list-style-image:**.

2. Then type **url(image.gif)**, where *image.gif* is the image you'd like to use for the list item's markers.

To remove custom markers:

Type **list-style-image: none**.

✔ Tips

■ By default, you've got about a 15 by 15 pixel square space for the marker.

■ If your image is larger than the line height of the list items, some browsers overlap them. You can adjust a list-item's margins *(see page 189)* if necessary.

■ There should be no space between *url* and the opening parentheses. Quotes around the URL are optional.

■ Note that relative URLs are relative to the location of the style sheet, not the Web page, except in Netscape 4 which (incorrectly) does the opposite. You can avoid problems by using absolute URLs.

■ Most browsers align custom markers to the right. IE for Windows (all versions) is the notable and annoying exception.

■ The list-style-image property overrides list-style-type. But, if for some reason the image can not be loaded, the marker specified with list-style-type is used.

■ The custom markers are inherited.

```
<ul>

<li>New or improved features marked with a solid bullet.</li>

<li class="new">One click page layout</li>

<li>Spell checker for 327 major languages</li>

<li>Image retouching plug-in</li>

<li>Special HTML filters</li>

<li>Unlimited Undo's and Redo's</li>

<li class="new">Automatic book writing</li>

</ul>
```

Figure 13.10 *I want to add a special marker for the new features in my list.*

```
li.new {
    list-style-image:url(http://www.cookwood.com/
    html5ed/examples/lists/rightarrow.gif)
}
```

Figure 13.11 *It's a good idea to use absolute URLs for specifying the location of the marker image to ensure that all browsers will understand.*

Figure 13.12 *It can be tricky mixing custom markers with default ones. You have to make sure the custom markers aren't too big.*

```
<ul>

<li>New or improved features marked with a solid
bullet.</li>

<li class="new">One click page layout. This is
particularly useful when you're under a heavy
deadline. You just select whether you want the end
product to be a book or a Web site, and poof, it's
done. </li>

<li>Spell checker for 327 major languages</li>

<li>Image retouching plug-in</li>

<li>Special HTML filters</li>

<li>Unlimited Undo's and Redo's</li>
```

Figure 13.13 *I've added a bit more text to the first "new" feature so that the effect of hanging markers inside is more obvious.*

```
li.new {
    list-style-image:url(http://www.cookwood.com/
    html5ed/examples/lists/rightarrow.gif);
    list-style-position:inside
    }
```

Figure 13.14 *I've added the inside list-style position to the style sheet rule shown in Figure 13.11 on page 208.*

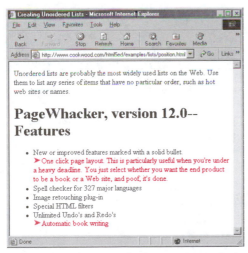

Figure 13.15 *The markers for the "new" features begin at the left margin of the list item, instead of outside it to the left.*

Controlling Where Markers Hang

By default, lists are indented from the left margin (of their parent). Your markers can either begin halfway to the right of that starting point, which is the default, or flush with the rest of the text (called *inside*).

To control where markers hang:

1. In the style sheet rule for the desired list or list item, type **list-style-position:**.

2. Then type **inside** to display the markers flush with the list item text, or **outside** to display the markers to the left of the list item text.

✔ Tips

- Markers are hung outside the list paragraph, by default.

- The `list-style-position` property is inherited.

Setting All List-Style Properties at Once

CSS has a shortcut property for the list-style features.

To set all the list-style properties at once:

1. Type **list-style:**

2. If desired, specify the kind of markers that should appear next to the list items, if any (as described on page 206).

3. If desired, specify the custom marker that should be used for list items (as described on page 208).

4. If desired, specify whether markers should be hung outside the list para-graphs or flush with the text (as described on page 209).

✔ Tips

■ You may specify any or all of the three list-style properties.

■ You might think that by omitting one of the three properties, you won't be affect-ing it, but that's not always the case. Any properties not explicitly set are returned to their defaults (disc for list-style-type, none for list-style-image, and outside for list-style-position).

■ The properties may be specified in any order.

■ The list-style property is inherited.

```
li.new {
    list-style:url(http://www.cookwood.com/
    html5ed/examples/lists/rightarrow.gif) inside
    square}
```

Figure 13.16 *This style rule is equivalent to setting the* list-style-image *to the* rightarrow.gif *file, the* list-style-position *to* inside *and the* list-style-type *to* square. *It's just shorter.*

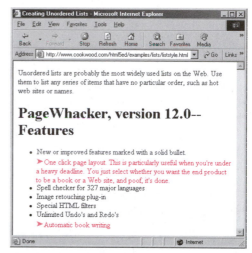

Figure 13.17 *As long as the image is available, the result is the same as in Figure 13.15 on page 209.*

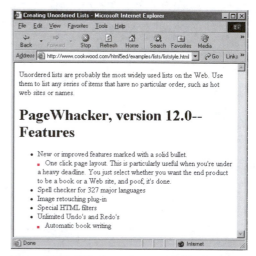

Figure 13.18 *If the image is not available, the square is used.*

```
<h1>Classical Greek Verb Tenses</h1>

<dl>

<dt>Present</dt>

<dd><span class="example">e.g. .luo,
luomai</span>. The present usually shows the pure
verb stem in verbs with strong stems. [snip]</dd>

<dt>Future</dt>

<dd><span class="example">e.g. luso, lusomai,
luthesomai</span>. The future has the[snip]</dd>

<dt>Aorist</dt>

<dd><span class="example">e.g. .elusa, eluthen,
elusamen</span>. The aorist (from [snip]</dd>

</dl>
```

Figure 13.19 *Each entry word is labeled with the* dt
tag, while the definition itself is labeled with a dd *tag.*

```
dt {font-weight:bold}

.example {font-style:italic}
```

Figure 13.20 *You may want to add formatting to your
definition term to help it stand out.*

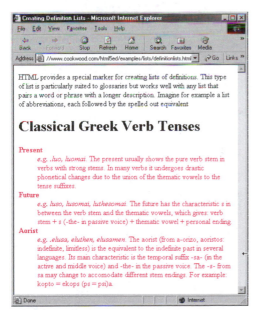

Figure 13.21 *By default, the defined word (the* dt *) is
aligned to the left and the definition (*dd*) is indented.*

Creating Definition Lists

(X)HTML provides a special tag for creating
definition lists. This type of list is particularly
suited to glossaries, but works well with any
list that pairs a word or phrase with a longer
description. Imagine, for example, a list of
Classical Greek verb tenses, each followed by
an explanation of proper usage.

To create definition lists:

1. Type the introductory text for the definition list.

2. Type **\<dl\>**.

3. Type **\<dt\>**.

4. Type the word or short phrase that will
be defined or explained, including any
logical or physical formatting desired.

5. Type **\</dt\>** to complete the definition
term.

6. Type **\<dd\>**.

7. Type the definition of the term that was
entered in step 4.

8. Type **\</dd\>** to complete the definition.

9. Repeat steps 3–8 for each pair of terms
and definitions.

10. Type **\</dl\>** to complete the list of
definitions.

✔ Tips

■ Browsers generally indent definitions on
a new line below the definition term.

■ You can create more than one dl line or
more than one dt line to accommodate
multiple words or multiple definitions.

Creating Definition Lists

Styling Nested Lists

You may insert one type of list in another. This is particularly useful with an outline rendered with ordered lists, where you may want several levels of items. While you can style nested lists using classes or ids, there's an easier way.

To style nested lists:

1. For styling the outermost list, type **toplevel li {style_rules}**, where *toplevel* is the list type of the outermost list (e.g., `ol`, `ul`, `dt`) and *style_rules* are the styles that should be applied.

2. For the second level list, type **toplevel 2ndlevel li {style_rules}**, where *toplevel* matches the *toplevel* in step 1 and *2ndlevel* is the list type of the second level list.

3. For the third level list, type **toplevel 2ndlevel 3rdlevel li {style_rules}**, where *toplevel* and *2ndlevel* match the values used in steps 1–2 and *3rdlevel* is the kind of list used for the third nested list.

4. Continue in this fashion for each nested list that you wish to style.

```
<h1>The Great American Novel</h1>
<ol>
    <li>Introduction
        <ol>
        <li>Boy's childhood</li>
        <li>Girl's childhood</li>
        </ol>
    </li>
<li>Development
    <ol>
    <li>Boy meets Girl</li>
    <li>Boy and Girl fall in love</li>
    <li>Boy and Girl have fight</li>
    </ol>
</li>
<li>Climax
    <ol>
    <li>Boy gives Girl ultimatum
        <ol>
            <li>Girl can't believe her ears</li>
            <li>Boy is indignant at Girl's
                indignance</li>
        </ol>
    </li>
    <li>Girl tells Boy to get lost</li>
    </ol>
</li>
<li>Denouement</li>
<li>Epilogue</li>
</ol>
```

Figure 13.22 *There are four nested lists here, one in the* Introduction *list item, one in the* Development *item, one in the* Climax *item and one, highlighted and in bold face, inside the* Boy gives Girl ultimatum *item (which is inside the* Climax *item).*

```
ol li {list-style-type:upper-roman;font-size:75%}

ol ol li {list-style-type:upper-alpha}

ol ol ol li {list-style-type:decimal}

li li {font-size:100%}
```

Figure 13.23 *You can format each level of nested list separately. If you use percentages for list text, be sure to add the* li li {font-size:100%} *so that it doesn't disappear on you (see last tip).*

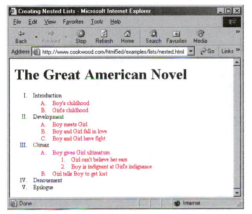

Figure 13.24 *The first level lists (*ol li*) have capital Roman numerals. The second level lists (*ol ol li*) have capital letters, and the third level lists (*ol ol ol li*) have Arabic numerals.*

✔ **Tips**

■ Your selectors should reflect the types of nested lists in your document, that is, you might need something like **ul ul ol li**.

■ Ordered lists always use Arabic numerals (1, 2, 3) by default, regardless of their nesting position. Use list-style-type to specify other numbering schemes *(see page 206)*. According to *The Chicago Manual of Style,* the correct nesting order for lists is I, A, 1, a, 1.

■ By default, the first level of an unordered list will have solid round bullets, the next will have empty round bullets and the third and subsequent levels will have square bullets. Again, use list-style-type to specify the type of bullets you want *(see page 206)*.

■ Since list items (li elements) can be nested within other list items, you have to be a bit careful with font sizes specified in relative values. If you use something like li {font-size: 75%}, the font size of the outermost list item will be 75% of its parent element, which, if the parent is a default 16 pixels high, will be 12 pixels, and not a problem. However, the font size of the first nested list item will be 75% of *its* parent (the first list item, which is 12 pixels), and thus will be only 9 pixels high. Each level gets quickly worse. One solution is to add li li {font-size:100%}. Now nested list items will always be the same size as top level ones. (Thanks to Eric Meyer.)

Styling Nested Lists

TABLES

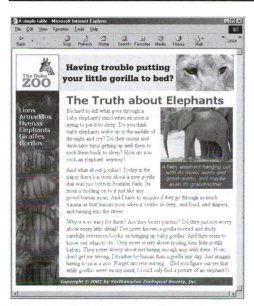

Figure 14.1 *Tables let you create fancy professional-looking layouts that will wow your visitors and be compatible with most older browsers.*

Tables have a storied history on the Web. While originally conceived just to hold tabular data, they were quickly appropriated for a much bigger task: serving as the foundation for complicated layouts, with multiple columns, sidebars and many other features that were simply impossible before the advent of CSS. The problem is that layouts with tables tend to be so complex that they are difficult to set up and cumbersome to update.

Now that CSS is here and well supported, you can create beautiful layouts without tables *(see page 175)*. However, those layouts will degrade, and sometimes not very gracefully, in older browsers. If you're not ready to give up on the 10% of the population who aren't using browsers with decent CSS support—some 50 million people (according to Nua, *http://www.nua.com/*)—use tables for layout.

And there's a middle road. As this chapter will illustrate, you can use tables for the basic structure of your page, but use CSS for all the text formatting, and much of the layout formatting (beyond the table itself). It will be that much easier to make the leap to full CSS when you (and your visitors) are ready.

One of the nice things about tables is that you can use them to create liquid design—design that expands and contracts proportionately to your visitor's browser window. The key is to use percentages instead of pixel-based widths and learn to let go of the need to control every last space.

Finally, if you want to use tables for tabular data, you still can. And CSS will help you make those tables shine.

Mapping Out Your Page

Before you create a complicated table, it's really important to have a vision of what you're about to construct. You need to know how many rows and columns you need, how big these should be, and where each of the items on your page should go.

To map out your page:

1. Design your page on a piece of paper—with a pen!

2. Figure out how many rows and columns you will need. Identify any rows or columns that will span more than one space.

3. If necessary, you can nest one table inside another. However, you should keep nesting to a minimum as it tends to slow browsers down—and sometimes causes them to break down altogether.

4. If you're going to make a static, fixed design, measure how wide your table should be (the standard is around 600 pixels) and then decide how many pixels wide each column should be. For liquid designs, use percentages.

5. Create the skeleton of your page with just the table tags but little or no content.

6. Finally, create or insert the content.

✔ Tip

■ One good way to get ideas for table structure is to look at how others do it *(see page 57)*. However, there are some very complicated setups out there. One way to get a handle on what's going on in someone else's page is to download the source code and then change the background color of each nested table *(see page 228)* so you can better see which parts of the layout belong to which table.

Figure 14.2 *Here's a map of the main example used in this chapter. I use one table for the top set of ads and logo and one table for the lower navigational bar and content area section. Note that there is a third table floating in the content text.*

```
<table>

<tr><td><img src="elephant.jpg" width="200"
height="150" alt="Elephant Baby"></td></tr>

<tr><td class="caption">A baby elephant hanging
out with its mom, aunts and great-aunts, and
maybe even its grandmother</td></tr>

</table>
```

Figure 14.3 *This very simple table has two rows, each of which has only one cell. Notice that I've added extra size formatting to the caption to keep it unobtrusive.*

```
.caption {font-size:.8em;font-style:italic;font-
family:"verdana", sans-serif}
```

Figure 14.4 *The style sheet contains only pure text formatting; nothing that would affect the table per se.*

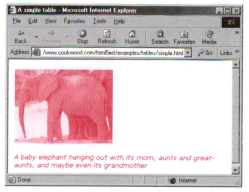

Figure 14.5 *Notice that by default, the table extends almost as far as the edge of the browser window.*

Figure 14.6
Here's the exact same table in a narrower browser window. The table simply contracts to fit better in the window.

Creating a Simple Table

Tables are made up of rows of cells. The number of cells in each row determines the table's shape.

To create a simple table:

1. Type **<table>**.

2. Type **<tr>** to define the beginning of the first row. If desired, press Return and Tab to visually distinguish the row elements.

3. Type **<td>** to define the beginning of the cell.

4. Type the contents of the cell.

5. Type **</td>** to complete the cell.

6. Repeat steps 3–5 for each cell in the row.

7. Type **</tr>** to complete the row.

8. Repeat steps 2–7 for each row.

9. To finish the table, type **</table>**.

✔ Tips

- The </table> tag is *not* optional. Netscape won't display tables without it.

- There is also a th tag for creating *header* cells. But, all it does is center the contents of a cell and format it in boldface. If you're mostly using tables to help lay out your page, th is not very useful. On the other hand, if you're organizing tabular data, header cells can help describe your table and make it more accessible.

- You can create a title for the table with the caption element. Use align= "direction", where *direction* is top, bottom, left, or right to align the caption. It's ugly and not well supported.

Adding a Border

A border helps distinguish your table from the rest of the page. However, if you're laying out your page with tables, you may not want to call so much attention to the border.

To create a border with (X)HTML:

1. Inside the initial table tag, type **border**.

2. If desired, type **="n"**, where *n* is the thickness in pixels of the border.

To create a border with styles:

1. In your style sheet, type **table** or **td**, or whichever selector denotes the part of the table that you want to apply a border to.

2. Type **{border: value}**, where *border* is the border property that you wish to apply and *value* is the type of border you want. For more details on the border property, consult *Setting the Border* on page 186.

✔ Tips

■ The CSS border property is discussed in detail (and there are a lot of details) on page 186. This page focuses on how the border property interacts with the (non-deprecated) (X)HTML border attribute.

■ The border attribute applies to both the table and the cells it contains. The CSS border property, in contrast, is not inherited. So, if you omit the border attribute but apply a CSS border to the table, the cells will have no borders. Conversely, if you use the border attribute but use table {border: none}, the cells will have borders, but the table won't.

■ If you use the border attribute with no value (border alone, or border="border" to be XHTML compliant) but no CSS border, you get a 1 pixel outset border.

```
<table border="10">

<tr><td><img src="elephant.jpg" width="200" height="150" alt="Elephant Baby"></td></tr>

<tr><td class="caption">A baby elephant hanging out with its mom, aunts and great-aunts, and maybe even its grandmother</td></tr>

</table>
```

Figure 14.7 *In this example, we set a 10 pixel wide border for the outside of the table. As long as you set the border attribute, regardless of its value, the cell borders are always 1 pixel wide.*

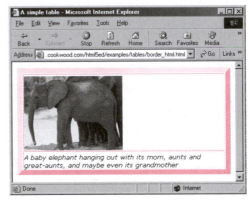

Figure 14.8 *Although borders are not usually shown in tables used for layout, they are often temporarily useful for showing exactly what's happening with a table. Here we can see we've got two rows and each row contains a single cell. The (X)HTML border attribute turns on borders around tables and cells indiscriminately.*

```
table {border:8px double red}


.caption {font-size:.8em;font-style:italic;font-family:"verdana", sans-serif}
```

Figure 14.9 *You can specify the width, color, and style with the single shortcut border property.*

Adding a Border *(side margin)*

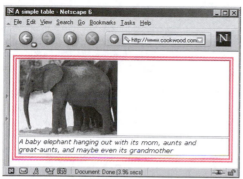

Figure 14.10 *This page is the result of the (X)HTML shown in Figure 14.7 and the CSS in Figure 14.9. Because we've applied the CSS* border *property only to the* table *element, the borders around cells are not affected at all. CSS borders are much more flexible and powerful than (X)HTML.*

Figure 14.11 *This page uses the same CSS as the previous illustration (Figure 14.10), but no* border *attribute in the (X)HTML. Notice that there are no borders around the cells.*

```
table, td {border:0}


.caption {font-size:.8em;font-style:italic;font-family:"verdana", sans-serif}
```

Figure 14.12 *Here is the CSS that we'll use with respect to borders in the rest of our example. So there!*

- The `border` attribute only controls whether or not the border exists *in the absence* of the CSS `border-style` property. If `border-style` is set to `none`, either explicitly (`{border-style:none}`) or implicitly (`{border:red 2px}` since `none` is the default style), there will be no border, regardless of the `border` attribute (except in IE for Windows which incorrectly lets the `border` attribute, if it's present, override the `border-style` default of `none`).

- If you don't set a border width with CSS, IE 5 for Mac uses the attribute value (if it's absent, that means no border), IE 6 for Windows uses the attribute value (but if it's absent, it uses a CSS default of `medium` which it interprets as 4 pixels), and Opera 5 and Netscape 6 use the CSS default of `medium` (which they interpret as *3* pixels) regardless of the attribute value. Conclusion: you should set the width explicitly if you want it to be consistent across browsers. (See next tip.)

- If you set the `border-width` in CSS, it overrides the (X)HTML `border` attribute.

- A border's default color is the color of the element itself (as specified with the CSS `color` property). Only IE for Mac and Netscape get that right. (Other browsers change only the color of the table's or cell's *content*.)

- Tables naturally expand to the edge of the elements they contain or to the edge of the browser window, whichever comes first. That's sometimes hard to see unless you view the border.

- It's not a bad idea to create a border while you're constructing your table and then banish it once you have everything in place.

Adding a Border

Setting the Width

By default, a browser will automatically determine the width of your cells by looking at the elements and text they contain. It will then expand each cell to the edge of its contents or to the edge of the browser window, whichever comes first. With images, that's pretty clear cut; the edge of the image will be the edge of the cell. Text, however, is stretched out until the first line break, or until the end of the paragraph, which can be very long indeed.

Instead of relying on the browser's sometimes unusual algorithms for determining table width, you can specify the width of the table or of individual cells manually, either in pixels or as a percentage of window size. For example, when designing liquid layouts with tables, it's very common to specify a table width of 100% in order to force the table to expand to the size of the browser window, no matter what size the visitor makes it. It's also quite common to specify the width of the navigational column in pixels so that it is not affected by the ebb and flow of browser size.

It's important to note that no browser will let you make a table or cell narrower than its images. It will simply stretch the cell or table as necessary to make the image fit, adjusting the rest of your table as best it can.

To set the width of a cell or table:

In the `td` or `table` tag, type **width="n"**, where *n* is the desired width of the cell or of the entire table, in pixels.

Or type **width="n%"**, where *n* is the portion of the browser window that the table should occupy.

To set the width with styles:

In the style sheet, type **width: value** where *value* is the desired width (for more details, see page 190).

```
<table border=0 width="200"
class="rightsidebar">

<tr><td><img src="elephant.jpg" width="200"
height="150" alt="Elephant Baby"></td></tr>

<tr><td class="caption">A baby elephant hanging
out with its mom, aunts and great-aunts, and
maybe even its grandmother</td></tr>

</table>
```

Figure 14.13 *This table has a 200 pixel wide image with no borders. We set the width of the table to 200 pixels to keep the text from stretching out.*

```
table, td {border:0}

.rightsidebar {width: 200px}

.caption {font-size:.8em;font-style:italic;font-
family:"verdana", sans-serif}
```

Figure 14.14 *You can use either the CSS, the (X)HTML or both. The CSS overrides the (X)HTML (though in this example, they're the same, so it doesn't matter.)*

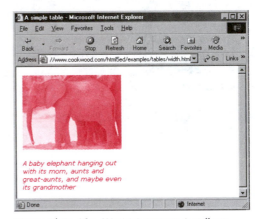

Figure 14.15 *The CSS* width *property is well supported. You can feel comfortable using it instead of the* width *attribute in the (X)HTML.*

```
.rightsidebar {width: 100px}
```

Figure 14.16 *In this case, the table is made narrower than the image it contains.*

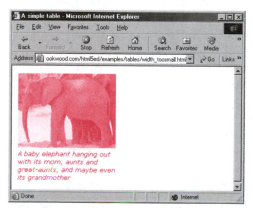

Figure 14.17 *The image (200px) overrides the* width *property and/or attribute (set to 100px). You can't make a table or cell too small for its images!*

```
.rightsidebar {width: 300px}
```

Figure 14.18 *In this case, the table is made wider than the image it contains.*

Figure 14.19 *Of course, you can make a table bigger than its contents. In that case, the text stretches out to fill the space.*

✔ Tips

- The CSS `width` property is described in detail on page 190. This page focuses on how the `width` property interacts with the (X)HTML `width` attribute (which has *not* been deprecated).

- A table sized with percentages will adjust as the browser window is resized. Tables sized with pixels will not.

- You can't make the table too small for its contents; the browser will just ignore you.

- You can keep a cell open to a certain width by putting a transparent pixel spacer inside it of the proper width *(see page 364)*.

- If you make the table too wide, visitors with smaller monitors (or visitors who don't use the entire screen for their browser) may have to scroll to see some parts of your table. If you must use a non-flexible layout, I don't recommend making tables any wider than 600 pixels.

- In IE 5.x for Windows the value of `width` is the sum of the content, cellspacing, cellpadding and borders. In browsers that properly follow the specifications (like IE 6, Netscape 6, and Opera)—in standards mode, see page 39—the value of the `width` property (or attribute) does not include padding or borders.

- The widest cell in the column determines the width of the entire column.

- You don't necessarily have to specify a width for every column.

- There is also a `height` attribute but it is non-standard, and not well supported.

- Netscape 4.x doesn't recognize the CSS `width` property. You'll have to use the (X)HTML `width` attribute instead.

Setting the Width

Centering a Table on the Page

You can draw attention to a table by centering it in the browser window.

To center a table on the page:

In the `table` tag, type **align= "center"**.

To center a table on the page with CSS:

1. Make sure you've specified the width of the table *(see page 220)*.

2. Add **margin-right: auto** and **margin-left: auto** to the table's style rule.

✔ Tips

■ Centering the table with CSS by setting the right and left margins to `auto` does not work in IE 5.5 or earlier or in Netscape 4.x or earlier.

■ You can also use the CSS `text-align` property in a surrounding `div` to center tables, but it seems a bit of a hack to me *(see page 171)*.

■ The `center` value for the `align` attribute has been deprecated by the W3C, though it continues to enjoy broad support.

■ You could also center the table by enclosing the entire table in opening and closing `center` tags *(see page 356)*, although they've also been deprecated.

■ You could conceivably center one table within another. For more information, consult *Combining Tables* on page 224.

■ You can also wrap text to the right or left of a table *(see page 223)*.

■ You can't align a table to the top or middle line of text as you can with images.

```
<table border=0 width="200" class="rightsidebar"
align="center">
```

Figure 14.20 *The simplest way to center a table is to add the deprecated (but still well supported)* center *value to the* align *attribute.*

```
table, td {border:0}

.rightsidebar {width:200px;margin-
right:auto;margin-left:auto }

.caption {font-size:.8em;font-style:italic;font-
family:"verdana", sans-serif}
```

Figure 14.21 *Setting the right and left margins to* auto *makes them equal—which is the essence of centering.*

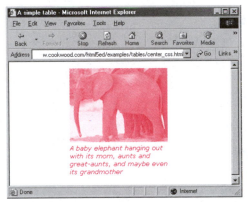

Figure 14.22 *Because support is so sketchy for centering with CSS, I recommend continuing to use the (X)HTML method (in addition to or instead of CSS, as you prefer).*

```
<h1>The Truth about Elephants</h1>

<table border=0 width="200" class="rightsidebar"
align="right">

<tr><td><img src="elephant.jpg" width="200"
height="150" alt="Elephant Baby"></td></tr>

<tr><td class="caption">A baby elephant hanging
out with its mom, aunts and great-aunts, and
maybe even its grandmother</td></tr>

</table>

<p>It's hard to tell what goes through a baby
elephant's mind when its mom is trying to put it to
sleep. Do you think baby elephants wake up in the
```

Figure 14.23 *When you align a table to the right, the text flows to the left. Notice also that in the markup, the table comes before the text that flows around it.*

```
table, td {border:0}

.rightsidebar {width:200px;float: right}

.caption {font-size:.8em;font-style:italic;font-
family:"verdana", sans-serif}
```

Figure 14.24 *You must specify a width when using the* float *property.*

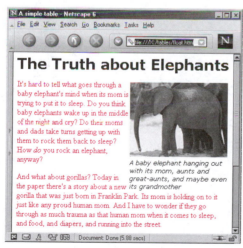

Figure 14.25 *Since the table is floated to the right, the text wraps around the left side.*

Wrapping Text around a Table

You can wrap text around a table in much the same way you can with images. While there are more sophisticated layout techniques, wrapping text around a table is helpful for keeping images together with captions in a long flow of text.

To wrap text around a table with (X)HTML:

1. In the `table` tag, either type **align="left"** to align the table to the left of the screen while the text flows to the right, or type **align="right"** to align the table to the right of the browser window while the text flows on the left side of the table.

2. After the closing `</table>` tag, type the text that should flow around the table.

To wrap text around a table with CSS:

1. Make sure you've specified the width of the table.

2. Add **float: right** or **float: left** to the table's style rule.

✔ Tips

- For more details about floating elements, see pages 110 and 194. For more details on controlling where elements float, see pages 112 and 195.

- The CSS `float` property is not supported by Netscape 4.x or earlier or Explorer 3 or earlier.

- The `right` and `left` values for the `align` attribute have been deprecated, though they continue to enjoy broad support.

- You can use one system or both, depending on how well supported or how standard you want your code to be.

Wrapping Text around a Table

Combining Tables

For more complex layouts, you may wish to combine tables. You can place combinations of tables and text in another table, you can nest tables within a specific cell of a larger table, or you can use multiple tables.

To nest one table in another:

1. Create the inner table and any text or other elements that should accompany it.

2. Create the outer table. Determine which cell of the outer table will hold the inner table and type **placeholder** (or some other easily identifiable text) there as a placeholder.

3. Test both tables separately to make sure they look the way you want them to.

4. Replace the word *placeholder* with the inner table content by copying and pasting.

The more complicated your tables become, the longer it will take for a browser to calculate their proper widths and display them. One way to simplify your code is to divide your layout into multiple tables that sit one on top of the next.

To use multiple tables:

1. Identify rows that could be separated into their own table.

2. Make sure the widths of the separate tables (and of the corresponding columns in each) match.

3. Use comments to identify the different parts of a layout.

```
<table width="100%" border="1">
<tr><td><!-- Left Navigation --></td>
<td><!-- Main Content -->
<h1>The Truth about Elephants</h1>
<table border=0 width="200" class="rightsidebar" align="right">
<tr><td><img src="elephant.jpg" width="200" height="150" alt="Elephant Baby"></td></tr>
<tr><td class="caption">A baby elephant hanging out with its mom, aunts and great-aunts, and maybe even its grandmother</td></tr>
</table>
<p>It's hard to tell what goes through a [snip]
</td>
</tr></table>
```

Figure 14.26 *Here I've created an outer table with a single row. The left column is devoted to a navigation bar and the right column contains the main content (what we've worked on so far in this chapter—which contains its own wrapped table).*

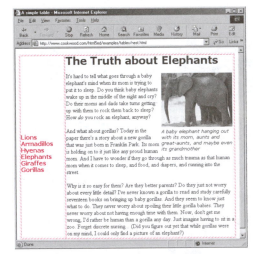

Figure 14.27 *Here I've combined the main content with the left navigation by placing them in a table in separate cells. I've added the border so you can see what's happening.*

Combining Tables

```
<!-- Top Logo Bar -->

<table width="100%">

<tr><td ><img src="logo.jpg" width="120"
alt="Northampton Zoo Logo"></td>

<td><img src="ad2.gif" width="320" alt="main
ad" ></td>

<td><img src="miniad.jpg" width="160"
height="100" alt="mini ad" ></td></tr></table>

<!--Left Nav and Main Content -->

<table width="100%">

<tr>

<!-- Left Navigation -->

<td class="toc"><img src="spacer.gif" alt=""
width="120" height="1">

<p><a href="lions.html">Lions</a>
```

Figure 14.28 *Instead of creating a new table to combine the logo bar and the table from Figure 14.27, the code will be cleaner, leaner, and faster if I create two independent tables. I link the two tables visually by ensuring that the width of the first column in each is the same (shown here in bold).*

Figure 14.29 *The new table sits right above the old one. Since the first columns have the same width, they look like part of the same layout.*

✔ Tips

- Creating the tables separately before combining them helps pinpoint where problems may lie, should they occur.

- Only nest tables where it's absolutely necessary. They can slow down a browser considerably or even make it crash. Whenever possible, use multiple tables as an alternative.

- Use ** ** in any cell that should remain empty. Otherwise, it may not display at all.

- Use background colors *(see pages 182 and 228)* to decipher which cells belong to which tables.

- Make sure to close each table with its own closing `</table>` tag, even if you usually scoff at XHTML. Otherwise, your table will be invisible in Netscape.

- You can keep a column open to a certain minimum by inserting a transparent spacer gif *(see page 364)* and setting its width to the desired width of the column. Otherwise, browsers will try to make the column as narrow as the text will allow.

Combining Tables

Aligning a Cell's Contents

By default, a cell's contents are aligned two ways: horizontally to the left and vertically in the middle. When you're designing a liquid layout, in which cells should stretch out over an extended browser window, it's particularly important to specify where things should be aligned.

To align the contents of cells with (X)HTML:

1. Place the cursor in the initial tag for the cell, row, or section, after the name of the tag but before the final >.

2. If desired, type **align="direction"**, where *direction* is left, center, or right.

3. Type **valign="direction"**, where *direction* is either top, middle, bottom, or baseline.

To align the contents of cells with CSS:

1. In the desired rule, add **text-align: direction**, where *direction* is left, right, center, or justify.

2. And/or add **vertical-align: position**, where *position* is baseline, top, bottom, or middle.

✔ Tips

- Although the align attribute has been deprecated for other properties, it is still valid for all table elements (except table itself). The valign attribute is also still valid. Both are well supported.

- The CSS text-align and vertical-align properties are very well supported. (Only version 3 browsers have trouble with them.)

```
<table width="100%" border="0">
<tr><td ><img src="logo.jpg" width="120" alt="Northampton Zoo Logo"></td>
<td align="center"><img src="ad2.gif" width="320" alt="main ad" ></td>
<td align="right"><img src="miniad.jpg" width="160" height="100" alt="mini ad" ></td></tr></table>
<table width="100%">
<tr>
<!-- Left Navigation -->
<td class="toc" valign="top"><img src="spacer.gif" alt="" width="120" height="1">
<p><a href="lions.html">Lions</a>
<br /><a href="armadillos.html">Armadillos</a>
```

Figure 14.30 *We need the middle image in the logo bar to stay centered and the right image to stay to the right regardless of the browser window size. The left navigation items should be at the top of their cell, not the middle, which is the default.*

```
h1 {font: bold 1.8em/1em "comic sans", "verdana", sans-serif;white-space:nowrap}
.rightsidebar {width:200px;float:right}
.caption {font-size:.8em;font-style:italic;font-family:"verdana", sans-serif;text-align:center}
.toc {font-family:"verdana", sans-serif;vertical-align:top}
[snip]
.center {text-align:center}
.right {text-align:right}
.top {vertical-align:top}
```

Figure 14.31 *For the caption to the elephant photograph and the left navigation bar, I just added the alignment properties to the existing classes. For the other cells, I had to create special classes to do the alignment (which frankly, seems like a bit of trouble).*

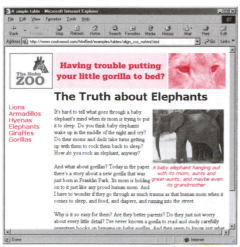

Figure 14.32 *Immediately obvious are the left navigation bar, which now sits at the top of its cell, and the caption to the photograph, which is nicely centered. Less obvious are the second and third cells of the logo bar table. But look what happens when the window is wider (Figure 14.33 below).*

Figure 14.33 *Notice how the middle cell in the top row stays centered even though the window is bigger. Perhaps more important, the right-hand cell (with the lion) stays aligned to the right, flush with the elephant picture and the rest of the text.*

- You can align all of the cells in a row by applying the `text-align` or `vertical-align` property to (or inserting the `align` or `valign` attribute in) the `tr` tag.

- The default value for `align` is *left*. The default for `valign` is *middle*.

- Note that you can justify a cell's contents with CSS but not with (X)HTML. In fact, the `justify` value exists for the `align` attribute, but I've never seen it working.

- Theoretically, you can align the contents with respect to any character you choose, for example to align monetary amounts with respect to the decimal point. In the (X)HTML, you'd use `align="char" char="x"`, where *x* is the character around which to align. In CSS, use `text-align:x`, again, where *x* is the desired alignment character. Unfortunately, no browser I've seen supports either method.

- The `baseline` value aligns the contents of each cell with the baseline of the first line of text that it contains. *Baseline* is the same as *top* when there are several lines of text and no images. *Baseline* is the same as *bottom* when the cells contain both images and text.

- The `vertical-align` property accepts a few other values (like `text-top`, `text-bottom`, `sub`, and `sup`) but these don't make sense with table cells, and so baseline is used in their place.

- For more information about `text-align`, see page 171. For more information about `vertical-align`, see page 196.

Aligning a Cell's Contents

Changing the Background

Changing the background color of one or more cells is a great way to add visual clarity and structure to your table.

To change a cell's background color with (X)HTML:

Within the desired tag, type **bgcolor= "color"**, where *color* is either a name or a hex color *(see page 46 and inside back cover)*.

To add a cell's background image with (X)HTML:

Within the desired tag, add **background = "image.url"**, where *image.url* is the image that should be displayed in the background.

To change a cell's background image or color with CSS:

In the desired rule, type **background: value**, where *value* is described in detail on pages pages 182–183.

✔ Tips

- The CSS background property is described in detail on pages 182–183. This section is devoted to explaining its peculiarities *with respect to tables*.

- The CSS background property with a color value is well supported, all the way back to IE and Netscape 3. Background images are supported back to version 4 of both browsers.

- The bgcolor attribute is deprecated in HTML 4. The background attribute for the table tag was never even officially a part of the HTML 4 specification. (It's been deprecated as an attribute to the body tag.). The W3C would prefer you use the CSS background property. Nevertheless, both bgcolor and background continue to be well supported.

```
<body text="#006666" bgcolor="white">

<table width="100%" border="0" class="logobar"
bgcolor="#ffff66">

<tr><td ><img src="logo.jpg" width="120"
alt="Northampton Zoo Logo"></td>

<td class="center"><img src="ad2.gif"
width="320" alt="main ad" ></td>

<td class="right"><img src="miniad.jpg"
width="160" height="100" alt="mini ad"
></td></tr></table>

<table width="100%">

<tr>

<!-- Left Navigation -->

<td class="toc" bgcolor="#339966"><img
src="spacer.gif" alt="" width="120" height="1">
```

Figure 14.34 *You can add the* bgcolor *attribute to any part of the table. Here I've matched the background of the logo bar to the color of the middle image so that it looks like it stretches with the browser window. And I've added a dark green background to the left navigation bar.*

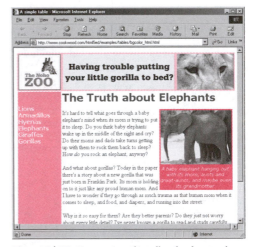

Figure 14.35 *You can see the yellow background around and between the images in the logo bar. Notice that the green background also surrounds the nested table and serves as the background for its text (that I've made white).*

Changing the Background

body {color:#006666; background:white}

h1 {font: bold 1.8em/1em "comic sans", "verdana", sans-serif;white-space:nowrap}

.rightsidebar {width:200px; float:right; background:#006666; color:white}

.caption {font-size:.8em; font-style:italic; font-family:"verdana", sans-serif; text-align:center;color:white}

.toc {background: #339966 url(longerfish.jpg); font-family:"verdana", sans-serif;vertical-align:top}

[snip]

.logobar {background:#ffff66}

Figure 14.36 In this example, I've created all the background colors with CSS instead of (X)HTML. In addition, I've added a background image for the left navigation bar.

Figure 14.37 Is the space around the cells bugging you yet? We're getting there next!

- You can add the `bgcolor` attribute to any table tag (`table`, `tr`, `thead`, etc.) to change the color of the cells in one or more rows or columns at once.

- The `bgcolor` attribute in an individual cell (`th` or `td`) overrides the color specified in a row (in a `tr` tag), which in turn overrides the color specified for a group of rows or columns (in `thead`, `colgroup`, etc.), which, as you might expect, overrides the color specified for the entire table (in the `table` tag).

- Consult *CSS Colors* on page 46 and the inside back cover for help choosing colors.

- You can add both a background image and a background color to a cell. The background color will both display before the image and then continue to shine through the transparent parts of the image, if there are any.

- If you set a background image for the whole table, beware! Netscape 4 copies the whole image into each cell individually instead of filling the entire table with a single image.

- You can also set the color of the contents of a cell. For information, consult *Changing the Foreground Color* on page 184. For information about changing the color of the borders, consult *Adding a Border* on page 218.

- Make sure that your background images do not distract from the content that is placed on top of them. I am continually amazed at how many sites use bizarrely busy backgrounds with text that is for all intents and purposes illegible.

Controlling the Space

(X)HTML has long had two attributes for the table tag that allow it to control spacing between the contents of a cell and its border (cellpadding) and between one border and the next (cellspacing). And while they're well supported and perfectly reasonable, they're not very flexible. You can't, for example, affect the cell spacing on a single side, or add cell padding just to a few cells in a table.

CSS on the other hand lets you use the now familiar padding property *(see page 188)* to control space on every side of a cell, as well as between paragraphs and other elements. It is a welcome substitute for cellpadding.

Unfortunately, the border-spacing property, which could stand in very well for cellspacing, is supported by Netscape 6 but not yet by Explorer (as of version 6).

To control the padding with (X)HTML:

In the table tag, type **cellpadding="n"**, where *n* is the number of pixels that should appear between the contents of a cell and its border.

To control the spacing with (X)HTML:

In the table tag, type **cellspacing="n"**, where *n* is the number of pixels that should appear between one cell border and the next.

To control the padding with CSS:

In the desired rule, type **padding: value**, where *value* is a length in pixels or a percentage of the parent element.

To control the space between cell borders with CSS:

In the desired rule, type **border-spacing: value**, where *value* is a length in pixels or a percentage of the parent element.

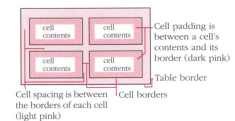

Figure 14.38 *Cell spacing adds space between cells. Cell padding adds space between a cell's contents and its border.*

```
<table width="100%" cellspacing="0"
cellpadding="0" border="0" class="logobar"
bgcolor="#ffff66">

<tr><td ><img src="logo.jpg" width="120"
alt="Northampton Zoo Logo"></td>
```

Figure 14.39 *I have set both the* cellpadding *and* cellspacing *to zero so that there is no extra space around or between the cells of my logo bar (and other elements).*

Figure 14.40 *Finally, the extra spaces between the cells disappear (especially in the logo bar) and the table appears seamless.*

```
<br /><a href="gorillas.html">Gorillas</a></p>
</td>
<td>     </td>
<td class="top">
<h1>The Truth about Elephants</h1>
```

Figure 14.41 *One way to make spaces on a single side of a cell or group of cells is to add a cell filled with non-breaking spaces (in our example, between the left navigation bar and the main content).*

Figure 14.42 *The extra space cell appears as requested. Of course, it will be invisible, not pink.*

```
h1 {font: bold 1.8em/1em "comic sans", "verdana",
sans-serif;white-space:nowrap;margin:10px 0px 5px}

p {margin:0px 0px 10px 0px}

table, td {border-spacing:0}

.rightsidebar {width:200px; float:right; color:white;
background:#006666; margin:0px 0px 5px 10px}

.caption {font-size:.8em;font-style:italic;font-family:
"verdana", sans-serif;text-align:center; color:white;
padding:5px;margin:0}

.toc {background: #339966 url(longerfish.jpg);
font-family:"verdana", sans-serif;vertical-align:top;
padding:25px 10px 0px}
```

Figure 14.43 *In this example, I use a combination of the* padding, margin, border-spacing *properties.*

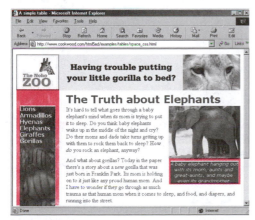

Figure 14.44 *The spacing looks much better now.*

✔ **Tips**

■ The default value for cell padding is 1. The default value for cell spacing is 2.

■ When using tables for layout, it's perhaps easiest to set both the `cellpadding` and `cellspacing` to zero and then selectively add padding with CSS.

■ Sometimes it's just simpler to create an empty cell and fill it with non-breaking spaces. It's a bit of a hack, but it's fast and easy **(Figures 14.41 and 14.42)**.

■ You can use the CSS `margin` property *(see page 189)* to control the spacing between h1 and p elements that may be contained in cells, or the space around a table.

■ Remember that the CSS alternative to `cellpadding` is called `padding`, while the CSS alternative to `cellspacing` is called `border-spacing`. The `padding` property can be used on any element; `border-spacing` is just for table cells.

■ The `border-spacing` property is inherited but `padding` is not.

■ Netscape 6 is so scrupulous with standards that it adds a bit of space under inline images in table cells—for descenders, one must presume. As long as you only have one image per cell, you can get rid of the space by making the images block level *(see page 28)*. Or you can trigger quirks mode *(see page 39)*.

■ Netscape 4, on the other hand, is sloppy with returns and spaces. Don't put any carriage returns in table cells.

■ Netscape 4 and up support the `hspace` and `vspace` attributes for the `table` element, which add extra space between the table and the text or elements next to it. Internet Explorer does not support these attributes. For more details, see page 113.

Controlling the Space

Spanning a Cell across Columns

With a table, it's often useful to straddle or *span* one cell across a few columns. For example, with multicolumn text, you could span a headline across the columns of text.

To span a cell across two columns:

1. When you get to the point in which you need to define the cell that spans more than one column, type **<td**.

2. Type **colspan="n">**, where *n* equals the number of columns the cell should span.

3. Type the cell's contents.

4. Type **</td>**.

5. Complete the rest of the table. If you create a cell that spans 2 columns, you will need to define one less cell in that row. If you create a cell that spans 3 columns, you will define two less cells for the row. And so on.

✔ Tips

- Each row in a table must have the same number of cells defined. Cells that span across columns count for as many cells as the value of their `colspan` attribute.

- Writing the HTML code for a table from scratch is, uh, challenging—especially when you start spanning columns and rows. It helps to sketch it out on paper first, as described on page 216, to get a handle on which information goes in which row and column. Or you can cheat and use a Web page authoring program like FrontPage or Dreamweaver to get started. You can always open the file and edit the (X)HTML by hand later.

- There is no CSS alternative for `colspan`.

```
<table width="100%" cellspacing="0"
cellpadding="0" border="0">

<tr><!-- Left Navigation -->

<td class="toc"><img src="spacer.gif" alt=""
width="100" height="1">[snip]</td>

<td>     </td>

<td class="top">

<h1>The Truth about Elephants</h1>

[snip]

mind, I could only find a picture of an
elephant?)</p>

</td></tr>

<tr><td colspan="3" class="copyright">
Copyright &copy; 2002 by Northampton
Zoological Society, Inc.</td></tr>

</table>
```

Figure 14.45 *The lower table now has two rows. The first row contains the left navigation cell, the non-breaking spaces cell, and the main content cell. The second row (highlighted) contains a single cell with copyright information that spans the three columns.*

Figure 14.46 *The new row spans all three columns.*

```
<table width="100%" cellspacing="0"
cellpadding="0" border="0">

<tr><!-- Left Navigation -->

<td class="toc" rowspan="2"><img
src="spacer.gif" alt="" width="100"
height="1">[snip]</td>

<td>     </td>

<td class="top">

<h1>The Truth about Elephants</h1>

[snip]

mind, I could only find a picture of an
elephant?)</p>

</td></tr>

<tr><td colspan="2" class="copyright"> Copyright
&copy; 2002 by Northampton Zoological Society,
Inc.</td></tr>
```

Figure 14.47 *I can make the left navigational bar span both rows, but then I have to adjust the second row's cell so that it only spans the second and third columns.*

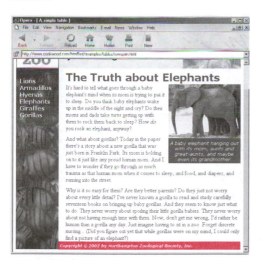

Figure 14.48 *Now the left navigational bar spans both rows and the copyright row only needs to span two columns.*

Spanning a Cell across Rows

Creating a cell that spans more than one row is essentially the same as spanning cells over more than one column—just from another direction.

To span a cell across two or more rows:

1. When you get to the point in which you need to define the cell that spans more than one row, type **<td**.

2. Type **rowspan="n">**, where *n* equals the number of rows the cell should span.

3. Type the cell's contents.

4. Type **</td>**.

5. Complete the rest of the table. If you define a cell with a rowspan of 2, you will not need to define the corresponding cell in the next row. If you define a cell with a rowspan of 3, you will not need to define the corresponding cells in the next two rows.

✔ Tips

- Each column in a table must have the same number of cells defined. Cells that span across rows count for as many cells as the value of their rowspan attribute.

- There is no CSS alternative for rowspan.

Dividing Your Table into Column Groups

When using tables for displaying tabular data (their classic purpose), you can divide your table into two kinds of column groups: structural and non-structural. The former control where dividing lines, or rules, are drawn *(see page 238)*. The latter do not. Both let you apply formatting to an entire column (or groups of columns) of cells all at once.

To divide a table into structural column groups:

1. After the `table` (and `caption`) tags, type **<colgroup**.

2. If the column group has more than one column, type **span="n"**, where *n* is the number of columns in the group.

3. If desired, define the attributes for the column group.

4. Type the final **>**.

5. If desired, define individual columns as specified below with `col`.

6. Type **</colgroup>**.

To divide a table into non-structural column groups:

1. After the `table` (and `caption`) tags, type **<col**.

2. If the column group has more than one column, type **span="n"**, where *n* is the number of columns in the group.

3. If desired, define the attributes for the column group.

4. Type the final **/>**.

5. Repeat steps 1–4 for each column group that you wish to define.

```
<table width="100%" border="1">

<caption align=top>Bear sightings in Western Massachusetts</caption>

<colgroup class="cities" />

<colgroup span="3" class="data" />


<tr>

<td> </td>

<td>Babies</td>
```

Figure 14.49 *I can make the left navigational bar span both rows, but then I have to adjust the second row's cell so that it only spans the second and third columns.*

Figure 14.50 *The* `colgroup` *element makes it easy to select all of the cells in a column and apply formatting to them in one fell swoop. Here we've applied a font, size, and right alignment to the column with the city names, and center alignment to the other three columns.*

Figure 14.51 *Netscape 6 does not support the* `colgroup` *element.*

```
<table width="100%" border="1">

<caption align=top>Bear sightings in Western
Massachusetts</caption>

<colgroup class="cities" />

<colgroup span="3" class="data" >

    <col span="2"/>

    <col class="totals" />

</colgroup>

<tr>

<td> </td>

<td>Babies</td>
```

Figure 14.52 *Now I divide the second column group into two separate non-structural column groups (with col) so that I can format an entire column at a time without affecting how rules are drawn (see page 237).*

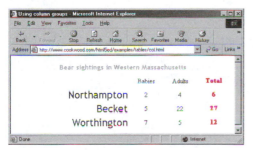

Figure 14.53 *I've used the non-structural column group to format the last column in bold type—without affecting where interior rules will be drawn.*

Figure 14.54 *Still nothing from Netscape.*

✔ Tips

- Both types of column group definitions are completely ignored by Netscape.

- Use `colgroup` when you want to determine where dividing lines (rules) should go. Use `col` for *everything but* deciding where dividing lines go. For more information on drawing dividing lines, consult page 238.

- You can use many attributes to format column groups, including `bgcolor`, `style`, and others.

- You can divide column groups (`colgroup`) into columns (`col`) in order to add non-structural information (like size, alignment, or whatever) to individual columns within structural column groups. Simply type the `col` tag *after* the parent `colgroup` tag **(Figure 14.52)**. Note that `col` tags' attributes override the attributes in the `colgroup` tag.

- If a column group is not divided into individual columns, you may combine the opening and closing tags: `<colgroup span="3" />`. In HTML, the closing tag for `colgroup` is optional.

- The `col` element is always empty. In HTML you may omit the `/`.

- If the column group only contains one column, you don't need to use the `span` attribute. Its default is 1.

- Header cells—those marked with the `th` tag—are not affected by the alignment specified in a column group. For more information on aligning cells, consult *Aligning a Cell's Contents* on page 226.

Dividing Your Table into Column Groups

Dividing the Table into Horizontal Sections

You can also mark a horizontal section of your table—one or more rows—and then format it all at once. You'll also be able to draw dividing lines between sections, instead of between individual rows (*see page 237*).

To divide the table into horizontal sections:

1. Before the first `tr` tag of the section you want to create, type **<thead**, **<tbody**, or **<tfoot**.

2. If desired, define the desired attributes for the section.

3. Type **>**.

4. If necessary, create the section's contents.

5. Close the section with **</thead>**, **</tbody>**, or **</tfoot>**.

✔ Tips

■ You can apply CSS (or indeed, formatting attributes) to horizontal sections of cells.

■ Horizontal section tags go *after* column group tags (*see page 234*).

■ At least one `tbody` tag is required in every table. Both XHTML, as long as it is served as an HTML file (e.g., with the .html extension) and HTML will create an *implicit* `tbody` if you omit it. XHTML served as XML (with the .xml extension) *requires* an explicit `tbody` element.

■ You can only have one `thead` and one `tfoot`.

■ In HTML, the closing tags are optional. A section is automatically closed when you begin the next.

```
<table width="100%" border="1">

<caption align=top>Bear sightings in Western Massachusetts</caption>

<colgroup class="cities" />
<colgroup span="3" class="data" >
    <col span="2"/>
    <col class="totals" />
</colgroup>

<thead class="titles">

<tr>
<td> </td>
<td>Babies</td>
<td>Adults</td>
<td>Total</td></tr></thead>

<tbody><tr>

<td>Northampton</td>
```

Figure 14.55 *Once the first row is in a* thead *section, I can define a class of styles for it which will be applied to each cell in the* thead.

Figure 14.56 *All of the elements in the* thead *section are formatted and they will be considered together when the interior borders are drawn.*

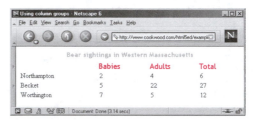

Figure 14.57 *Notice that Netscape does understand the horizontal section elements.*

```
<table width="100%" border="1" frame="vsides">

<caption align=top>Bear sightings in Western
Massachusetts</caption>

<colgroup class="cities" />
<colgroup span="3" class="data" >
    <col span="2"/>
    <col class="totals" />
</colgroup>

<thead class="titles">

<tr>

<td> </td>

<td>Babies</td>
```

Figure 14.58 *Add the* frame *attribute within the* table *tag.*

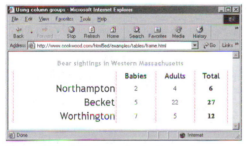

Figure 14.59 *With* frame="vsides", *Explorer incorrectly shows not only the external vertical sides of the table, but also the vertical sides of the individual cells. You can work around that by setting* rules *to* none *(next page), but meanwhile it's a bug.*

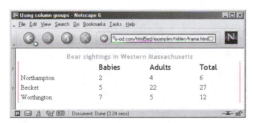

Figure 14.60 *Netscape gets* frame *right, showing only the external vertical sides. (Unfortunately it drops the ball with* rules *on the next page.)*

Choosing Which Borders to Display

When you use the border attribute *(see page 218)*, a border appears between each cell and also around the table itself. (X)HTML lets you choose which external sides of the table should have a border as well as which internal borders should be displayed.

To choose which external sides should have a border:

In the table tag, type **frame="location"**, where *location* is one of the values listed below:

- void, for no external borders

- above, for a single border on top

- below, for a single border on bottom

- hsides, for a border on both the top and bottom sides

- vsides, for a border on both the right and left sides

- rhs, for a single border on the right side

- lhs, for a single border on the left side

- box or border, for a border on all sides (default)

continued

Choosing Which Borders to Display

To choose which internal borders should be displayed:

In the table tag, type **rules="area"**, where *area* is one of the following values:

- none, for no internal rules

- rows, for horizontal rules between each row in the table

- cols, for vertical rules between each column in the table **(Figures 14.61 and 14.62)**

- groups, for rules between column groups (created with the colgroup element described on pages 234–235) and horizontal sections as defined by the tags described on pages 234–236 **(Figure 14.64)**

- all, for rules between each row and column in the table (default)

✔ Tips

- It is the groups value for rules that illustrates the difference between colgroup and col. The colgroup element defines what is considered a column group and therefore where lines are drawn with the groups value. The col element does not.

- It is also the groups value which makes this whole technique worthwhile. Otherwise, you can use the CSS border property to get much more control over borders *(see page 218)*.

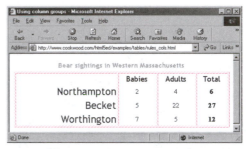

```
<table width="100%" rules="cols">

<caption align="top">Bear sightings in Western Massachusetts</caption>

<colgroup class="cities" />

<colgroup span="3" class="data" >
```

Figure 14.61 *The* rules *attribute determines which internal borders should be displayed. In this example, we will show the column borders.*

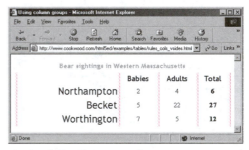

Figure 14.62 *Here we've got* rules="cols". *Explorer again mistakenly shows the external border as well as the interior column rules.*

Figure 14.63 *When we specify* frame="vsides" *and* rules="cols", *we get the desired effect: vertical external rules and vertical internal rules.*

Figure 14.64 *The attribute* rules="groups" *is particularly useful when you've divided the table into column and row groups (see pages 234–236). Instead of rules between each column, rules are only displayed between column groups.*

Choosing Which Borders to Display

Figure 14.65 *Imagine a table with several words in a column that you don't want split among several lines, no matter how narrow the browser window gets.*

```
<tr>

<td nowrap="nowrap">Worthington Center</td>

<td>7</td>

<td>5</td>

<td>12</td></tr></tbody>
```

Figure 14.66 *Just add the* nowrap *attribute to the* td *cell that should not be broken into multiple lines.*

Figure 14.67 *No matter how narrow the window and the table get, the cell's contents will stay on a single line, even if it means some of the table extends beyond the window.*

Controlling Line Breaks in a Cell

Unless you specify otherwise, a browser will divide the lines of text in a cell as it decides on the height and width of each column and row. The nowrap attribute forces the browser to keep all the text in a cell on one line.

To keep text in a cell on one single line:

In a td or th cell, type **nowrap= "nowrap"**.

✔ Tips

■ In HTML, but not XHTML, you can just type **nowrap** by itself.

■ Browsers will make the cell (and the table that contains it) as wide as it needs to accommodate the single line of text— even if it looks really ugly. I don't recommend using the nowrap tag with tables used for layout. It overrides the width attribute.

■ You can use regular line breaks (br) between words to mark where you *do* want the text to break.

■ You can also type ** ** instead of a regular space to connect pairs of words or other elements with non-breaking spaces.

■ For more information on line breaks, consult *Creating the Foundation* on page 62, *Keeping Lines Together* on page 358, and *Creating Discretionary Line Breaks* on page 359.

Speeding up Table Display

Although tables are extremely powerful, they can be very slow to appear in your visitor's browser. The major factor is that the browser must calculate the width and height of the table before it can begin to display the cells. So, if you can keep the browser's calculations to a minimum, the table will appear more quickly and your visitors may actually wait to see it.

To speed up table display:

■ Keep tables as small as possible. Where you can, divide large tables into smaller ones.

■ Specify the width of the table in pixels *(see page 220)*.

■ Use absolute values (in pixels) or percentages for determining cell width.

■ Only specify proportional widths for cells, columns, and horizontal sections when you've already set a fixed width in pixels for the entire table.

■ Divide your table into column groups.

■ Add `table-layout:fixed` to your `table` element's style rule **(Figure 14.68)**. This instructs browsers (IE 5+ and Netscape 6+) to look only at the first row of a table in order to determine the widths of the columns, instead of worrying about every cell in every row. While the contents of some cells may not fit (their display is governed by the `over-flow` property—see page 193), the table renders much more quickly.

```
table {table-display: fixed;}
```

Figure 14.68 *The* table-display *property with a value of* fixed *helps tables render more quickly. It is useful for tables whose cells are regular in size.*

FRAMES

One of the trickier parts of creating a Web site is giving your visitors an idea of the scope of information contained in your site and then making that information easily accessible without confusing or overwhelming them. By dividing a page, called a *frameset*, into frames, you allow the visitor to see more than one page at a time, without completely cluttering up their screen. Each frame contains its own Web page, and theoretically could be viewed independently in a separate window.

The beauty of having several Web pages open on a screen at a time lies in the ability to interrelate the information in each of the pages. For example, you can have a stationary banner frame across the top of the window that includes your company name and logo. Meanwhile, a dynamic frame on the left side of the window can include a table of contents. Finally, the main area of the window will be devoted to the *contents frame*, whose data changes each time your visitor clicks on a new topic in the table of contents.

Frames do have some disadvantages. They can be hard to navigate, their scroll bars can hog precious screen real estate, they can be hard to get indexed in a search engine like Google, and once indexed they may appear independently without benefit of their surrounding and supporting frames.

In fact, the W3C discourages the use of frames. Instead, they recommend embedding content on a page through fixed positioning *(see page 180)* and the use of the `object` element *(see page 260)*.

Creating a Simple Frameset

Think of a frameset as a window with individual panes. Each pane shows different information. You decide how many panes your window will have, what size each pane will be, how its borders should look and if it should have scroll bars or not. Once you've built the window, you create the initial landscape behind the window by assigning individual URLs to each pane, that is, frame.

First, you'll create a simple frameset with three horizontal rows all in the same column.

To create a simple frameset:

1. After the </head> tag, type **<frameset**.

2. Type **rows="a** where *a* is the height of the first row. The value may either be a percentage (40%), an exact number of pixels (35), or completely variable (with an asterisk *), depending on the size of the other rows.

3. Type **, b** where *b* is the height of the second row, again expressed as a percentage, an absolute value in pixels, or a variable (with an asterisk: *).

4. Repeat step 3 for each additional row.

5. Type **">** to complete the row definition.

6. Type **<frame** to assign a URL and other attributes to the top row/pane.

7. Type **name="name"** where *name* is a word that identifies this particular frame's use, like *banner*, *index*, or *contents*.

8. Type **src="content.html">** where *content.html* is the URL for the page that will be initially displayed in this frame when the visitor first navigates to this frameset.

9. Repeat steps 6–8 for each row you defined in steps 2–4.

```
<!DOCTYPE html PUBLIC "-//W3C//DTD XHTML
1.0 Frameset//EN" "http://www.w3.org/TR/
xhtml1/DTD/xhtml1-frameset.dtd">

<html xmlns="http://www.w3.org/1999/xhtml">

<head>

<title>Frames in Rows</title>

</head>

<frameset rows="65,*,60">

<frame name="banner" src="banner.html" />

<frame name="photos" src="openingpage.html"
/>

<frame name="buttons" src="buttons.html" />

</frameset>

</html>
```

Figure 15.1 *The frameset page has no actual content. Instead, it defines the frames and links them with the pages that hold the initial content. Notice that framesets use either the HTML or XHTML Frameset* DOCTYPE. *If you don't want to type it, you can copy it from my Web site (see page 24).*

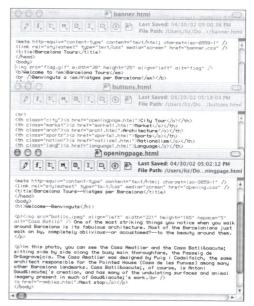

Figure 15.2 *Once you've created a frameset, the next step is to create the pages that will appear within the frames.*

Figure 15.3 *Viewed individually, the pages shown in Figure 15.2 appear just as any other Web page.*

Figure 15.4 *Here is the page from Figure 15.3 shown as one of three frames in a frameset.*

10. Type **</frameset>** to complete the frameset and the construction of your "window".

11. Create the pages that will be displayed initially in the frames, that is, those referenced by the `src` tag in step 8 **(Figures 15.2 and 15.3)**. This is the "landscape" behind the window.

✔ Tips

- You should use the Frameset `DOCTYPE` for frameset pages *(see page 38)*.

- Create a title in each framed page so that they are indexed by search engines *(see page 426)*.

- Don't forget the closing `</frameset>` tag! If you do, older versions of Netscape will display a blank page.

- The name you define in step 7 is used when you're targeting links to this frame. For more details, see page 255.

- Use an asterisk (*) to allocate to a frame whatever leftover space there is available in the window.

- You can use more than one asterisk at a time. The remaining space will be divided equally among the frames marked with an asterisk. To divide the remaining space unequally, add a number to the asterisk, e.g., **2***. In this case, two thirds of the remaining space will go to the frame marked 2* and the last third will go to the frame marked with just a plain asterisk.

- The `body` element is only used when offering alternatives to frames *(see page 259)*.

- To support visitors whose browsers don't understand frames, see page 259.

Creating a Simple Frameset

Creating Frames in Columns

Another simple way to divide a frameset is into columns instead of rows.

To create frames in columns:

1. Type **<frameset** after the </head> tag in the frameset page.

2. Type **cols="a,b">** where *a* and *b* (and any others) represent the width of the corresponding column, as a percentage, number of pixels, or variable (*).

3. Type **<frame** to define the leftmost frame/column.

4. Type **name="name"** where *name* is a word that identifies this particular frame's use, like *banner*, *index*, or *contents*.

5. Type **src="content.html">** where *content.html* is the URL of the page that you want to be displayed in this frame when the visitor initially navigates to this frameset.

6. Repeat steps 3–5 for each frame/column.

7. Type **</frameset>**.

8. Create the Web pages that will be shown initially in the frameset page.

✔ Tips

■ Consult the tips on page 243 for details on allocating the space among frames with variables (*).

■ A frame's name is used when you're targeting links to appear in the frame. For details, consult *Targeting Links to Particular Frames* on page 255.

```
</head>
<frameset cols="110,*,100">
<frame name="banner" src="bannercols.html" />
<frame name="photos" src="openingpagecols.html" />
<frame name="buttons" src="buttonscols.html" />
</frameset>
```

Figure 15.5 *To create a page with frames in columns, use the* cols *attribute instead of* rows.

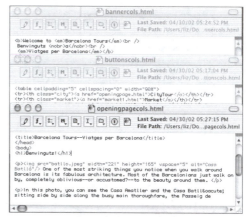

Figure 15.6 *Don't forget to create the content for the frames. Although these pages are very similar to the ones shown in Figure 15.2, they have been adjusted slightly to fit better vertically.*

Figure 15.7 *Browsers show the columns of frames in very much the same way as they show frames in rows.*

Creating Frames in Columns

```
</head>
<frameset frameborder="0" rows="*, 193, 104,
165, *" cols="*, 110, 110, 110, *">

<frame name="border1" src="border.html"
scrolling="no" marginwidth="1"
marginheight="1" />

[snip five more borders]

<frame name="border6" src="border.html"
scrolling="no" marginwidth="1"
marginheight="1" />

<frame name="topleft" src="balcony1.html"
scrolling="no" marginwidth="1"
marginheight="1" />

<frame name="topmiddle" src="balcony2.html"
scrolling="no" marginwidth="1"
marginheight="1" />
```

Figure 15.8 *You set the size of rows and columns in the* frameset *tag. Then define each row from left to right, and from top to bottom.*

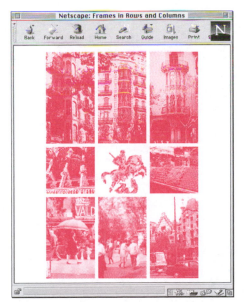

Figure 15.9 *Notice that the first and last rows and first and last columns of frames are set to take up all the left-over space not used up by the photos. Then I set each of those frames to display an empty page with a white background. No matter what size window my visitors look at this page with, the outside frames will expand or contract, but the photo filled frames will stay the same size.*

Creating Frames in Rows and Columns

Some information is best displayed horizontally while some looks better vertically. You can create both rows and columns in the same frameset to accommodate different kinds of information.

To create a frameset with both rows and columns:

1. Type **<frameset** to begin.

2. Type **rows="a, b"** where *a* and *b* (and any others) represent the height of the corresponding rows.

3. Type **cols="x, y"** where *x* and *y* (and any others) represent the width of the corresponding columns.

4. Type **>**.

5. Define the first frame in the first row by typing **<frame name="name" src="initialurl.html">**.

6. Define the rest of the frames in the first row from left to right.

7. Repeat steps 5–6 for each row, from top to bottom.

8. Type **</frameset>** to complete the frameset.

✔ Tips

- Defining rows and columns in this way limits you to the same number of frames in each row or column. To create one row with two frames and another row with three, you'll have to combine multiple framesets *(see page 246).*

- There is more about this technique (and this particular example) on my Web site *(see page 24).*

Combining Framesets

One of the most common layouts for frames you'll see on the Web is to have one row at the top that spans the width of the browser, and then a second row divided into two frames. This effect is achieved by inserting an additional frameset in the second row.

To combine framesets:

1. Make a sketch of your frameset and determine how many rows and columns you will need.

2. Type **<frameset** to begin.

3. Type **rows="a, b">** where *a* and *b* (and any others) represent the height of the corresponding rows.

4. In the example in Figure 15.10, the first and third rows are a single frame while the second row is divided into columns. For a row with just a single frame, type **<frame name="name" src="contents.html">** in the usual way.

5. For the second row, which is divided into columns in this example, type **<frameset cols="a, b">** where *a* and *b* (and any others) represent the width of each column in the row.

6. Type **<frame name="name" src= "contents.html">** where *name* is the reference for the frame and *contents.html* is the page that will be initially shown in that frame.

7. Repeat step 6 for each column in the frameset. (In this example, there are two columns, so you'll have to define two frames in the inner frameset.)

8. When you've finished defining the frames/columns in the divided row, type **</frameset>**.

```
<!DOCTYPE html PUBLIC "-//W3C//DTD XHTML
1.0 Frameset//EN" "http://www.w3.org/TR/
xhtml1/DTD/xhtml1-frameset.dtd">

<html xmlns="http://www.w3.org/1999/xhtml">

<head>

<meta http-equiv="content-type"
content="text/html; charset=iso-8859-1" />

<title>Combining Framesets</title>

</head>

<frameset rows="65,*,60">

<frame name="banner" src="banner.html" />

<frameset cols="120,*">

<frame name="index" src="indexcity.html" />

<frame name="photos" src="openingpage.html"
/>

</frameset>

<frame name="buttons" src="buttons.html" />

</frameset>

</html>
```

Figure 15.10 *First create the outer frameset. Then define each row from top to bottom. For rows that will be divided, use an inner frameset. The highlighted area here (the inner frameset) corresponds to the second row of the outer frameset.*

Figure 15.11 *In this example, the first and third rows are simple frames while the second row is a frameset divided into two columns.*

9. Continue defining each row individually. For a row with just one frame (i.e., just one column), just use a `frame` tag. For rows divided into multiple columns, repeat steps 5–8.

10. Type **</frameset>** to complete the outer frameset.

✔ Tips

- It's absolutely crucial that you add a closing `</frameset>` tag for each opening `<frameset>` that you create. Otherwise, Netscape 4.x won't show anything at all.

- Although I've defined the rows first and then the columns in this example, you can define the columns first if it works better for your particular layout. In fact, when adjusting the borders, both methods have distinct advantages (see the tips on page 253).

- It is important to stress that not every row need be divided into columns. For rows with a single frame (i.e., that span the entire window from left to right), just use a `frame` tag. For rows divided into columns, use an inner frameset.

- If you want to create the *same number* of frames in each row and each column, you don't need to combine multiple framesets. For details, consult *Creating Frames in Rows and Columns* on page 245.

- You can use combined framesets to change more than one frame at a time. For more information, consult *Changing Multiple Frames with One Link* on page 326.

Combining Framesets

Creating an Inline Frame

If you want to mix text, graphics, and a frame all on one page, you'll need to create a *floating* or *inline* frame.

To create an inline frame:

1. In the container page, type **<iframe src="frame.url"**, where *frame.url* is the page that should be initially displayed in the inline frame.

2. Type **name="name"**, where *name* is a word that identifies this inline frame.

3. Type **width="x" height="y"** where *x* and *y* represent the width and height, respectively, of the inline frame in pixels.

4. Type **>**.

5. Type the text that should appear if the browser can't display the frame.

6. Type **</iframe>**.

✔ Tips

- You can also use the `frameborder` *(see page 253)*, `hspace`/`vspace` *(see page 113)*, `scrolling` *(see page 250)*, and `marginwidth`/`marginheight` *(see page 249)* attributes with inline frames.

- You can use the deprecated `align` attribute *(see page 110)* or the CSS `float` property *(see page 194)* to wrap text around an inline frame.

- Netscape 4.x and Opera 5 for Mac do not support inline frames.

- For Explorer, you can also specify the `height` and `width` as a percentage of the parent window. Netscape 6.x can deal with a percentage `width` but flips out if you specify a percentage `height`.

</head>

<body bgcolor="#FFFFFF">

<h1>Barcelona Tours</h1>

Here's an idea of what the Barcelona Tours home page looks like:

<hr />

<iframe src="bcntourrc.html" name="bcntours" width="500" height="450">The <a href="bcntourrc.html">Barcelona Tours</a> page contains great photos and essential tips for making your vacation a success.</iframe>

</body>

</html>

Figure 15.12 *Specify at least the width of your inline frames in pixels (and not a percentage) so that Netscape 6 can view them properly.*

Figure 15.13 *Floating frames function similarly to images, flowing with the rest of the content on the page.*

Figure 15.14 *Note how the contents of each frame with default margins begins slightly down and to the right.*

```
</head>
<frameset rows="65,*,60">
<frame name="banner" src="banner.html"
marginheight="0" marginwidth="0" />
<frameset cols="120,*">
<frame name="index" src="indexcity.html"
marginheight="0" marginwidth="0" />
<frame name="photos" src="openingpage.html"
marginheight="0" marginwidth="0" />
</frameset>
```

Figure 15.15 *Adjust the margins of each frame by adding a* marginwidth *and/or* marginheight *tag to the desired* frame *tags. In this example, all the margins have been set to 0.*

Figure 15.16 *With the margins at 0, each frame's contents start in the top-left corner of each frame.*

Adjusting a Frame's Margins

All browsers display a frame's contents with a default margin of from 8 to 15 pixels on each side **(Figure 15.14)**. You can adjust the margin so that there is more space, or, if you prefer, so that the frame's contents begin in the top-left corner.

To adjust a frame's margins:

1. In the desired frame tag, before the final >, type **marginwidth="w"** where *w* is the desired amount of space, in pixels, between the left and right edges of the frame and the frame's contents **(Figure 15.15)**.

2. Type **marginheight="h"** where *h* is the desired amount of space, in pixels, between the top and bottom edges of the frame and the frame's contents.

✔ Tips

- The margin is transparent and thus always appears to be the same color as the background of the page displayed in the frame.

- While these two attributes have yet to be deprecated, you can also adjust the margin of the individual pages with the CSS margin property. For more information, consult *Setting the Margins around an Element* on page 189.

Showing or Hiding Scroll Bars

You can decide whether each individual frame should have a scroll bar all the time, never, or only when needed. *Only when needed* means that the scroll bars will appear only when there is more information than can be shown at one time in the frame. If the visitor makes the window big enough, these scroll bars will eventually disappear.

To show scroll bars all the time:

In the `frame` tag of the particular frame for which you wish to show the scroll bar, type **scrolling="yes"**.

To hide scroll bars all the time:

In the `frame` tag of the particular frame for which you wish to hide the scroll bar, type **scrolling="no"**.

✔ Tips

■ The default is for scroll bars to appear only when necessary, that is, when there is more information than can fit in the frame. To use the default, you can type **scrolling="auto"** or, more simply, don't type any `scrolling` tag at all.

■ There are few things more frustrating than jumping to a frameset page with tiny little frames that make it impossible to view the entire contents. Even worse is when you cannot scroll around (or make the frame bigger—see page 254) to make the hidden information visible. To avoid frustrating *your* visitors, make sure you test your frameset page in a small window and ensure that all the frames without scroll bars are big enough to display their entire contents.

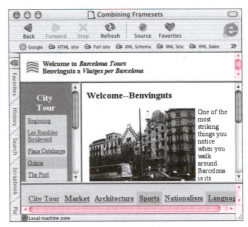

Figure 15.17 *These extra scroll bars are ugly!*

```
<frameset rows="65,*,60">

<frame name="banner" src="banner.html"
scrolling="no" />

<frameset cols="120,*">

<frame name="index" src="indexcity.html" />

<frame name="photos" src="openingpage.html"
/></frameset>

<frame name="buttons" src="buttons.html"
scrolling="no" /></frameset>
```

Figure 15.18 *So that the top and bottom frames never display scroll bars, add* `scrolling="no"` *to their* `frame` *tags.*

Figure 15.19 *Eliminating scroll bars from certain areas makes the information much clearer and more attractive. But be careful not to take away scroll bars from areas that need them. Remember, you can't control the size of your visitor's window.*

```
<frameset bordercolor="#ff0000"
rows="65,*,60">

<frame name="banner" src="banner.html"
scrolling="no"/>

<frameset cols="120,*" >

<frame name="index" src="indexcity.html"/>

<frame name="photos" src="openingpage.html" />

</frameset>

<frame name="buttons" src="buttons.html"
scrolling="no"/>
```

Figure 15.20 *You can add the* `bordercolor` *tag to any frameset or frame tag. Here it's been added to the topmost frameset tag so that it will affect all the frames contained within.*

Figure 15.21 *Both Netscape and Explorer support the non-standard* `bordercolor` *attribute. They also both add a bit of black to the bottom part of the border, regardless of the color you've chosen.*

Adjusting the Color of the Borders

In theory, you can change the color of each frame individually. In practice, however, since the borders are shared between frames, the possibilities are more limited. Unfortunately, the `bordercolor` attribute is not standard (X)HTML.

To adjust the color of all the borders in the frameset:

Inside the topmost `frameset` tag before the final >, type **bordercolor="color"**, where *color* is either one of the sixteen predefined colors or a hexadecimal color *(see page 46 or the inside back cover).*

To change the color of rows, columns, or individual frames:

In the appropriate `frameset` or `frame` tag, type **bordercolor="color"**.

✔ Tips

■ A `bordercolor` tag in an individual frame overrides a `bordercolor` tag in a row or column, which in turn overrides the tag defined in the topmost `frameset`. If two `bordercolor` tags at the same level conflict, the one that comes first in your (X)HTML file takes precedence.

■ When you change the border of an individual frame, other frames that share its borders are also affected.

■ The `bordercolor` tag is not standard (X)HTML but has been and continues to be supported by both Netscape and Explorer.

Adjusting the Frame Borders

By default, your visitor's browser will draw sculpted borders around each frame in your frameset. The border tag lets you control the width of the space between frames. The frameborder tag lets you choose to fill that space with sculpted borders or leave it blank.

To adjust the amount of space between frames:

Inside the topmost frameset tag, before the final >, type **border="n"** where *n* is the desired width of the space between frames, in pixels.

✔ Tips

- The border attribute is not standard (X)HTML, but is still well supported.

- IE supports the CSS border attribute when applied to frames and framesets, though that use is non-standard.

- You can use **border="0"** to make the borders completely disappear.

- The default border width is 5 pixels.

- You cannot set the thickness for individual frames.

- Explorer won't show borders between 1 and 5 pixels wide. Instead, it shows nothing but an empty space.

- The best way to make frames jut right up next to each other is to use border="0" *and* frameborder="0" *(see page 253)*.

- You can change the color of the borders (or the space between the frames) as well. For details, consult *Adjusting the Color of the Borders* on page 251.

- Explorer also supports a framespacing attribute which works essentially like the border attribute (which Explorer didn't support until version 4).

```
<frameset bordercolor="#ff0000" border="10"
rows="65,*,60">

<frame name="banner" src="banner.html"
scrolling="no" />

<frameset cols="120,*">

<frame name="index" src="indexcity.html" />

<frame name="photos" src="openingpage.html"
```

Figure 15.22 *Add the* border *tag to any* frameset *or* frame *tag to adjust its borders' thickness. Here, I've added the tag to the topmost* frameset *tag so that all the frames are affected.*

Figure 15.23 *Thick, colored borders can help divide information into understandable chunks.*

Figure 15.24 *With a value between 1 and 5, Explorer for Windows shows no borders at all (though it continues to leave the empty space for them).*

Adjusting the Frame Borders

```
<frameset bordercolor="#ff0000" border="0"
frameborder="0" rows="65,*,60">

<frame name="banner" src="banner.html"
scrolling="no" />

<frameset cols="120,*">

<frame name="index" src="indexcity.html" />

<frame name="photos" src="openingpage.html"
```

Figure 15.25 *If you want to be sure that your page has no borders, whether it is viewed in Netscape or Explorer, set both the* border *and* frameborder *tags to 0.*

Figure 15.26 *To have each frame right up next to the adjacent one, use* frameborder="0" border="0".

Figure 15.27 *With just* frameborder="0", *Explorer continues to leave space between frames. It's most noticeable below the left City Tour frame.*

To hide the sculpted borders:

Type **frameborder="0"** inside the topmost frameset tag, before the final >.

✔ Tips

■ The frameborder attribute is standard (X)HTML. Hurray!

■ If you use **frameborder="0"**, the sculpted borders disappear but Explorer continues to show space between frames. To get rid of both borders and space, use **frameborder="0"** and **border="0"**.

■ Type **frameborder="1"** in the desired frame or frameset tag to view *some* borders when the topmost frameset is set for none.

■ To make the horizontal borders disappear, define the columns in the outer frameset and the rows in the inner frameset and then type **frameborder="0"** within each of the frame tags in the desired column.

■ You can use the frameborder tag with individual frames. Explorer will display the border around an individual frame, but Netscape will show the border for the entire row.

Adjusting the Frame Borders

Keeping Visitors from Resizing Frames

Frames with relative or variable sizes are always resized when the visitor changes the size of the browser window. However, you can also choose whether to let the visitor resize individual frames.

To keep visitors from resizing your frames:

Type **noresize** in the `frame` tag for the desired frame.

✔ Tips

- Netscape 4 displays resizable frames with a small hash mark in the middle of the border. The mark disappears if you've used the `noresize` attribute. Explorer displays both resizable and non-resizable borders exactly the same way.

- If you use very small pixel values for your frames and the visitor views the frameset page in a very large window, the width of the frames will probably not be quite as you wished. The entire frameset is always stretched to fill the window.

- If you set the border width to 0 with the `border` attribute *(see page 252)*, visitors won't be able to resize the frames at all. (The same goes for the `frameborder` and `framespacing` attributes.)

- In Explorer, if you set the `border` width to less than 5, the borders disappear, and again visitors won't be able to resize frames at all, regardless of whether you use the `noresize` attribute or not.

Figure 15.28 *Normally when the visitor places the pointer over a border, it changes into a double-headed arrow with which she can change the size of the frame. Also notice the hash mark in Netscape 4 which indicates the frame can be resized.*

```
<frameset bordercolor="#ff0000" border="6"
rows="65,*,60">

<frame name="banner" src="banner.html"
scrolling="no" noresize="noresize" />

<frameset cols="120,*">
<frame name="index" src="indexcity.html" />
<frame name="photos" src="openingpage.html" />
</frameset>

<frame name="buttons" src="buttons.html"
scrolling="no" noresize="noresize" />
```

Figure 15.29 *Add the* `noresize` *tag to any frames that you don't want the visitor to be able to resize. Here, I've modified the top and bottom frames and left the middle frames flexible.*

Figure 15.30 *Once you've restricted the resizability, the pointer will not turn into a double-pointed arrow and the visitor can't change the size of the frame. (In Netscape, the hash mark disappears also.)*

Keeping Visitors from Resizing Frames

```
<frameset cols="120,*">
<frame name="index" src="indexcity.html" />
<frame name="photos" src="openingpage.html" />
```

Figure 15.31 *Targets will only work if the frame in which you want the page to appear has a name.*

```
<tr><td bgcolor="#F3D7E3"><a
href="openingpage.html" target="photos">
Beginning</a></td></tr>

<tr><td bgcolor="#F6D5C3"><a href=
"rambles.html" target="photos">Les Rambles
Boulevard</a></td>
```

Figure 15.32 *In the link, specify the name of the frame in which the destination page should open.*

Figure 15.33 *The original contents of the* photos *frame is the* Welcome *page. But when the visitor clicks the* Les Rambles *link (which is targeted to appear in the* photos *frame)...*

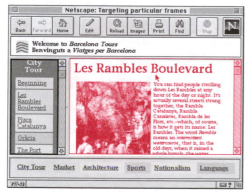

Figure 15.34 *...the* Les Rambles *page replaces the* Welcome *page in the* photos *frame.*

Targeting Links to Particular Frames

The initial content of a given frame is specified in the frameset page with the `src` tag. However, you can have other pages appear in that same frame. The trick is to add a pointer, called a *target*, to the links to those pages. The target says "open this link in the *photos* frame" (or whatever it's called).

To target a link to a particular frame:

1. Make sure the target frame has a name **(Figure 15.31)**. For more information, consult *Creating a Simple Frameset* on page 242.

2. On the page where the link should appear, type **<a href="page.html"** where *page.html* is the file that should be displayed in the target frame.

3. Type **target="name"** where *name* is the reference given to the target frame within the `frame` tag **(Figure 15.32)**.

4. Add any other attributes as desired to the link and then type the final **>**. For more information on creating links, see Chapter 7, *Links*.

✔ Tips

- By default, that is, without a specified target, a link will open in the same frame that contains the link.

- For some special targets, page 256.

- The frame must have a name to be targeted. For more information on naming frames, consult *Creating a Simple Frameset* on page 242.

- Frame names are case sensitive and must begin with an alphanumeric character (except the ones described on page 256).

Targeting Links to Particular Frames

Targeting Links to Special Spots

Although many times you'll be happy targeting a link to a particular frame, as described on page 255, other times you will want to make more general instructions, like having the link open in a new window. There are four special target names (each of which starts with an underscore).

To target a link to a special spot:

1. Type **<a href="contents.html"** where *contents.html* is the page that you wish to be displayed in the special spot.

2. Type **target="_blank"** to have the link open in a new, blank window. This is the ideal targeting for links to other sites which may not fit very well inside your frames.

   Or type **target="_self"** to open the link in the same frame that contains the link. The information in the frame (including the link itself) will be replaced by the *contents.html* file specified in step 1.

   Or type **target="_top"** to use the entire current window for the link, thus breaking out of frames altogether **(Figures 15.36 and 15.37)**.

   Or type **target="_parent"** to open the link in the frame that contains the current frameset. This will only be different from _top when you are using nested framesets. For more information on nested framesets, consult *Nesting Framesets* on page 258.

✔ Tip

■ So, use target="_top" if you want to *break out of* a frameset or *stop using* framesets, so to speak. The link will appear in the entire window.

stalls, younger people arguing at the political booths, mimes and bands, beggars and pickpockets (well, maybe you won't <em>see</em> them). If I were there, I'd be drinking an orxata at the Café de l'Ópera watching all the people go by.</p>

<p>Find out more at the <a href= "http://www.bcn.es/english/ihome.htm" target="_top">Official Barcelona Site</a>
<a href="plcat.html">Next stop</a></p>

Figure 15.35 *This link goes to another Web site and should not appear within my site's frames. Therefore, I use* target="_top" *to break out of frames and show this link in the entire browser window.*

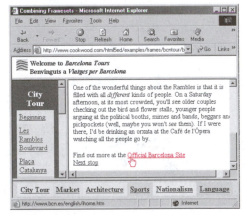

Figure 15.36 *When the visitor clicks a link that is targeted to the* _top...

Figure 15.37 *...the link is displayed in the full window without any frames.*

```
<title>Buttons</title>

</head>

<body bgcolor="white">

<table cellpadding="5" cellspacing="0"
width="100%">

<tr><th><font color="#FFFFFF" size="+1">City
Tour</font></th></tr>

<tr><td bgcolor="#F3D7E3"><a
href="openingpage.html"
target="photos">Beginning</a></td></tr>

<tr><td bgcolor="#F6D5C3"><a
href="rambles.html" target="photos">Les Rambles
Boulevard</a></td></tr>

<tr><td bgcolor="#D8E9D6"><a href="plcat.html"
target="photos">Pla&ccedil;a
Catalunya</a></td></tr>
```

Figure 15.38 *In the original document, I've set the target for each link individually.*

```
<title>Buttons</title>

<base target="photos" />

</head>

<body bgcolor="white">

<table cellpadding="5" cellspacing="0"
width="100%">

<tr><th><font color="#FFFFFF" size="+1">City
Tour</font></th></tr>

<tr><td bgcolor="#F3D7E3"><a href=
"openingpage.html">Beginning</a></td></tr>

<tr><td bgcolor="#F6D5C3"><a href="rambles.
html">Les Rambles Boulevard</a></td></tr>

<tr><td bgcolor="#D8E9D6"><a href="plcat.
html">Pla&ccedil;a Catalunya</a></td></tr>
```

Figure 15.39 *You can save a lot of typing by using the* base *tag to set the default target for every link on the page. This document is equivalent to the one shown in Figure 15.38.*

Changing the Default Target

If a frame contains a link, the link will open up in that same frame, by default, unless you change the target as described on pages 255–256. You can change the default target for all of the links on a page by using the base tag.

To change the default target:

1. In the head section of the page that contains the links, type **<base**.

2. Type **target="name"**, where *name* is the word that identifies the frame or window in which you want the links to appear, by default.

3. Type **/>** to complete the base tag.

✔ Tips

- You can override the target specified in the base tag by choosing a target in the link itself (*see page 255*).

- As ever, you can leave off the / at the end of the tag in HTML, but not in XHTML.

Nesting Framesets

As if frames and framesets weren't complicated enough, you can nest framesets inside
of frames to achieve special effects.

To nest framesets:

1. Build the child, or inner, frameset *(see
page 242)*.

2. Build the parent, or outer, frameset
(Figure 15.40). When you reach the
frame in which you wish to nest the child
frameset, type **src="child.html"** in the
`frame` tag, where *child.html* is the file
that you built in step 1.

✔ Tips

■ You can target a link to open in the parent frame of a frameset (in this example,
the right column is the parent frame of
the Barcelona tour frameset). For more
information, consult *Targeting Links to
Special Spots* on page 256.

■ You can't nest a frameset inside a frame
that is in that same frameset. Hey, and
why would you want to?

■ You can use nested framesets to change
two frames with one link (a common
desire). Simply create a special frameset
that references the two pages that you
want to appear. Then point the link at the
new frameset. It's a bit slower than the
JavaScript way, but it's pure (X)HTML
and relatively straight-forward. (For the
JavaScript way, consult *Changing Multiple Frames with One Link* on page 326.)

```
<frameset cols="*,4*">
<frame src="bigindex.html" />
<frame name="main" src="bcntourrc.html" />
</frameset>
```

Figure 15.40 *The frameset shown has two columns.
The first column will contain a simple index page,
while the second column will contain a distinct
frameset (in fact, the one used in most of the previous
examples in this chapter).*

Figure 15.41 *In this example, the Barcelona tour is
easily integrated into a larger group of topics just by
nesting its frameset into the larger one.*

```
<frameset rows="65,*,60">

<frame name="banner" src="banner.html"
noresize="noresize" scrolling="no" />

<frameset cols="120,*">

<frame name="index" src="indexcity.html" />

<frame name="photos" src="openingpage.html" />

</frameset>

<frame name="buttons" src="buttons.html"
noresize="noresize" scrolling="no" />

<noframes><body>

<p>The information on this page is displayed in
frames. Your browser can't view frames (or if you're
using Internet Explorer, you've turned frame
viewing off--go to Preferences under Edit and then
Web Content and check Show Frames). Sorry!</p>

</body></noframes>

</frameset>
```

Figure 15.42 *The* noframes *tags come after all of the framesets and frames have been defined.*

Figure 15.43 *Most browsers always display frames, and thus* never *show the* noframes *information.*

Figure 15.44 *When you turn frames off in Internet Explorer, the alternate information is displayed. This is a good way to test how this information will appear.*

Offering Alternatives to Frames

There are a few browsers that don't support frames, particularly text-based browsers like handhelds. You can create alternate content that will appear if your visitor's browser doesn't support frames.

To offer alternatives to frames:

1. Type **<noframes><body>** just before the last </frameset> tag (**Figure 15.42**).

2. Create the content that you want to appear if the frames do not.

3. When you've finished the alternate content, type **</body></noframes>**.

✔ Tips

- You can put a link in your noframes section that leads to a non-framed version of your site (*see page 262*).

- The noframes section will not be shown in browsers that can interpret frames, like Netscape (**Figure 15.43**) and Internet Explorer. Instead, the frames will be shown.

- Although this example is rather simple, don't be misled: you can put practically anything in the noframes section.

- Some visitors set up Explorer so that it doesn't view frames (by unchecking Frames in the Web Content preferences). They will see the noframes content.

- If you don't create a noframes section, beware! When visitors jump to your page with a browser that can't read frames, instead of an error message, they simply won't see anything! If nothing else, the noframes section can be used to explain what the problem is (**Figure 15.44**).

Offering Alternatives to Frames

Embedding Content with Objects

There are two principal alternatives to frames. The first is using fixed positioning as discussed in *Affixing an Element to the Browser Window* on page 180 in Chapter 11, *Layout with Styles*. The second is to use the `object` element to embed text or (X)HTML content in a page.

To embed content without frames:

1. Type **<object** to begin.

2. Type **type="text/html"**, where *text/html* is the MIME type for the embedded content.

3. Type **data="file.html"**, where *file.html* is the name of the (X)HTML file that you'd like to embed on your page.

4. Type **width="w" height="h"**, where *w* and *h* are the desired width and height in pixels of the embedded object.

5. Type **>** to complete the opening `object` tag.

6. Type the content that should appear if the browser doesn't support the object for whatever reason (see last tip).

7. Type **</object>** to finish.

```
</head>
<body bgcolor="#FFFFFF">
<h1>Barcelona Tours</h1>
<p>Here's an idea of what the first page of the Barcelona Tours site looks like: </p>
<hr />
<object type="text/html"
data="openingpage.html" width="500"
height="450" >

The <a href="openingpage.html"> Barcelona Tours</a> page contains great photos and essential tips for making your vacation a success.</object>
</body>
```

Figure 15.45 *You can embed one (X)HTML page in another by using the* object *element.*

Figure 15.46 *The referenced page is embedded on our Web page as if it were a frame. The links work and everything!*

```
<body bgcolor="#FFFFFF">

<h1>Barcelona Tours</h1>

Here's an idea of what the first page of the
Barcelona Tours site looks like:

<hr />

<object type="unsup/fake" data="superbcn.sup"
width="500" height="450" >

    <object type="text/html"
    data="openingpage.html" width="500"
    height="450" >

    The <a href="openingpage.html">Barcelona
    Tours</a> page contains great photos and
    essential tips for making your vacation a
    success.

    </object>

</object>

</body>
```

Figure 15.47 *Here are two nested object elements. The outer one could be in a new, experimental, but not very well supported MIME type. The inner is the old (X)HTML standby.*

Figure 15.48 *The browser doesn't yet support the unsup/fake MIME type (since I made it up), and so shows the second object instead.*

✔ Tips

■ You can find a list of MIME types on my Web site *(see page 24)*.

■ The `object` element is designed to be nested. Browsers are supposed to ignore the objects that they do not recognize and display *only* the first one they support. It's an ingenious system for serving alternate content to browsers in a format they can handle.

■ Netscape 6 and Opera 6 both support the `object` element properly.

■ IE 6 for Windows insists on adding unsightly scroll bars around every object (even images). In addition, if you nest objects as described on this page, it leaves an empty space and scrollbars for the objects it doesn't support instead of ignoring them completely as it's supposed to do. It's not pretty.

■ IE for Mac does slightly better. If it doesn't support an object, it doesn't leave an empty box for it. However, if it supports multiple objects, it displays them all (instead of displaying only the first one that it supports). It breaks the whole system of providing alternate content.

■ The `object` element is often used for embedding multimedia content in Web pages. For more details, Chapter 17, *Multimedia*.

■ Browsers may not support the `object` element itself, the MIME type of the object you're trying to display, or the method that you're using to display it. For example, IE 6 for Windows depends on proprietary ActiveX technology for its multimedia objects which other browsers do not support.

Embedding Content with Objects

Making Frames More Accessible

By combining several pages into one window, frames lose a lot of the transparency evident in other Web pages. For example, it's hard to figure out the URL or the title of the page that one is in, or where a given link might be displayed. While frames are discouraged in general, for these reasons, there are some things you can do to make them more accessible to people with disabilities.

To make frame-based sites more accessible:

1. Add the `title` attribute to each `frame` tag in order to identify the contents of the frame.

2. Provide more complete information about what each frame is for. For example, within the `frame` tag, type **longdesc="info.url"**, where *info.url* is the location on the server of a Web page that explains the purpose of this frame.

3. Add links to the `noframes` tag that describe the individual frames' functions.

4. Provide a full non-frame version of the frame-based site.

✔ Tip

■ Many of the world's governments, including the U.S. (with Section 508 of the Rehabilitation Act), have drawn up legislation requiring federal or state Web sites to be accessible to people with disabilities, including the blind. You can find more details at the W3C Web Accessibility Initiative site: *http://www.w3.org/ WAI/*. The United States government has an interesting site outlining the requirements of Section 508 at *http://www.section508.gov/*

```
</head>
<frameset rows="65,*,60">
<frame name="banner" src="banner.html"
title="The Welcome Banner" />
<frameset cols="120,*">
<frame name="index" src="indexcity.html"
title="The Table of Contents" />
<frame name="photos" src="openingpage.html"
title="Main Content and Photographs"
longdesc="frameinfo.html#photos" />
</frameset>
<frame name="buttons" src="buttons.html"
title="Larger Navigation System" />
<noframes><body>
<p>There is a <a href="plaintextversion.html">
non-frames version</a> of this site.</p>
<p>And here is <a href="frameinfo.html">more
information</a> about the way the frames work
together.</p>
</body></noframes></frameset>
</html>
```

Figure 15.49 *You can add* title *and* longdesc *information to each frame to help explain how the frames in the site work together.*

```
<body>
<h2>Information about the frames and
frameset</h2>
<p id="photos">The "Main Content and
Photographs" frame is situated in the center right of
the frameset. It will contain descriptions of
Barcelona monuments and buildings as well as
photographs of the same</p>
```

Figure 15.50 *The* longdesc *attribute links to an external document (like the (X)HTML document shown above) that provides additional information about how the site works.*

Making Frames More Accessible

FORMS

Forms

✓ What you can do with forms:

- get feedback

- have a guestbook

- take a survey

- see who's visiting you

- sell stuff

- and much more!

Up to now, all the (X)HTML you have learned has helped you communicate *your* ideas with your visitors. In this chapter, you'll learn how to create forms which enable your visitors to communicate with you.

There are two basic parts of a form: the structure or shell, that consists of fields, labels, and buttons that the visitor sees on a page and hopefully fills out, and the processing script that takes that information and converts it into a format that you can read or tally.

Constructing a form's shell is straightforward and similar to creating any other part of the Web page. You can create text boxes, special password boxes, radio buttons, checkboxes, drop-down menus, larger text areas, and even clickable images. You will give each element a name that will serve as a label to identify the data once it is processed. Constructing forms is discussed on pages 269–286.

Processing the data from a form is a bit more complicated. The principal tool, the *CGI script*, is typically written in Perl or some other programming language. Although Perl programming is beyond the scope of this book, and even explaining how to use existing Perl scripts stretches the limits a bit, I've added a few simple ready-made Perl CGI scripts for your use to get you started *(see page 267)*.

If this all seems a bit daunting, or if your ISP doesn't allow you to run CGI scripts, you might decide to have visitors submit form data via e-mail *(see page 270)* or use a public form host *(see page 271)*.

About CGI Scripts

If you're a non-programmer, the phrase *CGI script* may make you want to quickly close this book and forget about forms altogether. Hold on. What's CGI? What's a script? It's not as impossible as it sounds. First, a script is another word for a program, just like Microsoft Word or Adobe Photoshop. Of course, the scripts you'll use to process forms are a good deal simpler than commercial applications that cost hundreds of dollars. But they work in a similar way.

CGI, which stands for *Common Gateway Interface*, is simply a standardized way for sending information between the server and the script. So, to resume, a CGI script is a program (usually written in a programming language called Perl) that communicates with the server in a standard (CGI-like) way.

Perl is the most common language used for CGI scripts, partly because it's easily ported from one platform to another, partly because it's great for massaging data into understandable information, and partly because it has this reputation as a cool language—really! Perl programmers love to brag about how they can do anything with Perl, on one line, in a million different ways.

You can use other programming languages, like C++, tcl, Visual Basic, PHP, or even AppleScript to create CGI scripts. My advice is that if you know one of these languages, you should use it; otherwise, use Perl.

One extra nice thing about Perl programmers is that they often like to share. You can find tons of ready-to-use CGI scripts written in Perl all over the Web *(see page 266)*. Many are free, many are not.

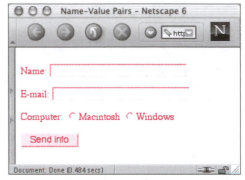

Figure 16.1 *Here's your basic form. There are two text fields, one set of radio buttons and a submit button. The words Name, E-Mail, Computer, Macintosh, and Windows are all labels. They do not affect the data that is collected in any way.*

```
<form method="post" action="none.cgi">

<p>Name: <input type="text"
name="visitor_name" size="30" /></p>

<p>E-mail: <input type="text"
name="visitor_email" size="30" /></p>

<p>Computer: <input type="radio"
name="computer" value="Mac" />Macintosh</p>

<input type="radio" name="computer"
value="Win" />Windows</p>

<p><input type="submit" name="submit"
value="Send info" /></p>

</form>
```

Figure 16.2 *Here's the (X)HTML code that is behind the form in Figure 16.1. Just focus on the* name *and* value *attributes for now. (You'll learn how to create form elements later on in the chapter.) First, notice how each form element has a* name *attribute, but only some have a* value. *The* value *attribute determines the data that is sent to the server for that element. Some form elements allow the visitor to type in any value (like text boxes) while others do not (like radio buttons). Form elements that work by checking or selecting must have the value specified in the* value *attribute.*

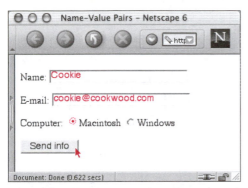

Figure 16.3 *When the visitor enters information in the text fields and chooses a radio button, the name-value pairs are set. Clicking the submit button (labeled here "Send info") will send the name-value pairs to the CGI script on the server.*

Label	Name	Value
Name	visitor_name	Cookie
E-Mail	visitor_email	cookie@cookwood.com
Computer	computer	Mac
Send info	submit	Send info

Figure 16.4 *These are the actual name-value pairs that will be sent when the visitor clicks the submit button in Figure 16.3. Be sure not to confuse label with name. Also, notice that the values for the first two fields correspond to what the visitor has typed. The value for the radio button—Mac (not Macintosh, which is the label)—was set by me, the author of this Web page (see Figure 16.2) since the visitor can only click the button (and not type).*

**visitor_name=Cookie&
visitor_email=cookie@cookwood.
com&computer=Mac&submit=
Send+info**

Figure 16.5 *This is what the data that is sent to the CGI script looks like. Notice that each name is linked with its value with an equals sign (=). An ampersand (&) separates each name-value pair and spaces are replaced with plus signs.*

What does the CGI script do?

Each element on your form will have a *name* and a *value* associated with it. The name identifies the data that is being sent. It might be something like *visitor_name*. The value is the data (say, *Cookie*), and can either come from you, the Web page designer, or from the visitor who types it in a field **(Figures 16.1 and 16.2)**. When a visitor clicks the submit button (or an active image—see page 286), each form element's name-value pair is sent to the server (for example, it might look like *visitor_name=Cookie*).

CGI scripts generally have two functions. The first is to take all those name-value pairs and separate them out into individual intelligible pieces. The second is to actually do something with that data—like print it out, multiply fields together, send an e-mail confirmation, store it on a server, or whatever. There are CGI scripts that create guestbooks, bulletin boards, chat areas, counters, games, postcard senders, image randomizers, scripts that work with databases, let you edit Web pages, and many, many more.

Security

Before you get too excited, you should know that CGI scripts can leave your server wide open to invaders. That's one reason some ISPs do not allow their users to use CGI scripts. If this is your case, one alternative is to use a form hosting service, as described on page 271.

If your ISP does allow you to run CGI-scripts, you should still read up on security issues. You might start with *http://www.w3.org/Security/Faq/* and in particular *http://www.w3.org/Security/Faq/wwwsf4.html* for more information on how CGI scripts can make you vulnerable, and how you can protect yourself.

About CGI Scripts

Getting a Script

If your ISP okays your use of CGI scripts, your next step is to get your hands on one. You might start with the scripts included with this book *(see page 267)*. Or you can either write your own or adapt one of the hundreds of scripts available on the Web. Some of these scripts are free, others require some sort of compensation to the programmer. While you can find scripts all over the Web, I've found four particularly good places to look.

CPAN

The Comprehensive Perl Archive Network (CPAN) is the official Perl script repository. You can find it at *www.cpan.org* (**Fig. 16.6**).

The CGI Resource Index

The CGI Resource Index lists hundreds of links to Perl CGI scripts, documentation, books, magazine articles, programmers, and jobs. It's at *www.cgi-resources.com.*

Extropia.com

Another famous source for free Perl CGI scripts is Extropia.com, created by Selena Sol and Gunther Birznieks. Extropia offers many useful scripts that its authors have generously released to the public domain. They now offer support for those scripts—for a fee. You can find them at *www.extropia.com.*

The WebScripts Archive

While not the biggest or perhaps the most popular, Darryl Burgdorf's site houses what I think is the best documented and easiest to implement collection of Perl CGI scripts. (I use his excellent WebBBS for my Question and Answer forums.) You can find The WebScripts Archive at: *www.awsd.com/scripts.*

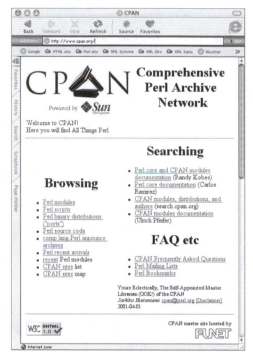

Figure 16.6 *The Comprehensive Perl Archive Network is the official Perl script repository.*

```
#!/usr/local/bin/perl
use strict;

use CGI ':standard';
my @param=param();

print "Content-type: text/html\n\n";

foreach my $name (param()) {
    my @value= param($name);
    print "<p>The field with the NAME
        attribute equal to <b>
        $name</b> had a VALUE equal
        to <b>@value</b></p>\n";
}
```

Figure 16.7 *This is an extremely simple script that uses CGI.pm to parse incoming form data and then prints out the results to the screen. It neither saves the form data, nor sends it anywhere. Its only use is to see how forms interact with scripts.*

Using the Scripts Included with This Book

With this book, I have included a set of very simple scripts that you can use to process the data that visitors submit to your Web site. These scripts are designed to help you understand how forms work and get you started. To really get some use out of them, you will have to know a little Perl (or be willing to learn). If you're just interested in getting the data from a form, you're probably better off using e-mail *(see page 270)*.

To use the scripts included with this book:

1. Download the desired scripts from my Web site: *www.cookwood.com/html/ cgiscripts/*.

2. Read and follow the instructions in *Preparing a Script* on page 268.

3. Reference the script (from your server) in step 2 on page 269.

4. Get a visitor to go to your site and press the submit button!

✔ Tips

■ To get more high-powered scripts, consult *Getting a Script* on page 266.

■ If you are intrigued by writing your own scripts, you might be interested in my other book: *Perl and CGI for the World Wide Web: Visual QuickStart Guide, Second Edition,* also published by Peachpit Press. With the same clear, concise, and visually oriented format as the book you have in your hands, it is a perfect starting place for non-programmers who want to make their Web pages interactive. For details, check out *www.cookwood.com/ perl/*. End of blurb.

Preparing a Script

Whether you've written your own script or are using someone else's, you'll have to do a couple of things to get the script ready for use with your form.

Adapting scripts for your use

If you're using a Perl script that you've downloaded from someone else, you'll have to open it up and see what variables and path names it uses. You will have to change these to reflect your particular situation.

Transferring the script to the server

The next step is to copy the script to the server, generally with an FTP program like WS_FTP *(see page 408)* or Fetch *(see page 410)*. Make sure you upload them in ASCII mode, not binary. Some servers require that all CGI scripts be located in a central cgi-bin directory. Others provide a personal cgi-bin directory for each user. Still others let you store CGI scripts wherever you want, as long as you add a particular extension to them for identification. You'll have to ask your ISP.

Permissions

If your page is on a Unix server, you will have to use a program called chmod to make the CGI script accessible and executable. For more details type **man chmod** at the Unix prompt. Some FTP programs (like Fetch, for instance) let you change permissions as well.

Add it to your form!

So you've got your CGI script on your server, ready to go. The only thing left is to add it to your form *(see page 269)*.

```
<form method="post" action="http://
www.cookwood.com/cgi-bin/display_results.pl">
```

```
<hr />

Please share any suggestions or comments with us:
<textarea

name="comments" rows="3" cols="65"
wrap="wrap">Comments?</textarea>

<hr />

<input type="submit" value="Order Bed"
name="submit" />

<input type="reset" value="Start Over"
name="startover" />

</form>
```

Figure 16.8 *Every form has three parts: the* form *tag, the actual form elements where the visitor enters information, and the submit button (or active image) that sends the collected information to the server.*

Figure 16.9 *A form gives you a great way to get information and feedback from your visitors.*

Creating a Form

A form has three important parts: the `form` tag, which includes the URL of the CGI script that will process the form; the form elements, like fields and menus; and the submit button which sends the data to the CGI script on the server.

To create a form:

1. Type **<form method="post"**.

2. Type **action="script.url">** where *script.url* is the location on the server of the CGI script that will run when the form is submitted (*see pages 264–268*).

3. Create the form's contents, as described on pages 272–292, including a submit button (*see page 282*) or active image (*see page 286*).

4. Type **</form>** to complete the form.

✔ Tips

■ In order for your visitor to send you the data on the form, you'll need either a submit button (if your form contains fields, buttons, and other elements that your visitors will fill in) or an active image. For more on submit buttons, consult *Creating the Submit Button* on page 282. For details on active images, consult *Using an Image to Submit Data* on page 286.

■ You can use CSS (*see page 175*) or tables (*see page 215*) to lay out your form elements more precisely.

■ You can also use the `get` method to process information gathered with a form. However, since the `get` method limits the amount of data that you can collect at one time, I recommend using `post`.

Creating a Form

Sending Form Data via E-mail

If you don't feel like messing with CGI scripts and can deal with not having your data perfectly formatted (or pre-processed by a script), you can have a visitor's data be sent to you via e-mail.

To send form data via e-mail:

1. Type **<form method="post"**.
2. Type **enctype="text/plain"** in order to format the incoming text.
3. Type **action="mailto:you@site.com"**, where *you@site.com* is the e-mail address where you want data from the form to be sent.
4. Type **>**.
5. Create the form's contents, as described on pages 272–292.
6. Type **</form>**.

✔ Tips

- This technique doesn't work with pre-version 4 browsers or with Outlook. Of course, it doesn't matter which browser or e-mail client *you* use, it only matters which ones your visitors use.
- When the visitor clicks the submit button, an alert appears warning them that their e-mail address will be submitted along with the data and that the data will not be encrypted. They have to click OK to continue submitting the data.
- The From field's value depends on what the visitor has entered in their browser's preferences. It may or may not be truthful.

```
<h2>Ordering your new bed</h2>
<form method="post" enctype="text/plain"
action="mailto:orderbed@cookwood.com">
Name: <input type="text" name="name" />
```

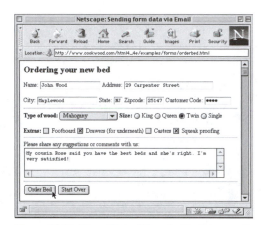

Figure 16.10 *One way to get around the complications of CGI scripts is to have the data that is submitted with the form sent to your e-mail address.*

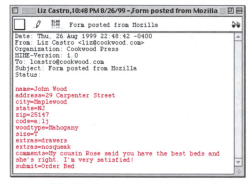

Figure 16.11 *Forms that will be submitted via e-mail look precisely the same as those that are processed with a CGI script.*

Figure 16.12 *The data is contained in the body of the e-mail message. Note that the default Subject line depends on the browser your visitor uses (in this example, it was Netscape, code name Mozilla). The From field should reveal the visitor's e-mail address. The To field will correspond to the address you entered for the* `action` *attribute.*

Figure 16.13 *This is Response-O-Matic's home page (www.response-o-matic.com).*

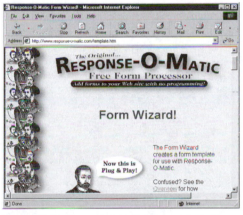

Figure 16.14 *Response-O-Matic gets you started by asking you a few questions and then creating a template, as shown in Figure 16.15.*

Figure 16.15 *Save the template to your hard disk and edit it as necessary. (Just don't change the hidden fields.)*

Using a Form Hosting Service

Another option for those who cannot or don't want to use a CGI script is a form hosting service. There are several such companies that create forms for you, give you access to CGI scripts that process the forms, or process the forms directly and send you the results via e-mail. You generally "pay" for the service by including some sort of advertisement on your page.

To use a form hosting service:

1. Search for a form hosting service on Google or Yahoo.

2. Connect to the form hosting service.

3. Read their site to answer the following questions:

   • Who creates the form: you or them?

   • What do you have to do in exchange for them processing your forms?

   • Is it OK to use their processing for commercial sites, or just personal ones?

4. Follow their instructions for setting up your form. Consult the rest of this chapter for more information about creating form elements.

✔ Tips

■ Most form hosting services send you the gathered data in an e-mail message.

■ Not all form hosting services are the same. Although they generally all process forms in exchange for advertising, some ads are not as intrusive as others.

Using a Form Hosting Service

Creating Text Boxes

Text boxes can contain one line of free-form text—that is, anything that the visitor wants to type—and are typically used for names, addresses, and the like.

To create a text box:

1. If desired, type the label that will identify the text box to your visitor (for example, **Name:**).

2. Type **<input type="text"**.

3. Type **name="name"**, where *name* is the text that will identify the input data to the server (and your script).

4. If desired, type **value="value"**, where *value* is the data that will initially be shown in the field and that will be sent to the server if the visitor doesn't type something else.

5. If desired, define the size of the box on your form by typing **size="n"**, replacing *n* with the desired width of the box, measured in characters.

6. If desired, type **maxlength="n"**, where *n* is the maximum number of characters that can be entered in the box.

7. Finish the text box by typing a final **/>**.

✔ Tips

■ Even if your visitor skips the field (and you haven't set the default text with the value attribute), the name attribute is still sent to the server (with an undefined, empty value).

■ The default size is 20. However, visitors can type up to the limit imposed by the maxlength attribute. Still, for larger, multi-line entries, it's better to use text areas *(see page 278)*.

Name: <input type="text" name="name" />

Address: <input type="text" name="address" size="30" />

<p>City: <input type="text" name="city" />

State: <input type="text" name="state" size="2" maxlength="2" />

Zipcode: <input type="text" name="zip" size="5" maxlength="5" />

Figure 16.16 *While it's essential to set the* name *attribute for each text box, you only have to set the* value *attribute when you want to add default values for a text box.*

Figure 16.17 *Text boxes can be different sizes to accommodate different types of fields.*

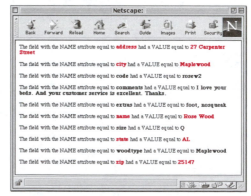

Figure 16.18 *It's important to give descriptive names to your text boxes (with the* name *attribute) so that you identify the information you're receiving.*

Customer Code: <input type="password"
name="code" size="8" /></p>

Figure 16.19 *The* name *attribute identifies the password when you compile the data.*

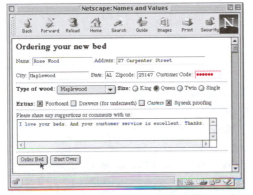

Figure 16.20 *When the visitor enters a password in a form, the password is hidden with bullets.*

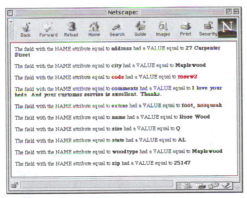

Figure 16.21 *The password data appears as regular text after processing by a form-parsing script. Password boxes are* not *high-security! (See second to last tip.)*

Creating Password Boxes

The only difference between a password box and a text box is that whatever is typed in the former is hidden by bullets or asterisks. The information is *not* encrypted when sent to the server.

To create password boxes:

1. If desired, type the label that will identify the password box to your visitor (for example, **Enter password:**).

2. Type **<input type="password"**.

3. Type **name="name"**, where *name* is the text that will identify the input data to the server (and your script).

4. If desired, define the size of the box on your form by typing **size="n"**, replacing *n* with the desired width of the box, measured in characters.

5. If desired, type **maxlength="n"**, where *n* is the maximum number of characters that can be entered in the box.

6. Finish the text box by typing a final **/>**.

✔ Tips

- Even if nothing is entered in the password box, the name is still sent to the server (with an undefined value).

- You could set default text for value (as in step 4 on page 272), but that kind of defeats the purpose of a password.

- The only protection the password box offers is from folks peering over your visitor's shoulder as she types in her password. Since the password box does not encrypt the data when it is sent to the server, moderately experienced crackers can discover the password without much trouble.

Creating Password Boxes

Creating Radio Buttons

Remember those old-time car radios with big black plastic buttons? Push one to listen to WFCR; push another for WRNX. You can never push two buttons at once. Radio buttons on forms work the same way (except you can't listen to the radio).

To create a radio button:

1. If desired, type the introductory text for your radio buttons. You might use something like **Select one of the following**.

2. Type **<input type="radio"**.

3. Type **name="radioset"**, where *radioset* both identifies the data sent to the script and also links the radio buttons together, ensuring that only one per set can be checked.

4. Type **value="data"**, where *data* is the text that will be sent to the server if the radio button is checked, either by you (in step 5) or by the visitor.

5. If desired, type **checked="checked"** to make the radio button active by default when the page is opened. You can only do this to one radio button in the set. (The **="checked"** is optional in HTML.)

6. Type the final **/>**.

7. Type the text that identifies the radio button to the visitor. This is often the same as value, but doesn't have to be.

8. Repeat steps 2–7 for each radio button in the set.

✔ Tip

- If you don't set the value attribute, the word "on" is sent to the script. It's not particularly useful since you can't tell which button in the set was pressed.

```
<b>Size:</b>

<input type="radio" name="size" value="K"
/>King

<input type="radio" name="size" value="Q"
/>Queen

<input type="radio" name="size" value="T"
/>Twin

<input type="radio" name="size" value="S"
/>Single
```

Figure 16.22 *The* name *attribute serves a dual purpose for radio buttons: it links the radio buttons in a given set and it identifies the value when it is sent to the script. The* value *attribute is crucial since the visitor has no way of typing a value.*

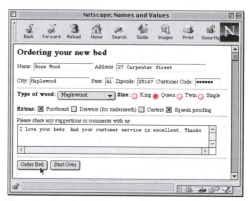

Figure 16.23 *The radio buttons themselves are created with the (X)HTML tags. The labels (King, Queen, etc.) are created with plain text alongside the (X)HTML tags.*

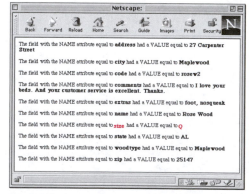

Figure 16.24 *Note that it is the* value *(Q) and not the label (Queen) that gets sent to the script.*

Creating Radio Buttons

```
<p><b>Extras:</b>

<input type="checkbox" name="extras"
value="foot" />Footboard

<input type="checkbox" name="extras"
value="drawers" />Drawers (for underneath)

<input type="checkbox" name="extras"
value="casters" />Casters

<input type="checkbox" name="extras"
value="nosqueak" />Squeak proofing</p>
```

Figure 16.25 *Notice how the label text (not high-lighted) does not need to match the* value *attribute. That's because the label text identifies the checkboxes to the visitor in the browser while the* value *identifies the data to the script.*

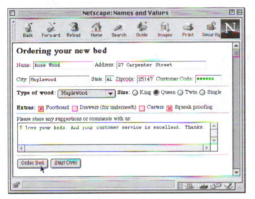

Figure 16.26 *The visitor can check as many boxes as necessary. Each corresponding value will be sent to the script, together with the checkbox set's name.*

Figure 16.27 *Since the visitor has chosen two check-boxes, both values (but not their labels, of course) are sent to the script. This particular script separates multiple values with a comma.*

Creating Checkboxes

While radio buttons can accept only one answer per set, a visitor can check as many checkboxes in a set as they like. Like radio buttons, checkboxes are linked by the value of the `name` attribute.

To create checkboxes:

1. If desired, type the introductory text (something like **Select one or more of the following**) for your checkboxes.

2. Type **<input type="checkbox"**. (Notice there is no space in the word *checkbox*.)

3. Type **name="boxset"**, where *boxset* both identifies the data sent to the script and also links the checkboxes together.

4. Type **value="value"** to define a value for each checkbox. The value will be sent to the server if the checkbox is checked (either by the visitor, or by you as described in step 5).

5. Type **checked="checked"** to make the checkbox checked by default when the page is opened. You (or the visitor) may check as many checkboxes as desired. (The **="checked"** is optional in HTML.)

6. Type **/>** to complete the checkbox.

7. Type the text that identifies the checkbox to the user. This is often the same as the `value`, but doesn't have to be.

8. Repeat steps 2–7 for each checkbox in the set.

✔ Tip

■ If you don't set the `value` attribute, the word "on" is sent to the script. It's not particularly useful since you can't tell which box in the set was checked.

Creating Menus

Menus are perfect for offering your visitors a choice from a given set of options.

To create menus:

1. If desired, type the text that will describe your menu.

2. Type **<select**.

3. Type **name="name"**, where *name* will identify the data collected from the menu when it is sent to the server.

4. If desired, type **size="n"**, where *n* represents the height (in lines) of the menu.

5. If desired, type **multiple="multiple"** to allow your visitor to select more than one menu option (with Ctrl or Command). (The **="multiple"** is optional in HTML.)

6. Type **>**.

7. Type **<option**.

8. Type **selected="selected"** if you want the option to be selected by default. (The **="selected"** is optional in HTML.)

9. Type **value="value"**, where *value* specifies the data that will be sent to the server if the option is selected.

10. If desired, type **label="name"**, where *name* is the word that should appear in the menu.

11. Type **>**.

12. Type the option name as you wish it to appear in the menu.

13. Type **</option>**.

14. Repeat steps 7–11 for each option.

15. Type **</select>**.

```
<b>Type of wood:</b>
<select name="woodtype">
<option value="Mahogany">Mahogany</option>
<option value="Maplewood">Maplewood
</option>
<option value="Pine">Pine</option>
<option value="Cherry">Cherry</option>
</select>
```

Figure 16.28 *Menus are made up of two HTML tags:* select *and* option. *You set the common* name *attribute in the* select *tag and the individual* value *attribute in each of the* option *tags.*

Figure 16.29 *There's no way for a visitor to select nothing in a menu unless you set the* size *attribute. The default selection is either the first option in the menu or the one you've set as* selected *in step 8.*

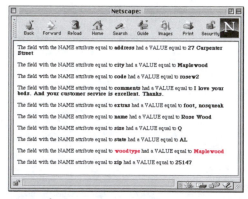

Figure 16.30 *Notice that the* name *attribute (woodtype) and not the label (Type of wood:) is what gets sent to the script.*

Creating Menus

```
<b>Type of wood:</b>
<select name="woodtype" >

<optgroup label="Hard woods">
<option value="Mahogany">Mahogany</option>
<option
value="Maplewood">Maplewood</option>
<option
value="Cherry">Cherry</option></optgroup>

<optgroup label="Soft woods">

<option value="Pine">Pine</option>

<option value="Fir">Fir</option>

</optgroup></select>
```

Figure 16.31 *Each submenu has a title, specified in the* label *attribute of the* optgroup *tag, and a series of options (defined with* option *tags and regular text).*

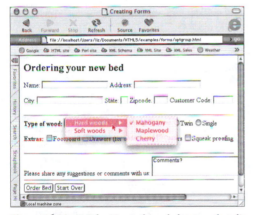

Figure 16.32 *IE 5 for Mac is the only browser that displays* optgroup *elements as true submenus. Snazzy!*

Figure 16.33 *IE 6 for Windows and Netscape 6 on both platforms show a single menu divided into groups.*

If you have a particularly large menu with many options, you may want to group the options into categories.

To group menu options:

1. Create a menu as described on page 276.

2. Before the first option tag in the first group that you wish to place together in a submenu, type **<optgroup**.

3. Type **label="submenutitle">**, where *submenutitle* is the header for the submenu.

4. After the last option tag in the group, type **</optgroup>**.

5. Repeat steps 2–4 for each submenu.

✔ Tips

■ If you add the size attribute in step 4, the menu appears more like a list, and there is no automatically selected option (unless you use selected—see step 8).

■ If size *(see step 4)* is bigger than the number of options, visitors can deselect all values by clicking in the empty space.

■ While the label attribute is a standard part of (X)HTML, only IE 5 for Mac—and mobile devices—support it. If there is no label attribute, the browser automatically uses the text enclosed in the option tag.

■ IE5 for Mac shows the optgroup tag as a submenu. IE 6 for Windows and Netscape 6 on both platforms simply divide the options into categories. No other browser supports optgroup at all.

■ The closing option tag in step 13 is optional in HTML 4 (but not in XHTML). You can also use the abbreviated selected and multiple in HTML, whereas XHTML requires selected= "selected" and multiple="multiple".

Creating Menus

Creating Larger Text Areas

In some cases, you want to give the visitor more room to write. Unlike text boxes *(see page 272)*, text areas may be as large as your page, and will expand as needed if the person enters more text than can fit in the display area. They're perfect for eliciting questions and comments.

To create larger text areas:

1. If desired, type the explanatory text that will identify the text area.

2. Type **<textarea**.

3. Type **name="name"**, where *name* is the text that will identify the input data to the server (and your script).

4. If desired, type **rows="n"**, where *n* is the height of the text area in rows. The default value is 4.

5. If desired, type **cols="n"**, where *n* is the width of the text area in characters. The default value is 40.

6. Type **>**.

7. Type the default text, if any, for the text area. No formatting is allowed here.

8. Type **</textarea>** to complete the text area.

✔ Tips

- There is no use for the `value` attribute with text areas.

- Visitors can enter up to 32,700 characters in a text area. Scroll bars will appear when necessary.

- Netscape 4.x doesn't wrap text automatically in large text areas. You can add the non-standard `wrap` attribute so that it will. Other browsers ignore it.

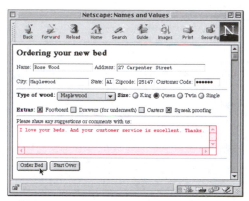

```
<hr />Please share any suggestions or comments with us:

<textarea name="comments" rows="3" cols="65" wrap="wrap">Comments?</textarea>
```

Figure 16.34 *The* value *attribute is not used with the* textarea *tag. Default values are set by adding text between the opening and closing tags (as in "Comments?" here).*

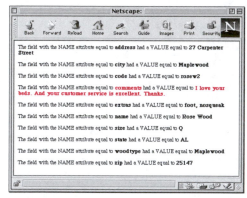

Figure 16.35 *The visitor can override the default text simply by typing over it.*

Figure 16.36 *Text areas are great for getting longer comments and suggestions from visitors. They are typically used in guestbooks and bulletin boards.*

Creating Larger Text Areas

```
<body>

<form method="post" action="http://
www.cookwood.com/cgi-bin/perl2e/uploading/
uploading.cgi" enctype="multipart/form-data" >

<h2>What files are you sending?</h2>

<p><input type="file" name="uploadfile"
size="40"/>

<p><input type="submit" name="submit"/>

</form>
```

Figure 16.37 *To allow visitors to upload files, you must make sure to set the proper* enctype *attribute, as well as create the* file *type* input *element.*

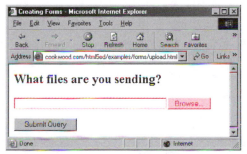

Figure 16.38 *When you create a file upload area, both a field where the visitor can type the path to the file and a Browse button (so the visitor can use an Open dialog box to choose the file) automatically appear on your page.*

Figure 16.39 *Once the file is uploaded, the visitor gets a confirmation message.*

Allowing Visitors to Upload Files

If the information you need from the folks filling out your form is complicated, you might want to have them upload an entire file to your server.

To allow visitors to upload files:

1. Type **<form method="post" action= "upload.cgi"** where *upload.cgi* is the URL of a special CGI script that processes incoming files. Most regular form parsing scripts won't be enough.

2. Type **enctype="multipart/form-data">**. The enctype attribute ensures that the file is uploaded in the proper format.

3. Type the caption for the file upload area so your visitors know what to do. Something like **What file would you like to upload?** would work well.

4. Type **<input type="file"** to create a file upload box and a Browse button.

5. Type **name="title"**, where *title* identifies to the server the files being uploaded.

6. If desired, type **size="n"**, where *n* is the width, in characters, of the field in which the visitor will enter the path and file name.

7. Type the final **/>**.

8. Complete the form as usual, including the submit button and final </form> tag.

✔ Tips

■ The size attribute is optional, but since most paths and file names are pretty long, it's a good idea to set it at 40 or 50. The default is 20.

■ You can't use the get method for forms that allow uploading.

Allowing Visitors to Upload Files

About Hidden Fields

(X)HTML forms allow for a special kind of field that doesn't appear in the browser, and yet is part of the form. These hidden fields seem counterproductive at first glance: if your visitors can't see them, how will they fill them in? The answer is they won't. Instead, you will use hidden fields to store information gathered from an earlier form so that it can be combined with the present form's data.

Imagine, for example, that on the first page, you ask for a visitor's name, address, and telephone number. You then want to send them to your catalog page where they can choose which piece of furniture they wish to order. Instead of asking them for their personal data a second time, you can use a CGI script to collect the data from the first form and then generate the hidden fields that will contain this data in the second form. Then, when you go to process the data from the second form, all of the fields, including both the items ordered and the personal data, will be analyzed.

Don't get carried away by the word *hidden*. While hidden fields are not shown by the browser, they still form part of the (X)HTML code that makes up the page (so the CGI script can get at them), and thus are not at all invisible if someone should look at the source code for your page *(see page 57)*.

```
<form method=post action="whatever.cgi">
<input type="hidden" name="name"
value="value" />
<input type=submit value="submit data" />
```

Figure 16.40 *An excerpt from the (X)HTML file used to create the form shows the syntax for hidden elements. It doesn't make much sense to write such code yourself and thus I'm reluctant to create such an example. Instead, your CGI script should generate this code.*

Adding Hidden Fields to a Form

Although you hardly ever add hidden fields to an (X)HTML document yourself, you'll have to know how to do it in order to write a CGI script that generates the code for the fields.

To add hidden fields to a form:

1. Within the form on your (X)HTML page, type **<input type="hidden"**.

2. Type **name="name"**, where *name* is a short description of the information to be stored.

3. Type **value="value"**, where *value* is the information itself that is to be stored.

4. Type **/>**.

✔ Tips

■ It doesn't matter where the hidden fields appear in your form since they won't appear in the browser anyway. As long as they are within the opening and closing form tags, you're OK.

■ In HTML, you don't have to use the quotation marks around the name and value if the name and value are comprised of only alphanumeric characters—that is, no spaces and no funny symbols. Since quotation marks have a special meaning in a Perl script and will thus need to be backslashed to get rid of that special meaning, it's often simpler to leave them out altogether where possible. (In XHTML, of course, you *always* have to use quotes around attribute values.)

■ To create an element that will be submitted with the rest of the data when the visitor clicks the submit button but that is also visible to the visitor, create a regular form element and use the readonly attribute *(see page 292)*.

Adding Hidden Fields to a Form

Creating the Submit Button

All the information that your visitors enter won't be any good to you unless they send it to the server. You should always create a submit button for your forms so that the visitor can deliver the information to you. (If you use images as active elements in a form area, see page 286.)

To create a submit button:

1. Type **<input type="submit"**.

2. If desired, type **value="submit message"** where *submit message* is the text that will appear in the button.

3. Type the final **/>**.

✔ Tips

■ If you leave out the value attribute, the submit button will be labeled *Submit Query*, by default.

■ The name-value pair for the submit button is only sent to the script if you set the name attribute. Therefore, if you omit the name attribute, you won't have to deal with the extra, usually superfluous submit data.

■ On the other hand, you can create multiple submit buttons (with both the name and value attributes) and then write your CGI script to react according to which submit button the visitor presses.

```
<input type="submit" value="Order Bed"/>
```

Figure 16.41 *If you leave out the* name *attribute, the name-value pair for the submit button will not be passed to the script. Since you usually don't need this information, that's a good thing.*

Figure 16.42 *The most important function of the submit button is to activate the script that will collect the data from the other fields. You can personalize the button's contents with the* value *attribute. (The phrase Order Bed is clearer for your visitors than the default Submit Query.)*

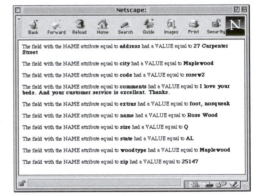

Figure 16.43 *If there is no* name *attribute specified for the submit button, not even the submit button's* value *attribute will be gathered by the script. But, hey, what do you need it for anyway?*

```
<h2>Ready to vote?</h2>

<form action="http://www.cookwood.com/cgi-
bin/vote.cgi" method="post">

<input type="radio" name="cats" value="W"
accesskey="w" />Woody<br />

<input type="radio" name="cats" value="C"
accesskey="c" />Cookie<br />

<input type="radio" name="cats" value="X"
accesskey="x" />Xixona<br />

<input type="radio" name="cats" value="L"
accesskey="l" />Llumeta<br />

<input type="radio" name="cats" value="A"
accesskey="a" />All of them (Don't make me
choose!)

<p><button type="submit" name="submit"
value="submit"><img src="check.gif" width="40"
height="40" alt="Vote button" />Vote</button>
```

Figure 16.44 *If you want a submit button with an image, you'll have to create it with the* button *tag.*

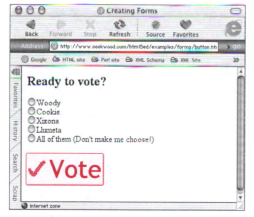

Figure 16.45 *The (X)HTML code for a submit button with an image is a little more complicated, but looks so good. (Although it would help if I could actually draw.)*

(X)HTML includes several tags that let you create prettier submit buttons. You can add an image, change the font, or even change the background color. That'll get them to submit that form!

To create a submit button with an image:

1. Type **<button type="submit" name="submit" value="submit"**

2. Type **>**.

3. Type the text, if any, that should appear on the left side of the image in the button.

4. Type **<img src="image.url"** where *image.url* is the name of the image that will appear on the button.

5. If desired, add any other image attributes.

6. Type **/>** to complete the image.

7. Type the text, if any, that should appear on the right side of the image in the button.

8. Type **</button>**.

✔ Tips

■ You can also use the button tag to create a submit button without an image. Just skip steps 4–6.

■ You can use CSS to style buttons.

■ For information on creating buttons with scripts, consult *Creating a Button that Executes a Script* on page 318.

■ Current browsers support the button tag quite well. Older browsers do not, despite it being a standard part of (X)HTML.

Resetting the Form

If humans could fill out forms perfectly on the first try, there would be no erasers on pencils and no backspace key on your computer keyboard. You can give your visitors a reset button so that they can start over with a fresh form (including all the default values you've set).

To create a reset button:

1. Type **<input type="reset"**.

2. If desired, type **value="reset message"** where *reset message* is the text that appears in the button. The default reset message is *Reset*.

3. Type **/>**.

✔ Tip

■ The name-value pair for the reset button is only sent to the script if you set the name attribute. Therefore, if you omit the name attribute, you won't have to deal with the completely superfluous reset data—which is usually something like "reset, Reset".

```
<input type="reset" value="Start Over" />
```

Figure 16.46 *You can use the* value *attribute to set any text you wish for the reset button.*

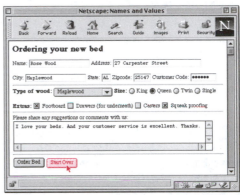

Figure 16.47 *If your visitor clicks the reset button, all the fields are set to their default values.*

```
<h2>Ready to vote?</h2>

<form action="http://www.cookwood.com/cgi-
bin/vote.cgi" method="post">

<input type="radio" name="cats" value="W"
accesskey="w" />Woody<br />

<input type="radio" name="cats" value="C"
accesskey="c" />Cookie<br />

<input type="radio" name="cats" value="X"
accesskey="x" />Xixona<br />

<input type="radio" name="cats" value="L"
accesskey="l" />Llumeta<br />

<input type="radio" name="cats" value="A"
accesskey="a" />All of them (Don't make me
choose!)

<p><button type="submit" name="submit"
value="submit"><img src="check.gif" width="40"
height="40" alt="Vote button" />Vote</button>

<button type="reset" name="reset" value="reset">
<img src="reset.gif" width="40" height="40"
alt="Reset button" />Reset</button></p>

</form>
```

Figure 16.48 *Make sure you set the* type *to reset. Otherwise, the button won't actually do anything at all.*

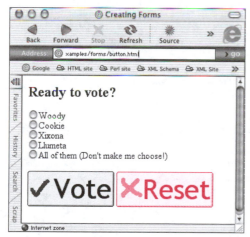

Figure 16.49 *Now both the submit and reset buttons really stand out. (It really works, by the way. Try it on my Web site—see page 24.)*

You can add images, font choices, and even a background color to your reset button.

To create a reset button with an image:

1. Type **<button type="reset" name="reset" value="reset"**

2. Type **>**.

3. Type the text, if any, that should appear on the left side of the image in the button.

4. Type **<img src="image.url"**, where *image.url* is the name of the image that will appear on the button.

5. If desired, add any other image attributes.

6. Type **/>** to complete the image.

7. Type the text, if any, that should appear on the right side of the image in the button.

8. Type **</button>**.

✔ Tips

■ You can also use the button tag to create a reset button without an image. Just skip steps 4–6.

■ For information on creating buttons with scripts, consult *Creating a Button that Executes a Script* on page 318.

■ Current browsers support the button tag quite well. Older browsers do not, despite it being a standard part of (X)HTML.

Using an Image to Submit Data

You may use an image—called an active image—as a combination input element and submit button. In addition to submitting the data from the other fields in the form, a click on the image sends the current mouse coordinates to the server in two name-value pairs. The names are generated by adding .x and .y to the value of the `name` attribute. The values correspond to the actual horizontal and vertical locations (where the top-left corner is 0,0) of the cursor.

To use an image to submit data:

1. Create a GIF or JPEG image *(see page 83)*.

2. Type **<input type="image"**.

3. Type **src="image.url"**, where *image.url* is the location of the image on the server.

4. Type **name="name"**, where *name* will be added to the mouse's *x* and *y* coordinates and sent to the server, when the visitor clicks the image.

5. Type **alt="description"**, where *description* will appear if the image does not.

6. Type the final **/>** to finish the active image definition for the form.

✔ Tips

- Setting the `value` attribute has no effect. The values are set to the mouse coordinates automatically.

- *All* the form data is sent when the visitor clicks the active image **(Figure 16.52)**. Therefore, it's a good idea to explain how to use the active image and to place the image at the end of the form so that the visitor completes the other necessary form elements before clicking the image and sending the data.

```
<form action="http://www.cookwood.com/cgi-
bin/zonemap.cgi" method="post"><br>

<input type="radio" name="infotype"
value="time" />Local time

<input type="radio" name="infotype"
value="weather" />Local weather

<input type="radio" name="infotype"
value="directions" />Directions

<input type="radio" name="infotype"
value="statistics" />City statistics

<p><input type="image" src="zonemap.gif"
name="coord" alt="U.S. Map" /></p></form>
```

Figure 16.50 *If you use an active image, you don't need a submit button.*

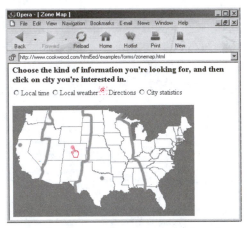

Figure 16.51 *You can have both regular form elements (like the radio buttons) and an image map in the same form. When the visitor clicks the map, all of the data is sent to the script.*

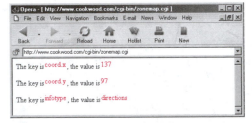

Figure 16.52 *The browser appends a period and an x to the* name *attribute (coord) and uses this name (coord.x) to identify the x coordinate of the location where the visitor clicked. The same thing happens with the y coordinate. Notice that the information from the radio button is also collected.*

Using an Image to Submit Data

```
<form action="processform.cgi" method="post">

<fieldset><legend>Personal Information</legend>

<p>Name: <input type="text" name="firstname"
size="15" /><br />

E-mail: <input type="text" name="email"
size="25" /></p>

</fieldset>

<fieldset><legend align="right">Comments
</legend> Please let us

know what you think:<br />

<textarea cols="40" rows="7"
name="comments">I think your cats are...

</textarea></fieldset>

<input type="submit" name="Submit" value="Send
```

Figure 16.53 *The* fieldset *tag is ideal for separating your form into smaller, more easily understood chunks.*

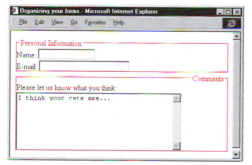

Figure 16.54 *By default, in Explorer, the fieldsets are outlined with a thin line. The legend appears at the top right or top left. Of course, you can apply CSS to them to create practically whatever look you want.*

Organizing the Form Elements

If you have a lot of information to fill out on a form, you can group related elements together to make the form easier to follow. The easier it is for your visitors to understand the form, the more likely they are to fill it out correctly.

To organize the form elements:

1. Below the form tag but above any form elements that you wish to have contained in the first group, type **<fieldset>**.

2. Type **<legend**.

3. If desired, type **align="direction"** where *direction* is left or right.

4. Type **>**.

5. Type the text for the legend.

6. Type **</legend>** to complete the legend.

7. Create the form elements that should belong in the first group. For more information, see pages 272–286.

8. Type **</fieldset>** to complete the first group of form elements.

9. Repeat steps 1–8 for each group of form elements.

✔ Tips

■ You don't have to create a legend. To omit it, skip steps 2–6. In fact, you don't have to organize your form into groups at all. While it is a useful tool, it's completely optional.

■ While the align attribute for legend has been deprecated, it's still supported by Netscape 6 and IE (from 4 on). It's default value is left. There were supposedly top and bottom values as well, but I've never seen a browser support them.

Organizing the Form Elements

Formally Labeling Form Parts

As you've seen, the explanatory information next to a form element is generally just plain text. For example, you might type "First name" before the Text field where the visitor should type her name. (X)HTML provides a method for marking up labels so that you can formally link them to the associated element and use them for scripting or other purposes.

To formally label form parts:

1. Type **<label**.

2. If desired, type **for="idname">**, where *idname* is the value of the id attribute in the corresponding form element.

3. Type the contents of the label.

4. Type **</label>**.

✔ Tips

- If you use the for attribute, you must also add the id attribute to the associated form element's tag in order to mark it with a label. (Otherwise, the document will not validate.) For more details about the id attribute, consult *Naming Elements* on page 67.

- If you omit the for attribute, no id attribute is required in the element being labeled. The label and the element, in that case, are then associated by proximity, or perhaps by being placed in a common div element.

- You can use CSS to format your labels.

- Another labeling technique is to use the title attribute. For more information, consult *Labeling Elements in a Web Page* on page 72.

```
<form action="processform.cgi" method="post">

<fieldset><legend>Personal Information</legend>

<p><label for="name">Name:</label> <input
type="text" name="firstname" size="15"
id="name"/><br />

<label>E-mail:</label> <input type="text"
name="email" size="25" /></p>

</fieldset>

<fieldset><legend
align="right">Comments</legend> Please let us
know what you think:<br />

<textarea cols="40" rows="7"
name="comments">I think

your cats are...

</textarea></fieldset>
```

Figure 16.55 *You link a label to its form element with the* for *and* id *attributes. You can also label an element without a* for *attribute (as with E-mail) in which case you can also skip the* id *attribute or not label a field at all (as with the Comments).*

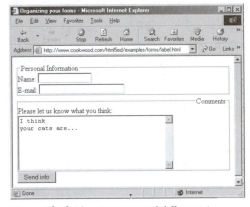

Figure 16.56 *There's no outward difference in appearance when you use labels—unless you style them with CSS.*

```
<body>

<a href="moreinfo.html" tabindex="4">About our company</a>

<h2>Please tell us more about yourself:</h2>

<form method="post" action="processform.cgi">

Name: <input type="text" name="firstname" size="20" tabindex="1" /><br />

E-mail address: <input type="text" name="email" tabindex="2" /><br />

Hobbies: <input type="text" name="hobbies" tabindex="3" /></form>

</body>
```

Figure 16.57 *You can add the* tabindex *attribute to links, form elements, and client-side image maps.*

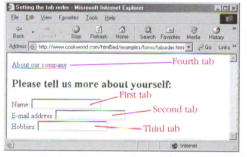

Figure 16.58 *With forms on a page that begins with a link, you may want to change the tab order so that the first tab takes you to the first field, not the first link.*

Setting the Tab Order in a Form

By pressing the Tab key, visitors can move the focus through the fields in your form from top to bottom (and then select the desired one by pressing Return). Depending on your form's layout, you may prefer to set the tab order yourself so that the visitor fills out all the fields in a particular group before going on to the next group.

To set the tab order:

In the form element's tag, type **tabindex="n"**, where *n* is the number that indicates the tab order.

✔ Tips

■ *Getting the focus* means the form element is selected but not activated. Activation requires pressing the Return key (or a keyboard shortcut—see page 290).

■ The value for tabindex can be any number between 0 and 32767.

■ By default, the tab order depends on the order of the elements in the (X)HTML code. When you change the tab order, the lower numbered elements get the focus first, followed by higher numbered elements.

■ In a form, you can assign tab order to text fields, password fields, checkboxes, radio buttons, text areas, menus, and buttons.

■ You can also assign tab order to links *(see page 127)* and client-side image maps *(see page 130).*

■ OK, I cannot tell a lie. The first time your visitor hits the Tab key, the Address or Location field—where the current URL is displayed—gets the focus (even if its toolbar is hidden). Then, the next tab brings the visitor where *you* say.

Adding Keyboard Shortcuts

Keyboard shortcuts let your visitors select and activate links without using a mouse.

To add a keyboard shortcut to a form element:

1. Inside the form element's tag, type **accesskey="**.

2. Type the keyboard shortcut (any letter or number).

3. Type the final **"**.

4. If desired, add information about the keyboard shortcut to the text so that the visitor knows that it exists.

✔ Tips

- On Windows systems, to invoke the keyboard shortcut, visitors use the Alt key plus the letter you've assigned. On Macs, visitors use the Control key.

- Explorer for Windows has supported keyboard shortcuts since version 4. IE5 for Mac and Netscape 6 also support them now. Opera has its own keyboard navigation system and will ignore yours.

- When a visitor uses a keyboard shortcut it not only gives the element the focus, but actually activates it. In the case of radio buttons and checkboxes, this means the item is selected. If it's a text box, the cursor is placed inside (after any existing text). If it's a button, the button is activated.

```
<h2>Ready to vote?</h2>

<p>Choose any option from the keyboard by
pressing Alt (Ctrl for Macintosh) plus its first letter.
So Alt-W/Ctrl-W would choose <em>Woody
</em> (he's awful cute). (Use "T" for the comments
box.)</p><hr />

<form action="http://www.cookwood.com/cgi-
bin/vote.cgi" method="post">

<input type="radio" name="cats" value="W"
accesskey="w" />Woody<br />

<input type="radio" name="cats" value="C"
accesskey="c" />Cookie<br />

<input type="radio" name="cats" value="X"
accesskey="x" />Xixona<br />

<input type="radio" name="cats" value="L"
accesskey="l" />Llumeta<br />

<input type="radio" name="cats" value="A"
accesskey="a" />All of them (Don't make me
choose!)

<p><textarea name="comments" cols="40"
rows="3" accesskey="t">Any special comments?
</textarea></p>
```

Figure 16.59 *Add keyboard shortcuts to your form elements with the* accesskey *attribute.*

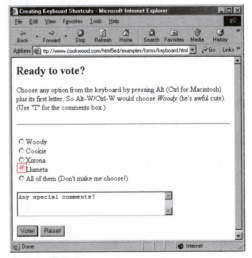

Figure 16.60 *It's a good idea to tell your visitors about any available keyboard shortcuts. Otherwise, they won't know they're there.*

```
<form action="http://www.cookwood.com/cgi-
bin/vote.cgi" method="post" name="vote">

<input type="radio" name="cats" value="W"
onclick="document.vote.submit.disabled=false"
accesskey="w"/>Woody <br />

<input type="radio" name="cats" value="C"
onclick="document.vote.submit.disabled=false"
accesskey="c" />Cookie <br />

<input type="radio" name="cats" value="X"
onclick="document.vote.submit.disabled=false"
accesskey="x" />Xixona <br />

[snip]

<p><input name="submit" type="submit" value
="Vote!" accesskey="v" disabled="disabled" />

<input type="reset" value="Reset" accesskey="r"
onclick="document.vote.submit.disabled=true" />
</p>
```

Figure 16.61 *You can use the (X)HTML* disabled *attribute to make the submit button inaccessible until other options are selected. Here, I've added a bit of very simple JavaScript to each option so that when something is selected, the submit button is enabled.*

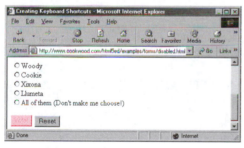

Figure 16.62 *When the visitor first views the form, nothing is selected and the submit button is disabled.*

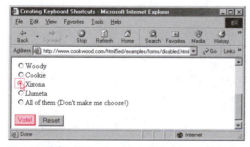

Figure 16.63 *When the visitor clicks on one of the buttons, the submit button becomes enabled.*

Disabling Form Elements

In some cases, you may not want visitors to use certain parts of your form. For example, you might want to disable a submit button until all the required fields have been filled out.

To disable a form element:

In the form element's tag, type **disabled="disabled"**.

✔ Tips

- In HTML, you can just use disabled by itself. XHTML requires the redundant value.

- You can change the contents of a disabled form element with a script. For more information on scripting, consult Chapter 18, *Scripts*. You'll also need some JavaScript expertise. The very simple way I've added here is to add **onclick= "document.vote.submit.disabled=false"** to each radio button (where *vote* is the value of the form's name attribute, *submit* is the value of the disabled button's name attribute, and *disabled* is the attribute in that button whose value I want to change to *false*). So when one of the radio buttons is clicked, the Vote button will be enabled.

- If you disable a form element, its keyboard shortcut is also disabled. For more information on keyboard shortcuts, consult *Adding Keyboard Shortcuts* on page 290.

Disabling Form Elements

Keeping Elements from Being Changed

Sometimes it may be necessary to automatically set the contents of a form element and keep the visitor from changing it. For example, you could have the visitor confirm information, or you could show a past history of transactions and then submit that information again with the new data collected. You can do this by making the element "read-only".

To keep elements from being changed:

Type **readonly="readonly"** in the form element's tag.

✔ Tips

■ In HTML, you can just use `readonly` by itself. XHTML requires the redundant value.

■ You can use the `readonly` attribute in text boxes, password boxes, checkboxes, radio buttons, and text areas.

■ Setting the `readonly` attribute is something like using a hidden field without making it hidden. For more information on hidden fields, consult *About Hidden Fields* on page 280.

```
<form action="http://www.cookwood.com/cgi-
bin/vote.cgi" method="post" name="vote">

<br>So far you've voted for

<p><textarea name="votehistory" cols="40"
rows="3" readonly="readonly">Woody on
Monday, Cookie on Tuesday, Xixona on Thursday,
and Llumeta on Wednesday</textarea></p>

<input type="radio" name="cats" value="W"
onclick="document.vote.submit.disabled=false"
accesskey="w" />Woody <br />

<input type="radio" name="cats" value="C"
onclick="document.vote.submit.disabled=false"
accesskey="c" />Cookie <br />

<input type="radio" name="cats" value="X"
onclick="document.vote.submit.disabled=false"
accesskey="x" />Xixona <br />

<input type="radio" name="cats" value="L"
onclick="document.vote.submit.disabled=false"
accesskey="l"/>Llumeta <br />

<input type="radio" name="cats" value="A"
onclick="document.vote.submit.disabled=false"
accesskey="a" />All of them (Don't make me
choose!)
```

Figure 16.64 *Add the* `readonly` *attribute to any form element that you want to show to visitors but that you don't want them to change.*

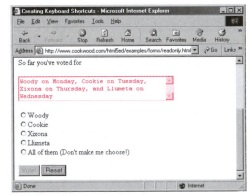

Figure 16.65 *In this example, the visitor's prior votes are displayed in the read-only text area. They can be viewed by the visitor and then submitted with the new vote.*

MULTIMEDIA

One of the things that has made the Web so popular is the fact that you can add graphics, sound, animations, and movies to your Web pages. While in the past the prohibitive size of such files limited their effectiveness, newer technologies—including streaming audio and video, Flash, and Shockwave—make pages with dynamic multimedia effects much more accessible to those of us who don't have the latest, fastest Pentiums and G4s.

Multimedia files, however, continue to be very large, and as technology improves, they seem to get bigger still. Ten seconds of medium quality sound take up more than 200K, which will take your average visitor about a minute to download. A ten second file of a movie displayed in a tiny 2" x 3" window would be about three times as big.

In addition, since the Web population is diverse, and uses many different kinds of computers, you have to make sure that the files you provide can be viewed and heard by your visitors (or the largest number of them possible). The fact that the developers of multimedia technologies can't seem to agree on standards doesn't help in the least.

Please note that this chapter is meant to be an introduction to multimedia Web files, with a strong emphasis on the (X)HTML code you need. It does not teach you how to create Flash animations or QuickTime movies, only how to make them available to your visitors.

Multimedia

Of Plugins and Players

Early Web browsers could show only black and white text, with no images. Netscape quickly put an end to that, adding internal support to their browser for color and images. But there are thousands of different kinds of files that a person might want to show in a Web page, including movies, sounds, even spreadsheets, just to mention a few. Instead of trying to add support for all of these files inside the browser, Netscape developed a system that matches the extension and MIME type of the desired file to an appropriate piece of software—a *helper application* or *player*—outside the browser.

Netscape also created the `embed` element—that together with a specialized application called a *plugin*—enables a browser to show multimedia and other types of files right in a Web page. Other browsers, including, Microsoft, with a mere 25% of the market back then, followed Netscape's lead and supported the `embed` tag.

The W3C meanwhile, perhaps annoyed with Netscape's non-standard, albeit innovative approach, ignored the success of the `embed` tag and instead created the `object` element, which it thought was a more generic and thus more powerful tool for embedding diverse types of files in a Web page.

While Netscape floundered in success, clever Microsoft started to support the newly standard `object` element, but in a non-standard way—together with its proprietary ActiveX controls which it does not share with other software companies. And with version 5.5, Explorer for Windows (but not Mac) stopped supporting Netscape's `embed` tag.

Netscape 6, for its part, now fully supports the `object` element—actually better than Explorer—and continues to support the `embed` tag for backward compatibility.

```
<object classid="clsid:02BF25D5-8C17-4B23-
BC80-D3488ABDDC6B"
width="240"height="196"

codebase="http://www.apple.com/qtactivex/
qtplugin.cab">

<param name="src" value="madmax.mov" />

<param name="autoplay" value="false" />

<param name="controller" value="true" />

<object data="madmax.mov" type=
"video/quicktime" width="240" height="196"

codebase="http://www.apple.com/qtactivex/
qtplugin.cab">

<param name="src" value="madmax.mov" />

<param name="autoplay" value="false" />

<param name="controller" value="true" />

</object>

</object>
```

Figure 17.1 *The first* `object` *tag uses Explorer's proprietary ActiveX controls, the second (highlighted) uses standard MIME types and extensions to determine the proper plugin.*

Figure 17.2 *Explorer fails to ignore the standardly coded object tag that it doesn't understand, instead displaying a big, ugly, empty box.*

Figure 17.3 *Netscape properly ignores the ActiveX controlled* `object` *and displays just the one it understands.*

Of Plugins and Players

```
<object classid="clsid:02bf25d5-8c17-4b23-
bc80-d3488abddc6b" width="240"height="196"

codebase="http://www.apple.com/qtactivex/qtpl
ugin.cab">

<param name="src" value="madmax.mov">

<param name="autoplay" value="false">

<param name="controller" value="true">

<embed src="madmax.mov" width="240"
height="196" autoplay="false" controller="true"
pluginspage="http://www.apple.com/quicktime/
download/">

</embed>

</object>
```

Figure 17.4 *Here I use the ActiveX-controlled* object *element together with the non-standard* embed *element. It is the most universal—yet least standard—solution.*

Figure 17.5 *Explorer is happy when fed just its* object *element with ActiveX controls. It ignores the* embed *element.*

Figure 17.6 *Netscape ignores the ActiveX controlled* object *as usual, but supports the* embed *tag just fine.*

So, simple, if both major browsers support the object tag, that's what we should use, right? Unfortunately, not quite yet. Explorer only supports the object element when used with its proprietary ActiveX controls. But those same controls, off limits to Netscape and other browsers, make Netscape ignore the non-standard implementation of the object element.

Luckily, the object element is designed to be nested in order to allow several options to browsers **(Figure 17.1)**. If the first object is unreadable, they can ignore it and try the next until they find one they understand. Alas, Explorer's support of the object tag is incomplete. Instead of ignoring the standard object elements it for some reason cannot understand, it shows big, ugly boxes **(Figure 17.2)**. Netscape 6, for its part, handles nested object elements perfectly, ignoring the one with proprietary ActiveX controls and displaying the standard one **(Figure 17.3)**.

In fact the only way to offer embedded multimedia files for both Explorer 5.5+ for Windows and the *other* browsers, including Netscape and Opera on both platforms as well as Explorer for Macintosh, is to combine the object element with the non-standard embed tag **(Figure 17.4)**. Explorer happily ignores the embed element since it has its ActiveX-laced object element **(Figure 17.5)**, while standards-supporting browsers ignore the non-standard use of object in favor of the familiar, if also non-standard embed tag **(Figure 17.6)**. I explain this technique throughout this chapter.

Nonetheless, this solution is far from satisfactory to those of us who would like to write standard, validated code. However, until Explorer offers complete support for the object tag, I think it's the best we've got.

Getting Players for Your Visitors

When a browser goes looking for a player or plugin on the visitor's computer, it doesn't always find one. While browsers often come bundled with one or more players, software developers, always competing for market share, continually come out with new versions. Depending on the file format and extension of the file on your site, the visitor may have to download a new player with which to view it.

On Explorer for Windows, the ActiveX control can automatically install the appropriate plugin without making the visitor close and restart their browser. It is perhaps its major positive feature. Other browsers will alert your visitor that a new player is required and will direct them to the proper page (as specified by you) where the necessary plugin or player can be found.

There are two important pieces here. First, it's a good idea to use standard formats (and versions of those formats) for which it's likely your visitors will already have an appropriate plugin or player installed. That way, they don't need to do anything special to see your multimedia files. Second, you might want to add explanatory information on your Web page about which player is required to properly view your multimedia files and even where users need to go to download them.

Visitors can also customize their browsers to open particular types of files (identified by their extension, and thus their MIME type) with the program of their choice. On Netscape, they must choose Preferences > Navigator > Helper Applications. In Explorer for Windows, from a folder on the Desktop, they should choose Tools > Folder Options > File Types. And on Explorer for Mac, they should select Preferences > Receiving Files > File Helpers.

Figure 17.7 *With Internet Explorer 5.5+ for Windows, when the visitor goes to view a multimedia file that requires a player that's not already on the visitor's system, the ActiveX control asks whether the appropriate player should be downloaded and installed. Since such actions could be a security risk, the wording of the dialog box can be a little scary: "Security Warning".*

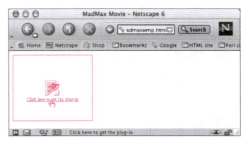

Figure 17.8 *On most browsers (other than IE5.5+ for Windows), a broken plugin icon or an alert about the missing plugin will appear. When the visitor clicks the broken icon...*

Figure 17.9 *...they are immediately directed to the Web page where they can download the necessary software and then install it themselves.*

Getting Multimedia Files

The most common multimedia files embedded on Web pages are sounds and videos. You can create sounds with a microphone and digitizing software (like SoundRecorder for Windows and Amadeus for Macintosh). And there are many programs that create MP3s from CDs.

With the advent of digital camcorders, getting video on the Web has gotten easier and easier. On the Mac you have the unbeatable and free iMovie which lets you input digital video via the incorporated Firewire port, add special effects and transitions, and then automatically convert it to QuickTime format which is easily embedded on a Web page *(see page 298)*. Folks with Windows ME can use Windows Movie Maker (though they'll also have to get the appropriate hardware for connecting their digital camcorder since most PCs don't have Firewire ports).

You can also find some free sounds and movies on the Web, although you should read their license agreements carefully. (For more information about copyrights and Web files, see *http://www.ivanhoffman.com.*)

But don't limit yourself to sounds and video. You can also embed PDF files (created with Adobe Acrobat), playable sheet music (with Sibelius Scorch), Java applets (with Sun's Java), Flash animations (with Macromedia Flash) and much more.

One limitation to multimedia madness is your visitors' willingness to download and install plugins or players for viewing unfamiliar formats. While you may have all the latest and greatest multimedia helper applications, your visitors may not. Leaving your page to download a viewer may distract them so much that they never come back.

Getting Multimedia Files

Embedding QuickTime Movies

You can add QuickTime movies to your Web site that are compatible with Explorer and Netscape on both Mac and Windows and that automatically stream from any server.

To add internal video with QuickTime:

1. Create a movie (perhaps with iMovie) and save it in QuickTime format with the .mov extension.

2. In your Web page, start by inserting the endless number that calls Explorer's ActiveX control for QuickTime, by typing **<object classid= "clsid:02bf25d5-8c17-4b23-bc80-d3488abddc6b" codebase= "http://www.apple.com/qtactivex/qtplugin.cab"**.

3. Next, without closing the initial `object` tag yet, type **width="w" height="h"**, where *w* and *h* are the desired width and height, respectively, in pixels, of the box that will hold the movie.

4. Type **>** to complete the initial `object` tag.

5. Next, type **<param name="src" value="filename.mov">**, where *filename.mov* is the name of your movie file.

6. Type **<param name="autoplay" value="true">**, to make the movie start playing automatically when the visitor jumps to this page (or use a value of `false` to keep the movie from starting automatically).

7. If you want control buttons to appear under the movie, type **<param name= "controller" value="true">**. Or use a value of `false` to hide the controls (in which case you better use `true` in step 6).

```
<body>

<p>Here's my movie:</p>

<object classid="clsid:02bf25d5-8c17-4b23-
bc80-d3488abddc6b"

codebase="http://www.apple.com/qtactivex/
qtplugin.cab"

width="240"height="196">

<param name="src" value="madmax.mov">

<param name="autoplay" value="false">

<param name="controller" value="true">

<embed src="madmax.mov" width="240"
height="196" autoplay="false" controller="true"
pluginspage="http://www.apple.com/quicktime/
download/">

</embed>

</object>
```

Figure 17.10 *The* `object` *tag is used by Internet Explorer 5.5+ for Windows, which no longer supports the* `embed` *tag. The* `embed` *tag is used by all other browsers* .

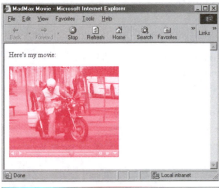

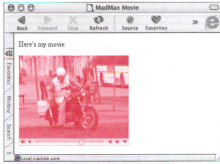

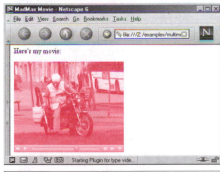

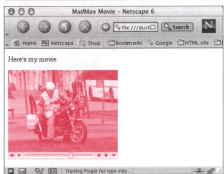

Figure 17.11 *The movie shows up in the big two browsers on both platforms. No small feat.*

8. For browsers besides IE5.5+, type **<embed src="filename.mov" width="w" height="h" autoplay="true" controller= "true" pluginspage= "http:// www.apple.com/quicktime/download/">** **</embed>**, where *filename.mov*, *w*, *h*, and the values for `autoplay` and `controller` have the same values as you specified in steps 2–7.

9. Finally, type **</object>**.

✔ Tips

■ You can download a template file from my Web site in order to save yourself from typing that incredible classid. What were they thinking?

■ You can find the size of the movie in the QuickTime player by choosing Window > Show Movie Info (and clicking the triangle, if necessary).

■ The height and width determine the size of the box that contains the movie. If the box is too small, the movie will be cropped (or scaled if you've set a scale factor—page 300). If the box is too big, there will be empty space around it.

■ You should include an additional 16 pixels in the `height` to allow for the control box.

■ The default value for `autoplay` is defined by the visitor in their QuickTime settings. The default value for `controller` is true.

■ Explorer 5.5+ for Windows will use the information in the `object` tag while other browsers (including Explorer for Mac) will use the information in the `embed` tag. While the values of the two elements should probably match, it's not absolutely required. You could even combine the `object` element for the Windows Media Player *(see page 304)* with the `embed` tag for the QuickTime player.

Embedding QuickTime Movies

Scaling a QuickTime Movie

You can adjust the size of a QuickTime movie in the (X)HTML code.

To scale a QuickTime movie:

1. After the initial `object` tag *(step 2 on page 298)*, type **<param name="scale" value="factor">**, where *factor* is:

tofit, if you want the movie to be reduced or expanded to fit its box.

Or **aspect**, if you want the movie to be reduced or expanded to fit its box while maintaining its original proportions.

Or **n**, where *n* is the number with which the original height and width of the movie will be multiplied to get the final height and width.

Type **">** to complete the `param` tag.

2. Next, in the `embed` element add **scale="value"**, where *value* is the same as the value you used in step 1.

✔ Tips

■ You may wish to also adjust the height and width of the movie's box *(see page 298)*.

■ The `scale` parameter changes the size of the movie, not the size of the movie's box, which you specified in step 3 and step 8 on page 299. If you use a numerical scale factor and the box is too small or too big, the movie will be cropped, or empty space will appear around the movie.

■ If you make the box smaller than the movie, the scale parameter gives you control over how the movie should be adjusted to fit. If you don't specify the scale parameter, the movie is simply cropped.

```
<body>

<p>Here's my movie:</p>

<object classid="clsid:02bf25d5-8c17-4b23-
bc80-d3488abddc6b"

codebase="http://www.apple.com/qtactivex/
qtplugin.cab"

width="480"height="392">

<param name="src" value="madmax.mov">

<param name="autoplay" value="false">

<param name="controller" value="true">

<param name="scale" value="2">

<embed src="madmax.mov" width="480"
height="392" autoplay="false" controller="true"
pluginspage="http://www.apple.com/quicktime/
download/" scale="2">

</embed>

</object>
```

Figure 17.12 *I've made the space for the movie bigger (using the* width *and* height *attributes in both the* object *and* embed *tags). Then, I add the* scale param *element to double the size of the movie itself.*

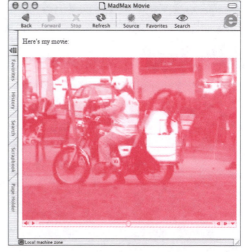

Figure 17.13 *The movie appears at twice its original size. Note that I also made the movie's box twice its original size so that the movie itself wouldn't be cropped.*

Scaling a QuickTime Movie

```
<body>

<p>Here's my movie:</p>

<object classid="clsid:02bf25d5-8c17-4b23-
bc80-d3488abddc6b"

codebase="http://www.apple.com/qtactivex/
qtplugin.cab"

width="480"height="392">

<param name="src" value="madmax.mov">

<param name="autoplay" value="false">

<param name="controller" value="true">

<param name="scale" value="2">

<param name="loop" value="true">

<embed src="madmax.mov" width="480"
height="392" autoplay="false" controller="true"
pluginspage="http://www.apple.com/quicktime/
download/" scale="2" loop="true">

</embed>

</object>
```

Figure 17.14 *Don't forget to add both the* param *element within the* object *element as well as the* loop *attribute to the* embed *tag.*

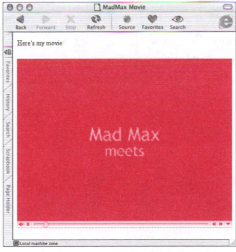

Figure 17.15 *With a* loop *value of* true, *the movie automatically starts over when it reaches the end.*

Looping a QuickTime Movie

You can make a QuickTime Movie play over and over again.

To loop a QuickTime movie:

1. After the initial object tag *(step 2 on page 298)*, type **<param name="loop" value="option">**, where *option* is true if you want the movie to loop continuously, false if you want the movie to play just once and palindrome if you want the movie to play forwards and then backwards, continuously.

2. Add the loop attribute to the embed tag with the same value as you've specified in step 1.

Putting QuickTime Sounds on a Page

You can save sound files in QuickTime format. (They simply have no video track.) You can also use QuickTime to play MP3s and many other sound formats. Sounds can either be controlled by the visitor or hidden so that they play in the background.

To put QuickTime sounds on a page:

1. Follow the instructions for putting regular QuickTime movies on a page *(see page 298)*.

2. Use a value of 16 for the height and a width of 240 for the sound-only controller.

✔ Tip

■ You can hide QuickTime sounds altogether *(see page 303)*.

```
<p>Listen to Barcelona street sounds:</p>

<object classid="clsid:02bf25d5-8c17-4b23-bc80-d3488abddc6b" width="240" height="16"
codebase="http://www.apple.com/qtactivex/qtplugin.cab">

<param name="src" value="madmax_sound.mov">

<param name="autoplay" value="true">

<param name="controller" value="true">

 <param name="loop" value="true">

<embed src="madmax_sound.mov" width="240" height="16" autoplay="true" controller="true" pluginspage="http://www.apple.com/quicktime/download/" loop="true">

</embed>

</object>
```

Figure 17.16 *Set the height to 16 if you're just embedding sounds.*

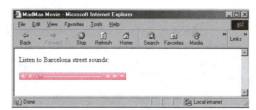

Figure 17.17 *The 16 pixel high controller is shown.*

Putting QuickTime Sounds on a Page

```
<param name="hidden" value="true">

<embed src="madmax_sound.mov" width="240"
height="16" autoplay="true" controller="true"
pluginspage="http://www.apple.com/quicktime/
download/" loop="true" hidden>
```

Figure 17.18 *You can also hide the controller altogether if you want a background sound.*

Hiding QuickTime Sounds

You can hide a QuickTime sound, essentially creating background music for your site.

To hide QuickTime sounds:

1. Follow the instructions for putting regular QuickTime movies on a page *(see page 298)*.

2. Hide the control buttons altogether, thus creating a background sound, by typing after the initial object tag, **<param name="hidden" value="true">** and adding the stand-alone attribute **hidden** to the embed tag.

✔ Tips

■ Explorer will hide the controller if you use the hidden parameter, but it leaves an empty space for it. (Thanks a lot!) Since Apple cautions against using a height less than 2 pixels due to problems in some browsers, my recommendation would be to either use a value of 3 pixels (!) or put the hidden sound at the end of your (X)HTML page where it won't mess up your layout.

■ It's probably a good idea to keep background sounds at the end of your code in all cases. That way, your visitors can look at your page while they're waiting for the sound to download.

■ I might note that I hate background sounds. There is little more annoying to me than jumping to a page and having to actually wait while it downloads some tinny rendition of a song I'm embarrassed to admit that I might like in other circumstances. They're even more awkward and annoying in office environments.

Embedding Windows Media Player Files

Inserting Windows format movies and sounds on your Web page is quite similar to embedding QuickTime movies. The principal differences are the value of the classid, and the names and values of the param elements.

To embed Windows Media Player files:

1. Create the desired movie or sound.

2. In your (X)HTML document, type **<object classid="CLSID:22D6F312-B0F6-11D0-94AB-0080C74C7E95" codebase= "http://activex.microsoft.com/activex/ controls/mplayer/en/nsmp2inf.cab# Version=6,4,5,715"**.

3. Next type **width="w" height="h"**, where *w* and *h* are the size in pixels of the media player that you'd like to embed.

4. Type **type="application/x-oleobject"** so that the browser knows what to expect.

5. Type **>** to complete the initial object tag.

6. To tell the player where the media file is, type **<param name="filename" value="movie.avi">**, where *movie.avi* is the name and extension of the multimedia file.

7. If desired, you can type **<param name= "autostart" value="false">** in order to keep the file from playing automatically. The default is true.

8. If desired, you can type **<param name="showcontrols" value="false">** to hide the play, rewind and other control buttons. The default value is true.

9. If desired, you can type **<param name="showstatusbar" value="true">** in order to display a little status bar at the bottom of the player. The default is false.

```
<body>
<object id="MediaPlayer1"
classid="CLSID:22D6F312-B0F6-11D0-94AB-
0080C74C7E95"
codebase="http://activex.microsoft.com/activex/
controls/mplayer/en/nsmp2inf.cab#Version=6,4,
5,715"
width="240" height="252"
type="application/x-oleobject">
  <param name="autostart" value="false">
  <param name="filename" value="madmax.avi">
  <param name="showcontrols" value="true">
  <param name="ShowStatusBar" value="true">
<embed type="application/x-mplayer2"
pluginspage="http://www.microsoft.com/
Windows/MediaPlayer/" src="madmax.avi"
width="240" height="252" autostart="0"
showcontrols="1" showstatusbar="1"></embed>
</object>
```

Figure 17.19 *Here's the code for embedding the Windows Media Player.*

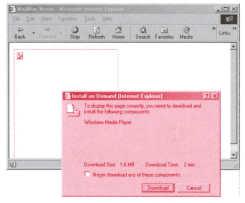

Figure 17.20 *One of the purported advantages of Windows' reliance on ActiveX is that it allows visitors to easily download the plug-in should it not already be installed.*

Figure 17.21 *However, the ActiveX control doesn't work on the systems that are most likely not to have Windows Media Player already installed, like folks who use Netscape and/or Macintosh. These visitors have to click the broken link and then manually download the plugin from the page that appears.*

Figure 17.22 *Once the plugin is installed, the movie plays correctly.*

Figure 17.23 *If Windows Media Player is not installed and the ActiveX control is not functioning, some browsers, including Internet Explorer for Macintosh shown here, will simply display the movie with whatever player is available (in this case the QuickTime player).*

10. Now, for browsers besides Explorer 5.5+, type **<embed type="application/x-mplayer2" pluginspage="http://www.microsoft.com/Windows/MediaPlayer/"**.

11. Type **src="madmax.avi"**, where *movie.avi* is the name of the desired multimedia file.

12. Type **width="w" height="h"**, where *w* and *h* are the size in pixels of the desired embedded Media Player.

13. If desired, add the `autostart`, `showcontrols` and `showstatusbar` attributes to the `embed` tag with values of 1 for true and 0 for false.

14. Type **</embed></object>** to complete the embedded player.

✔ Tips

■ I would also recommend advising Netscape 6 visitors to go to Microsoft's site to download version 7.1 of Windows Media Player. Microsoft's earlier installers (including 6.4) only recognize Netscape version 4.x and earlier and so do not properly install the plugin for Netscape 6.

■ You can personalize the Windows Media Player with custom skins and scripting. See Microsoft's site for details.

■ Internet Explorer 5.5+ for Windows will use the information in the `object` tag while other browsers (including Explorer for Mac) will use the information in the embedded `embed` tag. While the values of the two elements should probably match, it's not absolutely required. You could even use the `object` element described on this page in conjunction with the `embed` tag described for the QuickTime player *(see page 298)*.

Inserting Java Applets

Java applets are little applications (hence the term *applets*) that can run in your browser to create special effects on your page, like clocks, calculators, and interactive events. There are whole books devoted to Java; here we'll restrict the topic to how to insert applets on your page once you've written or copied them from another source.

To insert an applet:

1. Type **<object codetype="application/ java" classid="java:file.class"**, where *file.class* is the name of the applet you want to embed.

2. Then type **width="w" height="h"**, where *w* and *h* are the applet's size in pixels.

3. Close the opening `object` tag with **>**.

4. Include any parameters, with **<param name="parameter" value="value_of_ parameter" />**.

5. Finally, type **</object>** to finish.

✔ Tips

■ You can get more information about Java applets at: *http://java.sun.com/applets/*.

■ You don't need to know Java to be able to use applets on your page.

■ You can also use the deprecated, but still well-supported `applet` element to embed Java applets on a page: **<applet code="applet.class" width="w" height= "h"><param name="param_name" value="param_value" /></applet>**, where *applet.class* is the name of the applet to be embedded and the other values are the same as described above.

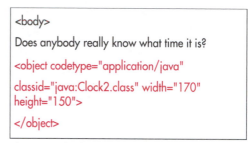

Figure 17.24 *This applet doesn't have any parameters to adjust. Everything is in the opening* `object` *tag.*

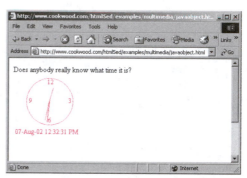

Figure 17.25 *Applets you create interactive, multimedia effects on your page without having to know how to program or script.*

Inserting Java Applets

Figure 17.26 *Go the player manufacturer's home page and search for "embed".*

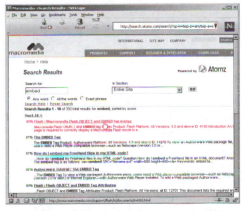

Figure 17.27 *Follow the link that gives more information about embedding the player.*

Figure 17.28 *Since companies want to make it easy to embed their player, they usually offer complete details, including the* `classid` *attribute and other controls.*

Embedding Other Multimedia Files

Other common types of multimedia files that you might want to embed on a page include Flash animations, Real audio and video, Scorch music files, and more.

To embed other multimedia files:

1. Go to the Web site of the company that develops the player for the multimedia files you want to embed. For example, for Flash, go to Macromedia's site *(http://www.macromedia.com)*.

2. Look for developer information on the Web site or search for "embedding files". Most sites offer information about the exact value of the `classid` that you'll need for embedding multimedia for IE5.5 for Windows as well as the MIME types you'll need for embedding those same files for all other browsers.

3. Create an outer `object` tag with the proper `classid` that calls the appropriate ActiveX control.

4. Create the `param` elements that control the appearance of the embedded player.

5. Create an inner `embed` tag with the MIME types and other information needed by browsers that don't support Windows' proprietary ActiveX controls.

6. Close the `embed` element and then the `object` element.

✔ Tip

■ If you can't find information on the site, try looking at the source code of a page that contains an embedded player. You should be able to find the value of the `classid` attribute there, as well as other attributes for controlling the player.

Linking to Multimedia Files

While embedding multimedia files gives your pages a more coherent look, linking to external helper applications or players can give your visitors welcome control over large multimedia downloads. A link gives them the choice about whether to see the file or not.

To link to multimedia files:

1. Type **<a href="multimedia.ext">**, where *multimedia.ext* is the name of the multimedia file that should open in an external player.

2. Type the text that the visitor will click on to activate the link.

3. Type **</a>** to complete the link.

✔ Tips

■ You may wish to also include information about the player with which they should view the file as well as a link to that player's download page.

■ On most browsers, if the visitor has an appropriate plugin installed, the multimedia file will be opened in a new browser window with an embedded player. If the visitor does not have an appropriate plugin but does have a player, the linked file is opened in the external player. And, if there is neither a plugin nor a player available, most browsers will let visitors download the file and/or choose another program with which to open it. Finally, some browsers give visitors choices along the way.

■ The important point is that the browser won't load the multimedia file unless the visitor expressly requests it.

```
<head>
<title>MadMax Movie</title>
</head>
<body>
<p>Here's my <a
href="madmax.mov">movie</a>.
</body>
</html>
```

Figure 17.29 *Create a link to the movie.*

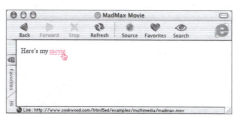

Figure 17.30 *When the visitor clicks the link...*

Figure 17.31 *...an independent QuickTime player appears. It is not within the browser window.*

Linking to Multimedia Files

```
<head>

<meta http-equiv="refresh" content="5;
url=page2.html" />

<style> p {width:200px}</style>

<title>Slide Show Page 1</title>

</head>

<body>

<p><img src="tree1.jpg" alt="Tree in September"
width="200" height="293" /></p>

<p>I love autumn in New England. Last year,
```

Figure 17.32 *The* meta *tag must be in the* head *section. It won't work if you place it anywhere else.*

Figure 17.33 *The first page loads as usual. But wait five seconds, and...*

Figure 17.34 *...the second page loads automatically. And so on.*

Creating an Automatic Slide Show

And now for something completely different! You can use a special feature of the meta attribute, within the head section, to automatically move the reader from one page to another. If you set up a series of pages in this way, you create a Web slide show.

To create an automatic slide show:

1. In the first page, within the head section, type **<meta http-equiv="refresh"**. (That's a regular hyphen between http and equiv.)

2. Type **content="n;** where *n* is the number of seconds the current page should display on the screen.

3. Type **url=nextpage.html" />** where *nextpage.html* is the URL of the next page that you want the visitor to jump to automatically.

4. Repeat these steps for each page in the series.

✔ Tips

- Omit the meta tag in the last page of the series if you don't want to cycle around again to the beginning.

- Make sure you use a display time long enough for all of your pages to appear on screen.

- This is a great way to show a portfolio or other series of images without having to create a lot of links and buttons.

- Be careful with the quotation marks. Notice that there is one set before content and the closing set after the URL.

Creating an Automatic Slide Show

Creating a Marquee

A marquee is text that starts at one part of the screen and floats across to the left, rather like the messages that advertise sales in the window of a 24-hour gas station. Internet Explorer for both Mac and Windows lets you put marquees on your Web page.

To create a marquee:

1. Type **<marquee**.

If desired, type **behavior="type"** where *type* is scroll, for text that starts at one side of the screen and disappears off the other, slide for text that starts at one side of the screen and stops when it reaches the other, or alternate for text that starts at one side of the screen and bounces back when it reaches the other side.

2. To determine which direction the text starts from, type **direction="left"** or **direction="right"**.

3. If desired, type **loop="n"**, where *n* is the number of times the text will pass across the screen. Use **loop="infinite"** to have the text appear continuously.

4. Type **scrollamount="n"** to determine how much space, in pixels, is left between each pass of the text.

5. Type **scrolldelay="n"** to determine how much time, in milliseconds, passes before the text scrolls again.

6. Use the **height**, **width**, **hspace**, **vspace**, **align**, and **bgcolor** attributes as usual, if desired.

7. Type the final **>**.

8. Type the scrolling text.

9. Type **</marquee>**.

```
<html>

<head>

<title>Untitled</title>

</head>

<body>

<h1>The Quabbin Reservoir</h1>

They had to flood four towns and three <snip>
<marquee width="75%" height="15"
behavior="scroll" direction="left" loop="infinite"
bgcolor="yellow">

Attention: Quabbin Enthusiasts General Meeting
Dec 9 at 7pm

</marquee>

</body></html>
```

Figure 17.35 *Notice that there's not much point in adding a* DOCTYPE *since this document contains proprietary tags that are not part of any specifications.*

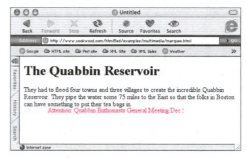

Figure 17.36 *With the* direction *set to* left *and* behavior *to* scroll, *the text starts at the right and moves toward the left before disappearing off the page.*

Figure 17.37 *Netscape and other standards-supporting browsers completely ignore Microsoft's extensions.*

```
<html><head>

<title>Background Sound for Explorer
Only</title></head>

<body>

<h1>Dakota</h1>

<bgsound src="dakota.mp3" loop="2">

<p>Dakota is Kevin's lovable golden lab. I haven't
actually met him, though I'm looking forward to it.
But I know he sounds something like this.

</p>

</body>

</html>
```

Figure 17.38 *Again, there's not much point in using the* DOCTYPE *with non-standard, proprietary tags.*

Figure 17.39 *Woof, woof. You can't see sound, but trust me, if you play it loud enough, your cats will disappear.*

Adding Background Sound

Internet Explorer for both Mac and Windows has a special, non-standard tag that lets you link a sound to a page and have the sound play automatically whenever a visitor jumps to the page.

To add background sound:

1. In the (X)HTML document, type **<bgsound src="sound.url"** where *sound.url* is the complete file name, including the extension of the sound.

2. If desired, type **loop="n"** where *n* is the number of times you wish the sound to be played. Use **loop="-1"** or **loop= "infinite"** to play the sound over and over.

3. Type the final **>**.

✔ Tips

■ I include this technique only for its historical value. This is a non-standard, proprietary tag with little support among non-Explorer browsers. It can be easily duplicated with the standard `object` tag (*see page 302*).

■ Don't use a really obnoxious, annoying, or long sound (or even a particularly loud one) if you want people to come back to your page with any regularity.

■ The `bgsound` tag recognizes WAV, AU, MP3, or MIDI formatted sounds.

Adding Background Sound

18

SCRIPTS

Scripts are little programs that add interactivity to your page. You can write simple scripts to add an alert box or a bit of text to your page, or more complicated scripts that load particular pages according to your visitor's browser or change a frame's background color depending on where they point the mouse. Because scripts are perfect for moving elements around on a page, they are the backbone of dynamic HTML, also known as DHTML.

Most scripts are written in JavaScript, since JavaScript is the scripting language that is supported by most browsers, including Netscape and Explorer.

Of course, there are entire books written about JavaScript—and some very fine ones indeed, including *JavaScript for the World Wide Web: Visual QuickStart Guide* by Dori Smith and Tom Negrino. In this chapter, rather than talking about how to write scripts, I'll stick to explaining how to insert those scripts, once created, into your (X)HTML documents.

For a look at a few important scripts that you can use in your pages, consult Chapter 19, *JavaScript Essentials*.

Scripts

313

Adding an "Automatic" Script

There are two kinds of scripts—those that are executed without the visitor having to do anything and those that react to something the visitor has done. The first group might be called "automatic scripts" and are executed by the browser when the page is loaded. You can have as many automatic scripts as you like on a page. They will run in the order they appear. (The second group, "triggered scripts", is discussed on page 316.)

To add an automatic script:

1. In your (X)HTML document, type **<script**.

2. Type **type="text/language-name"**, where *language-name* identifies the scripting language you're using: *javascript*, *vbscript*, etc.

3. Type **language="script"**, where *script* is the name of the scripting language you'll be using: *JavaScript*, *VBScript*, etc.

4. Type **>**.

5. Type the content of the script.

6. Type **</script>**.

✔ Tips

- The `language` attribute is deprecated and thus only valid in (X)HTML transitional (*see page 38*). Nevertheless it is often used to maintain compatibility with older browsers.

- The location of the script on the (X)HTML page determines when it will load. Scripts are loaded in the order in which they appear in the (X)HTML file. If you want your script to load before anything else, be sure to place it in the `head` section.

- For hiding scripts in XHTML pages from XML parsers, see page 321.

```
<head>
<meta http-equiv="content-type"
content="text/html; charset=iso-8859-1" />
<title>Simple Scripts</title>
</head>
<body>
<script type="text/javascript"
language="JavaScript">

document.write("Visca Catalunya!")

</script>

<p>Here's the rest of the page.</p>
</body>
</html>
```

Figure 18.1 *A script may appear anywhere in your (X)HTML document, however, where it appears determines when it will be executed.*

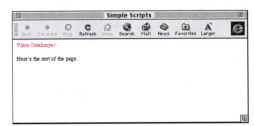

Figure 18.2 *This simple JavaScript script is output to the browser window itself. Other scripts send their results elsewhere.*

```
document.write("Visca Catalunya!")
```

Figure 18.3 *Here I've created an independent text file with the same script as in Figure 18.1. I can reference this external script from inside any (X)HTML file.*

```
<head>
<meta http-equiv="content-type"
content="text/html; charset=iso-8859-1" />
<title>Accessing external scripts</title>
</head>
<body>
<script type="text/javascript"
language="JavaScript" src="extscript.txt">

</script>

<p>Here's the rest of the page.</p>
</body>
</html>
```

Figure 18.4 *The* src *attribute not only references the script, it also automatically hides it from browsers that don't recognize the* script *tag.*

Figure 18.5 *External scripts work the same way as internal ones. But they are often much more convenient.*

Calling an External Automatic Script

If you use a script in several different Web pages, you'll save time and avoid typos by creating an external script (in Text Only format) and then calling the script from each page where it is used.

To call an external automatic script:

1. Type **<script**.

2. Type **type="text/language-name"**, where *language-name* identifies the scripting language you're using: *javascript, vbscript,* etc.

3. Type **language="script"**, where *script* is the name of the scripting language you'll be using: *JavaScript, VBScript,* etc.

4. Type **src="script.url"**, where *script.url* is the location on the server of the external script.

5. If desired, type **charset="code"**, where *code* is the official name for the set of characters used in the external script.

6. Type **>**.

7. Type **</script>**.

✔ Tips

- Using external scripts is a great way to keep older browsers from displaying your scripts as text. Since they don't understand the script tag, they ignore it (and the src attribute) completely. Use noscript to give those visitors using the older browsers an idea of what they're missing *(see page 319)*.

- The language attribute is deprecated. Nevertheless it is often used to maintain compatibility with older browsers.

Triggering a Script

Sometimes you won't want a script to run until the visitor does something to trigger it. For example, perhaps you want to run a script when the visitor mouses over a particular picture or link, or when a page is loaded. These actions—mousing over or loading a page—are called *intrinsic events*. There are currently 18 predefined intrinsic events. You use them as triggers to determine when a script will run.

To trigger a script:

1. Create the (X)HTML tag that the intrinsic event depends on **(Figure 18.6)**.

2. Within the tag created in step 1, type **event**, where *event* is an intrinsic event as defined below **(Figure 18.7)**. Unless otherwise noted, most events can be used with most (X)HTML tags.

    onload occurs when a browser loads a page or frameset. **onunload** occurs when it unloads. They can be used in the body or `frameset` tags.

    onclick occurs when the visitor clicks an element. **ondblclick** occurs when they double click it.

    onmousedown occurs when the visitor points at an (X)HTML element and presses the mouse button down. **onmouseup** occurs when they let go.

    onmouseover occurs when the visitor points at an element. **onmousemove** occurs when the visitor moves the pointer that is already over an element. **onmouseout** occurs when the visitor moves the pointer away from the element.

    onselect occurs when the visitor selects some text in a form element.

```
<head>
<meta http-equiv="content-type"
content="text/html; charset=iso-8859-1" />
<title>Triggering scripts</title>
</head>
<body>
<p>What <a href="time.html">time</a> is it?
</p>

<p>Here's the rest of the page.</p>
</body>
</html>
```

Figure 18.6 *First, create the (X)HTML tag that the intrinsic event depends on. In this case, I want the script to occur when a visitor clicks the link. Therefore, I have to start with the link tag.*

```
<head>
<meta http-equiv="content-type"
content="text/html; charset=iso-8859-1" />
<title>Triggering scripts</title>
</head>
<body>
<p>What <a href="time.html"
onclick="alert('Today is '+ Date())">time</a> is it?
</p>

<p>Here's the rest of the page.</p>
</body>
</html>
```

Figure 18.7 *The event name and the script itself go right inside the (X)HTML tag. Make sure to enclose the script in double quotation marks.*

Figure 18.8 *A triggered script doesn't run until the visitor completes the required action. In this case, they have to click the link.*

Figure 18.9 *Once the visitor clicks the link, the script runs. In this case, an alert appears, giving the current date and time.*

onfocus occurs when the visitor selects or tabs to an element. **onblur** occurs when the visitor leaves an element that was "in focus".

onkeypress occurs when the visitor types any character in a form element. **onkeydown** occurs even before the visitor lets go of the key and **onkeyup** waits until the visitor lets go of the key. As you might imagine, these only work with form elements that you can type in.

onsubmit occurs when the visitor clicks the submit button in a form *(see page 282)*. **onreset** occurs when the visitor resets the form *(see page 284)*.

onchange occurs when the visitor has changed the form element's value and has left that element (by tabbing out or selecting another).

3. Next, type **="script"**, where *script* is the actual script that should run when the event occurs.

✔ Tips

- If your script requires quotation marks, use single quotation marks so that they're not confused with the quotation marks that enclose the entire script (in step 3).

- If you need to use quotes within text that is already enclosed in single quotation marks, you can backslash them. So, you could use **onclick="alert('Here is today\'s date:' + Date())"**. Without the backslash, the apostrophe in *today's* would mess up the script.

- For a complete listing of which intrinsic events work with which (X)HTML tags, consult the table on page 448.

- Also see *Setting the Default Scripting Language* on page 322.

Triggering a Script

Creating a Button that Executes a Script

You can associate a button with a script to give your visitor full control over when the script should be executed.

To create a button that executes a script:

1. Type **<button type="button"**.

2. Type **name="name"**, where *name* is the identifier for the button.

3. Type **onclick="script"**, where *script* is the code (usually JavaScript) that will run when the visitor clicks the button.

4. If desired, type **style="font: 14pt Lithos Regular; background:red"** (or whatever) to change the appearance of the text on the button.

5. Type **>**.

6. If desired, type the text that should appear on the button.

7. Type **</button>**.

✔ Tips

■ You can use other intrinsic events with buttons, but `onclick` makes the most sense.

■ You can also add images to buttons. Simply insert the image between the opening and closing `button` tags (that is, after step 5 or 6).

■ You can also use buttons with forms (*see pages 283 and 285*).

■ Although `button` is standard (X)HTML, only current browsers support it.

```
<!DOCTYPE html PUBLIC "-//W3C//DTD XHTML
1.0 Transitional//EN"
    "http://www.w3.org/TR/xhtml1/DTD/xhtml1-
transitional.dtd">
<html xmlns="http://www.w3.org/1999/xhtml">
<head>
<meta http-equiv="content-type"
content="text/html; charset=utf-8" />
<title>Associating scripts with a button</title>
</head>
<body>
<button type="button" name="time"
onclick="alert('Today is '+ Date())" style="font:
24px 'Helvetica', 'Arial', sans-serif;
background:yellow;color:red;padding:4px">What
time is it?</button>
</body>
</html>
```

Figure 18.10 *Notice that the script is the same as the one used in the example in Figure 18.7. The style information here is optional, but it does make the button stand out. I also could have added an image.*

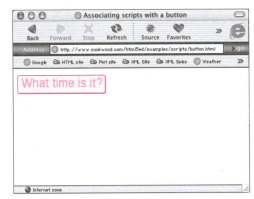

Figure 18.11 *Although the* button *tag is a standard part of (X)HTML, only current browsers support it (with or without scripts).*

Figure 18.12 *A click on the button executes the script, as shown here.*

```
<title>Llumi's big cat dreams</title>
<script type="text/javascript"
language="javascript">
   <!--
     littlecat = new Image(143,83)
     littlecat.src = "real.jpg"
     bigcat = new Image(143,83)
     bigcat.src = "dream.jpg"
   // -->

</script>
</head>
<body>
<noscript>Your browser isn't running scripts, so you
can't see what Llumi's thinking.</noscript>
<p>Point at Llumi to see what she's thinking. <a
href="llumipage.html"
onmouseover="document.catpic.src = bigcat.src"
```

Figure 18.13 *The* noscript *tag helps you take care of visitors who use really old browsers or who have scripting turned off in their browser.*

Figure 18.14 *If your visitor uses a browser that doesn't support scripts (like Mosaic, shown here), they'll get a message explaining what's missing.*

Figure 18.15 *Or if your visitor has turned off Java-script support (in Communicator here), the* noscript *text will clue them in to the problem.*

Adding Alternate Information

If you give your visitors access to information through scripts, you may want to provide an alternate method of getting that data if your visitor uses a browser that can't run the scripts.

To add alternate information for older browsers:

1. Type **<noscript>**.

2. Type the alternate information.

3. Type **</noscript>**.

✔ Tips

■ If a browser doesn't understand the script tag, what hope is there that it will understand noscript? Actually it won't. It will completely ignore it and treat its contents as regular text—which, curiously, is exactly what you want. Only the browsers that understand script (and thus can run the script) will understand noscript as well. And as long as they've got JavaScript on, they'll *ignore* the contents of the noscript tag—which is also what you want. Clever, indeed.

■ Current browsers (and some older ones) allow your visitors to disable JavaScript. The noscript tag is perfect for telling those visitors what they're missing **(Figure 18.15)**.

■ The noscript tag will not help if the browser doesn't support the scripting language or if there is a problem with the script.

Adding Alternate Information

Hiding Scripts from Older Browsers

Older browsers don't always understand the `script` tag. If they don't, they'll just ignore it and display your script as if it were part of the body of the (X)HTML document. To keep that from happening, it's a good idea to use commenting to hide scripts from older browsers.

To hide scripts from older browsers:

1. After the initial `script` tag, type **<!--**.

2. Write the script as usual.

3. Right before the final `script` tag, type your scripting language's comments symbol. For JavaScript, type **//**. For VBScript, type **'** (a single quotation mark). For TCL, type **#**.

4. If desired, add text to remind yourself why you're typing all these funny characters. Something like **end comments to hide scripts** will work just fine.

5. Type **-->**.

✔ Tips

■ The code in step 1 and in step 5 is for hiding the script from the browsers. The code in step 3 is for keeping the final **-->** from being processed as part of the script, and thus must be specific to the particular scripting language you're using.

■ I have to admit I had a hard time finding a browser old enough not to understand scripts. Hiding scripts from browsers is a good idea, but I'm not sure it's essential.

■ External scripts *(see page 315)* are automatically hidden from old browsers. They simply don't follow the URL.

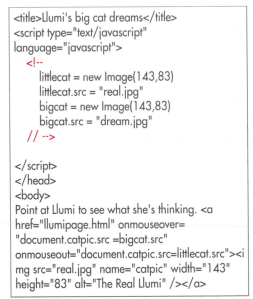

Figure 18.16 *This is Mosaic 1. Because it doesn't understand the* `script` *tag, it ignores it and prints out the script as if it were regular text. Ugly!*

```
<title>Llumi's big cat dreams</title>
<script type="text/javascript"
language="javascript">
  <!--
    littlecat = new Image(143,83)
    littlecat.src = "real.jpg"
    bigcat = new Image(143,83)
    bigcat.src = "dream.jpg"
  // -->

</script>
</head>
<body>
Point at Llumi to see what she's thinking. <a
href="llumipage.html" onmouseover=
"document.catpic.src =bigcat.src"
onmouseout="document.catpic.src=littlecat.src"><i
mg src="real.jpg" name="catpic" width="143"
height="83" alt="The Real Llumi" /></a>
```

Figure 18.17 *This JavaScript script comes from Figure 19.18 on page 330. It preloads the images into cache to ensure speedy rollovers.*

Figure 18.18 *By commenting out the script, it is hidden from old browsers like this one. (Hey, it may not handle scripts, but this old version of Mosaic displays normal pages without trouble and runs on less than 1Mb of RAM.)*

Hiding Scripts from Older Browsers

```
<body>
<script type="text/javascript"
language="javascript">

<![CDATA[
    document.write("<p
align='right'><i>"+Date()+"<\/i><\/p>")
 ]]>

</script>

<h1>The Big Ben Home Page</h1>
```

Figure 18.19 *This JavaScript script is adapted from Figure 19.1 on page 324. The* CDATA *section removes the special meaning from the characters in the script, essentially hiding them from the XML parser.*

Hiding Scripts from XML Parsers

Scripts sometimes contain symbols that have special meaning in XHTML documents, namely the & and the >. If you use these symbols in a script, you should enclose them in a CDATA section to hide them from *XML parsers* (the programs that ensure that the XML, or XHTML in this case, is properly written).

To hide internal scripts from XML parsers:

1. Type **<script>** to begin your script as usual.

2. Type **<![CDATA[** to hide the script from the XML parser.

3. Insert the script itself.

4. Type **]]>** to complete the CDATA section.

5. And then type **</script>** to complete the script element.

✔ Tips

■ This is only necessary for XHTML documents with internal scripts. External scripts are automatically hidden from XML parsers.

■ You can also hide internal style sheets in a CDATA section *(see page 151)*.

Hiding Scripts from XML Parsers

Setting the Default Scripting Language

According to the (X)HTML specifications, if you don't say what language you're using for the scripts on a page, your Web page is "incorrect". While you can use the `type` attribute to set the scripting language for internal and external scripts, the only mechanism for declaring the language of triggered scripts *(see page 316)* is with a `meta` tag.

To set the default scripting language:

1. In the `head` section of your (X)HTML document, type **<meta http-equiv= "Content-Script-Type"** (with both hyphens).

2. Then type **content="type"**, where *type* indicates the default format and language for your scripts. Use **text/javascript** for JavaScript, **text/vbscript** for VBScript, and **text/tcl** for TCL.

3. Type **/>**.

✔ Tips

■ The `Content-Script-Type` value sets the default scripting language for all of the scripts in a page, including the intrinsic events, internal scripts, and external scripts.

■ The scripting language indicated with the `type` attribute in the `script` tag *(see page 314)* overrides the `meta` tag specification. That means you can set the default scripting language, but still use scripts written in other languages, if desired.

■ While this `meta` tag is theoretically required for pages that contain intrinsic events, its absence generates no validation errors nor problems in browsers.

```
<!DOCTYPE html
    PUBLIC "-//W3C//DTD XHTML 1.0 Strict//EN"
    "http://www.w3.org/TR/xhtml1/DTD/xhtml1-strict.dtd">
<html xmlns="http://www.w3.org/1999/xhtml">
<head>
<meta http-equiv="content-type"
content="text/html; charset=utf-8" />
<title>Triggering scripts</title>
<meta http-equiv="Content-Script-Type"
content="text/javascript" />
</head>
<body>
<p>What <a href="time.html"
onclick="alert('Today is '+ Date())">time</a> is it?
</p>
<p>Here's the rest of the page.</p>
</body>
</html>
```

Figure 18.20 *The* `meta` *tag is always placed in the* `head` *section of your (X)HTML document. It specifies the default scripting language for all of the scripts on a page.*

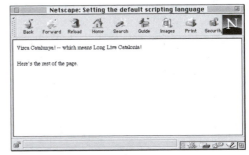

Figure 18.21 *The result of the script itself is not changed.*

JavaScript Essentials

Many of the most popular effects created on Web pages these days have little or nothing to do with (X)HTML and everything to do with *JavaScript*, a scripting language originally developed by Netscape Communications and now supported by all major browsers. There are entire books—and lots of them!—that go into JavaScript in full detail. This is not one of them.

This chapter, in contrast with the rest of this book, is not meant to teach you how, why, and when to do something. Instead, I want to give you some simple scripts that you can easily paste into your pages in order to create a few cool effects. Please note that there are probably much more elegant methods of achieving these effects that make the script more flexible and more powerful. But that would require a level of JavaScript that would not fit in a book about (X)HTML. If you'd like to find out more about what you can do with JavaScript, you might try the latest edition of *JavaScript for the World Wide Web: Visual QuickStart Guide*, by Tom Negrino and Dori Smith *(http://www.javascriptworld.com)*.

There are a couple of things to keep in mind while writing JavaScript. You should be very careful with spaces, returns, and all the funny punctuation. If you have trouble typing the scripts in yourself, feel free to download these examples from my Web site *(see page 24)*. I've personally tested these scripts—and they work fine—on Explorer 4.5 and 5 for Mac, Explorer 5 and 6 for Windows, and Netscape 4.6 and 6.2 for both Mac and Windows.

JavaScript Essentials

Adding the Current Date and Time

Nothing makes your page seem more current than adding the date and the time. While they're a bit more complicated to format in a particular way, just adding them is not difficult at all.

To add the current date and time to your page:

1. In a separate text document, on the first line, type **document.write(**

2. If desired, type **"<tag>"+**, where *tag* is the (X)HTML structure you'd like to apply to the date.

3. Next type **Date()** to call JavaScript's internal date function.

4. If you've added an element in step 2, type **+"<\/tag>"**, where *tag* is the corresponding closing tag. Notice the extra backslash that hides (X)HTML's forward slash / from JavaScript.

5. Type **)** to finish the *document.write* function **(Figure 19.1)**.

6. Save the document as text only, using the file name *time.js*.

7. In your (X)HTML document, place the cursor where the time should appear.

8. Type **<script type="text/javascript" language="javascript" src="time.js"> </script>** to call the script from that location **(Figure 19.2)**.

✔ Tip

■ When you know more JavaScript, you can format the date, add the full name of the week and month, and change the order of the elements to better suit the situation at hand.

```
document.write("<p align='right'><i>"+
Date()+"<\/i><\/p>")
```

Figure 19.1 *I recommend creating your JavaScript scripts in independent, external documents. They should be saved as text only with the .js extension. For example, this file is called* time.js. *Notice that there is no return; it wraps here in order to fit in this narrow width column.*

```
<body>

<script type="text/javascript"
language="javascript" src="time.js"></script>

<h1>The Big Ben Home Page</h1>

<img src="bigben.gif" alt="A very rudimentary
picture of Big Ben" width="75" height="133"
align="left" /> <br />
```

Figure 19.2 *Put the script element in the place in your (X)HTML document where you'd like the time to appear. Note that the* language *attribute is deprecated and thus only valid in (X)HTML transitional (see page 315).*

Figure 19.3 *The illustration is amateurish but the current time in the upper right-hand corner makes up for everything.*

```
<meta http-equiv="Content-Script-Type"
content="text/javascript" />

<title>Status bar labels</title></head>

<body>

<img src="noho.gif" alt="Main Street,
Northampton" align="left" width="384"
height="256" border="0" hspace="5" vspace="0"
onmouseover="window.status='Main Street,
Northampton'; return true" />

<a href="noho.html"
onmouseover="window.status='Click here for more
information about Northampton\'s sights'; return
true">Northampton</a> is a great place to visit.
```

Figure 19.4 *Note that the highlighted lines above are all on one line with no returns.*

Figure 19.5 *Adding the* onmouseover *line to links gives visitors extra information before they actually click the link.*

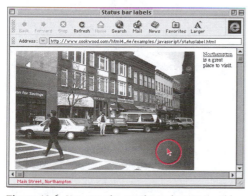

Figure 19.6 *You can also use this technique to add information to images.*

Changing a Link's Status Label

When a visitor points to a link, usually the link's URL appears in the status area of the browser window. If you want something else to appear there, you can use this easy technique to add your own status label.

To change a link's status label:

1. Create the link as usual. For more details, consult Chapter 7, *Links*.

2. In the link tag, type **onmouseover = "window.status='**. (First double quotes, then a single one.)

3. Type the text that you want to appear in the status area of the browser window when the visitor points at the link.

4. Type **'; return true"**. (That's a *single quote, semicolon,* and then the rest.)

✔ Tips

■ If there are quotation marks (single or double) or apostrophes in the text entered in step 3, you must precede them with a backslash **(Figure 19.4)**. Otherwise, the browser will probably confuse them with the quotation marks that delimit the script itself (in steps 2 and 4).

■ Make sure you don't add any returns to the status label text. They'll break the script.

■ Current browsers also support the use of the onmouseover attribute to add labels to images. Simply add the line to the img tag **(Figure 19.6)**. For some reason, Netscape 4 doesn't support it.

■ You can also make text move through the status area like a marquee, but the code is a bit involved to go into here.

Changing a Link's Status Label

Changing Multiple Frames with One Link

When you've set up a frameset, it's often nice to change the contents of more than one frame at a time.

To change multiple frames with just one link:

1. First, set up your frameset as described in Chapter 15, *Frames*. Make sure each of the frames has a name *(see step 7 on page 242)*.

2. Type **<a href="** to begin the link.

3. Type **javascript:location='url.html'**, where *url.html* is the page that you want to appear in the frame that contains the link. (If you don't want this frame to change, use the URL of the page that is currently in the frame.)

4. Type **;** (a semicolon) to separate this first statement from the next.

5. Type **parent.framename.location= 'new-page.html'**, where *framename* is the name of the frame that will contain the page specified by *newpage.html*.

6. Repeat steps 4 and 5 for each additional frame whose contents you wish to change.

7. Type **">** to complete the link tag.

8. Type the clickable text.

9. Type **</a>**.

✔ Tip

- If you don't feel like messing with JavaScript, you can get this effect by creating a special frameset that holds the right-hand frames and then set the link to open that frameset. (It's not as fast, but it works.)

```
<h1>Wild Animals</h1>

<br /><a href="javascript:location='toc.html';
parent.topright.location='birdbuttons.html';
parent.bottomright.location='parrots.html'">

Birds</a> <br />

<a href="javascript:location='toc.html';
parent.topright.location='catbuttons.html';
parent.bottomright.location='tiger.html'">

Cats</a>
```

Figure 19.7 *There are no spaces or returns in the JavaScript lines. The file shown here is called "toc.html" and is referenced in the first part of the script so that when the visitor clicks the link, this TOC remains visible in the left frame (while the two right hand frames are updated).*

Figure 19.8 *When the visitor clicks the Cats link in the left-hand frame...*

Figure 19.9 *...both the top-right and bottom-right frames are updated while the left-hand frame remains constant.*

```
if (top.location !=
"http://www.cookwood.com/html5ed/examples/
javascript/wildanimals.html" & top.location !=
"http://www.cookwood.com/html5ed/examples/
javascript/wildanimals_geese.html")

{top.location.href =
"http://www.cookwood.com/html5ed/examples/
javascript/wildanimals_geese.html"}
```

Figure 19.10 *Here's the* keepinframes.js *file. In the requested page* (geese.html) *we check to see if this same page is being displayed in the* wildanimals *frameset or in the* wildanimals_geese *frameset. If it's not in one of those, we'll display the* wildanimals_geese *frameset instead of the geese.html page which was requested. Note that there are only two lines in this script (It is wrapped to fit in the column.)*

```
<title>Geese</title>

<script type="text/javascript" language=
"javascript" src="keepinframe.js"></script>

</head>
```

Figure 19.11 *Call the script from the* head *section of your (X)HTML page.*

Figure 19.12 *The visitor types the URL of the desired page...*

Figure 19.13 *...and instead of displaying the* geese.html *page, the browser shows the* wildanimals_geese.html *page (which is the frameset that contains the* geese.html *page).*

Keeping Frames in Their Framesets

If your frames get indexed in a search engine like Google or Yahoo, it's possible that a visitor will attempt to see an individual frame without its supporting frameset. You can use JavaScript to ensure that a frame is always, well, *framed*.

To keep frames in their framesets:

1. In a text document, on the first line, type **if (top.location != "frameset.url"**, where *frameset.url* is the frameset that the page in question should always be displayed in.

2. If desired type **& top.location != "frameset2.url"** where *frameset2.url* is another frameset in which the page is allowed to be displayed.

3. Repeat step 2 for each possible frameset.

4. Type **)** to complete the condition.

5. Then type **{top.location.href= "frameset.url"}**, where *frameset.url* is the Web page that should be displayed instead of the requested page, and must be one of the ones noted in steps 1–2, and (hopefully) contains the requested page.

6. Save the script as text only with the name *keepinframe.js*.

7. In the head section of your (X)HTML document, type **<script type="text/ javascript" language="javascript" src= "keepinframe.js"></script>** to call the script **(Figure 19.11)**.

✔ Tip

■ This script says "if the requested page isn't displayed in one of the allowed framesets, display *this* frameset instead".

Keeping Frames in Their Framesets

Changing an Image When a Visitor Points

You can make an image change when the visitor points at it. This is commonly called a "rollover".

To change an image when the visitor points at it:

1. Type **<a href="page.html"**, where *page.html* is the page that will be displayed if the visitor actually clicks the link (as opposed to just pointing at it).

2. Type **onmouseover="document. imgname.src=**, where *imgname* is the value of the `img` tag's `name` attribute (see step 11, below). Note that there are no spaces before or after the periods.

3. Type **'image-in.jpg'**, where *image-in.jpg* is the name and extension of the image file that should be displayed when the visitor *points at* the image.

4. Type **"** to complete the attribute.

5. Type **onmouseout="document. imgname.src=**, where *imgname* is the value of the `img` tag's `name` attribute (see step 11, below). Note that there are no spaces before or after the periods.

6. Type **'image-out.jpg'**, where *image-out.jpg* is the name and extension of the image file that should be displayed when the visitor points *away from* the image.

7. Type **"** to complete the attribute.

8. Add other link attributes as desired *(see Chapter 7, Links)*.

9. Type **>** to finish the link.

```
<!DOCTYPE html PUBLIC "-//W3C//DTD XHTML
1.0 Transitional//EN"

"http://www.w3.org/TR/xhtml1/DTD/xhtml1-
transitional.dtd">

<html xmlns="http://www.w3.org/1999/xhtml">

<head>

<meta http-equiv="content-type"
content="text/html; charset=iso-8859-1" />

<meta http-equiv="Content-Script-Type"
content="text/javascript" />

<title>Llumi's big cat dreams</title>

</head>

<body>

Point at Llumi to see what she's thinking. <a
href="llumipage.html" onmouseover=
"document.catpic.src='dream.jpg'"
onmouseout="document.catpic.src='real.jpg'">
<img src="real.jpg" name="catpic" width="143"
height="83" alt="Llumi"/></a>

</body>

</html>
```

Figure 19.14 *Notice that the file names of the two images are enclosed in single quotes, since the script itself is contained in double quotes.*

Figure 19.15 *The image that appears initially is the one specified by the* img *tag.*

Figure 19.16 *When the visitor passes the mouse over the image (which is also a link—notice the status bar), the image referenced by the* onmouseover *attribute is revealed.*

Figure 19.17 *When the visitor points the mouse away from the image, the image referenced by the* onmouse- out *attribute is displayed (in this case, it's the same as the original image specified by the* img *tag).*

10. Type **<img src="initialimage.jpg"**, where *initialimage.jpg* is the file name for the image that should appear before the visitor even picks up their mouse.

11. Type **name="imgname"**, where *imgname* identifies the space for the images that will be loaded.

12. Type **width="w" height="h"**, where *w* and *h* represent the width and height of the images, respectively.

13. Type **alt="alternate text"**, where the *alternate text* describes the initial image.

14. Add other attributes to the img tag as desired *(see Chapter 6, Using Images).*

15. Type **/>** to complete the img tag.

16. Type **</a>** to complete the link tag.

✔ Tips

- The images should be the same size. If they're not, the second one will be shoehorned in to fit.

- Note that the img element's name attribute is used in both step 2 and step 5. That's because the name attribute identifies the space (the particular img element) that will be replaced with both of the other images. The name must match exactly, including case.

- If you don't want the image to be part of the link, after step 9, type some clickable text, then do step 16 before completing steps 10–15.

- You can preload the images involved in a rollover so that the effect is immediate. For more details, consult *Loading Images into Cache* on page 330.

Changing an Image When a Visitor Points

Loading Images into Cache

You can use JavaScript to load all of the images into your browser's cache as the page is initially displayed on the screen. One benefit is that rollovers *(see page 328)* are instantaneous.

To load images into cache:

1. In a separate text document, on the first line, type **label=**, where *label* is a word that identifies the image.

2. Type **new Image(h,w)**, where *h* and *w* are the image's height and width, in pixels.

3. On the next line, type **label**, where *label* matches the label used in step 1.

4. Directly following the name in step 3 (i.e., with no extra spaces), type **.src="image.url"**, where *image.url* is the location of the image on the server.

5. Repeat steps 1–4 for each image you wish to load into cache **(Figure 19.18)**.

6. Save the script in text only format and call it *loadimages.js*.

7. In the `head` section of the (X)HTML document that uses the images, type **<script type="text/javascript" language="javascript" src="loadimages.js"></script>**, where *loadimages.js* is the name of the file you saved in step 6.

8. When you refer to the images in other scripts, use **label.src** (without quotes), where *label* is the word you used to describe the images in step 1 **(Figure 19.19)**.

```
littlecat = new Image(143,83)
littlecat.src = "real.jpg"
bigcat = new Image(143,83)
bigcat.src = "dream.jpg"
```

Figure 19.18 *Here's the* loadimages.js *file that I use to load the cat images into cache in order to make the rollover effect appear more fluidly. You can preload as many images as you'd like. There should be two lines for each image—one to create the image space and one to fill it with the corresponding URL*

```
<!DOCTYPE html PUBLIC "-//W3C//DTD XHTML
1.0 Transitional//EN"
    "http://www.w3.org/TR/xhtml1/DTD/xhtml1-
transitional.dtd">
<html xmlns="http://www.w3.org/1999/xhtml">
<head>
<meta http-equiv="content-type"
content="text/html; charset=iso-8859-1" />
<meta http-equiv="Content-Script-Type"
content="text/javascript" />
<title>Llumi's big cat dreams</title>
<script type="text/javascript" language=
"javascript" src="loadimages.js"></script>
</head>
<body>
Point at Llumi to see what she's thinking. <a
href="llumipage.html"
onmouseover="document.catpic.src=bigcat.src"
onmouseout="document.catpic.src=littlecat.src"><i
mg src="real.jpg"
name="catpic" width="143" height="83"
alt="Llumi"/></a>
</body>
</html>
```

Figure 19.19 *Notice that the scripts in the body of the page (explained on page 328) now references the* big-cat.src *and* littlecat.src *objects. You don't need to enclose these labels in quotes, as you do with the actual file names (step 3 on page 328).*

```
<h1>Nathaniel Hawthorne</h1>

Nathaniel Hawthorne was one of the most
important writers of 19th century
America. His most famous character is <a href=
"javascript:location='hawthorne.html';
window.open('hester.html', 'characters',
'height=150, width=150, scrollbars=yes')">
Hester Prynne</a>, a woman living in Puritan New
England. Another famous object
of Hawthorne's writing was <a
href="http://www.ripon.edu/dept/pogo/presiden
```

Figure 19.20 *The file name of the document shown here is* hawthorne.html. *The first part of the JavaScript statement says "keep displaying the* hawthorne.html *document right where it is". The second part of the JavaScript code says "and then open a window labeled* characters *that's 150 pixels by 150 pixels, with scrollbars, and display the* hester.html *file in it".*

Figure 19.21 *When the visitor clicks a link...*

Figure 19.22 *...the link is displayed in the new window. Contrast this example with the one shown in Figure 7.13 on page 122.*

Controlling a New Window's Size

In Chapter 7, you learned how to open a link in a new window. JavaScript lets you control how big that window should be.

To control the size of a new window:

1. Type **<a href="javascript:location='current.html';**, where *current.html* is the URL of the page that contains the link.

2. Type **window.open('nextpage.html',**, where *nextpage.html* is the URL of the page to be opened in the new window.

3. Type **'label',**, where *label* is the name of the new window.

4. Type **'height=h,width=w**, where *h* and *w* are the desired height and width for the new window. (No spaces!)

5. If desired, type **,chrome=yes**, where *chrome* is scrollbars, toolbar, status, menubar, location, or resizable.

6. If desired, type a **,** (comma) and repeat step 5 as desired. Each window part should be separated from the previous one with a comma but no spaces.

7. Type **'** (a straight apostrophe)—whether or not you've set the window parts.

8. Type **)"** to finish the JavaScript code.

9. Type **>clickable text</a>**.

✔ Tip

■ To open a new window automatically as the main page loads (with no link at all), type **onload="javascript:** and then follow steps 2–8 above within the body tag of your main page's (X)HTML code. Then open other links in the new window by using **target="label"**, where *label* matches step 3. For details, see page 122.

Controlling a New Window's Size

SYMBOLS AND NON-ENGLISH CHARACTERS

20

Global Reach *(http://www.glreach.com/ globstats/)* estimates that only 40% of the Web surfing public speaks English. That means that roughly 60% hopes that your Web page is written in some other language. And while many languages (particularly in Western Europe and the United States) are written with the same alphabet, many are written with scripts of their own: Cyrillic, Greek, and Chinese, just to mention a few. In addition, there are many useful symbols—common to English as well as other languages—that are not available in the current default system, known as ASCII.

Fortunately, (X)HTML is designed to support every symbol and character in every language in the world. When creating a Web page that will contain symbols and non-English characters, it's important to take into account the file's encoding (that is, the system used to convert the characters on the screen into the computer's internal system), the browser's support for such encodings (generally good in current browsers from versions 4 on) and the fonts that your visitors will have available.

Special thanks to Alan Wood for his help understanding how multilingual Web pages work. His site *(http://www.alanwood.net/ unicode/)* is an excellent resource.

About Character Encodings

When you type, a computer translates each character into bits. The system it uses for doing this is called a *character encoding*. The most basic character encoding is called ASCII and has 128 characters: the letters of the English alphabet, the numbers, and some common symbols.

In non-English speaking countries, ASCII is clearly insufficient. Instead, they use slightly larger encodings sometimes encompassing more than one language. In order to maintain compatibility with English, these encodings treat the first 128 characters in the same way as ASCII and assign 128 new characters to positions 129–256. The only problem is that each regional encoding does it in a different way. So, for example, if you want to write in Spanish, you might use the ISO-8859-1 encoding but if you want to write in Cyrillic, you need the ISO-8859-5 encoding. And if you want to write Spanish and Cyrillic together, or send a Spanish document to a Russian computer, it's a big problem.

One rather cumbersome solution is to use *character references* to include characters in a document whose encoding otherwise wouldn't allow such characters. While this system continues to be used today *(see page 340)*, it is perhaps most useful for largely English documents that contain a few foreign letters or unusual symbols, whose writers don't want to worry about the encoding.

A more definitive solution is *Unicode*. Unicode is designed to be a universal system for encoding all of the characters in all of the world's languages. By assigning each character in each language a unique code, Unicode lets you include in a document any character from any language, and indeed multiple characters from multiple languages, without fear that it (or they) will be misinterpreted.

δ The Greek *sigma* is character E4 in the ISO-8859-7 encoding.

ה The Hebrew *hay* is character E4 in the ISO-8859-8 encoding.

ä The Germanic *umlaut a* is character E4 in the ISO-8859-1 encoding.

Ф The Cyrillic *small letter ef* is character E4 in the ISO-8859-5 encoding.

Figure 20.1 *Each of these characters has the same code (E4) in its respective local encoding, which makes it impossible, for example, to have both a Greek sigma and a Hebrew hay.*

δ The Greek *sigma* is character 03B4 in Unicode.

ה The Hebrew *hay* is character 05D4 in Unicode.

ä The Germanic *umlaut a* is character 00E4 in Unicode.

Ф The Cyrillic *small letter ef* is character 0424 in Unicode.

Figure 20.2 *In Unicode, each character has a unique code, and thus they may all appear in the same document without confusion (as long as that document is encoded with UTF-8).*

```
<head>

<meta http-equiv="Content-Type"
content="text/html; charset=shift_jis" />

<title>The importance of encodings</title>

</head>

<body>

<p>Here's the title of my book in Japanese (I hope):

<br />

HTML4クイックスタートガイド </p>

<p>Here's a quote from its <a

href="http://www.mdn.co.jp/Books/html4qsg/">

Web page:</a></p>

<blockquote><p>サポートサイトについて</p>
```

Figure 20.3 *Here's part of an XHTML document that contains both English and Japanese. Since I'm going to save it in the* shift-jis *encoding, I declare that encoding with the* meta *tag (details on page 338).*

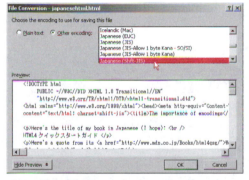

Figure 20.4 *When I save the document, I am sure to choose the same encoding:* shift-jis, *in this case.*

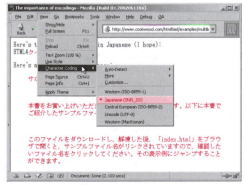

Figure 20.5 *When the visitor goes to this page, their browser will see the* meta *tag and automatically view the page with the proper encoding (*shift-jis*).*

The form of Unicode used in HTML and XHTML is called UTF-8, which has the added advantage of encoding ASCII characters in the same way that ASCII does. That means that older browsers that may not recognize UTF-8 will still understand the English portion of the page, and indeed any character numbered 1–128. Its principal disadvantage is that pages written in double-byte languages (like Chinese, Japanese, and Korean) take up almost twice as much file space as they would with a local, more limited encoding.

As a Web page designer, you must choose a proper encoding that encompasses all of the characters in your document, declare that encoding in the (X)HTML code **(Figure 20.3)**, and specify the encoding when you save your file **(Figure 20.4)**. If you've never specified an encoding before, your text editor selected one for you—probably the default encoding for your operating system. For example, most text editors on Windows in the U.S. will save "text-only" files in the Western ANSI encoding, whose official name is windows-1252.

Once you've done your part, your visitors still need a browser that recognizes the encoding you've used as well as a font that includes the characters in your page **(Figure 20.5)**. Most current browsers, including IE and Netscape for both Mac and Windows from version 4 on, support UTF-8, as well as many regional encodings, although they often require the installation of an additional *language kit* of some sort. Older browsers may only be able to support individual regional encodings.

You may want to suggest that your visitors go to Alan Wood's excellent Unicode Resources site (*http://www.alanwood.net/unicode/*) which includes information about getting the appropriate language kits and fonts, as well as how your visitors should set up their browsers to use such fonts, once they've been downloaded.

About Character Encodings

Saving Your Page with the Proper Encoding

Saving Your Page with the Proper Encoding

At the beginning of this book, I said you had to save your Web pages as "text-only" documents, and made little mention of the encoding *(see page 50)*. That's because most of my readers create Web pages in the same language as their operating system and because most text editors automatically save files with the default system encoding. You only need to manually choose the encoding as you save if your document contains characters that *don't belong* to your system's default character encoding.

To save your page with the proper encoding:

1. When you go to save your document, choose the appropriate option for selecting an encoding.

In Word, it's called Encoded Text, and you'll find it in the Save as type box.

In BBEdit, it's a button called Options.

2. Choose the desired encoding from the list or options that appear **(Figures 20.7 and 20.8)**.

3. Finish saving the document.

✔ Tips

■ Which is the proper encoding? My first choice would be UTF-8. My second choice would be the regional encoding for the main language used on your page. For a list of common encodings, see *http://www.w3.org/International/O-charset-lang.html*.

■ Once you've saved your file with the proper encoding, you *must* declare that encoding in the code with the `meta` tag *(see page 338)*.

Figure 20.6 *In Microsoft Word, first choose Encoded Text in the Save as type box, then enter the file name (with the .html extension). Finally, click Save.*

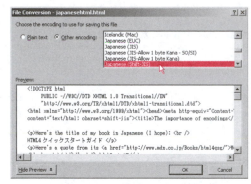

Figure 20.7 *Choose the desired encoding from the list that appears. In Word (shown), this dialog box appears after clicking Save in the Save As dialog box shown in Figure 20.6 and insisting in the next alert that appears that you really, really want to encode your text.*

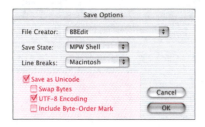

Figure 20.8 *In BBEdit on the Mac, click the Options button in the Save As dialog box, and then check both Save as Unicode and UTF-8 Encoding to save in UTF-8. I don't recommend checking Include Byte-Order Mark since some browsers (notably Internet Explorer) choke on it.*

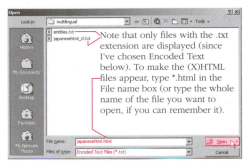

Note that only files with the .txt extension are displayed (since I've chosen Encoded Text below). To make the (X)HTML files appear, type *.html in the File name box (or type the whole name of the file you want to open, if you can remember it).

Figure 20.9 *When you go to open a file for editing, choose Encoded Text in the Files of type box, and then type the name of the file in the File name box. (Or make all your (X)HTML files appear by typing *.html in the File name box, and then click the desired file.)*

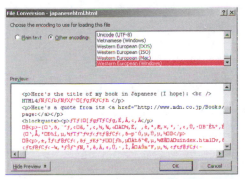

Figure 20.10 *Text editors (including Word) can't tell which encoding a file is in. If they guess incorrectly and use the wrong encoding (like here), the characters look pretty awful.*

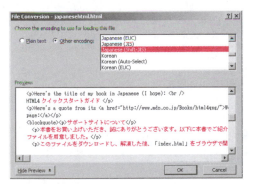

Figure 20.11 *Luckily, you know which encoding the file is in. Select it from the menu and the characters are again displayed properly.*

Editing a Page with the Proper Encoding

Once a file is encoded, there's no easy way to figure out which encoding was used. I haven't seen a browser or text editor than can figure it out on its own. So, if you save a file with a particular encoding you have to manually open the file with that encoding in order to edit it. Otherwise, the characters that differ between your system's default encoding and the encoding in which you originally saved the file will turn into garbage.

To edit a page with the proper encoding:

1. Choose File > Open in your text editor.

2. Choose the appropriate option for decoding an encoded file.

In Word, choose Encoded Text from the Files of type box (and note tip below).

In BBEdit, choose the proper encoding from the Read as pop-up menu.

3. Depending on the program, you may have to select the desired encoding from a list that appears.

4. Then choose your file and click Open.

✔ Tips

■ You have to make Word *ask* you for the proper encoding—choose Tools > Options, click the General tab, and check "Confirm Conversion at Open"—otherwise it uses your system's default encoding.

■ BBEdit comes with a handy AppleScript (in the BBEdit Utilities folder) that you can drop files on in order to open them as UTF-8. I've got it on my OS X Dock.

■ If you open the file and see garbage, close it without saving and try again.

Declaring Your Page's Character Encoding

Saving your file with the proper encoding is only half the battle. You must next include information in the (X)HTML code about which encoding you used to save the page.

To declare your page's character encoding:

1. In the `head` section of your page, type **<meta http-equiv="Content-Type" content="text/html;**.

2. Then type **charset=code"**, where *code* is the name of the encoding with which you saved your page.

3. Type **/>** to complete the `meta` tag.

✔ Tips

■ The encoding you declare *must* match the encoding with which your page was saved. Otherwise, characters that differ between the encodings will display incorrectly.

■ If you have saved your files without explicitly choosing an encoding, your text editor probably used the default encoding for your system. You must still declare the encoding using the `meta` tag as described above. On Windows in the U.S. and Western Europe, the default encoding is `windows-1252`. On Macintosh in the U.S. and Western Europe, it's `x-mac-roman`.

■ Fetch, the most popular FTP program for Macintosh, changes the encoding from MacRoman to ISO-8859-1 *by default* upon uploading (*see page 411*). Therefore, unless you change that setting, you should declare the files to be ISO-8859-1 even if you save them as MacRoman with your text editor (which is the default for most Mac text editors).

```
<!DOCTYPE html PUBLIC -//W3C//DTD XHTML 1.0
Transitional//EN" "http://www.w3.org/TR/xhtml1/
DTD/xhtml1-transitional.dtd">
<html xmlns="http://www.w3.org/1999/xhtml">
<head>
<meta http-equiv="Content-Type"
content="text/html; charset=shift_jis" />
<title>The importance of encodings</title>
</head>
<body>
<p>Here's the title of my book in Japanese (I hope):
<br />
HTML4クイックスタートガイド </p>
<p>Here's a quote from its <a
href="http://www.mdn.co.jp/Books/html4qsg/">
Web page:</a></p>
<blockquote><p>サポートサイトについて</p>
<p>本書をお買い上げいただき、誠にありがと
うございます。以下に本書でご紹介したサンプル
ファイルを用意しました。</p>
<p>このファイルをダウンロードし、解凍した
後、「index.html」をブラウザで開くと、サンプ
ルファイル名がリンクされていますので、確認し
たいファイル名をクリックしてください。その表
示例にジャンプすることができま
す。</p></blockquote>
</body></html>
```

Figure 20.12 *In the* `head` *section of your Web page, create a* `meta` *tag that describes the encoding you used to save the file.*

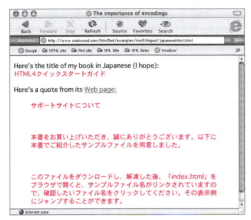

Figure 20.13 *When you tell the browser what encoding to expect, and as long as it supports that encoding and the visitor's system has an appropriate font, the characters display properly.*

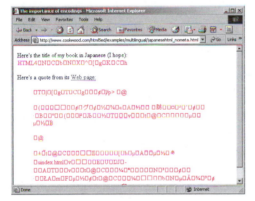

Figure 20.14 *If you don't tell the browser what to expect, it makes an attempt, but often doesn't know how to display the characters properly. The result is not pretty.*

- If you don't specify your page's encoding, the browser (and search engines) will guess, based on the visitor's preferences, information from the server (see next tip), the `charset` attribute (see last tip), or by examining the document. You have a better chance of the browser getting it right if you just make its life easy and tell it.

- Apache server users can add a line to their *.htaccess* file that indicates the default encoding of files with a particular extension. The line should look like **AddType text/html;charset=code.html**, where *code* is the character encoding that files with the .html extension should be assumed to have. See page 370 for another example of changing the *.htaccess* file. Thanks to Don Tobias: *http://webtips.dantobias.com/char.html*

- To write a page in a different language from that of your operating system, you'll also need keyboard layouts (or possibly an IME, *input method editor*) that let you input the characters, and a text editor that supports the desired languages and that can save the page in the proper encoding. If the text editor can at least save the file in Unicode, you can use IE for Windows to convert the file to any of the encodings that it recognizes (by opening the file and choosing File > Save As).

- IE 6 for Windows, when browsing a page with an encoding it's not set up for, will automatically ask the visitor if they'd like to download the appropriate resources. This is an important reason to include the proper encoding.

- You can theoretically also add the `charset` attribute to a link or script to describe the associated files' encodings. However, this feature is not yet widely supported.

Declaring Your Page's Character Encoding

Adding Characters from Outside the Encoding

If most of the characters on your page belong to one encoding and you just want to add a few characters from another, you can set the main encoding for the document *(see page 338)* and then use *character references* for characters outside of the main encoding.

A character reference can represent any character in the Universal Character Set (UCS) by giving the character's unique code within that set. A character's code can be represented as either a regular (base 10) number or as a hexadecimal number. Some characters also have associated *entities*, that is, unique identifying words, that you can use instead of the number.

You can find a character's code, in hexadecimal form (which is the most common), at the Unicode site: *http://www.unicode.org/charts/*. You can find the complete list of characters that have associated entities in Appendix D or at my site: *www.cookwood.com/entities/*

To add characters from outside the encoding:

1. Type **&** (an ampersand).

2. Next, type **#x*n***, where *n* is the hexadecimal number that represents the desired character **(Figure 20.15)**.

   Or type **#*n***, where *n* is the base 10 number for your character **(Figure 20.16)**.

   Or type **entity**, where *entity* is the name of the entity that corresponds to your character **(Figure 20.17)**.

3. Finally, type **;** (a semicolon).

✔ Tips

■ In general, you only *need* to use character references for characters that are *not* part of the document's character encoding.

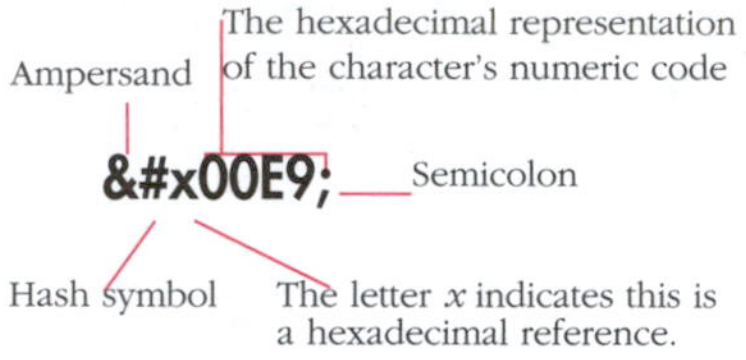

Ampersand | The hexadecimal representation of the character's numeric code

é — Semicolon

Hash symbol | The letter *x* indicates this is a hexadecimal reference.

Figure 20.15 *A hexadecimal reference is comprised of an ampersand, a hash symbol (#), the letter x, the hexadecimal representation of the numeric code for the character, and a semicolon. You can use hexadecimal references to insert any character from the Universal Character Set. This particular character is an é.*

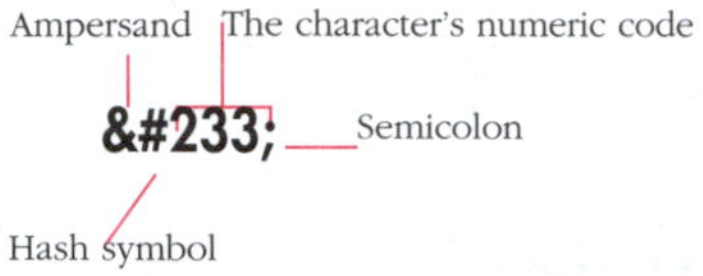

Ampersand | The character's numeric code

é — Semicolon

Hash symbol

Figure 20.16 *A numeric reference is comprised of an ampersand, a hash symbol (#), the numeric code for the character, and a semicolon. You can use numeric references to insert any character from the Universal Character Set. This reference is also for an é.*

Ampersand | The character's name | Semicolon

é

Figure 20.17 *An entity reference, also known as character entity references or named references, is made up of an ampersand, the character's name, and a semicolon. There are 252 named references that you can use in your (X)HTML pages. They are case-sensitive. This reference is also for an é.*

```
<!DOCTYPE html PUBLIC "-//W3C//DTD XHTML
1.0 Transitional//EN" "http://www.w3.org/TR/
xhtml1/DTD/xhtml1-transitional.dtd">

<html xmlns="http://www.w3.org/1999/xhtml">

<head>

<meta http-equiv="content-type"
content="text/html; charset=windows-1252" />

<title>Character References</title>

<style>p {font-size:24px}</style>

</head>

<body>

<p> &ldquo;Parla vost &eacute;
angl &egrave;s? &rdquo;he asked.</p>

<p> &ldquo;Yes, a little, &rdquo;she said.</p>

<p> &ldquo;How much is that in euros? &#8221;he
asked.</p>

<p> &#x201C;&euro;25, &#x201d;she
replied.</p>

</body>

</html>
```

Figure 20.18 *You can use any combination of named, numeric, or hexadecimal references in your document. It doesn't matter which encoding the document is in.*

Figure 20.19 *The characters display properly. Note that the visitor's browser must have an appropriate font for the characters.*

- The only exception to the first tip is the & symbol. In XHTML documents, when used as text (as in *AT&T*), you *must* use its character reference (&).

- The greater than, less than, and double quotation mark symbols also have special meaning in (X)HTML. You may use their character references—>, <, and ", respectively—where they might otherwise be misconstrued (as in the case of showing (X)HTML code on a Web page).

- While using references for characters like é and £ is valid, using the proper encoding (e.g., ISO 8859-1) is much faster for large chunks of text.

- The most common default encodings, including windows-1252 and x-mac-roman lack several useful symbols. You can use character references to create these symbols without touching the default encoding.

- If you're using a hexadecimal or numeric reference, don't forget the **#** between the ampersand and the number. And if you're using a hexadecimal, don't forget the lowercase letter **x**, that indicates that the hexadecimal is coming.

- While there are hex and numeric references for *every* character in Unicode, there are named entity references for only 252 of them. They are case-sensitive. See Appendix D for a complete listing.

- Your visitors will only be able to view the characters for which they have adequate fonts installed. While you can specify a particular font *(see page 158)*, it's not required; in its absence browsers should search the available fonts for one that includes the characters in question.

- You may also insert small quantities of special characters by using gif images *(see page 104)*.

Adding Characters from Outside the Encoding

Specifying Your Page's Language

While saving with the proper encoding and declaring that encoding is essential, it can also be useful to specify the main language in which your page is written. This information may be used by search engines to determine which pages satisfy a language-limited match, or perhaps by a server so that it can serve the appropriate version of a document.

To specify a page's language:

Within the opening `html` tag, type **xml:lang= "xx" lang="xx"**, where *xx* is the two letter abbreviation for your page's main language.

✔ Tips

■ The value of `xml:lang` overrides the value for `lang`.

■ You may add the `xml:lang` and `lang` attributes to almost any element to define the language for that element and override the language noted in the `html` tag).

■ Browsers may use this information to determine hyphenation, assist spell checkers and speech synthesizers, etc.

■ Search engines *may* use this information, but they also use proprietary algorithms to determine which language a page is in.

■ Note that since encodings often encompass more than one language, this tag lets you be more explicit about which language you've actually used.

■ You can find a list, officially called *ISO 639-2*, of the two-letter abbreviations for most languages at: *http://www.loc.gov/ standards/iso639-2/langcodes.html* and also at *http://www.w3.org/WAI/ER/IG/ert/ iso639.htm*. Be sure to use the two-letter, not the three-letter abbreviations.

```
<!DOCTYPE html PUBLIC "-//W3C//DTD XHTML
1.0 Transitional//EN"

    "http://www.w3.org/TR/2000/REC-xhtml1-
20000126/DTD/xhtml1-transitional.dtd">

<html xmlns="http://www.w3.org/1999/xhtml"
xml:lang="fr" lang="fr">

<head>

<meta http-equiv="content-type"
content="text/html; charset=utf-8" />

<title>Quotes in French</title>

<style>p {font-size:24px}</style>

</head>

<body>

<p>Alceste dit <q>Mais enfin, vos soins sont
superflus.</q> </p>

<p xml:lang="en" lang="en">Alceste says <q>But
in the end, what you want is superfluous.</q></p>

</body></html>
```

Figure 20.20 *Specify the principal language in the* `html` *tag. Here I've used* fr *for* French*. You can override that value in individual elements, as I've done for the English paragraph at the bottom of this Web page. Note that this page was encoded with UTF-8 so I wouldn't have had to use character references had there been any accented characters.*

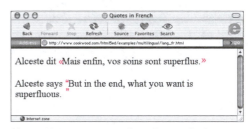

Figure 20.21 *Internet Explorer for Mac displays guillemet quotes when the language specified is French but curly quotes if the language is English.*

FORMATTING: THE OLD WAY

21

Back in the days when CSS was still poorly supported by most browsers, most folks controlled the appearance of the text in their Web pages with HTML elements. Partly due to the browser wars—and the balkanization of the Web that ensued—and partly because of the push towards CSS and XHTML, the W3C decided to *deprecate* a number of formatting elements, that is, to mark them for eventual removal from the standard (X)HTML specifications.

Still, it has been a bit like locking the chicken coop after the fox has gotten inside; most of the pages on the Web today already use one or more of the deprecated tags. While CSS is more powerful, more efficient, and easier to update, for most people, (X)HTML is still easier to understand and is often easier to use as well. Further, while CSS support has increased dramatically, it still doesn't rival the universal support enjoyed by almost all (X)HTML tags.

Note that the formatting tags, despite being deprecated, continue to be a valid and legal part of the transitional flavor of both HTML 4 and XHTML 1.0 *(see page 38)*. And while some might say that using deprecated tags is akin to heresy, there are so many pages that already use them, that it's important to at least know how they work. And if you decide to use one here or there in new work, well, I won't tell.

343

Choosing Default Characteristics for Text

You can select the default font, size, and color for all the text on your page with the `basefont` tag. You can then change the characteristics of individual sections or words as described in later sections of this chapter.

To choose default characteristics for body text:

1. Right after the opening body tag, type **<basefont**.

2. Type **size="n"**, where *n* is a number from 1 to 7. The default is 3.

3. If desired, type **color="color"**, where *color* is a hex color or proper color name.

4. If desired, type **face="fontname"**, where *fontname* is the preferred font that should be used for the text.

5. Type **/>**.

✔ Tips

- The `size` attribute is required. You may omit both the `color` and `face` attributes.

- The value you choose for the `size` attribute is always relative to the text's default size set in the visitor's browser. A value of 3 will display text at the same size as the browser's default size, 1 and 2 will be smaller than the default and 4–7 will be larger. If the visitor changes the size of the text, either with the View > Text Size option or with Preferences, the `basefont` values are adjusted accordingly.

- On older browsers, text appears larger on Windows than on a Mac. In current browsers on both platforms, browsers are set up by default to display at 96 pixels per inch, making text more uniform across platforms.

```
<body>

<basefont size="5" color="red" face="Trebuchet MS"/>

<h1>Barcelona Night Life</h1>

<p>Barcelona is such a great place to live. People there really put a premium on <b>socializing</b>. Imagine it being more important to go out with your friends than to get that big promotion. Even when you're, gasp, <i>pushing 30</i>. They say there are more bars in <a href="http://www.bcn.es/english/ihome.htm" target="_blank">Barcelona</a> than in the rest of the European community <i>combined</i>. Don't get me wrong, I don't mean that everyone gets drunk all the time--bars are for hanging out and talking or for having a cup of coffee (espresso, of course).</p>

<p>The opinions expressed on this page are mine and mine alone.</p>

</body>
```

Figure 21.1 *The* basefont *element should come directly after the opening* body *tag.*

Figure 21.2 *In Internet Explorer 4+, on both Mac and Windows, the* basefont *tag sets the default size (5), color (this is red), and font face (Trebuchet MS) of the text. Note that the headers gain only the color and font, but are unaffected by the* basefont *element's size value.*

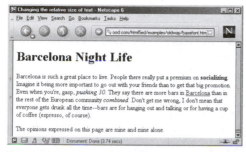

Figure 21.3 *Netscape 6 (like Opera, not shown) completely ignores the* basefont *element.*

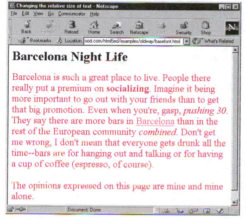

Figure 21.4 *Netscape 4.x supports only the* size *attribute for* basefont, *but ignores the* color *and* face *attributes.*

■ You may specify more than one font as a value for `face`. For more details, follow the syntax described under *Formatting Bits of Text* on page 346.

■ Only use one `basefont` tag in each (X)HTML document. To change individual characters, use the `font` element *(see page 346)*, or preferably styles *(see page 157)*.

■ Netscape 4 only supports the `basefont` element with the `size` attribute. Netscape 6 does not support the `basefont` element at all.

■ Headers are not affected by the `size` attribute, though they do gain the color and face specified by the `basefont` element (though only in Explorer).

■ Links are not affected by the `color` attribute, though they do gain the size and face specified by the `basefont` element. To change the color of links, see page 349.

■ The `font` element *(see page 346)* overrides the `basefont` element which overrides the `text` attribute of the `body` tag *(see page 348)*. Where do styles fit in, you might ask? They override `basefont` (and `text`) but not `font`.

■ In HTML, you can omit the forward slash from the end of the tag. In XHTML, of course, it's required.

■ The `basefont` element is deprecated and as you can see is extremely inconsistent from one browser to the next. It should be avoided. Use style sheets instead *(see page 157)*.

Choosing Default Characteristics for Text

Formatting Bits of Text

While the `basefont` element can be used to set the size, color, and font of your entire page, the `font` element is used to format discrete sections of your text.

To format bits of text:

1. Type **<font**

2. If desired, type **size="n"**, where *n* is a number from 1 to 7.

   Or, you may use a relative value, as in +2 or -3, with respect to the default size.

3. If desired, type **face="fontname1, fontname2"**, where *fontname1* is your first choice of fonts and fontname2 is your second choice of fonts. Each successive font should be separated from the previous one by a comma. You can specify as many as you like.

4. If desired, type **color="color"**, where color is a valid color name or hex color *(see page 46 and the inside back cover).*

5. Type **>** to complete the opening `font` tag.

6. Type the text that should be formatted.

7. Type **</font>** to complete the element.

✔ Tips

- You may specify all three attributes, or any combination thereof. None is required.

- The `font` tag has been deprecated. For information on using style sheets to control font usage (and to download fonts for your visitors), see page 158.

```
<body>

<basefont size="5" color="red" face="Trebuchet MS"/>

<h1>Barcelona Night Life</h1>

<p><font size="+2">B</font>arcelona is such a great place to live. People there really put a premium on <b>socializing</b>. Imagine it being more important to go out with your friends than to get that big promotion. Even when you're, gasp, <i>pushing 30</i>. They say there are more bars in <a href="http://www.bcn.es/english/ihome.htm" target="_blank">Barcelona</a> than in the rest of the European community <i>combined</i>. <font color="#660000">Don't get me wrong,</font> I don't mean that everyone gets drunk all the time--bars are for hanging out and talking or for having a cup of coffee (espresso, of course).</p>

<p><font face="Copperplate, Univers, Arial Black" size="-2">The opinions expressed on this page are mine and mine alone.</font></p>

</body>
```

Figure 21.5 *The `font` element is useful for localized formatting. Here we enlarge the initial B in the first paragraph, highlight a phrase in the text with a different color, and set a new font and size for the disclaimer at the bottom.*

Figure 21.6 *IE 4+ supports the `font` element. Note that the initial B is two sizes larger than the `basefont` size of 5, not the default text size.*

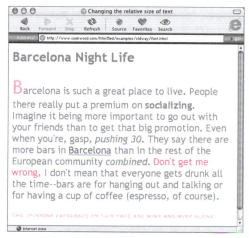

Figure 21.7 *The support on Explorer for Mac is the same, but notice how the first choice font is used, since it was available on this Mac, while the third choice was used on the PC in Figure 21.6.*

Figure 21.8 *Netscape 6 supports the* font *element, but since it ignores the* basefont *element, the effect is very different in this example. (Netscape 4 also supports the* font *element.)*

- A value of 3 for the `size` attribute represents the browser's default size for text—usually Times at 16 pixels. The tricky part is that every visitor can change their own browser's default text by tweaking the preferences or by choosing the View > Text Size (or Text Zoom) option.

- Relative sizes are calculated with respect to the `basefont` element, or to the default of 3 in `basefont`'s absence.

- The `font` element overrides the `basefont` element. The `font` element also overrides any formatting applied with style sheets.

- See page 46 and the inside back cover for a listing of common colors and for instructions for creating your own.

- You can also set the color of all of the body text with the `text` attribute in the `body` element. The `color` attribute of the `font` element overrides the `text` attribute in the `body` element.

- The `font` tag can change a link's size and the face, but its color. To change a link's color, see page 349, or better yet, use styles *(see page 166)*.

- The `font` element *does* affect the size of headers (in contrast with `basefont`, which does not—see page 345).

- Note that `font` is an inline element and should only contain other inline elements or text. You cannot, therefore, span font information across paragraphs, table cells, or any other block-level element. When you get sick of writing **<font>** and **</font>**, you start using style sheets.

Another Way to Choose Default Colors

Another way to change the default color for text is by setting the `text` attribute in the body tag. You can still change the color of individual words or paragraphs with the `font` tag *(see page 346).*

To choose a default color for text:

1. Inside the body tag, type **text**.

2. Type **="#rrggbb"**, where *rrggbb* is the hexadecimal representation of the color.

   Or type **="color"**, where *color* is one of the 16 predefined colors.

✔ Tips

■ The `body` tag's `text` attribute works the same way as the `basefont` tag's `color` attribute. However the `text` attribute is supported by all major browsers (and probably most minor ones), in contrast with `basefont/color`, which is not supported by Netscape (including 6).

■ Both `basefont` and `font` override the `text` attribute.

■ See the inside back cover for a listing of hexadecimal values and common color representations.

■ You can also specify the color of the background *(see page 354)* and of links *(see page 349).* Make sure all the colors work well together.

■ The `text` attribute is deprecated. For details on changing text color with styles, see page 166.

■ Most browsers allow users to override the colors that you might specify for the Web page.

```
<body text="red">

<h1>Barcelona Night Life</h1>

<p>Barcelona is such a great place to live. People
there really put a premium on <b>socializing</b>.
Imagine it being more important to go out with your
friends than to get that big promotion. Even when
you're, gasp, <i>pushing 30</i>. They say there
are more bars in <a href="http://www.bcn.es/
english/ihome.htm" target="_blank">Barcelona
</a> than in the rest of the European community
<i>combined</i>. Don't get me wrong, I don't
mean that everyone gets drunk all the time--bars
are for hanging out and talking or for having a cup
of coffee (espresso, of course).</p>

<p>The opinions expressed on this page are mine
and mine alone.</p>

</body>
```

Figure 21.9 *You can also set the default color for the text by using the* text *attribute in the* body *element.*

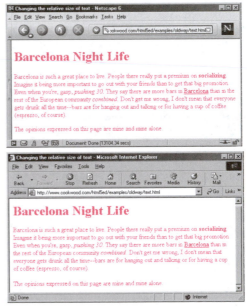

Figure 21.10 *The* text *attribute is almost universally supported. Shown are Netscape 6 (above) and Explorer 6 (below), both for Windows.*

```
<body text="red" link="gray" vlink="green"
alink="yellow" >

<h1>Barcelona Night Life</h1>

<p>Barcelona is such a great place to live. People
there really put a premium on <b>socializing</b>.
Imagine it being more important to go out with your
friends than to get that big promotion. Even when
you're, gasp, <i>pushing 30</i>. They say there
are more bars in <a href="http://www.bcn.es/
english/ihome.htm" target="_blank">Barcelona
</a> than in the rest of the European community
<i>combined</i>. Don't get me wrong, I don't
mean that everyone gets drunk all the time--bars
are for hanging out and talking or for having a cup
of coffee (espresso, of course).</p>

<p>The opinions expressed on this page are mine
and mine alone.</p>

</body>
```

Figure 21.11 *You can change the color of new links, visited links, and active links.*

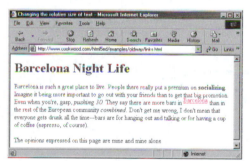

Figure 21.12 *The* link, vlink, *and* alink *attributes are all well supported. Making them obvious in a two-color book is another thing. You can view this example—and indeed all of the examples—online at my Web site (see page 24).*

Changing the Color of Links

Since a link has to stand out and call attention to itself, its color is an important and special quality. None of the elements that we've discussed so far in this chapter affect a link's color.

To change the color of links:

1. Place the cursor inside the body tag.

2. To change the color of links that have not yet been visited, type **link**.

    To change the color of links that have already been visited, type **vlink**.

    To change the color of a link when the user clicks on it, type **alink**.

3. Type **="color"**, where *color* is a hex color or color name *(see page 46 and inside back cover)*.

4. Repeat steps 2–3 for each kind of link.

✔ Tips

■ See page 46 and the inside back cover for a list of common colors and instructions for creating your own.

■ Make sure you test the colors of your text, links, and background together.

■ Be careful when choosing different colors for links from page to page. If your visitors can't tell what to click on or which pages they've already visited, they may decide not to click on anything.

■ The basefont and font elements *can* change a link's size or font face *(see pages 344–347)*.

■ The link, vlink, and alink attributes have been deprecated. You can use styles to control the colors of links *(see pages 141 and 174)*.

Striking Out or Underlining Text

Most browsers can display lines either through or under text. Strike out text is most useful to show revisions to text. Underlining is another way of emphasizing text, especially newly added text.

To strike out or underline text:

1. Type **<strike>** or **<u>** for strike out text and underlining, respectively.

2. Type the text that should appear with a line through or under it.

3. Type **</strike>** or **</u>**.

✔ Tips

- Both the `strike` and `u` tags have been deprecated. There is also a shorthand `s` tag for `strike` that has also been deprecated.

- There are two tags that have not been deprecated that you can use for strike out and underline text: `del` (for deleted) and `ins` (for inserted) respectively *(see page 81)*. They are not supported by Netscape 4.

- Although fonts and colors let designers indicate links in new ways, most Web sites continue to use underlining to show links to other Web pages *(see page 117)*. You may confuse visitors by underlining text that is not a link.

- Lynx displays `em` and `strong` text with an underline.

- You can apply (or remove) underlining, strike out, and even overlining with styles. For more details, consult *Decorating Text* on page 174.

```
<body link="gray" vlink="green" alink="yellow" >

<h1>Barcelona Night Life</h1>

<p>Barcelona is such a <u>great</u> place to live.
People there really put a premium on
<b>socializing</b>. Imagine it being more
important to go out with your friends than to get that
big promotion. Even when you're, gasp,
<i>pushing 30</i>. They say there are more bars
in <a href="http://www.bcn.es/english/
ihome.htm" target="_blank">Barcelona</a> than
in the rest of the European community
<i>combined</i>. Don't get me wrong, I don't
mean that everyone gets drunk all the time--bars
are for hanging out and talking or for having a cup
of coffee (espresso, of course).</p>

<p>The opinions expressed on this page are
mine<strike> and mine alone</strike>.</p>

</body>
```

Figure 21.13 *Note that besides adding the underline and strike through text, I've also removed the default red color—for simplicity's sake.*

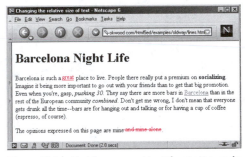

Figure 21.14 *Most browsers support the* `strike` *and* `u` *elements.*

```
<body>

<h1>Famous Catalans</h1>

<p><font size="+3">E</font>ver heard of
Montserrat Caball&eacute;, Josep Carreras, and
Vict&ograve;ria dels &Agrave;ngels? (You may
know these last two by their Spanish names:
Jos&eacute; Carreras and Victoria de los
&Aacute;ngeles.) Did you know they were
<blink>all Catalans</blink>? The things you
learn!</p>

</body>
```

Figure 21.15 *The* blink *element only works on text.*

Figure 21.16 *Blinking text appears normal (top), then disappears (bottom), then reappears.*

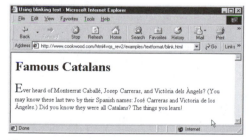

Figure 21.17 *Internet Explorer does not now and probably never will recognize the* blink *tag.*

Making Text Blink

 Another way to make text stand out is to make it blink. You can apply the blink tag to anchors, links, or any important text that you have on the page.

To make text blink:

1. Type **<blink>**.

2. Type the text that you want to blink.

3. Type **</blink>**.

✔ Tips

■ The blink element is not a valid part of (X)HTML, but it is so infamous, I had to mention it. Honestly, I think it helped get people excited about the Web in its own garish, annoying way.

■ You should omit the DOCTYPE if you're going to use the non-standard blink.

■ Blinking text—and other high contrast images on your page—can provoke seizures in folks with epilepsy. It's also considered a bit gauche in the sophisticated world of Web design. You might want to be careful where and how much you use it.

■ You can include an image in your blinking definition, but it won't blink.

■ You may not use blinking text in the title.

■ Internet Explorer does not recognize the blink tag and probably never will. Could it be because the blink tag was one of the driving factors behind arch-rival Netscape's rise to fame?

■ You can use styles to create valid blinking text. For more information, consult *Decorating Text* on page 174.

Making Text Blink

LAYOUT: THE OLD WAY

There are several deprecated and proprietary (X)HTML tags that apply to an entire page, instead of being limited to just a few words or paragraphs. I call these elements *page layout* features and restrict them to this chapter.

Included among these features are setting margins and columns, controlling the spacing between the elements on a page, changing the background color for the entire page, dividing a page into logical sections, positioning elements in layers, and determining when line breaks should, and shouldn't, occur.

Note that all of the elements discussed in this chapter are either deprecated *(see page 343)* or non-standard and should be avoided in favor of styles. In each section, I'll point you to the page that discusses the standard method for achieving the effect.

Using Background Color

Tired of basic gray? The `bgcolor` tag lets you set the background color of each Web page you create.

To set the background color:

In the `body` tag, after the word `body` but before the final >, type **bgcolor="color"**, where *color* is either one of the standard color names or is a hex color *(see page 46 and the inside back cover).*

✓ Tips

- See the inside back cover for a list of the 16 predefined colors as well as a selection of other colors together with their hexadecimal values. For more information about creating your own colors, see page 46.
- For more information on setting the link colors, consult *Changing the Color of Links* on page 349. For more information on setting the text color, consult *Choosing Default Characteristics for Text* on page 344 or *Another Way to Choose Default Colors* on page 348.
- To use an image for the background, consult *Using Background Images* on page 355.
- Most browsers let your visitors override any background color set by you, the page designer **(Figure 22.3)**.
- The `bgcolor` attribute has been deprecated. I recommend using styles to control the background *(see page 182).*

```
<body bgcolor="#FF00FF">
You can change the color of the background of your page--but make sure your
users can still read the text on top of it. That is the point, right?
</body>
```

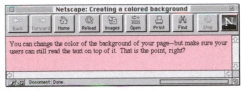

Figure 22.1 *Add the* `bgcolor` *attribute to the* `body` *tag to set the background color for the page.*

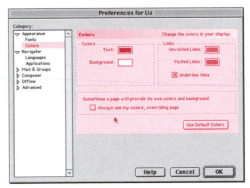

Figure 22.2 *Changing the background color is an easy way to give your pages a distinctive flavor. Beware though of visitors who view pages with their own colors (see Figure 22.3 below)—especially if the color of your text depends on your background color.*

Figure 22.3 *This is Netscape's preferences dialog box in which your visitors can choose not to use the colors that you, the designer, have specified for a page. (Explorer has a similar option.)*

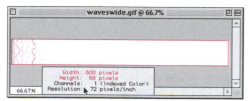

Figure 22.4 *In this example, I've created a background image that is 68 pixels high and 600 pixels wide. It compresses beautifully to less than 2K, but since browsers automatically tile images smaller than the window, it will fill the background as completely as any bigger image.*

```
<body background="waveswide.gif">
<table cellspacing="2" cellpadding="1">
<tr>
<td width="80" valign="top"> </td>
<td valign="top">
<h2>The Mardi Gras Home Page</h2>
Mardi Gras is gearing up to be the best ever this
year. Come down to New Orleans and see how we
throw a party!
<p><a href="calendar.html">Calendar</a></p>
```

Figure 22.5 *To keep text from overlapping my background image along the left side, I've placed the text in a table with two columns, and left the first column empty. For more information about tables, consult Chapter 14, Tables. Notice you can't add extra image attributes (like* width *or* height, *for example) to the body tag.*

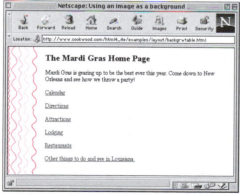

Figure 22.6 *Because the image is so wide, it does not repeat horizontally (and leaves room for text that is easy to read).*

Using Background Images

You can use one image as the backdrop for your entire page. *Backdrop* is the operative word here. A background image should not detract from the readability of your page, but instead make it more attractive.

To use a background image:

1. In the body tag at the beginning of your page, type **background=**.

2. Type **"bgimage.gif"**, where *bgimage.gif* is the location on the server of the image you want to use.

3. If desired, type **bgproperties= "fixed"** to make the image a stationary watermark.

✔ Tips

■ Take advantage of the fact that browsers automatically tile smaller images when creating your background **(Figure 22.6)**.

■ With an image editing program, try increasing the brightness and lowering the contrast to soften the background image so it doesn't distract from your page's content.

■ Save your visitor loading time by using the same background image on a series of pages. After the image has been loaded for the first page, each subsequent page uses a cached version which loads much more quickly.

■ The background attribute is deprecated. For details on using styles to create a background image, see page 182.

Centering Elements on a Page

The center tag is perhaps the most missed of the deprecated elements, and the least satisfactorily replaced with CSS. In other words, when centering with CSS seems like too much of a hassle, many continue to use the center tag. It remains well supported and can be used with virtually any element on your page.

To center elements on a page:

1. Type **<center>**.

2. Create the element that you wish to center.

3. Type **</center>**.

✔ Tips

- For information on using styles to center text, consult *Aligning Text* on page 171.

- You can use the center tag with almost every kind of (X)HTML element, including paragraphs, headers, images, and forms.

- For more details on aligning paragraphs, consult *Starting a New Paragraph* on page 66. For more information on aligning headers, consult *Creating Section Headers* on page 65.

- For information on aligning images with text, consult *Aligning Images* on page 114.

- For details on dividing your document into sections that you can then align, consult *Breaking up a Page into Divisions* on page 68.

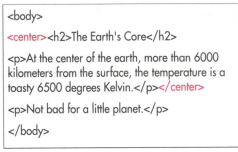

Figure 22.7 *The center element can contain block-level elements, inline elements, or both.*

Figure 22.8 *Centering a bit of text is a good way to call attention to it. The center tag is supported by practically all browsers (despite having been deprecated by the W3C) and is sorely missed by standards advocates.*

```
<body leftmargin="0" topmargin="0"
marginwidth="0" marginheight="0">

If you set all the margin attributes to 0, the page will
start in the top leftcorner, leaving no margin at all.

</body>
```

Figure 22.9 *Inside the* body *tag, set values for both Netscape's and Explorer's attributes.*

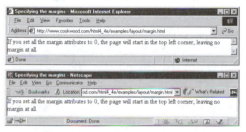

Figure 22.10 *Each browser ignores the other one's particular attributes so you have to use all four to have the browsers display the margins correctly.*

```
<body marginwidth="0" marginheight="0">

If you set all the margin attributes to 0, the page will
start in the top leftcorner, leaving no margin at all.

</body>
```

Figure 22.11 *If you only use say, the attributes that Netscape recognizes (*marginwidth *and* margin-height*), then Netscape will display the margins properly but Explorer will not. And if you only use IE's proprietary attributes, then Explorer will understand and Netscape will not.*

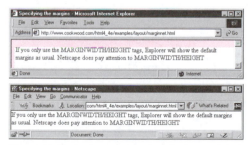

Figure 22.12 *Explorer goes back to displaying default margins (top) while Netscape is still happy with just the* marginwidth *and* marginheight *attributes.*

Specifying the Margins

Both Netscape and Internet Explorer add a certain amount of space, by default, between the contents of a page and the edges of the window. And both let you specify how much space you want there to be. Unfortunately, since they don't understand each other's methods, you'll have to use both.

To specify the margins:

1. For your Internet Explorer users, in the body tag, after the word body but before the final >, type **leftmargin="x" topmargin="y"**, where *x* is the width in pixels of the space between the left border of the window and the contents of the page and *y* is the height in pixels between the top of the window and the contents of the page.

2. For Netscape folks, in the body tag, after the word body but before the >, type **marginwidth= "x", marginheight="y"**, where *x* and *y* are the same values as in step 1.

✔ Tips

- You can set only the left or only the top margin if you wish.

- The leftmargin and topmargin tags were developed by Microsoft and are completely non-standard.

- The attributes marginwidth and marginheight are part of the standard (X)HTML specifications when used with frame (*see page 249*), but not with body.

- Thank goodness for CSS which lets us set the margins in a standard way that all current browsers understand. For more details, consult *Setting the Margins around an Element* on page 189.

Specifying the Margins

Keeping Lines Together

You may have certain phrases in your document that you don't want separated. Or you may want to keep a word and an image together, no matter what.

To keep elements on one line:

1. Type **<nobr>**.

2. Create the text or elements that should appear all on one line.

3. Type **</nobr>**.

✔ Tips

■ Elements within nobr tags will not be separated, unless there is a wbr tag *(see page 359)*, even if the size of the window causes them to be displayed off the screen, and thus invisible to the user **(Figure 22.14)**.

■ Unlike the nowrap attribute used in tables to keep a cell's contents on a single line *(see page 239)*, the nobr tag must have an opening and closing tag and only affects the text contained within the two.

■ The nobr element is not standard (X)HTML (and thus will not validate). Nevertheless, most browsers (current and otherwise) support it.

■ You can also insert a non-breaking space (type ** **) between words that should not be separated.

■ You also use styles to keep lines together. Consult *Setting White Space Properties* on page 170 for details.

```
<body>

<h1><nobr>The Worldwide Conference on
Keeping It Together</nobr></h1>

<p>Opening Hymn:</p>

<p>We have to keep it together<br />

Never come apart,<br />

Birds of a feather,<br />Close to our heart.</p>

<p><em>12 December 1996. London.</em> The
Worldwide Conference on Keeping It Together met
today for the first time as a group. They had
originally met separately in their respective states.
Discussed today was whether or not the group
should vote on a charter together or whether each
sovereign state should vote separately. They
couldn't quite keep it together.</p>
```

Figure 22.13 *I have placed* nobr *tags around the header text to ensure that the entire sentence is displayed on one line in the browser.*

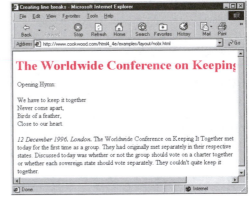

Figure 22.14 *With the* nobr *tags, the headline is kept on one line, even when it extends past the width of a visitor's browser window.*

Keeping Lines Together

```
<body>

<h1><nobr>The Worldwide Conference on <wbr>
Keeping It Together</nobr></h1>

<p>Opening Hymn:</p>

<p>We have to keep it together<br />

Never come apart,<br />

Birds of a feather,<br />Close to our heart.</p>

<p><em>12 December 1996. London.</em> The
Worldwide Conference on Keeping It Together met
today for the first time as a group. They had
originally met separately in their respective states.
Discussed today was whether or not the group
should vote on a charter together or whether each
sovereign state should vote separately. They
couldn't quite keep it together.</p>
```

Figure 22.15 *The* nobr *tag keeps all the enclosed elements on the same line. The* wbr *tag allows a line break—if necessary—depending on window size.*

Figure 22.16 *When the visitor makes the window too narrow for the entire header to fit, the line is divided where you inserted the* wbr *tag.*

Figure 22.17 *If the visitor expands the window so that the entire line can fit, the line break is not used.*

Creating Discretionary Line Breaks

Regular line breaks *(see page 70)* are permanent. No matter how big the visitor makes her window, the poem will never be displayed on one line. However, there are many situations in which you'd like to control where a line breaks—if the break is necessary—but keep the line together if the break is not necessary. This kind of line break is called *discretionary*.

To create discretionary line breaks:

1. Enclose the text in nobr tags as described on page 358.

2. Type **<wbr>** where you'd like the line to break, if a break is necessary.

✔ Tips

- It doesn't make sense to use the wbr tag without the nobr tags.

- Line breaks created with wbr only appear if the window is small enough to warrant them. Otherwise, the elements will not be separated.

- The wbr tag is not part of the standard (X)HTML specifications. Just the same, both Netscape and Explorer support it.

Creating Discretionary Line Breaks

Specifying the Space Between Paragraphs

Before CSS, when you used the p or br tags, the amount of space between paragraphs was only controlled by the size of the surrounding text. Larger text had larger spaces. Smaller text had smaller spaces. Netscape's spacer tag let you specify exactly how much space should appear between one line and another.

To specify the space between paragraphs:

1. Place the cursor between the two lines to be separated.

2. Type **<spacer**.

3. Type **type="vertical"**.

4. Type **size="n"**, where *n* is the amount of space, in pixels, that should appear between the two lines.

5. Type the final **>**.

✔ Tips

- The spacer tag with vertical type works only in Netscape 4.x. Styles are much more flexible and much better supported *(see pages 188 and 189)*.

- The spacer tag with a value of *vertical* for the type attribute creates an automatic line break. You do not need to use the p tag—it will create the same amount of space it always has, in *addition* to the spacer element's space.

```
<html><head>
<title>Creating space between paragraphs</title>
</head>
<body>
You can use vertical spacers to specify the exact amount of space between each paragraph.
<spacer type="vertical" size="48">
However, they are only supported by Netscape 4.x and so should be avoided like the plague.
</body>
</html>
```

Figure 22.18 *You might want to take out any p tags when using vertical spacers. Otherwise, the paragraphs will have both the space allotted by the spacer tag as well as that from the p tag. Clearly, this is a compatibility nightmare.*

Figure 22.19 *Since we haven't used a p tag, the two paragraphs run together in Internet Explorer, which doesn't understand the spacer tag.*

Figure 22.20 *On a 96 dpi screen, there will be exactly 1/2 inch of white space between the two paragraphs—as long as they're viewed in Netscape 4.x.*

```
<html ><head>

<title>Using spacers</title></head>

<body>

<spacer type="horizontal" size="36">You can use
spacers as a substitute of tabs (which don't exist in
HTML) in order to indent paragraphs.

<p><spacer type="horizontal" size="36">
However, since the spacer tag is only supported by
Netscape 4.x, it should be avoided.</p>

</body>

</html>
```

Figure 22.21 *Use horizontal spacers for indenting paragraphs, or any place you need to add an invisible, horizontal block of space.*

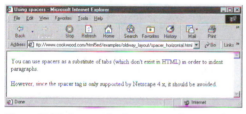

Figure 22.22 *Internet Explorer ignores horizontal spacers completely, aligning all text to the left. To indent text for Explorer, use styles (see page 168) or if you really have to, use pixel shims (see page 364).*

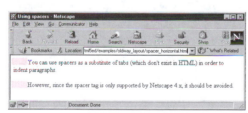

Figure 22.23 *Horizontal spacers work only in Netscape 4.x.*

Creating Indents

 You can't type a tab, or specify a tab stop in (X)HTML documents. However, there are a number of ways to create indents for your paragraphs for Netscape browsers.

To create indents:

1. Place the cursor where you want the space to appear.

2. Type **<spacer**.

3. Type **type="horizontal"**.

4. Type **size="n"**, where *n* is the desired indent size, in pixels.

5. Type the final **>** tag.

6. Type the text of the indented paragraph.

✔ Tips

■ You can use horizontal spacers anywhere you want, not just at the beginning of a text paragraph.

■ The spacer element has no real advantages over styles. I describe it here purely for historical reasons, and in case you need to update someone's old code. I recommend using styles to add indents *(see page 168)*. Even pixel shims *(see page 364)* are better than the spacer element.

■ The spacer tag, with type set to horizontal, is only supported by Netscape 4.x.

■ You can also use the spacer element to create vertical spacing *(see page 360)*.

Creating Indents

Creating Indents (with Lists)

Old HTML editors used to kludge paragraph indents that worked on most any browser. Looking at the code revealed the secret: the indents were created with lists.

To create indents with lists:

1. Place the cursor where you'd like to create indented text.

2. Type **<ul>**.

3. Type the contents of the indented text. You can type as many paragraphs as you want.

4. Type **</ul>**.

✔ Tips

- ■ According to the (X)HTML specifications, the ul and ol tags may only contain li elements, and not text. In other words, this rather common, but old-fashioned technique is not valid HTML.

- ■ This method won't work for hanging indents or first-line indents.

- ■ For real indents using style sheets, consult *Adding Indents* on page 169.

```
<body>

<h2>Sneaky ways to create indents</h2>

<p>Using lists to create indents is not exactly legal
but it does work--in any browser. The W3
Consortium would prefer that you use styles. But
until you do, list indents will come in handy.</p>

<ul>The basic technique is to create a list for each
section that you want to indent. Don't create any list
items--since they are always marked with a bullet.
Oh, and there's no way to make hanging indents or
first-line indents. If you want to get fancy, use
styles.</ul>

</body>
```

Figure 22.24 *You can use lists (without the* li *tag) to create indented paragraphs.*

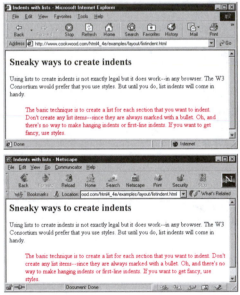

Figure 22.25 *List indents work on most browsers but they have two disadvantages: the W3C wishes you wouldn't use them and they don't offer much flexibility in the way of hanging or first-line indents.*

Creating Indents (with Lists)

```
<html><head><title>Creating blocks of
space</title></head><body>

<spacer type="block"  width="100" height="100"
align="left">If you like to create big margins
around your text, spacers are ideal for the job.

<p>Just use the spacer tag as if it were an invisible
image. And wrap the text right around it as usual.

</body></html>
```

Figure 22.26 *When creating a block-shaped space, you have to specify the width and the height, along with an alignment, to determine where the space will appear.*

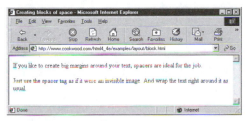

Figure 22.27 *Don't forget: the spacer tag has absolutely no effect in Internet Explorer (shown here). It only works with Netscape browsers.*

Figure 22.28 *Block shaped spaces are ideal for setting large, invisible margins—in Netscape. (I've colored the space to illustrate it in this book, but it's really invisible.)*

Creating Blocks of Space

 Netscape's spacer tag can also be used to create blocks of space that you can wrap text around.

To create blocks of space:

1. Place the cursor where the space should appear, before any text that will wrap around it.

2. Type **<spacer**.

3. Type **type="block"**.

4. Type **width="w" height="h"**, where *w* and *h* are the width and height, respectively, of the block, in pixels.

5. To wrap text around the block, type **align="left"** or **align="right"**, depending on which side of the block you want the text.

    To align the block next to the text, without wrapping the text around it, type **align="direction"**, where *direction* is top, middle, or bottom.

6. Type the final **>**.

✔ Tips

■ Internet Explorer does not support spacer. Netscape 6 only supports spacer with the type attribute set to block. I recommend avoiding spacer like the plague, in favor of the better supported, more powerful, and more flexible styles.

■ For more information on wrapping text, consult *Making Images Float* on page 110. For more information on the alignment options, consult *Aligning Images* on page 114.

■ To create a *colored* block of space, use a pixel shim (*see page 364*).

Using Pixel Shims

A shim in the physical world is a little piece of wood (or sometimes paper) that you stick under one of the legs of your table (for example) to make it stop wobbling. A *pixel shim* is a wedge of pixels, sometimes in color, that can be inserted between elements on a page to shore up the balance and alignment.

To use a pixel shim:

1. Create a 1 pixel by 1 pixel GIF image in the desired color *(see page 90)*.

2. In your HTML document, type **<img src="pixelshim.gif"**, where *pixelshim.gif* is the name of the image created in step 1.

3. Type **width="w" height="h"**, where *w* and *h* are the *desired* width and height, in pixels, of the desired space.

4. To wrap text around the shim, type **align ="left"** or **align="right"** *(see page 110)*.

    Or you can align the shim next to the text (and not around it) by typing **align="direction"**, where *direction* is top, middle, or bottom *(see page 114)*.

5. Add other image attributes, as desired.

6. Type the final **/>**.

✔ Tips

■ Pixel shims are well supported since they're just images, forced to work in a new way. They are, however, unwieldy and inflexible. Use styles instead.

■ Pixel shims are tiny (and thus, load quickly) and can be made any color you want—or they can be transparent.

■ You can download pixel shims from my site *(see page 24)*.

```
<body>

<img src="pixelshim.gif" width="100"
height="150" hspace="3" alt="" align="left" />

<p><b>Or, perhaps better yet, use a pixel shim. It
has the advantage of being recognized by most
browsers, and you can make it any color you
want.</b></p>

</body>
```

Figure 22.29 *A pixel shim is nothing more than a one pixel by one pixel image, of any color you like, expanded to the desired size, and aligned as necessary.*

Figure 22.30 *The principal advantage of pixel shims is that they work in almost any browser. In addition, they are small and load quickly and they can be made any color you need. Notice, however, that Explorer (top) leaves slightly more space to the right of the image than Netscape.*

Using Pixel Shims

```
<html><head><title>Creating
columns</title></head><body>

<multicol cols="2" gutter="30" width="85%">

<p><font size="-1">A multicolumn layout is typical
of newspaper articles. You start reading down the
first column and when you read [snip]</font></p>

<p><font size="-1">Use returns where necessary
to start a new line. Or use a line break instead. Or
insert images, or whatever.</font></p>

<p><font size="-1">Hey, the headline's a joke, get
it? </font></p></multicol>

<font size="-1">After the final multicol tag, you can
```

Figure 22.31 *The only required attribute in the* mul-ticol *tag is* cols*: you must determine how many columns you want. (I've reduced the size of the text in this illustration to better fit on the page.)*

Figure 22.32 *Columns are perfect for newspaper style articles. These take up 85% of the screen, as defined in the HTML document. In addition, I've made the text one size smaller so as to better fit in the columns.*

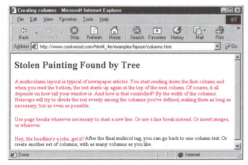

Figure 22.33 *Internet Explorer does not recognize the* multicol *tag. The last paragraph runs into the column text, since there was no* p *tag.*

Creating Columns

Netscape tried to resolve the thirst for columns with this badly implemented `multicol` tag. Among its limitations: it works only in Netscape 4.x, all columns must be the same width, and perhaps worst of all, if you make the columns too narrow, they overlap and look horrible.

To create columns:

1. In your HTML document, type **<multicol**.

2. Type **cols="n"**, where *n* is the number of columns desired. Each column will be the same size.

3. If desired, type **gutter="n"**, where *n* is the width of the space between the columns, in pixels or as a percentage.

4. If desired, type **width="n"**, where *n* is the width of the entire column set, including the gutter, in pixels or as a percentage of window size.

5. Type the final **>** to finish the column definition.

6. Create the elements (text or images) that will go into the columns.

7. Type **</multicol>**.

✔ Tips

- If you omit the `width` attribute, the columns will expand to fit whatever size window the user has created.

- You can nest one set of columns with another. Simply repeat steps 1–7 when you reach step 6 of the outer set.

- If you don't use the `gutter` attribute, Netscape automatically leaves 10 pixels between columns.

- Only Netscape 4.x supports `multicol`.

Creating Columns

Positioning Elements with Layers

 Although they had already promised to work towards a universal standard for HTML, Netscape developed a set of proprietary tags for positioning HTML elements in early 1997. Now that Netscape 6 leads the pack in supporting CSS positioning techniques *(see page 177)*, you can forget about layers.

To position elements with layers:

1. Type **<layer**.

2. If desired, type **id="name"**, where *name* identifies the layer to JavaScript.

3. Type **top="m"**, where *m* is the number of pixels the layer's contents should be off-set from the top edge of the browser window.

4. Type **left="n"**, where *n* is the number of pixels the layer's contents should be off-set from the left edge of the browser window.

5. If desired, type **width="w"**, where *w* is the width of the layer in pixels.

6. If desired, type **height="h"**, where *h* is the height of the layer in pixels.

7. If desired, type **src="source.html"**, where *source.html* is the initial HTML content that should appear in the layer **(Figure 22.37)**.

8. If desired, type **clip="t,l,r,b"** where *t, l, r,* and *b* are the offsets in pixels from the top, left, right, and bottom.

9. If desired, type **z-index="z"**, where *z* is a number indicating the layer's level if it overlaps other layers. The higher the value of z, the higher the layer.

```
<body>

<layer id="layer1" top="10" left="50"
width="100" height="100" bgcolor="yellow"
z-index="1">This is the very bottom layer. It's
yellow.</layer>

<layer id="layer2" top="20" left="60"
width="160" height="80" bgcolor="orange"
z-index="2">This is the second layer from the
bottom. It's orange.</layer>

<layer id="layer3" top="40" left="80" width="40"
height="40" bgcolor="black" z-index="3">
<font color="white">This is layer 3. It's
black.</font></layer>

<layer id="layer4" top="70" left="200"
width="100" height="100" bgcolor="red"
z-index="1">This layer is at the same level as the
first one, that is, the bottom.</layer>

<nolayer>This page contains elements positioned
with layers. It only works in Netscape
Communicator 4.</nolayer>

</body>
```

Figure 22.34 *Each layer is defined separately with its own coordinates. I've just entered plain text as the contents of each layer, but you can add any other HTML tags you like, except frames.*

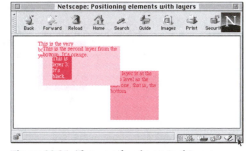

Figure 22.35 *There are four layers in this example. Layers become really useful when combined with JavaScript.*

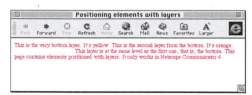

Figure 22.36 *Explorer makes a total mess of layers with content—despite the* `nolayer` *option.*

```
<body>

<layer id="layer1" top="10" left="300"
width="50" height="60" bgcolor="aqua" z-
index="1" src="layer1.html"></layer>

<layer id="layer2" top="50" left="30"
width="300" height="80" bgcolor="magenta" z-
index="2" src="layer2.html"></layer>

<nolayer>This page contains elements positioned
with layers. It only works in Netscape
Communicator 4.</nolayer>

</body>
```

Figure 22.37 *If you know Explorer users are going to try to view your page, you should use the* `src` *attribute in the* `layer` *tags to insert content and then the* `nolayer` *tags to alert Explorer users to the fact that they won't see the effect.*

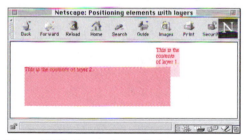

Figure 22.38 *Communicator displays the contents from the files in the* `src` *attribute.*

Figure 22.39 *Since Explorer completely ignores* `layer` *tags, it won't try to insert the content of layers defined by the* `src` *attribute. Instead, it simply and cleanly displays the contents of the* `nolayer` *tags.*

10. If desired, type **bgcolor="color"**, where *color* is a hex color or one of the predefined colors listed on the inside back cover.

11. If desired, type **background= "image.gif"**, where *image.gif* is the image that you'd like to use for the background of the layer.

12. Type **>**.

13. Create the contents of the layer.

14. Type **</layer>**.

✔ Tips

- Layers were designed to be combined with JavaScript to create dynamic pages. For more information, check out *http:// developer.netscape.com/docs/manuals/ communicator/dynhtml/layers3.htm*. My basic examples don't quite do it justice.

- You can create content for browsers (like Explorer) that don't recognize the `layer` tags. Simply enclose it in opening and closing `nolayer` tags **(Figure 22.39)**.

- To create relatively positioned elements (that is, elements that are offset with respect to their natural position in the flow), use opening and closing `ilayer` tags instead of `layer` tags.

- The official way to position elements precisely is with styles *(see Chapter 11, Layout with Styles)*, not this non-standard and poorly supported `layer` tag. Now that Netscape 6 supports CSS, you can forget about the `layer` element forever. I include the information here solely so that you can decipher old code.

Positioning Elements with Layers

WML: WEB PAGES FOR MOBILE DEVICES

Figure 23.1 *I used Openwave (right) and Nokia simulators to create the illustrations for this chapter. They are an essential tool for developing mobile Web sites. Download information is on page 392.*

Because mobile devices (like cell phones) are so small and their connection to the Internet is so slow (and costly), they are just not very good at browsing regular Web pages, written with (X)HTML and full of complex layouts and striking images (not to mention sounds, videos, and Flash animations).

Instead, the standard language for writing Web pages for mobile devices is WML, or *Wireless Markup Language*. Based on XML— indeed, it's an *application* of XML—WML insists you follow the same syntax rules that you've learned for XHTML: lowercase tag and attribute names, quoted attributes, end tags, in short, valid and well-formed documents. In addition, WML asks that you be extremely careful about size. Images should be kept to a minimum and the files themselves should be tiny (under 2K).

Actually, WML looks remarkably like a scaled down version of XHTML, with many of the same elements (p, br, em, etc.), although some of those elements have distinct attributes. You'll learn all the rules for writing WML files in this chapter.

While the promise of XHTML and CSS is that you can create a single file that can be served properly both to a desktop browser and to a microbrowser on a mobile device, the reality is that most phones simply don't support XHTML (or even WML plus CSS) yet. Nevertheless, the similarity between WML and XHTML makes WML an ideal first step towards XHTML for mobile devices.

WML: Web Pages for Mobile Devices

Preparing Your Server

When a visitor types in the URL of an HTML page, the server looks at the file name, goes and fetches the document, compares the .html (or .htm) extension against the MIME types it's familiar with and treats it accordingly. Since HTML is so popular, all servers are set up to handle HTML files. You may have to help your server know what to do with WML files by associating the file extensions with the proper MIME types.

To prepare an Apache server to serve WML files and images from a particular directory:

1. On the first line of a text file, type **DirectoryIndex** followed by a space and then **index.wml**, where *index.wml* is the name of the file that should be displayed if a visitor types the URL of the directory.

2. Press the Return key.

3. Type **addtype mime extension**, where *mime* is the MIME type for the desired kind of file, and *extension* is the three or four letter extension those kinds of files will have. Press Return.

4. Repeat step 3 for each type of file that you want to be able to serve.

5. Save the file as text only and upload it to the directory from which you wish to serve the WML files. Its name in the directory should be *.htaccess* (with that initial period).

✔ Tips

- You may need to give the file a different local name if your system does not permit initial periods in the name.

- You can download a sample (but valid) *.htaccess* file from my site *(see page 24)*.

```
DirectoryIndex  index.wml
addtype text/vnd.wap.wml wml
addtype text/x-hdml  hdml
addtype image/vnd.wap.wbmp wbmp
```

Figure 23.2 *Here is a typical* .htaccess *file. You can ask your ISP to set this up, or you can simply add the file to the directories that contain your WML files.*

```
<?xml version="1.0"?>

<!DOCTYPE wml PUBLIC "-//WAPFORUM//DTD
WML 1.3//EN"
"http://www.wapforum.org/DTD/wml13.dtd">



<wml>




</wml>
```

Figure 23.3 *Don't forget the closing* </wml> *element. Nothing will work without it.*

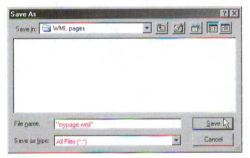

Figure 23.4 *When saving the file, choose All Files (*.*) if available and enclose the file name in double quotes to keep Windows from adding extraneous extensions to your files (and making them inoperable).*

Starting Your WML Page

A collection of related Web pages for mobile devices (like cell phones) is stored in a Web page called a *deck*. It is a single XML file, written in WML (Wireless Markup Language).

To start your WML page:

1. At the very top of a blank page in any text editor, type **<? xml version="1.0" ?>**.

2. Next type **<!DOCTYPE wml PUBLIC "-//WAPFORUM//DTD WML 1.3//EN" "http://www.wapforum.org/DTD/wml13.dtd">** so that browsers know that the page is written in WML (version 1.3) and is designed for WAP browsers.

3. Next type **<wml>** to begin the actual content of your page.

4. Create the page, using the techniques described throughout this chapter.

5. Type **</wml>** to finish your page.

6. Make sure to save your document as text only with the .wml extension.

✔ Tips

■ Windows users, you may want to enclose the file name in double quotation marks so that Windows doesn't add any extra extensions to your file name as you save **(Figure 23.4)**.

■ Since WML is an XML application, you must follow all those persnickety syntax rules, including using all lowercase letters for tags, attributes, and preset values, quoting all values, using end tags, etc. For an overview, consult *HTML vs XHTML* on page 36. For a complete reference, you might try my *XML for the World Wide Web: Visual QuickStart Guide*, also published by Peachpit Press.

Starting Your WML Page

Creating a Card

A WML file or deck can be divided into one or more cards, which are analogous to individual Web pages.

To create a card:

1. Within the WML document, after the <wml> element, type **<card**.

2. Next type **id="label"**, where *label* is a unique word that will identify the card as the target of links from other cards.

3. Type **title="header"**, where *header* is the text that should appear at the top of the Web page.

4. If desired, type **newcontext="true"** to unset all variables *(see page 383)* and to clear the history stack.

5. Type **>**.

6. Create the card's content, as described on the following pages.

7. Type **</card>** to complete the card.

✔ Tips

■ A deck (WML document) may have as many cards as you like. When the visitor loads the deck, all the cards will be available to the mobile browser without having to go back to the server.

■ While all the cards in a deck are downloaded together, only one card at a time is displayed on a mobile browser.

■ A card's id serves as the target of a link. You may not use the same id twice in the same deck (WML file).

■ Your titles should be no more than about 18 characters long. Longer titles may simply be truncated to fit.

```
<?xml version="1.0"?>

<!DOCTYPE wml PUBLIC "-//WAPFORUM//DTD
WML 1.3//EN"
"http://www.wapforum.org/DTD/wml13.dtd">

<wml>

<card id="welcome" title="Welcome"
newcontext="true">


</card>

</wml>
```

Figure 23.5 *You must use a unique value for the* id *attribute in the* card *element.*

Figure 23.6 *The* title *attribute is displayed at the top of the microbrowser. (Openwave on left, Nokia at right.)*

```
<?xml version="1.0"?>

<!DOCTYPE wml PUBLIC "-//WAPFORUM//DTD
WML 1.3//EN"
"http://www.wapforum.org/DTD/wml13.dtd">

<wml>

 <card id="welcome" title="Welcome"
newcontext="true">

<p align="center">

<big><b>The Cat and Otter<br />
Bistro/Pub</b></big>

</p>

</card>

</wml>
```

Figure 23.7 *All text, formatted or not, must be enclosed in* p *tags.*

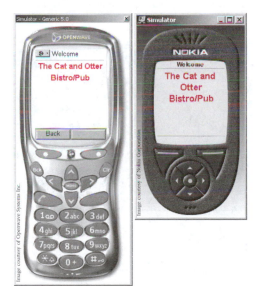

Figure 23.8 *Not all microbrowsers support all of the formatting options, though both of these simulators do.*

Creating Basic Content

The actual content of your card will be enclosed in elements that look a lot like (X)HTML.

To create basic content:

1. Right after the opening card tag, type **<p**.

2. If desired, you can align the content by adding **align="direction"**, where *direction* is left, right, or center.

3. If desired, type **mode="nowrap"** to force the paragraph to display without automatic line breaks. The default is wrap.

4. Type **>** to complete the opening p tag.

5. Create the rest of the card, using the following familiar elements: p, br, em, strong, b, i, u, big, small, table, tr, td, and comments (<!-- -->).

6. Be sure to end your card by typing the closing **</p>** that matches the one you opened with in step 1.

✔ Tips

■ Remember that your average microbrowser on a cell phone has room for only three lines of content (along with the title area and the button text line). If your card has extra text, your visitors will have to scroll to see it. (The simulators shown here are taller than average.)

■ Most microbrowsers don't support all of the formatting elements.

■ The mode attribute is most useful for displaying tables *(see page 375)*.

■ For more details about p, br, em, strong, b, i, u, big, small, table, tr, td, and comments, consult the corresponding section for (X)HTML elements of the same name.

Creating Basic Content

Including an Image

Some browsers can display (very small) images. You must include alternate text for browsers which cannot.

To include an image:

1. Type **<img src="image.wbmp"**, where *image.wbmp* is the name and location of the WBMP format file that you wish to insert in the card.

2. Type **alt="label"**, where *label* is a word that describes the image and will be displayed if the image is not.

3. If desired, add the `height`, `width`, `hspace`, `vspace`, or `align` attributes.

4. Type **/>**.

✔ Tips

- Most microbrowsers only support images in WBMP format.

- Adobe Photoshop 7 can create new or convert existing images to WBMP format. Once your image is ready, choose File > Save for Web. Then choose WBMP in the format menu under Settings on the right side of the window that appears.

- Use the smallest size images you can stand. For some perspective, the cat in Figure 23.10 is a scant 54 pixels wide and 45 pixels high.

- You can use percentages to specify the height and width. Note that percentages are relative to the screen size, not to the intrinsic size of the image itself.

- Make sure your server is prepared to serve WBMP images *(see page 370)*.

```
<?xml version="1.0"?>

<!DOCTYPE wml PUBLIC "-//WAPFORUM//DTD
WML 1.3//EN"
"http://www.wapforum.org/DTD/wml13.dtd">

<wml>

<card id="welcome" title="Welcome"
newcontext="true">

<p align="center">

<img src="cat.wbmp" alt="logo" /><br />

<big><b>The Cat and Otter<br />
Bistro/Pub</b></big>

</p>

</card>

</wml>
```

Figure 23.9 *You must create alternate text (with the* `alt` *attribute) for all* `img` *elements.*

Figure 23.10 *Images should be no larger than 100 pixels across. Be restrained!*

Including an Image

```
<card id="specials" title="Today's Specials">

<p>

<table columns="2" align="RL">

<tr><td><b>Soup</b></td><td>Cream of
Mushroom</td></tr>

<tr><td><b>Entree</b></td><td>Seafood
Fideua, specialty of the house</td></tr>

</table>

</p>

</card>
```

Figure 23.11 *Here is a new card in the same deck as the previous examples. Notice that the table must be enclosed in p tags.*

Figure 23.12 *The first column is aligned to the right while the second column is aligned to the left* (align="RL").

Creating a Table

You can use a table to align several columns of text on a page.

To create a table:

1. After an initial p tag, type **<table** to begin.

2. Type **columns="n"**, where *n* is the number of columns your table will have.

3. If desired, type **align="xy..."**, where *x* sets the alignment for the first column, *y* sets the alignment for the second column, and so on, and each value is one of L (for left), R (for right), or C (for center).

4. Type **>** to complete the initial table tag.

5. Type **<tr>** to begin the row.

6. Type **<td>** to start the cell.

7. Enter the contents of the cell.

8. Type **</td>** to finish the cell.

9. Repeat steps 6–8 for each cell in the row.

10. Type **</tr>** to complete the row.

11. Repeat steps 5–10 for each row.

12. Type **</table>** to complete the table.

✔ Tips

■ Not all microbrowsers support tables.

■ You may not nest tables.

■ You may not use any other table attributes besides the ones described here.

■ You may have to set the enclosing paragraph's mode to nowrap *(see page 373)* in order for the table to display properly.

Creating a Link

There are two principal ways for your visitors to get from one card to another. You can either create links within the page, or you can assign functions to a mobile device's buttons.

To create a link in the page:

1. Type **<anchor**

2. If desired, type **title="label"**, where the browser will use the *label* to identify the anchor in some way, often as the label for the button the visitor will have to click to activate the link. (The default is Link.)

3. If desired, type **accesskey="n"**, where *n* is the number on the mobile device keypad that the visitor should type to activate the link.

4. Type **>**.

5. Type the text and/or insert the image that should identify the anchor in the text.

6. Type **<go href="#cardid">**, where *cardid* is the value of the id attribute of the card that should be displayed when the visitor clicks the link (*see step 2 on page 372*).

   Or type **<prev>** to have the link go to the previous card viewed.

   Or type **<refresh>** to have the link refresh the card, and any variables it contains.

7. Create any additional actions that should happen. For example, with all three tasks, you could set a variable (*see page 383*), and in go tasks you can also post data to an external script (*see page 388*).

8. Type **</go>**, **</prev>**, or **</refresh>** depending on what you used in step 6.

9. Type **</anchor>**.

```
<card id="welcome" title="Welcome"
newcontext="true">

<p align="center">

<img src="cat.wbmp" alt="logo" /><br />

<big><b>The Cat and Otter<br />

Bistro/Pub</b></big>

</p>

<p><a href="#specials" title="Go">Specials</a>

<br /><anchor title="Reserve">Reservations<go
href="#res"></go></anchor>

<br /><anchor title="Where?">Directions<go
href="#dir"></go></anchor>

</p>

</card>
```

Figure 23.13 *Here are three simple links. In the first one, I've used the familiar a tag (see second tip). In the second and third, I use the more WMLish anchor tag. There's no difference between the two methods unless you want to do more than just show a different card.*

Figure 23.14 *Notice that when the link is highlighted, the button is labeled with the title attribute (of either the a or anchor element)—it is the word "Go" in this example.*

Figure 23.15 *The microbrowser now shows the card referenced by the link (the* Specials *page in this case).*

✔ Tips

- You can also create links to cards in other decks by using the deck's URL in step 6. Be default, the new deck's first card will be displayed. Or use **URL#cardid** to jump to a specific card in a different deck.

- If you don't need to add any actions to the go task, you can use the a tag to create simple links: **<a href="destination.wml">Click me</a>**.

- The anchor element may also contain images, line breaks (br elements), and text, but not p elements or formatting.

- The refresh action is most commonly used to set a variable. For more details about variables, consult *Setting and Using Variables* on page 383.

- Only the go task can be used to send data to a server (with postfield). For more details, consult *Processing Data from Visitors* on page 388.

- If you don't specify an additional action in step 7, you can combine the opening and closing elements of the go, prev, or refresh tasks: e.g., <prev /> or <go href="#cardid" />.

- Note that the anchor element creates a link that appears in the main body (skimpy as it is) of the microbrowser and which must be selected by the visitor and then activated with one of the buttons. The do element, described on page 378, assigns a link directly to one of the phone's physical buttons and does not affect the main content at all.

- In some browsers, the accesskey is output just before the link as a visual clue to the visitor. In others, it's invisible.

Creating a Link

Programming Buttons

Although the WML specifications say that browsers are not bound to display the do element in a given way, it seems that mostly, it's used to format the buttons (sometimes called *soft keys*) on a mobile device.

To use buttons:

1. Type **<do type="kind"**, where *kind* is one of accept, prev, (or others depending on the device) and gives the mobile device a hint about the button's purpose.

2. If desired, type **label="button word"**, where *button word* is a descriptive word that will identify the button to the visitor. The label should be six letters or less.

3. If desired, type **name="identifier"** where *identifier* is a word that distinguishes this button from others in your code.

4. Type **>** to complete the opening do tag.

5. Type **<go href="#cardid">**, where *cardid* is the value of the id attribute of the card that should be displayed when the visitor clicks the button *(see step 2 on page 372)*.

   Or type **<prev>** to have the button go to the previous card viewed.

   Or type **<refresh>** to refresh the card, and any variables it contains.

   Or type **<noop>** to disable the button.

6. Create any additional actions that should happen. For example, with all three tasks you could set a variable *(see page 383)*, and with just the go task, you can post data to an external script *(see page 388)*.

7. Type the end tag that matches the opening one you used in step 5.

8. Type **</do>** to complete the button.

```
<card id="welcome" title="Welcome"
newcontext="true">

<p align="center">

<img src="cat.wbmp" alt="logo" /><br />

<big><b>The Cat and Otter<br />

Bistro/Pub</b></big>

</p>

<p><a href="#specials" title="Go">Specials</a>

<br /><anchor title="Reserve">Reservations<go
href="#res"></go></anchor>

<br /><anchor title="Where?">Directions<go
href="#dir"></go></anchor>

</p>

<do type="accept" name="Help"
label="Help"><go href="#help" /></do>

</card>
```

Figure 23.16 *I've created a Help button that will bring visitors to a card with extra information about how to use this site.*

Figure 23.17 *On most microbrowsers, the* accept *type buttons are created on the left side.*

✔ **Tips**

■ The type attribute that you specify for the do element is supposed to help the mobile device figure out what kind of button you're creating. On some phones, for example, you use the accept type to program the left button and the prev type for the right button. Others list all the do elements, regardless of type, under a general Options button. The WML specifications do not require user agents to map types to particular buttons.

■ No two do elements may have the same values for the name attribute.

■ If you omit the name attribute, the value for the type attribute is used by default.

■ The difference between the do element and the anchor element? See the last tip under *Creating a Link* on page 376.

■ Some browsers override any URL specified in the go action of a do element with type prev and insist on creating a standard Back button that goes to the previously visited page. If you create two prev do elements, then you can specify the URL in the second one (although this isn't a real solution if what you wanted was to change the Back button's destination).

■ You cannot set an accesskey for a do element.

■ The default label for the prev type is *BACK*. For the accept type it's *OK*. While there are other valid types, these are the most common and best supported.

■ If you do not create additional actions in step 6, you may combine steps 5–7 into a single tag: e.g., <go href="#cardid" /> or <noop />, or whatever.

Programming Buttons

Creating Conditional Actions

You can have something happen depending on whether the visitor *comes* to a page with a link or menu or *returns* to the page with a prev element.

To specify a conditional action:

1. Within the card element, after the opening card tag, type **<onevent type=**

2. Next type **"onenterforward"** if you want the action to occur only if the visitor has entered the card from a link or menu.

   Or type **"onenterbackward"** if you want the action to occur only if the visitor has entered this page by clicking a Back button or link (created with the prev element).

3. Type **>** to complete the opening onevent tag.

4. Create a go, prev, refresh, or noop action, as described in steps 5–7 on page 378.

5. Type **</onevent>**.

✔ Tips

■ For example, you might want to set a variable only if the visitor jumps to the page, but not if she returns. In that case, use a go action in step 4 that includes a setvar element *(see page 383)*.

■ If you only want to (conditionally) jump to another page, you can use this shortcut: <card onenterforward= "destination.url">. (You can use onenterbackward this way as well.)

■ You can also have an action occur after a certain amount of time. For details, consult *Scheduling an Action* on page 381.

```
<card id="welcome" title="Welcome"
newcontext="true">

<onevent type="onenterforward">

<go href="#help" /></onevent>

<p align="center">

<img src="cat.wbmp" alt="logo" /><br />
```

Figure 23.18 *The* onevent *goes right after the opening* card *element.*

Figure 23.19 *When your visitors go the main page, they are immediately shuttled to the Help screen.*

```
<card id="help" title="Help">

<onevent type="ontimer">

<prev />

</onevent>

<timer value="30" />

<p>Choose the <b>Specials</b> link to see what
delicious food we've got today. Choose the
<b>Reservations</b> link to have us reserve you a
table.

Click <b>Where?</b> to get directions to our
restaurant and click the <b>Help</b> button to get
this screen.

</p>

</card>
```

Figure 23.20 *Now, in the Help card, we create an* ontimer *event so that whenever a user comes to this card, they will have 3 seconds (30 tenths of a second), to read the information and then they will be automatically returned from whence they came.*

Figure 23.21 *Since your visitors return to the home page via a* prev *action, the* onenterforward *condition is not fulfilled (and they don't get whisked back to the Help page). I should probably add that sending your visitors around like this is a good way to annoy them. Instead, use onevents for setting variables (see page 383) and posting data to the server (see page 388).*

Scheduling an Action

You can make certain actions happen after a specified amount of time. This can be useful, for example, to show a splash page, or to automatically close a window after a few seconds.

To schedule an action:

1. Within a card, type **<onevent type="ontimer">**

2. Create a go, prev, refresh, or noop action, as described in steps 5–7 on page 378.

3. Type **</onevent>**.

4. Within the same card, type **<timer**.

5. If desired, type **name="var"**, where *var* is the name of the variable that contains the amount of time (in tenths of seconds) that should pass before the action in step 2 occurs.

6. Type **value="default"**, where *default* is the amount of time (in tenths of seconds) that should be used if the name attribute in step 5 is omitted, or if its corresponding variable is not set.

7. Type **>** to complete the timer element.

✔ Tips

■ Only one timer element is permitted in each card.

■ If you only want to send the visitor to another card when the timer goes off (and not, for example, set a variable or post field data), you can use this shortcut: <card ontimer="destination.url"> and then follow steps 4–7 above to set the timer.

Scheduling an Action

Making a Call

You can take advantage of the fact that many mobile browsers also happen to be telephones and allow your visitors to make calls. To do so, you use a thing called WTAI (Wireless Telephony Applications Interface) to connect from the browser to the telephone (roughly speaking). First, you create a card that makes the call, using WTAI. Then, you link to that card from the card on your deck from which you want to make the call.

To create the card that makes a call:

1. Type **<card id="callcard" title="Call"**, where *callcard* and *Call* are the id and title attribute values *(see page 372)*.

2. Within the card, add **onenterforward= "wtai://wp/mc;number"**, where *number* is the phone number that should be dialed.

3. Type **>** to finish the opening card tag.

4. Then type **</card>**. (The card is never shown to your visitors, so it needs no content.)

To make a call:

Create an anchor, do element, or onevent that goes to the card you created above. For example, **<do type="accept" name="call" label= "Call"><go href="#callcard" /></do>** would create a button labeled *Call* that would call the number specified in step 2 above.

✔ Tips

■ The WTAI instruction can go anywhere a normal URL would go, for example as the value of a href attribute in a go element.

■ The card with the WTAI instruction can be in the same deck or in a different deck as the one that references it.

```
Click <b>Where?</b> to get directions to our
restaurant and click the <b>Help</b> button to get
this screen. If you get really stuck, just <anchor
title="Call">call us<go href="#callcard"
/></anchor>

</p>

</card>

<card id="callcard" title="Call"
onenterforward="wtai://wp/mc;8002839444">

</card>
```

Figure 23.22 *Put the WTAI instruction in an* onenterforward *attribute in a separate card. Then link to the card to make the call.*

Figure 23.23 *When the visitor clicks the* call us *link at the end of the* help *screen (top left and top right), they then see a screen similar to the one on the right asking them to confirm that they'd like to make the call. Once the visitor clicks OK, the browser sends the information to the phone and asks it to try to complete the call.*

Making a Call

```
<card id="res" title="Reserve a Table">

<onevent type="onenterforward">

<refresh><setvar name="number" value="2" />

</refresh>

</onevent>

<p>

Would you like us to reserve a table for

$(number)?</p>

</card>
```

Figure 23.24 *You might want to set a default variable when the visitor enters a card. Then, you can output variables within other text, as shown here, or even as attribute values.*

Figure 23.25 *The content of the variable ("2", that we set earlier) is output instead of the variable name.*

Setting and Using Variables

You can store information in one card and then use it in another, or even send it to a server for processing.

To set a variable explicitly:

Within a go, prev, or refresh element, add **<setvar name="var" value="value" />**, where *var* is the name that will identify the variable and *value* is its content.

To display a variable's content:

1. Place the cursor where you want the current value of the variable to appear.

   You can output variables by themselves, in a larger block of text, or as the value of an attribute.

2. Type **$(var)**, where *var* is the name that identifies the variable.

✔ Tips

- You can clear all variables in a new card by adding newcontext="true" to the opening card tag.

- You can also set (or let your visitor set) variables with text boxes *(see page 384)* and menus *(see page 386)*.

- One typically sets a variable within a refresh element. You can add a refresh element to an anchor *(see page 376)*, to a do element *(see page 378)*, or to an onevent element *(see page 380)*.

- Variables set or updated in one card work in other cards, and even in other decks.

- There are a slew of special codes for escaping (or not) the variables. You can find them in the WML specifications at *http://www.wapforum.org* or on my Web site *(http://www.cookwood.com)*.

Creating Input Boxes

Input boxes are created in almost the same was as for (X)HTML *(see page 272)*. There are a few special attributes and some familiar attributes have special qualities.

To create input boxes:

1. Type **<input type="text"** to begin.

2. Next type **name="var"**, where *var* is the name of the variable that will hold the data from this input box.

3. If desired, type **format="code"**, where *code* is comprised of any combination of the following:

   A (for an uppercase letter or symbol)

   a (for a lowercase letter or symbol)

   N (for a number)

   n (for a number or symbol)

   X (for an uppercase letter, number, or symbol)

   x (for a lowercase letter, number, or symbol)

   M (for any letter, number, or symbol). Note: the mobile device may display in uppercase.

   m (any letter, number, or symbol). Note: the mobile device may display in lowercase.

   *f, where *f* is one of the preceding codes (for any quantity of the desired type of character). Note: this can only be used once, and must be the last part of the full code.

   n*f*, where *n* is a number from 0–9 and *f* is one of the preceding codes (for up to the desired quantity of the desired type of character). Note: this can only be used once, and must be the last code used.

```
<card id="res" title="Reserve a Table">
<onevent type="onenterforward">
<refresh><setvar name="number" value="2" />
</refresh>
</onevent>
<p>Number in party?<input type="text"
name="number" format="2N" /></p>
</card>
```

Figure 23.26 *Note that text and input boxes must be enclosed in* p *tags (while* onevent *elements need not be). I've set the format to 2N to allow numbers up to 99 (in other words, up to 2 digits).*

Figure 23.27 *Since we've already set the number variable with* setvar, *it has a default value (2).*

4. If desired, type **emptyok="true"** if you don't want to require that the visitor enter an answer.

5. If desired, type **accesskey="n"**, where *n* is the key the visitor should type to activate the input box.

6. If desired, type **value="default"**, where *default* is the value of the input box's variable (named in step 2) if none is entered by the visitor.

7. If desired, type **type="password"** to have the visitor's input hidden on screen as they type it.

8. Type **/>** to complete the input box.

✔ Tips

■ You can require that data be entered in a particular pattern using the format attribute. For example, you could insist on a 2 digit (and *not* 1 digit) number by using format="NN".

■ The default value for emptyok is false. However, whether or not input is required for the input box also depends on the value of the format attribute. Since the *f format allows for *any* number of characters to be entered, including zero, it implies that no input is acceptable, regardless of the emptyok attribute.

■ You may also specify the standard (X)HTML input attributes: size, maxlength, tabindex, and title. For more details about input attributes, consult *Creating Text Boxes* on page 272.

■ If a variable with the same name as that specified in step 2 has already been set *(see page 383)*, its value will be the default value for the input box, and will override the contents of the value attribute.

Creating Input Boxes

Creating Menus

WML pages can also include menus for offering choices to your visitors. There are a few special features for menus.

To create menus:

1. Type **<select** to begin.

2. Next type **name="var"**, where *var* is the name of the variable that will hold the data from this input box.

3. If desired, type **value="default"**, where *default* is the value of the menu's variable (named in step 2) if no option is chosen by the visitor.

4. If desired, type **iname="var_index"**, where *var_index* is the name of the variable that will contain the number of the option that the visitor has selected. (Each option is numbered in order, starting with 1. If no option is selected, the var_index variable will contain "0".)

5. If desired, type **ivalue="default_option"**, where *default_option* is the number of the option that should be selected by default.

6. If desired, type **multiple="true"** to allow the visitor to choose more than one option. The default is false.

7. If desired, type **tabindex="n"**, where *n* indicates the order in which elements in the page should be tabbed through. For more details, see page 289.

8. Type **>**.

9. Next, type **<option**.

10. If desired, type **value="var_value"**, where *var_value* is the value that the menu's variable (named in step 2) will get if the visitor chooses this option.

```
<p>Number in party?<input type="text"
name="number" format="2N" />

Smoking?<select name="smoke"
title="Smoking?">

<option value="no">No</option>

<option value="yes">Yes</option>

</select>
```

Figure 23.28 *Here we create a menu titled* Smoking *with two options,* Yes *or* No.

Figure 23.29 *Some browsers show menus as radio buttons (above), while others use a separate screen to give the options (right).*

```
Order your entree:<select name="entree"
title="Dinner" iname="dinner_index" ivalue="4">

<optgroup title="Meat">

<option value="chicken">Chicken
Parmesian</option>

<option value="steak">Filet Mignon</option>

<option value="veal">Veal Cutlets</option>

<option value="fish">Seafood Fideua</option>

</optgroup>

<optgroup title="Vegetarian">

<option value="rice">Rice and Beans</option>

<option value="pasta">Pasta Primavera</option>

<option value="ravioli">Spinach Ravioli</option>

</optgroup>

</select>
```

Figure 23.30 *Two separate things are going on here. First, I've set the* iname *attribute to store the index number of the chosen entree. I also set the default entree by specifying an* ivalue *of 4 (which corresponds to the fourth option,* Seafood Fideua*). Secondly, I've divided the menu into two subsections or option groups to make it easier for visitors to find what they're looking for.*

Figure 23.31 *The* Seafood Fideua *entree is chosen by default. Nokia browsers use the* optgroup *element to divide menu options. Openwave browsers ignore it.*

11. If desired, type **title="label"**, where *label* may be used by the microbrowser to identify the option to the visitor.

12. If desired, type **onpick="url"**, where *url* is the file that should be loaded if the visitor chooses this option.

13. Type **>**.

14. Enter text that identifies the option.

15. Type **</option>**.

16. Repeat steps 9–15 for each option.

17. Type **</select>** to complete the menu.

✔ Tips

- Different browsers treat the `option` element's `title` in distinct ways. (Surprise!) Some browsers use the `title` to label the button that activates the option, others use it to create the menu itself, or ignore it completely if you've added text in step 14. (However, if you don't set the text in step 14, some browsers will show nothing at all for that option in the menu.)

- You may group `option` elements with `optgroup` *(see page 277)*. Use a `title` attribute for identification (and not a `label` attribute as for (X)HTML). Some browsers ignore `optgroup` elements.

- Add an `onevent` element with `type="onpick"` to an `option` element (instead of step 12 above) if you want to set a variable *(see page 383)* and/or post data to the server *(see page 388)* when the visitor chooses the option.

- If a variable with the same name as that specified in step 2 has already been set *(see page 383)*, its value will be the default value for the input field, and will override the contents of the `value` attribute (but not the `ivalue` attribute).

Creating Menus

Processing Data from Visitors

Once you have requested data from your visitors, perhaps through a text box or menu, you can then send the data to the server for processing. You may also, of course, send variables that you've set yourself.

To process data from visitors:

1. Create a text box *(see page 384)* or menu *(see page 386)*, or set a variable yourself *(see page 383)*. Pay special attention to the name (or iname) attribute of the input, select, or setvar elements, respectively. The name (or iname) attribute identifies the variable that will contain the data.

2. In an anchor, do element or onevent, type **<go href="formscript.cgi" method="post">**, where *formscript.cgi* is the name of the script that will process the data from your visitors and perhaps create a response WML page from that data.

3. Next, type **<postfield name="var" value="$(var)" />**, where *var* is the value of the name (or iname) attribute used in the input, select, or setvar elements in step 1.

4. Repeat step 3 for each variable whose data you want to send to the server.

5. Type **</go>**.

6. Then close the anchor, do, or onevent element you opened in step 2.

```
<option value="ravioli">Spinach Ravioli</option>
</optgroup>
</select>
<do type="accept">
<go href="http://www.cookwood.com/cgi-bin/reserve_table.cgi" method="post">
<postfield name="number" value="$(number)" />
<postfield name="smoke" value="$(smoke)" />
<postfield name="dinner_index" value="$(dinner_index)" />
</go>
</do></p>
</card>
```

Figure 23.32 *You must use the* postfield *element for each variable whose value you wish to send to the server. They must be located within a* go *element that references the processing script. (The* go *element, in turn, must be in either a* do, anchor, *or* onevent *element).*

Figure 23.33 *When the visitor activates the OK button (created with the* accept*-type* do *element), the values of the three variables are sent to the* reserve_table.cgi *script.*

Processing Data from Visitors

```
#!/usr/local/bin/perl

use strict;

use CGI ':standard';

print "Content-type: text/vnd.wap.wml\n\n";

print '<?xml version="1.0"?>

<!DOCTYPE wml PUBLIC "-//WAPFORUM//DTD
WML 1.1//EN"

"http://www.wapforum.org/DTD/wml_1.1.xml">

<wml><card>';

my $number = param('number');

my $smoke = param('smoke');

my $dinner_index = param('dinner_index');
```

Figure 23.34 *Here's a bit of the Perl script for processing the dinner reservations. Note that I print out both the content headers for WML documents and the proper* DOCTYPE, *as well as all of the pertinent opening and closing elements.*

Figure 23.35 *The Perl script confirms the reservation for the visitor by returning a (valid and well-formed) WML page with the appropriate information.*

✔ Tips

■ You may also use the `get` method in step 2. It may be better-supported on some browsers but purportedly cannot handle more than 127 characters at a time.

■ You can use Perl or ASP or any other scripting language to gather information and then use the results to dynamically generate a response. Note that the script has to create a well-formed WML document with the proper headers. For example, the content-type header should look like this: `Content-type: text/vnd.wap.wml`, followed by two new lines. Don't forget to create the proper `DOCTYPE` and opening and closing `wml` elements and `card` elements **(Figure 23.34)**.

■ You may also have to let your server know you may be serving WML MIME types from your cgi-bin directory *(see page 370)*.

■ You can test the results of a such a script on a regular Web browser. Pass variables to the script by affixing them to the URL in the form `script.url?name=value&name2=value2`. The browser should tell you that it doesn't know what to do with a WML file, but it will let you save it. Save the result file and open it with your text editor to see the file that will be sent back to the mobile device. First and foremost, check its syntax to see if it's a well-formed WML document. Then check to see if it does what you want it to do. Once you get the major bugs worked out, you can start testing it on a simulator or real mobile device (both of which are a lot slower).

■ For more information about testing WML pages, consult *Testing WML pages* on page 392.

Processing Data from Visitors

Creating Elements on Multiple Pages

If you want to add the same buttons to all of the cards in your deck or have the same action occur upon entering all the cards in a deck, WML offers the `template` element shortcut.

To create elements on multiple pages:

1. Directly before the initial `<card>` element, type **<template>**.

2. Program a button *(see page 378)*, create a conditional action *(see page 380)*, or schedule an action *(see page 381)* that should occur on all cards.

3. Type **</template>**.

✔ Tips

■ You can have only one `template` element per deck.

■ You may override `template` instructions by specifying identically named events in individual cards.

■ You can theoretically deactivate programmed buttons on individual cards by using the `<noop />` element *(see the last part of step 5 on page 378)* though I've had varying success doing so.

■ You can also create conditional or scheduled actions in each card by adding one of the following attributes to the opening `template` tag: `onenterforward="url"`, `onenterbackward="url"`, or `ontimer="url"`, in which case, skip step 2 above.

■ The `timer` element goes in the individual card *(see page 381)*, even if you set `ontimer` with the `template` element.

```
<?xml version="1.0"?>

<!DOCTYPE wml PUBLIC "-//WAPFORUM//DTD
WML 1.3//EN"
"http://www.wapforum.org/DTD/wml13.dtd">

<wml>

<template>

<do type="prev"><prev /></do>

</template>

<card id="welcome" title="Welcome"
newcontext="true">

<p align="center">

<img src="cat.wbmp" alt="logo" /><br />

<big><b>The Cat and Otter<br />
```

Figure 23.36 *This* `template` *element adds a Back button to every card in the deck. (Thing is, most browsers do that anyway.)*

Figure 23.37 *Now every card has a Back button.*

```
<?xml version="1.0"?>

<!DOCTYPE wml PUBLIC "-//WAPFORUM//DTD
WML 1.3//EN"
"http://www.wapforum.org/DTD/wml13.dtd">

<wml>

<head><access domain="www.cookwood.com"
path="/html5ed" />

</head>

<template>

<do type="prev"><prev /></do>

</template>

<card id="welcome" title="Welcome"
newcontext="true">
```

Figure 23.38 *Only pages on* www.cookwood.com *in the top-level* html5ed *directory will be able to link to this page.*

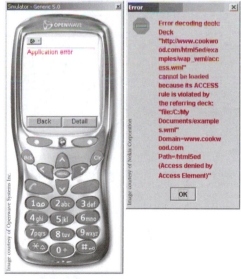

Figure 23.39 *If someone tries to link to this page from outside the domain or path, they get an error. (Nokia's simulator just shows an error box, but doesn't show anything in the phone. Nevertheless, I imagine real Nokia phones do give an error of some sort.)*

Restricting Access to a Deck

You can specify the domain and path information that a deck must have in order to be allowed to link to the cards in your deck. Any decks located in other domains or paths will not be able to link to your deck's cards.

To restrict access to a deck:

1. Directly after the opening <wml> element, type **<head><access**.

2. If desired, type **domain="location"**, where *location* is the URL of the domain in which a deck must reside in order to be able to link to this deck's cards.

3. If desired, type **path="location"**, where *location* is the path in which a deck must reside on the server in order to be able to link to this deck's cards.

4. Type **/></head>** to complete the access element and close the head area.

✔ Tips

- Remember that a deck's access attributes refer to the location of the page that is trying to access the deck, not to the deck's location itself.

- If you limit access with a domain like www.mydomain.com, decks from both domains like *www.mydomain.com* and *mydomain.com* (but not *domain.com* or *yourdomain.com*) will be able to access the deck

- The path should begin at the root WML directory and should start with a slash. A path like /html5ed would match decks with URLs like *http://www.cookwood.com/html5ed/* as well as *http://www.cookwood.com/html5ed/examples*, but not *http://www.cookwood.com/perl/html5ed/*.

Testing WML Pages

Testing WML pages makes you appreciate the sheer paucity of browsers for desktop systems! As always, think about who your audience is, and what sort of phone they're liable to use. Test as much as you can, but don't go crazy.

To test WML pages:

1. Download a software development kit (SDK) from the developer's area of the microbrowser manufacturer you're interested in:

   Nokia: *http://www.forum.nokia.com/ main.html*

   Openwave: *http:// developer.openwave.com/*

   Ericsson: *http://www.ericsson.com/ mobilityworld/*

2. Use a syntax checker in your text editor or a validator to make sure you have written valid and well-formed WML.

3. Open your WML page with the simulator from the SDK.

✔ Tips

■ Some SDKs let you write your code in an incorporated text editor. They usually will check and validate your code as well. The downside? They're so slow!

■ Unfortunately, I have yet to see a WML SDK that runs on a Mac. I use Connectix' Virtual PC to bridge the gap.

■ Different phones have different microbrowsers. Openwave, for example, lists the phones that use its browsers on its Web site: *http://upmkt.openwave.com/ dev_phones/phones.cfm*

■ Or, buy a phone!

Figure 23.40 *Openwave's SDK 5.0 for WAP includes all sorts of goodies, including a simulator (right), a WML editor (left), and output and error logs (bottom).*

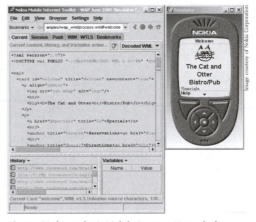

Figure 23.41 *Nokia's Mobile Internet Kit includes a simulator, editing window, History pane, and the rather useful Variables pane, for keeping track of the value of your variables.*

TESTING AND DEBUGGING WEB PAGES

24

So, you've written up a spanking new page and you fire up your browser only to find that it doesn't look anything like you expected. Or it doesn't display at all. Or maybe it looks great in your default browser but when you call your client she says it looks, well, kind of funny on her computer.

Between HTML, XHTML, CSS and the multitude of browsers and platforms on which you can view them, it's easy to have a bit of trouble. This chapter will alert you to some common errors, and will also help you weed out your own homegrown variety.

Once your code is correct, you should then thoroughly test your site to see if each page works the way you want it to.

Validating Your Code

The first step to perfecting your page is to run it through a validator. An (X)HTML validator will look at the DOCTYPE to see which version of HTML or XHTML you say you're using *(see pages 38 and 60)*, compare your code against the actual specifications of that version, and then display any inconsistencies it finds. A CSS validator works similarly.

To validate your code:

1. First check your (X)HTML with the W3C's *http://validator.w3.org/*

2. Once your (X)HTML validates, you can make sure your CSS is free of errors with *http://jigsaw.w3.org/css-validator/*

✔ Tips

■ Validators have a hard time getting the big picture. While they're good at noticing missing closing tags or missing quotes, they're not always so smart about what that means in the rest of the file. For example, a missing closing tag can trigger lots of error messages throughout your document. Fix the closing tag, and all of those subsequent "errors" go away. The trick, then, is to fix a few errors at a time, starting at the top of the file, and then immediately revalidate the file to see if other problems are also resolved **(Figure 24.2)**.

■ Many text editors, like BBEdit, have incorporated syntax checkers. They are great for catching errors before you get to the official validator.

■ Use the DOCTYPE to tell the validator which specifications to judge your HTML and XHTML with *(see page 60)*.

■ There are other validators out there. I think the ones from the W3C are the best.

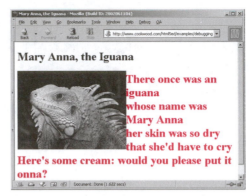

Figure 24.1 *That text to the right of the image isn't supposed to be so big. What's the problem?*

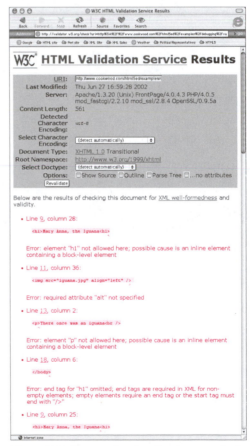

Figure 24.2 *The error found on Line 9 seems to be the problem—instead of a closing </h1> tag, I've put in another opening <h1> tag by mistake. Notice the erroneous message about line 13. This one will disappear when I fix the closing </h1> tag.*

```
<img scr="image.gif" alt="Woody the cat" />
```

Figure 24.3 *Can you see where the problem is? I've misspelled* src. *I can't tell you how many times I've torn apart a table or some other complicated construction only to find a miserable little typo like this.*

```
<img src="image.gif" alt="Woody the cat">
```

Figure 24.4 *The corrected version shows the src attribute spelled correctly, plus I've removed the final / that is used only in XHTML, not HTML.*

Checking the Easy Stuff: HTML

While validators can usually point you to the errors in your code, sometimes it's hard to figure out what they're complaining about (and sometimes they're offline and unavailable). Here are some common problems with HTML code.

To check the easy stuff with HTML:

- Make sure you've spelled everything right. I can't tell you how many times I write scr instead of src (which stands for *source*, by the way).

- Be careful about nesting. If you open <h2> and then use <b> make sure the closing </b> comes before the final </h2>.

- The final / in empty XHTML tags is not part of the HTML specification. If you want the file to validate as HTML, you'll have to get rid of it. (Better yet, switch to XHTML.)

- Make sure the DOCTYPE matches the HTML you're actually using. For example, if you want to use deprecated tags, don't use HTML strict, use HTML transitional *(see pages 38 and 60)*.

- Avoid non-standard tags. Their support across browsers is notoriously spotty.

- Be aware that most valid DOCTYPE declarations will make IE and Netscape go into standards mode. If you're relying on old quirky behavior, you may be disappointed *(see page 39)*.

- If accented characters or special symbols are not displaying properly, see Chapter 20, *Symbols and Non-English Characters*.

Checking the Easy Stuff: HTML

Checking the Easy Stuff: XHTML

If you're making the jump to XHTML, it's easy to miss a few of its syntax rules. Make sure you check them first.

To check the easy stuff with XHTML:

- Be sure all attribute values are enclosed in straight, not curly, quotes. If the value itself contains quotes, use references *(see page 340)*. Also note that a value can contain single quotes if the value is enclosed in double quotes, or double quotes if the value is enclosed in single quotes **(Figures 24.5 and 24.6)**.

- Make sure all elements have opening and closing tags, or one combination tag (with a final /). Always put a space before the / to ensure compatibility with older browsers.

- Don't combine opening and closing tags for elements that usually have content. For example, while `<p />` is technically correct in XHTML, browsers won't always know what to do with it. In the same vein, don't use separate opening and closing tags for empty elements as in `<img src="woody.gif" alt="cat"> </img>`. Again, while this is perfectly valid XHTML, browsers will be confused **(Figures 24.7 and 24.8)**.

- Be careful about case. All elements, attributes, and predefined values should be in lowercase.

- Don't leave out the # when specifying hexadecimal colors.

- If symbols or accented characters are not displaying properly, see Chapter 20, *Symbols and Non-English Characters*.

```
<img src="jungle.jpg" alt="Llumi's jungle" />
```

Figure 24.5 *If an attribute's value contains a single quote, you can just enclose it in double quotes as usual.*

```
<img src="cookie.jpg" alt="Cookie's saying &quot;Enough! &quot;" />

<img src="tough_llumi.jpg" alt='Llumi replies, "This is _my_ jungle."' />
```

Figure 24.6 *If an attribute's value contains double quotes, either use references (top), or enclose the attribute value in single quotes (bottom).*

```
<p />

<img src="jungle.jpg" alt="Llumi's jungle" >
</img>
```

Figure 24.7 *Here are two examples of valid XHTML that will give most browsers a headache.*

```
<p></p>

<img src="jungle.jpg" alt="Llumi's jungle" />
```

Figure 24.8 *Instead, don't combine the opening and closing tags of elements that aren't usually empty (like p) and don't use individual opening and closing tags for elements that are usually empty (like img).*

```
p {font-size=24px}
```

Figure 24.9 *Bad! It's hard to break the habit of separating properties and values with the equals sign. But you must, otherwise it'll incapacitate your CSS.*

```
p {font-size: 24px}
```

Figure 24.10 *Much better. Always use a colon between the property and the value. Note that it doesn't matter if you add extra spaces before and after the colon.*

```
p {font-size:24px font-weight:bold; ; font-style:italic}
```

Figure 24.11 *Bad! You must put one and only one semicolon between each property-value pair. Here there's one missing and one extra.*

```
p {
    font-size: 24px;

    font-weight:bold;

    font-style:italic;

}
```

Figure 24.12 *One way to make sure that each property-value pair is separated by the next with a semicolon is to give each one its own line. It's easier to see the semicolons when they're not in a sea of properties, values, and colons. (While a semicolon after the final property-value pair is optional, it's a good habit to get into.)*

```
p {font-style: "italic"; font: "Trebuchet MS";}
```

Figure 24.13 *Bad! Get rid of those quotes around* italic, *CSS doesn't need them.*

```
p {font-style:italic; font: "Trebuchet MS";}
```

Figure 24.14 *The only CSS values that are enclosed in quotes are multi-word font names.*

Checking the Easy Stuff: CSS

While CSS syntax is pretty straightforward, it has some common pitfalls, especially if you've gotten used to writing HTML or XHTML.

To check the easy stuff with CSS:

- Make sure you separate your properties from their values with a colon (:) not an equals sign, like you do in (X)HTML **(Figures 24.9 and 24.10)**.

- Be sure to complete each property-value pair with a semicolon (;). Make sure there are no extra semicolons **(Figures 24.11 and 24.12)**.

- Don't forget to close your brackets.

- Don't quote values—as you do in (X)HTML. The only values that have quotes in CSS are multiword font names **(Figures 24.13 and 24.14)**.

- Make sure you're using an accepted value. Something like `font-style: none` isn't going to work since the "none" value is called `normal`. You can find a complete list of CSS properties and values in Appendix B, *CSS Properties and Values*.

- Don't forget the closing `</style>` tag with internal style sheets *(see page 151)*.

- Make sure you've linked the (X)HTML document to the proper CSS file, and that the URL points to the desired file. Remember that URLs are relative to the CSS file, not to the (X)HTML, except for Netscape 4.x *(see page 149)*.

- Watch the spaces and punctuation between the selectors.

- Make sure the browser supports what you're trying to do *(see page 402)*. Support for CSS varies widely.

Testing Your Page

Even if your code validates, your page still may not work the way you want it to. Or it may work properly in one browser, but not in the next. It's important to test your page in as many browsers as possible, on as many platforms as possible. At the very least, test your page on current versions of both Explorer and Netscape on both Windows and Macintosh.

Figure 24.15 *This page validates but it doesn't look anything like it's supposed to. What's the problem?*

To test your (X)HTML pages:

1. Validate your (X)HTML and CSS *(see page 394)*. Make any necessary changes.

2. Open a browser, and choose File > Open File.

3. Find the Web page on your hard disk that you want to test and click Open. The page appears in the browser.

4. Go through the whole page and make sure it looks exactly the way you want it. For example:

   • Is the formatting like you wanted?

   • Does each of your URLs point to the proper document? (You can check the URLs by clicking them if the destination files are located in the same relative position on the local computer.)

   • Is your CSS file referenced properly?

   • Do all of your images appear? Are they placed and aligned properly?

   • Have you included your name and e-mail address so that your users can contact you with comments and suggestions? (Or, to avoid spambots, have you included a form that people can use to submit comments?)

```
<!DOCTYPE html PUBLIC "-//W3C//DTD XHTML
1.0 Transitional//EN"
    "http://www.w3.org/TR/xhtml1/DTD/xhtml1-
transitional.dtd">
<html xmlns="http://www.w3.org/1999/xhtml">
<head>
<meta http-equiv="content-type"
content="text/html; charset=utf-8" />
<title>Mary Anna, the Iguana</title>
<link rel="stylesheet" type="text/css"
href="testerpage.css" />
</head>
<body>
<img src="iguana.jpg" alt="Iguana" width="220"
height="165" />
<h1>Mary Anna, the Iguana</h1>
<p>There once was an iguana
whose name was <em>Mary Anna</em>
her skin was so dry
that she'd have to cry
Here's some cream: would you please put it
onna?</p>
</body>
</html>
```

Figure 24.16 *The problem is the link to the CSS file—the file is named* testpage.css *and here I'm linking to* testerpage.css. *It should be no surprise that the browser can't find the CSS and thus displays the page wrong.*

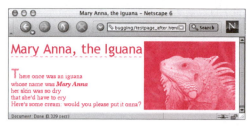

Figure 24.17 *Now that the link to the CSS is corrected, the page is displayed properly.*

5. Without closing the page in the browser, open the appropriate (X)HTML or CSS document and make any necessary changes.

6. Save the changes.

7. Switch back to the browser and press Refresh or Reload to see the changes.

8. Repeat steps 1–7 until you are satisfied with your Web page. Don't get discouraged if it takes several tries.

9. Revalidate the code to make sure you haven't introduced any new errors.

10. Upload the files to the server *(see page 405)*.

11. Return to the browser and choose File > Open.

12. Type your page's URL and click Open. The page will appear in the browser.

13. With your page on the server, go through your page again to make sure everything is all right.

✔ **Tips**

■ Again, if you can, test your (X)HTML documents in several browsers on various platforms. You never know what browser (or computer) your visitors will use. The major browsers are discussed on pages 15–16.

■ The rest of this chapter deals with common problems that can occur in validated code as well as their solutions.

■ Sometimes it's not your fault—especially with styles. Make sure a browser supports the feature you're having trouble with before assuming the problem is with your code.

Testing Your Page

When the Browser Displays the Code

Although you may be proud of your (X)HTML code, when you view your file with a browser, you want that code converted into a beautiful Web page, not displayed for all to see.

When the browser displays the code instead of the page:

■ Have you saved the file in Text Only (sometimes called "Text Document") format? Sometimes, if you've saved the file previously as a, say, Word document, saving it as Text Only isn't enough. You have to create a brand new document, copy and paste the code to that new document, and then save it as Text Only.

■ Have you saved the file with an .htm or .html extension? You must *(see page 50)*.

■ Have you begun the page with the proper DOCTYPE? *(see page 60)*.

■ Do you shun Word's (or some other word processor's) "Save as Web Page" or "Save as HTML" command? That command, in all its incarnations, is only for converting regular text into Word's idea of a Web page **(Figures 24.18 and 24.19)**. If you're writing your own code, this command will "code your code" *(see page 52)*. Instead, choose Save As and then save the file as Text Document with the .htm or .html extension.

■ Is Windows adding .txt extensions to the files you save as "page.html", creating something like "page.html.txt"? Find out by viewing file extensions in the folder. To avoid it, enclose the file name in double quotation marks in the Save As dialog box.

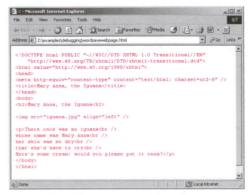

Figure 24.18 *This page, shown here in Internet Explorer, was created with Word's Save as Web Page option. Since it already contained code, Word simply makes a Web page that contains that code. I would bet it's not what you expected.*

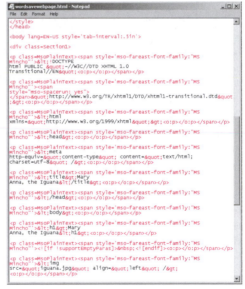

Figure 24.19 *If you select View Source, you can see how Word coded your code, changing your < and > symbols to < and >, converting quotation marks to " and adding all sorts of extra junk.*

```
<body>

<img src="Iguana.jpg" alt="Iguana" width="220"
height="165" />

<h1>Mary Anna, the Iguana</h1>

<p>There once was an iguana
```

Figure 24.20 *The file name for the image is* iguana.jpg *but here it is incorrectly referenced as* Iguana.jpg, *with a capital* I.

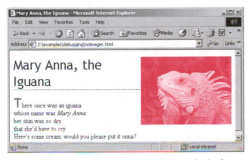

Figure 24.21 *On your computer, the page looks fine because your computer isn't picky about upper- and lowercase letters.*

Figure 24.22 *When the page is published to the server, which is case sensitive, the image cannot be found.*

When Images Don't Appear

Little red x's, broken icons, alternate text, or nothing at all. Regardless, it's a drag if what you really wanted was a picture of an iguana.

When images don't appear:

- First, check that the file name of the image on the server matches the name you've referenced in the `img` tag *exactly*, including upper- and lowercase letters, and the extension **(Figure 24.20)**. For more information, consult *File Names* on page 32.

- Don't use spaces in file names. While they make work locally (on your personal computer), servers have a tough time with them.

- Next, make sure the path to the image on the server is reflected in the path that you've got in the `img` tag. One easy test is to put an image in the same directory as the HTML page. That means you'll just need the proper file name referenced in the `img` tag (but no path information). If it shows up, you can be pretty sure that the problem with your image is the path. For more information about paths, consult *URLs* on page 33.

- Have you saved the image as GIF or JPG? I've seen Windows users create images in BMP format (which Internet Explorer for Windows has no trouble with) and then not understand when Netscape (on Windows *or* Mac) displays a broken image icon instead of the graphic. For more information, see Chapter 5, *Creating Web Images*.

- Have you saved the image in RGB format (as opposed to CMYK which is strictly for printed images)?

Differences from Browser to Browser

This one's probably not your fault. Unfortunately, no browser supports the standard specifications 100 percent. While most support virtually all of HTML 4, their support of CSS varies widely. Netscape 6 currently has the best support, followed by Opera and then IE 6. Unfortunately, older browsers (versions 4 and earlier) have notoriously bad or buggy CSS implementations.

When your page looks different from one browser to the next:

- Test your page on as many browsers and platforms as you can. Read your server logs to see which browsers your visitors use and which browsers they don't so that you can make informed choices about which browsers to focus on.

- Be aware of which CSS properties are supported by current browsers and which are the most problematic. There are a number of good resources. Check my Web site for details.

- Design your page so that even if something you use is not supported, your page still functions. This is called "degrading gracefully".

- Cater your page to your desired audience. Web designers can be expected to have all the latest plug-ins, members of the American Iguana Club might not.

✔ Tip

- Check out The Web Standards Project page *(www.webstandards.org)* for more information on what you can do to promote the adoption of standards by the major Web browser manufacturers (as well as by any newcomers to the game).

```
h1 {font: 2em "Trebuchet MS", "Helvetica", "Arial
Black"; border-bottom: 2px dashed red}

img {border: none; float:right}

p {white-space:pre}

p:first-letter {font: bold 200% "Trebuchet
MS";color:green}

p>em {font-weight:bold}
```

Figure 24.23 *Here is the CSS I've applied to this page.*

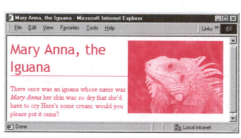

Figure 24.24 *Explorer 5 doesn't understand the dashed border, gets float a bit wrong (notice that some of the border is beyond the image), and doesn't recognize the first-letter selector.*

Figure 24.25 *Netscape 4.7 doesn't get* border-bottom *nor the* first-letter *selector, though it gets* float *and* white-space *right.*

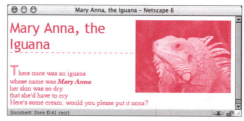

Figure 24.26 *Netscape 6 (for both Mac and Windows) has excellent CSS support. You may question my esthetics (and my poetry) but this is the way the page is supposed to look.*

```
<table border="0">
<tr><th colspan="2">
<h1>Mary Anna, the Iguana</h1>
</th></tr>
<tr>
<td><img src="iguana.jpg" align="left" /> </td>
<td>There once was an iguana<br />
whose name was Mary Anna<br />
her skin was so dry<br />
that she'd have to cry<br />
Here's some cream: would you please put it
onna?</td>
</tr></body></html>
```

Figure 24.27 *There is no closing `</table>` tag.*

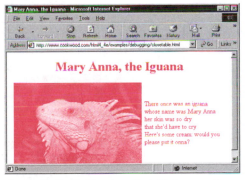

Figure 24.28 *Most browsers don't blink an eye if you leave off a closing `</table>` (or `</frameset>`) tag.*

Figure 24.29 *Netscape 4, on the other hand, is very strict. The entire table (or frameset) disappears from view.*

When Nothing Appears in Netscape 4

You're up all night coding this complicated page, with tables or frames. You upload it to the server, view it with Explorer, smile smugly at your prowess, and go to sleep only to be awakened by your Netscape 4-using client who wants to know why the page is completely (or mostly) blank. What's gone wrong?

When the page looks fine in other browsers, but doesn't appear in Netscape 4:

- If you're using tables, you must be sure to create a closing `</table>` tag to match each and every opening one.

- If your page is set up with several framesets *(see page 246)*, make sure you insert a closing `</frameset>` tag for each and every opening one. I think this one is easy to miss because you've got all those `<frame>` tags that don't require a closing tag. Remember that the `<frameset>` tag *does* require a closing tag, and Netscape 4 won't forgive you if you leave it out.

- If the problem is that the page looks great in Explorer but cruddy in Netscape 4 (as opposed to *nothing* in Netscape 4), check *Differences from Browser to Browser* on page 402.

- Note that the closing `</table>` and `</frameset>` tags are always required and should always be used.

- Only Netscape 4 (and earlier) is this picky about the closing tags.

Still Stuck?

If you've gotten to this page, you're probably frustrated. Don't think I'm being patronizing when I suggest you go take a break. Sometimes the best thing you can do for a problem is leave it alone for a minute. When you come back, the answer may be staring you in the face. If it's not, let me offer you these additional suggestions.

1. Check again for typos. Revalidate your code *(see page 394)*.

2. Check the easy pieces first. So many times I've spent hours fiddling with an exciting new tag that just wouldn't work only to find that the problem was a typo in some tag that I'd used a thousand times before. Familiarity breeds contempt—check the stuff you think you know really well before you harass the newcomers.

3. Simplify the problem. Go back to the most recent version of your page that worked properly (which might be a blank page in some cases). Then test the page after adding each new element.

4. Read through this chapter again.

5. Check one final time for typos.

6. Post the piece of code that doesn't work on my Question and Answer board *(www.cookwood.com/html/qanda/)*. Be sure to include the relevant code (or a URL), a description of what is happening and a description of what you think should be happening.

7. If you're at the end of your rope, write me directly at *helphtml@cookwood.com*. But please note that I get a lot of e-mail and while I have the best intentions, I'm sometimes too swamped to answer. I'm much more inclined to try if you assure me you've tried everything else first.

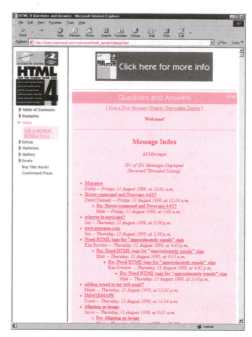

Figure 24.30 *If you get stuck, try posting a question to my HTML Question and Answer board (http://www.cookwood.com/html/qanda/)*

PUBLISHING YOUR PAGES ON THE WEB

25

Once you've finished your masterpiece and are ready to present it to the public, you have to transfer your pages to your Web host server so that people can get to them.

You may also want to contact your Web host (or Internet Service Provider) to ask them about the best way to upload your files.

Be sure to thoroughly test your pages before publishing them. For more details, consult Chapter 24, *Testing and Debugging Web Pages*.

Finding a Host for Your Site

Unless you have your own server, you'll probably have to pay someone to host your site. There are hundreds, maybe thousands of companies that provide Web site hosting. Most charge a monthly fee that depends on the services they offer. Some offer free Web hosting in exchange for advertising from your site. Although you can search on the Internet for a Web host, I recommend talking to friends or looking in your local yellow pages.

When considering a host, there are a number of things—besides price—to keep in mind.

- How much disk space will they let you have for your Web site? Don't pay for more than you need. Remember that HTML files take up very little space while images, sounds, and videos take up successively larger quantities.

- Do they offer technical support? If so, is it by telephone or by e-mail? How long will it take them to get back to you?

- Will they register a domain name *(see page 407)* for you? How much will they charge?

- How fast is their connection to the Internet? This will determine how fast your pages are served to your visitors. Do they have multiple connections in case one of them should become inoperable?

- Do they include dial-up access to the Internet? (They don't usually.) Will they if you need it?

- Will they let you run custom CGI scripts, Server Side Includes, FrontPage extensions, RealAudio, Telnet/SSh, PHP, MySQL, and other advanced features?

- Do they offer a Web hit statistics service to let you know how many people have been visiting your site?

Figure 25.1 *Verisign (which bought Network Solutions in 2000) is one of the accredited registrars of domain names. You can use their site to see if a desired domain name is available.*

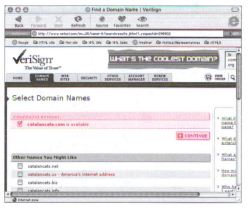

Figure 25.2 *If the name is available, you can either register it through Verisign or call your Web host and get them to do it for you. (Now you know: the very useful* www.catalancats.com *domain can be yours!)*

Getting Your Own Domain Name

Generally a Web page's address or URL is made up of the name of the server along with the path to the file on that server. When you use a Web hosting service, they rent you a piece of their server and your Web pages take the name of that Web host, by default. For example, in my case, my Web host's server name is *www.crocker.com* and thus the URL for my pages might look something like *www.crocker.com/~lcastro/*.

However, if you don't want your Web host's server name to appear in your Web page's URL, you can register your own domain name (for a fee, always for a fee) and then ask your Web hosting company to create a *virtual domain* on their server with your domain name. In my case, while my pages are still on Crocker's server, they *look like* they're on my own server: *www.cookwood.com*. Even if your visitors don't know about servers and where the files actually reside, having your own domain name makes your URLs simpler and easier to type, and thus easier to visit.

They also have one very important advantage. If you ever decide to change your Web host (or if they go out of business), you can move your domain to another server and all of your URLs will stay exactly the same.

To get your own domain name:

1. Point your browser at a domain registrar (see *http://www.internic.net/alpha.html* for a list) and check to see if the domain you want is available.

2. Once you've found a domain name, ask your Web hosting service to set it up for you. Charges vary from host to host. While it used to cost $35/year for a domain, some places offer domain registration as part of a discounted hosting fee.

Getting Your Own Domain Name

Transferring Files to the Server

In order for other people on the Internet to see your pages, you have to upload them to your Web host's server. One easy way to do that is with an FTP program, like WS_FTP for Windows *(see below)*, or Fetch for Macintosh *(see page 410)*. Many Web page editors offer publishing features as well. (AOL members can either use AOL's rather awkward FTP tools, or an FTP program like those described here. For details, see page 412.)

To define a new FTP site's properties:

1. In the Connect to Remote Host window (which appears upon launching WS_FTP Pro), click Create Site **(Figure 25.3)**.

2. In the WS_FTP Pro Site Profile Wizard boxes, name your connection so you can find it in the list **(Figure 25.4)**, specify the FTP server (ask your ISP if you're not sure), and enter your user name and password. Click Next for each screen and click Finish when you're done.

To set up WS_FTP to transfer HTML files as text (in ASCII mode):

1. Click Options at the bottom of the WS_FTP's main window.

2. Click the Extensions tab in the WS_FTP Pro Properties dialog box that appears.

3. In the text box, type **htm** and click the Add button. Then repeat this step for html, css, js, pl, and cgi **(Figure 25.5)** This ensures that all your (X)HTML, CSS and scripting files will be transferred in ASCII mode (which is how they should be transferred). If you're uploading any other kind of text file, be sure to add its extension to this box as well.

Figure 25.3 *In the Connect to Remote Host window, click Create Site to set up your account. (If this window doesn't appear, click Connect in the main window.)*

Figure 25.4 *Insert the appropriate information in each screen and then click Next to continue. Click Finish when you're done. Note that it doesn't matter what you name the site. You enter the proper FTP name in the Host Name/Address field (which appears after you click Next).*

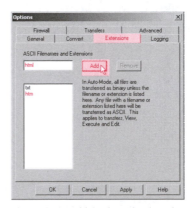

Figure 25.5 *Add the .htm, .html, and .css extensions to the list so that (X)HTML files will be transferred in ASCII mode. (Images and other multimedia files should be transferred as Binary.)*

Transferring Files to the Server

Figure 25.6 *In WS_FTP's main window, click Connect. Then choose your site (that you set up on page page 408) in the Connect to Remote Host window.*

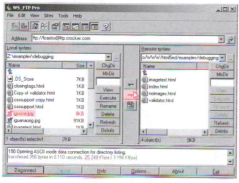

Figure 25.7 *In the left frame, select the files from your hard disk that you want to upload. In the right frame, select the destination directory on the server. Then click the right-pointing arrow to transfer the files.*

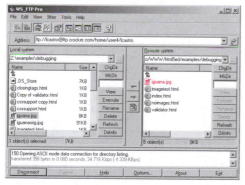

Figure 25.8 *The newly transferred files appear in the right frame. Notice the status messages in the lower-left portion of the window.*

To transfer files to the server with WS_FTP (for Windows):

1. Connect to the Internet and open WS_FTP.

2. Click Connect in the lower-left corner of WS_FTP's main window **(Figure 25.6)**.

3. Choose your site in the list and click Connect. The server is accessed.

4. On the right side of the window, navigate to the directory on the server to which you want to upload files **(Figure 25.7)**.

5. On the left side of the window, navigate to the directory on your hard disk that has the files you want to upload.

6. Select the desired files in the left frame and click the right-pointing arrow in the middle of the screen. The files are transferred **(Figure 25.8)**.

7. Click Disconnect to close the connection to the server.

✔ Tips

- (X)HTML, CSS, CGI, and JavaScript files should be transferred in ASCII mode. All other files, including images, sounds, and videos should be transferred in Binary mode. The Auto button means that any file with an extension *not listed* in the Extensions tab **(Figure 25.5)** will be transferred in Binary mode.

- You can create a new directory by clicking the MkDir button.

- You can find WS_FTP's home page at *www.ipswitch.com/products/ws_ftp/*.

- There are many other file transfer programs for Windows besides WS_FTP. Do a search at CNET's shareware site *(www.shareware.com)* if you'd prefer to use some other program.

Transferring Files to the Server

Fetch is the leading FTP client for Macintosh. There's an excellent new version available for OS X.

To transfer HTML files to the server with Fetch (for the Mac):

1. Open your Internet connection.

2. Open Fetch.

3. Choose Customize > Preferences **(Figure 25.9)**, click the Upload tab in the Preferences box that appears, and make sure the Add .txt suffix to Text Uploads box is *not* checked **(Fig. 25.10)**.

4. Click OK.

5. Choose File > New Connection.

6. In the New Connection window, enter the server name in the Host box, your user name in the User ID box, your password in the Password box, and, if desired, the path to the directory where you plan to save the Web pages in the Initial directory box **(Figure 25.11)**.

7. Click OK to open the connection. Fetch will make the connection to the server you requested and open the designated directory (or the top directory if you haven't specified one).

8. If necessary, navigate to the desired directory where you wish to place your Web files **(Figure 25.12)**.

9. Click the Put Files button or press Command-T **(Figure 25.13)**.

10. In the dialog box that appears, choose the files that you wish to transfer to the server. Select multiple files holding down the Shift key. Select multiple non-contiguous files holding down the Command key. When you have selected all the files you wish to transfer, click Choose **(Figure 25.14)**.

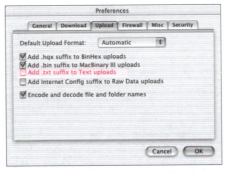

Figure 25.9 *Choose Preferences in Fetch's Customize menu to open the Preferences dialog box.*

Figure 25.10 *Click the Upload tab and make sure that the Add .txt suffix option is unchecked.*

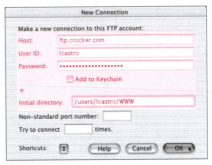

Figure 25.11 *In the New Connection window, type the server name (Host), your User ID and password, and the directory where you want to transfer the files.*

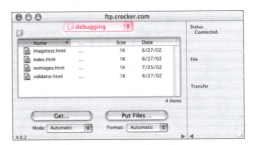

Figure 25.12 *Make sure the proper directory on the server (where you want to transfer the files) is showing in the Fetch window before transferring the files (in this case, debugging).*

(Side margin, rotated) **Transferring Files to the Server**

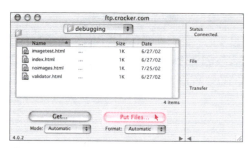

Figure 25.13 *Click the Put Files button (or choose Command-T).*

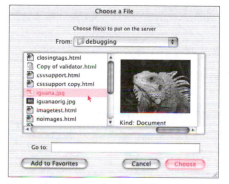

Figure 25.14 *Select the desired file or folder. (In Mac OS X, you can select more than one by holding down the Shift or Command key.) Then click Choose.*

Figure 25.15 *Confirm the file name and format for the desired files.*

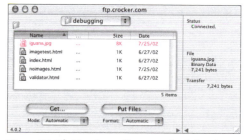

Figure 25.16 *The chosen files are uploaded to the current directory.*

11. In the Put File dialog box that appears, confirm the appropriate file names and formats for the files. The Automatic format correctly uses the Text format for (X)HTML and other text documents and Raw Data for other files **(Figure 25.15)**.

12. Click OK. The files are transferred to the server and maintain the hierarchy they had on the local system **(Figure 25.16)**.

✔ Tips

- (X)HTML, CSS, CGI, and JavaScript files should always be transferred as Text (in ASCII mode). Any other file, including images, sound, and video, should be transferred as Raw Data.

- Fetch used to belong to Dartmouth University but was bought back by its principal engineer, Jim Matthews (thanks to winnings from a stint on the television show, *Who Wants to Be a Millionaire?*). You can find Fetch's great new Web site, complete with upgrades, documentation and support at *http://fetchsoftworks.com*.

- You can resize the main window so that it shows more files at one time. Just click and drag the bottom-right corner.

- Relative URLs *(see page 35)* are maintained when you transfer a folder to the server. Absolute URLs *(see page 34)*, must be updated to reflect the files' new locations.

- By default, Fetch converts characters from the default MacRoman to ISO-8859-1. If you've saved your document as anything other than MacRoman *(see pages 50 and 336)*, you'll want to turn this feature off (Customize > Preferences > Misc and then uncheck Translate ISO Characters). If you *do* use this feature, your files' `meta` tags should specify the ISO 8859-1 character set, *not* MacRoman *(see page 338)*.

Transferring Files to the Server

Transferring Files to AOL

If you are an AOL member, AOL gives you a certain amount of free disk space from which you can host a Web site. AOL offers a very basic, rather clunky interface for uploading files which I describe here. But note the second to last tip in this section which explains how to use the much more robust Fetch and WS_FTP for uploading files to AOL.

To transfer a file with AOL's tools:

1. Go to keyword **myftpspace**.

2. In the window that appears, click the See My FTP Space button **(Figure 25.17)**.

3. Create any desired directories (using the Create Directory button) and then navigate to where you want to upload the file **(Figures 25.18 and 25.19)**.

4. Once you're in the desired directory, click the Upload button **(Figure 25.20)**.

5. Under Remote Filename in the window that appears, type the exact name and extension that the file should have on the AOL server. (The path appears just above "Remote Filename". To change the path, navigate to a different directory in step 3.)

6. Click ASCII for text documents (including XHTML, HTML, CSS, and scripting files), and Binary for everything else.

7. Finally, click Continue **(Figure 25.21)**.

8. In the Upload File dialog box that appears, click Select File **(Figure 25.22)**, and then choose the desired file from your hard disk and click OK.

9. The Upload File dialog box returns with the selected file listed in the File box. Click Send to upload the file **(Figure 25.23)**.

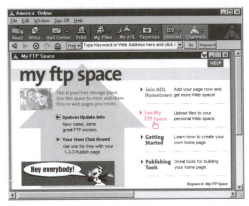

Figure 25.17 *Click See My FTP Space to get to the FTP Upload area.*

Figure 25.18 *Create and navigate to the desired directory, if necessary.*

Figure 25.19 *If you click the Create Directory button, AOL will allow you to name the new directory.*

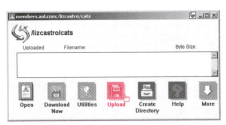

Figure 25.20 *Once you're in the desired directory, click the Upload button at the bottom of the screen.*

Transferring Files to AOL

Figure 25.21 *Type the file name and extension (but not the directory) that the file should have on the AOL server, choose ASCII or Binary, depending on the nature of the file, and then click Continue.*

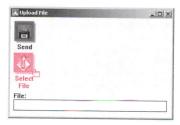

Figure 25.22 *Click Select File to choose the file that you want to upload from your hard disk.*

Figure 25.23 *The selected file is listed in the File box at the bottom of the screen. Click Send to upload the file to AOL.*

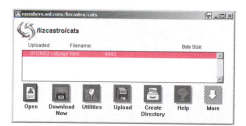

Figure 25.24 *The chosen file is uploaded to the current directory with the name specified in the Remote Filename box. This particular file will now be accessible at: http://members.aol.com/lizcastro/cats/catpage.html (until I cancel my AOL account).*

✔ Tips

- The URL of your pages on AOL is *http://members.aol.com/screenname/filename*. You can publish up to 2MB *per screenname* (for a total of 14MB). If you publish files on AOL's Hometown (and thus allow AOL to advertise on your site), they give you a bit more space.

- It seems unreasonably laborious to me, but AOL's FTP tool only lets you upload one file at a time.

- Delete or rename files by selecting the desired file, clicking the Utilities button, and then choosing Delete or Rename.

- The remote file name that you specify in step 5 is the name that the file will have on the server (and in URLs that your visitors type). It doesn't necessarily have to match the name of the file on your hard disk. Of course it must match any URL that refers to it.

- Many of AOL's dialog boxes just sit there on the screen instead of disappearing when you're done with them. Don't be afraid to click their close boxes.

- The good news is that you can also use external (and infinitely better) FTP clients like Fetch and WS_FTP to upload files to AOL. Follow the instructions on pages 408–411, using **members.aol.com** for the Host name, **anonymous** as the User name, and your AOL email address for your password. You must be connected to AOL when you use the external FTP program for security reasons.

- Also note that any files in your AOL server space (except those in the *private* folder) are visible to anyone who can use an external FTP client. They can't delete, change, or upload new files, but they can see what's there.

Transferring Files to AOL

GETTING PEOPLE TO VISIT

With more than two billion Web pages in existence and thousands more being created every day, you may have to shout a little to get your page noticed. This chapter explains the (X)HTML tags you can use to identify your page to search engines like Google and Yahoo as well as a few strategies you can use to get noticed by these portals to the Web.

There are a number of good resources on the Web for improving one's ranking in search engines. For this chapter, I am indebted to two excellent WebMonkey articles written by Paul Boutin *(hotwired.lycos.com/webmonkey/ 01/23/index1a.html* and *www.hotwired.com/ webmonkey/99/31/index1a.html)* and to the site put together at *searchenginewatch.com* by Danny Sullivan.

There are several *search engine optimization* companies who would like to charge you for completing the steps I outline in this chapter —while making big promises about search engine results. Unfortunately, some of them go too far and spend much too much energy (not to mention your money) trying to trick visitors into coming to your site (or trying to trick search engines into listing your site). Their slimy techniques, apart from annoying potential visitors, can even get you removed from some search engines. If you have real (non-pornographic, non-gambling) content on your site, you can do just as good or better without them.

About Keywords

When prospective visitors go to a search engine to find information, they type a few identifying *keywords* that describe what they're looking for. The more those words are honestly reflected on your page, the better your chances are that your page will appear in a search engine's results. So, it's a good idea to think about what your page is about, decide on some keywords that describe your page (and that might be used to find it), and then use your keywords consistently.

Do

- Use keywords in your title *(see page 64)*.

- Use keywords in headers *(see page 65)*.

- Keep the content of your page as specific and focused on your topic as possible, and be sure to include your keywords.

- Specify keywords in a `meta` tag *(see page 417)*.

- Use keywords in an image's `alt` tag, where applicable *(see page 105)*.

But...

- Don't create headers out of GIF images if they contain keywords since search engines cannot understand the text in an image. At the very least, add keywords to such an image's `alt` tag *(see page 105)*.

- Don't use keywords where they don't make sense. It is their *natural* and consistent use which is rewarded.

- Don't repeat keywords endlessly and meaninglessly, perhaps in a small font or with the same color as the background. This is called *spamming* and can get you banned from a search engine's results.

```
<head>

<meta http-equiv="content-type"
content="text/html; charset=utf-8" />

<title>Barcelona's Market</title>

<link rel="stylesheet" type="text/css"
href="barcaeng.css" />

</head>

<body>

<h1>Barcelona's Market</h1>

<img src="mercat1.gif" height="167"
width="144" alt="Entrance to Barcelona's
Boquería Market" class="right" />

<p>This first picture shows the stalls in the
entranceway to the <em>Mercat de la
Boquería</em>, the Barcelona central market that
is just off the Rambles. It's an incredible place, full
of every kind of fruit, meat, fish, or whatever you
might happen to need. It took me a long time to get
up the nerve to actually take a picture there. You
might say I'm kind of a chicken, but since I lived
there, it was just sort of strange. Do you take
pictures of your supermarket?</p>
```

Figure 26.1 *In this document, I've used the keywords* Barcelona *and* market *in the title, headers, alternate text for images, and in the first paragraph. Try searching for* Barcelona market *on Google.*

Figure 26.2 *Use keywords as consistently and naturally as you can. If you do it right, there's no reason to cheat.*

```
<head>

<meta http-equiv="content-type"
content="text/html; charset=utf-8" />

<meta name="keywords" content="Barcelona,
market" />

<title>Barcelona's Market</title>

<link rel="stylesheet" type="text/css"
href="barcaeng.css" />

</head>

<body>

<h1>Barcelona's Market</h1>

<img src="mercat1.gif" height="167"
width="144" alt="Entrance to Barcelona's
Bouquería Market" class="right" />

<p>This first picture shows the stalls in the
entranceway to the <em>Mercat de la
Bouquería</em>, the Barcelona central market that
is just off the Rambles. It's an incredible place, full
of every kind of fruit, meat, fish, or whatever you
might happen to need. It took me a long time to get
up the nerve to actually take a picture there. You
might say I'm kind of a chicken, but since I lived
```

Figure 26.3 *If you want to be absolutely sure that a search engine knows what your page is about, you can specify the keywords with a* meta *tag.*

Explicitly Listing Keywords

You can explicitly tell search engines exactly what your page is about by specifying a list of relevant keywords.

To explicitly list keywords:

1. In the head section of your page, type **<meta name="keywords" content="**.

2. Type a few words or phrases that concisely describe the topic discussed on your page. Separate each word or phrase with a comma and a space.

3. Type " **/>** to complete the meta tag.

✔ Tips

- Use a combination of very unique and more general words to describe the contents of your page. *Chihuahua* is unique, but *dog* may also net you some visitors who didn't realize they were interested in Chihuahuas (or couldn't spell it).

- Actually, adding misspelled keywords (in *addition* to correctly spelled ones) is not such a bad idea. You might offer several alternative spellings for foreign words.

- More words is not necessarily better. According to Paul Boutin *(see page 415)*, the closer you match what a prospective visitor types (with no extra words), the higher up you'll get listed in the results.

- If you're using frames, include keywords in each frame and in the frameset itself.

- Some search engines offer specific tips on using the meta tag to describe your site. Check out: *http://help.altavista.com/ search/faq_web#9.*

- Google ignores keywords specified with a meta tag. It's more interested in keywords that appear in the page's content.

Explicitly Listing Keywords

Providing a Description of Your Page

Search engines try to help visitors distinguish between results by adding information about the individual pages next to their URLs. Some search engines let you specify the description that should appear next to your page.

To control your page's summary:

1. In the `head` section of your page, type **<meta name="description" content="**.

2. Type a concise sentence or two that describes your page and hopefully persuades folks to click through.

3. Type **" />** to complete the `meta` tag.

✔ Tips

- When a visitor sees a list of links that match their keywords, the description of your page may help it outshine the competition. Be careful to describe your page succinctly and descriptively. Avoid generic marketing hype in favor of specific features that set your site apart from the rest.

- AltaVista limits the length of the description to 1024 characters.

- If your page is set up with frames, be sure to include a description in every frame page, as well as the frameset itself.

- Google does not pay any attention to the description you include with the `meta` tag. Instead, it shows visitors the specified keywords in the context of the matching pages.

```
<head>

<meta http-equiv="content-type"
content="text/html; charset=utf-8" />

<meta name="keywords" content="Barcelona,
market" />

<meta name="description" content="An insider's
view of the Barcelona market, complete with
photos." />

<title>Barcelona's Market</title>

<link rel="stylesheet" type="text/css"
href="barcaeng.css" />

</head>

<body>
```

Figure 26.4 *You can offer search engines a concise description of your site.*

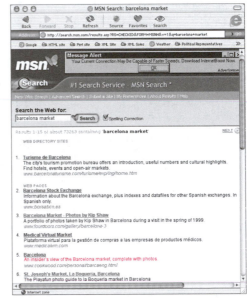

Figure 26.5 *Instead of using the first few lines of the page, or showing where the keywords appeared, MSN uses the description given in the `meta` tag.*

```
<head>

<meta http-equiv="content-type"
content="text/html; charset=utf-8" />

<meta name="keywords" content="Barcelona,
market" />

<meta name="description" content="An insider's
view of the Barcelona market, complete with
photos." />

<meta name="generator" content="BBEdit 6.5.2"
/>

<meta name="author" content="Liz Castro" />

<meta name="copyright" content="&copy; 2002
Liz Castro" />

<title>Barcelona's Market</title>

<link rel="stylesheet" type="text/css"
href="barcaeng.css" />

</head>

<body>

<h1>Barcelona's Market</h1>
```

Figure 26.6 *Use as many* meta *tags as you need.*

Figure 26.7 *The* meta *information is always invisible in the browser.*

Controlling Other Information

You can also add information to your page about who wrote it, what program was used (if any) to generate the (X)HTML code, and if it is copyrighted. Note, however, that search engines do not currently use this information (though they may some day), and browsers don't display it.

To control other information about your page:

1. In the head section of your Web page, type **<meta name="author" content= "name" />**, where *name* is the person who wrote the (X)HTML page.

2. In the head section of your Web page, type **<meta name="generator" content= "program" />**, where *program* is the name of the software that created (or edited) the (X)HTML page.

3. In the head section of your Web page, type **<meta name="copyright" content= "© year holder" />**, where *year* is the calendar year of the copyright, and *holder* is the name of the person or entity who holds the copyright to the page.

✔ Tips

■ The generator is created automatically by most Web page editors. You can delete it if you prefer not to give them credit.

■ If you browse a page with Internet Explorer 5 for Windows and then save the source to your hard disk, Explorer will actually add meta information to the file, claiming to be its generator. (For more information on saving the source code from a page on the Web, consult *The Inspiration of Others* on page 57.)

Controlling Other Information

Keeping Visitors Away

Search engines employ little programs called *robots* or *spiders* to hang out on the Web and look for new pages to add to the engine's index. But sometimes, you don't want search engines to know your page exists. Perhaps it's a personal page designed only for your family or an internal page for your company. You can add information to the page so that most search engine robots will stay out.

To keep search engine robots out:

1. In the head section of your page, type **<meta name="robots" content="**.

2. If desired, type **noindex** to keep the robot from adding the page to its index.

3. If desired, type **nofollow** to keep the robot from following the links on the page and indexing those pages.

4. Type **" />** to complete the tag.

✔ Tips

■ Separate multiple values with a comma and a space.

■ With about one billion Web pages in existence, the easiest way to keep people away from your page is to never create any link *to* that page from any other page on your or anyone else's site (and, obviously, don't submit it to a search engine).

■ If a page has already been indexed, you'll have to go to the search engine's Web site and use the Remove URL page.

■ You can use the values all and index to have robots add the current page (and its links) to the search engine's index. However, these are the default values and so leaving them out is the same as specifying them (but faster).

```
<head>
<meta http-equiv="content-type"
content="text/html; charset=utf-8" />
<meta name="copyright" content="&copy; 2002
Liz Castro" />
<meta name="robots" content="noindex,
nofollow" />
<title>Untitled</title>
</head>
<body>
This is my personal page! I don't want it to be
indexed by search engines.
</body>
</html>
```

Figure 26.8 *When a search engine's robot encounters this page, it will ignore both the page and the page's links.*

Figure 26.9 *Some search engines, like Google shown here, keep a copy of most of the pages that they index so that visitors can see what's on the page even if the page is not available.*

```
<head>

<meta http-equiv="content-type"
content="text/html; charset=utf-8" />

<meta name="copyright" content="&copy; 2002
Liz Castro" />

<meta name="robots" content="noarchive" />

<title>Untitled</title>

</head>

<body>

This is a page I update frequently (or perhaps it's a
temporary page). I don't want search engines to
keep a copy of it in their archives.

</body>

</html>
```

Figure 26.10 *When a search engine's robot encounters this page, it will continue to index the page, but it won't archive it (and thus won't be able to offer a cached version should your page (or server) be unavailable).*

Keeping Pages From Being Archived

Some search engines save a copy of your Web page and offer it as an alternative if your site is down or otherwise inaccessible. However, there is no guarantee that this cached version is up to date. If you'd rather your page not be archived on a search engine's server, you can tell the robot not to archive it.

To keep search engines from archiving your pages:

In the `head` section of your page, type **<meta name="robots" content="noarchive" />**.

✔ Tip

■ Presently, Google is the most important search engine that archives Web pages. If you'd like to keep only Google from archiving your pages, you can specify `googlebot` instead of `robots` as the value of the `name` attribute above.

Keeping Pages From Being Archived

Creating a Crawler Page

Most search engines, like AltaVista or Yahoo, ask that you submit just one URL and promise that they will follow all the links and find the rest of the pages on your site. But why make it difficult for them? You can create a page with links to all of the most important sections of your site and then submit that to the search engine, thus ensuring that the proper pages will be noticed.

To create a crawler page in Explorer:

1. Choose Favorites > Organize Favorites.

2. In the dialog box that appears, click Create Folder **(Figure 26.11)**.

3. Type the name of the crawler page (it appears in the right hand box).

4. Close the dialog box.

5. Navigate to the important pages on your site that you want to be sure the search engine finds.

6. Choose Favorites > Add to Favorites.

7. Select your crawler page folder from the list and then click OK **(Figure 26.12)**. If your folder doesn't appear, click the Create in button to see the list of folders.

8. When you've added all the desired pages, choose File > Import and Export.

9. Use the Wizard to create an HTML file of your crawler page favorites folder **(Figure 26.13)**.

10. Upload the page to your server *(see page 408)*.

11. And then don't forget to submit it to the desired search engines *(see page 424)*.

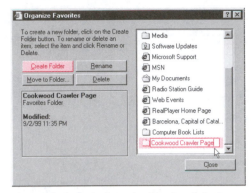

Figure 26.11 *In the Organize Favorites dialog box, click Create Folder and give the new folder a name. Then click Close.*

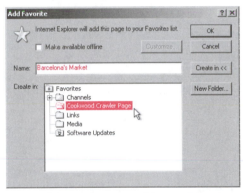

Figure 26.12 *After choosing Add to Favorites, select the crawler page folder in which the link should be added.*

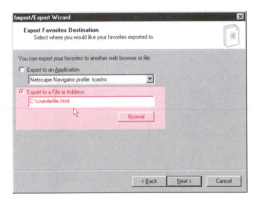

Figure 26.13 *In the Import/Export Wizard, be sure to choose the Export to a File or Address option and then choose a simple name for your crawler file.*

Creating a Crawler Page

Figure 26.14
Choose Bookmarks > Manage Bookmarks to make the Bookmarks window appear.

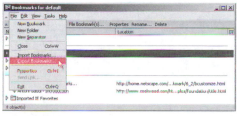

Figure 26.15 *Once the Bookmarks window is open and active, click the New Folder button.*

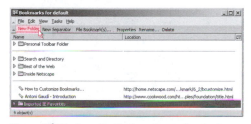

Figure 26.16 *Once you've created bookmarks for all the important pages on your site, choose File > Export Bookmarks to save the bookmarks file as an HTML file.*

Figure 26.17 *A crawler page should contain links to all of the pages on a site that you want indexed by a search engine.*

To create a crawler page with Netscape:

1. Choose Bookmarks > Manage Bookmarks (**Figure 26.14**).

2. Click the New Folder button in the Bookmarks window to create a new folder to hold the bookmarks for your most important pages (**Figure 26.15**).

3. Select the new folder in the Bookmarks window and choose View > Set as New Bookmarks Folder so that all new bookmarks will be automatically added to this folder.

4. Close the Bookmarks window.

5. Navigate to the important pages on your site that you want to be sure the search engine finds.

6. Choose Bookmarks > Add Bookmark (Ctrl/Command+D) to add the desired pages to your bookmarks folder.

7. When you've added all the desired pages, choose Bookmarks > Manage Bookmarks to open the Bookmarks window again.

8. Choose File > Export Bookmarks to save the bookmarks in an HTML file (**Figure 26.16**). Unfortunately, you can't choose a particular folder to save.

9. Open the bookmarks file and delete everything except the links to the important pages on your site.

10. Continue with step 10 on page 422.

✔ Tips

- Crawler pages can double as site maps.

- I got the idea of using a crawler page from Paul Boutin (*see page 415*).

Creating a Crawler Page

Submitting Your Site to a Search Engine

Once you have carefully used keywords and added `meta` tags to all of the desired pages on your site and perhaps created a crawler page (as described on page 422) that lists those pages, you'll want to invite a search engine to visit your site in order to add your pages to its database.

To submit your site to a search engine:

1. Connect to the search engine of your choice.

2. Find their Add URL page.

3. Google's is at *http://www.google.com/ addurl.html* **(Figure 26.18)**.

Yahoo's is at *http://docs.yahoo.com/ info/suggest/*

AltaVista's is at: *http://www.altavista.com/ sites/search/addurl/*

4. Type your (crawler) page's URL in the appropriate text box and click the Submit button.

5. Go back to the search engine in two weeks and search for your site. If it doesn't appear, submit it again.

✔ Tips

■ The most popular general search engines are Google and Yahoo. Also see *http:// www.useit.com/about/searchreferrals.html*.

■ You might also want to register your site with a search engine that specializes in a particular topic. So, if your page is about Star Trek, you might want to register it with *http://www.treksearch.com*. Yahoo has a very complete list of specific topic search engines.

Figure 26.18 *Go to the search engine's Add URL page. This is Google. You can add comments about your page, though they are not used in the search results.*

Improving Your Ranking by Getting Linked

While matching a visitor's search criteria might get your page among the results, one of the key factors in bubbling your page to the top of those results is its *popularity*, as measured by the number of similar pages (outside your site) that link to it. In short, if you get other sites to link to your site, your page will appear higher up in the rankings.

To improve your ranking by getting linked:

- Ask sites with similar content if they would link to your site.

- Join Web rings of sites with similar content.

- Offer to exchange links with sites of similar content.

- Make sure to submit your site to major as well as specific search engines.

✔ Tips

- Don't create bogus domains and then link to your page from there. Search engines can spot this scam from a mile away.

- Links from authoritative sites of the same topic are more valuable than links from less authoritative or more generic sites.

- You can find out who links to you by typing **link:yourdomain.com** in Google.

- Note that the wording of the link and the keywords on the originating page can be almost as important in determining how and whether a page gets listed as the keywords on the page itself. (For more details, do a search for *googlebombing*.)

Improving Your Ranking by Getting Linked

Writing Pages That Are Easy to Index

There are three major Web design practices that can sabotage your efforts to get noticed by search engines: frames, image maps, and dynamically generated pages.

Frames

While frames can be useful for showing more than one page at a time *(see page 241)*, this flexibility can also keep them from getting indexed by search engines. Some search engines will ignore a frameset's frames in favor of its alternate content (as marked by the `noframe` tag). And if they do index an individual frame, search engines often give the individual frame as a result, which may or may not make sense without the enclosing frameset (**Figures 26.19, 26.20, and 26.21**).

Image maps

Some search engines don't know what to do with image maps and ignore them altogether. Any linked pages may thus not get indexed. It's always a good idea to repeat the links from an image map as text, both for search engines and for visitors who cannot use images.

Dynamically generated pages

While you can create fancy, customized effects by dynamically creating pages based on information you've collected from your visitors, these pages are hard for search engines to deal with. On the one hand, they may be suspicious that you're trying to serve different versions to search engines than you are to regular visitors (a big no-no that can also get your page removed from a search engine). On the other hand, the page is a moving target; there's no place to link to once a prospective visitor says they're interested in going back. At the very least, use URLs that search engines can digest, preferably without ? or & (as may appear in CGI instructions).

Figure 26.19 *So inspired by the endless Catalan examples in this book, you go searching for* Catalan grammar and vocabulary *at Google and find this page.*

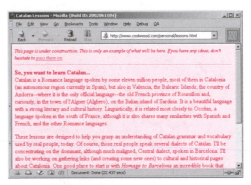

Figure 26.20 *You click on the link, and unbeknownst to you, see only an individual frame, instead of the entire frameset. You're missing a huge part of the site.*

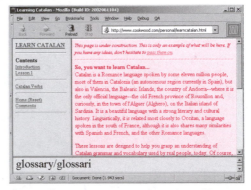

Figure 26.21 *You might never see the rest of the site. The person who designed this frame-based site (yes, it was me) should have given you a way to get to the frameset from the individual frame (or used JavaScript, see page 327).*

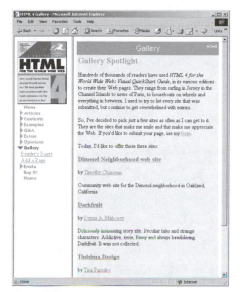

Figure 26.22 *Adding your page to my gallery is just one of a number of techniques you can use to get people to come visit your site.*

Other Techniques for Publicizing Your Site

Although getting your site to appear at the top of the list when a prospective visitor looks for related topics at Google is a laudable goal, there are several additional ways to let people know your page exists.

- Add your URL to your signature so that it will be included in all outgoing e-mail.

- Answer questions or post information on a related newsgroup and make sure your URL is prominently included in your signature. (On the other hand, it's also considered good form to keep your signature relatively brief and humble.)

- Post a note in the moderated newsgroup *comp.infosystems.www.announce* or the in the unmoderated *comp.internet.net-happenings*. (The hyphen is part of the address.)

- Join a Web ring. A Web ring is a group of related Web sites that have links that go from one site to the next. Web rings encourage visitors from one site to explore related ones. You can search for pertinent Web rings at Yahoo.

- Even simpler than a Web ring is to exchange links with other sites that have similar content.

- Submit your page to my readers' gallery: *www.cookwood.com/html/gallery/*.

- Make sure your Web site's URL appears on your stationery, business cards, pamphlets and other promotional material, and advertisements.

- And of course, you can always pay someone to advertise your page for you.

Other Techniques for Publicizing Your Site

(X)HTML Elements and Attributes

As we mentioned way back in Chapter 1, *Web Page Building Blocks*, there are three flavors of (X)HTML: strict, transitional, and frameset. Each flavor is defined by a DTD *(document type definition)* which lists which elements, attributes, and even values are permitted. The strict version does not allow the use of any deprecated or frameset elements, the transitional (sometimes called *loose*) lets you use deprecated elements, but not frameset ones, and the frameset version lets you use all the elements of the transitional flavor as well as the frameset elements.

On the following pages, you'll find a list of the (X)HTML elements and attributes described in this book. In the "Vers." or *version* column, I've used a *D* to mark elements or attributes that have been deprecated (and thus not allowed in strict), and an *F* to mark elements and attributes that are only allowed in the frameset flavor. Thus, only elements with *no code* in the version column may be used in strict (X)HTML. You should use a DOCTYPE that corresponds to the elements used in your Web page *(see pages 38 and 60)*.

Proprietary tags are marked with an N if only recognized by Netscape, an IE if only recognized by Internet Explorer, or with N+IE if supported by both. You should omit the DOCTYPE when using proprietary tags, since they are not valid in any DTD.

(You can now find intrinsic events in Appendix C, *Intrinsic Events*.)

(X)HTML Elements and Attributes

TAG/ATTRIBUTE(S)	DESCRIPTION	VERS.
--MOST TAGS--	The following attributes may be used with most (X)HTML tags	
class	For identifying a set of tags in order to apply styles (pp. 67, 68, 69)	
event	For triggering a script (p. 316). Also see *Intrinsic Events* on page 448	
id	For identifying particular tags for JavaScript functions and styles (pp. 67, 68, 69)	
lang	For specifying the language an element is written in (p. 342)	
style	For adding local style sheet information (p. 153)	
title	For labeling elements with tool tips (p. 72)	
!--	For inserting invisible comments (p. 71)	
!doctype	Theoretically required. For indicating version of HTML used (p. 60)	
a	For creating links and anchors (p. 118)	
accesskey	For adding a keyboard shortcut to a link (p. 126)	
event	For triggering a script (p. 316)	
href	For specifying URL of page or name of anchor that link goes to	
name	For marking a specific area of page that a link might jump to (p. 120)	
tabindex	For defining the order in which the Tab key takes the visitor through links and form elements (p. 127)	
target	For specifying a particular window or frame for a link (pp. 122, 123)	D
abbr	For explaining meaning of abbreviations (p. 82)	
acronym	For explaining meaning of acronyms (p. 82)	
address	For formatting the e-mail address of the Web page designer (p. 74)	
applet	For inserting applets (p. 306)	D
code	For specifying the URL of the applet's code	D
width, height	For specifying width and height of an applet	D
area	For specifying coordinates of image maps (p. 130)	
accesskey	For adding a keyboard shortcut to a particular region of the map	
alt	For giving information about an area	
coords	For giving coordinates of area in image map	
href	For specifying destination URL of link in area in image map	
nohref	For making a click in image map have no effect	
shape	For specifying shape of area in image map	
target	For specifying window or frame that link should be displayed in	D
b	For displaying text in boldface (p. 74)	

Page numbers are omitted for those attributes discussed on the same page as the tag to which they belong.

TAG/ATTRIBUTE(S)	DESCRIPTION	VERS.
base		
href	For specifying the URL to be used to generate relative URLs (p. 123)	
target	For specifying the default target for the links on the page (p. 123)	D
basefont	For specifying default font specifications throughout page (p. 344)	D
color	For specifying the default color for text	D
face	For specifying the default font for text	D
size	For specifying the default size for text	D
bgsound	For inserting background sound for page (p. 311)	IE
loop	For specifying how many times sound should play	IE
src	For specifying URL of sound	IE
big	For making text bigger than surrounding text (p. 75)	
blink	For making text disappear and reappear (p. 351)	N
blockquote	For setting off block of text on page (p. 78)	
cite	For giving the URL of the source of the quote	
body	For enclosing main section of page (p. 62)	
alink, link, vlink	For specifying color of active links, new links, and visited links (p. 349)	D
background	For specifying a background image (p. 355)	D
bgcolor	For specifying the background color (p. 354)	D
leftmargin, topmargin	For specifying left and top margins (p. 357)	IE
text	For specifying color of text (p. 348)	D
br	For creating a line break (p. 70)	
clear	For stopping text wrap (pp. 112, 223)	D
button	For creating buttons (pp. 283, 285, 318)	
accesskey	For adding a keyboard shortcut to a button	
disabled	To gray out a button until some other event occurs	
event	For associating the button with a script	
name	For identifying buttons (perhaps for a JavaScript function)	
type	For using the button as a form element	
value	For specifying what kind of button to create	
caption	For creating a caption for a table (p. 217)	
align	For placing caption above or below table	D
center	For centering text, images, or other elements (p. 356)	D
cite	For marking text as a citation (p. 74)	
code	For marking text as computer code (p. 76)	

Page numbers are omitted for those attributes discussed on the same page as the tag to which they belong.

TAG/ATTRIBUTE(S)	DESCRIPTION	VERS.
col	For joining columns in a table into a non-structural group (p. 234)	
align, valign	For specifying alignment of columns in column group	
span	For specifying number of columns in column group	
width	For specifying a column's width	
colgroup	For joining columns in a table into a structural column group (p. 234)	
align, valign	For specifying alignment of columns in column group	
span	For specifying number of columns in column group	
width	For specifying the default width for the enclosed col elements	
dd	For marking a definition in a list (p. 211)	
del	To mark deleted text by striking it out (p. 81)	
div	For dividing a page into logical sections (p. 68)	
align	For aligning a given section to left, right, or center	D
class	For giving a name to each class of divisions	
id	For giving a unique name to a particular division	
dl	For creating a definition list (p. 211)	
dt	For marking a term to be defined in a list (p. 211)	
em	For emphasizing text, usually with italics (p. 74)	
embed	For adding multimedia (pp. 298, 304, 307)	N+IE*
align	For aligning controls	N+IE*
autostart	For making multimedia event begin automatically	N+IE*
controls	For displaying play, pause, rewind buttons	N+IE*
loop	For determining if multimedia event should play more than once	N+IE*
src	For specifying URL of multimedia file	N+IE*
width, height	For specifying size of controls	N+IE*
fieldset	For grouping a set of form elements together (p. 287)	
font	For changing the size, face, and color of text (p. 346)	D
color	For changing text color	D
face	For changing text font	D
size	For changing text size	D
form	For creating fill-in forms (p. 269)	
action	For giving URL of CGI script for form	
enctype	For uploading files in the proper format (pp. 270, 279)	
method	For determining how form should be processed	

Page numbers are omitted for those attributes discussed on the same page as the tag to which they belong.

*the embed element, while non-standard, used to be universally accepted. Internet Explorer 5.5+ for Windows no longer supports it.

TAG/ATTRIBUTE(S)	DESCRIPTION	VERS.
frame	For creating frames (p. 242)	F
border	For determining thickness of frame borders (p. 252)	N+IE
bordercolor	For determining color of frame borders (p. 251)	N+IE
frameborder	For displaying or hiding frame borders (p. 253)	F
framespacing	For adding space between frames (p. 252)	IE
longdesc	For linking to a document with more information (p. 262)	F
name	For naming frame so it can be used as target (p. 242)	F
noresize	For keeping users from resizing a frame (p. 254)	F
marginwidth, marginheight	For specifying a frame's left and right, and top and bottom margins (p. 249)	F
scrolling	For displaying or hiding a frame's scrollbars (p. 250)	F
src	For specifying initial URL to be displayed in frame (p. 242)	F
target	For specifying which frame a link should be opened in (pp. 255, 256)	F
title	For indicating a frame's purpose (p. 262)	F
frameset	For defining a frameset (p. 242)	F
border	For determining thickness of frame borders (p. 252)	N+IE
bordercolor	For determining color of frame borders (p. 251)	N+IE
cols	For determining number and size of frames (pp. 244, 245)	F
frameborder	For displaying or hiding frame borders (p. 253)	F
framespacing	For adding space between frames (p. 252)	IE
rows	For determining number and size of frames (pp. 244, 245)	F
h1, h2, h3, h4, h5, h6	For creating headers (p. 65)	
align	For aligning headers	D
head	For creating head section of page (p. 62)	
hr	For creating horizontal rules (p. 115)	
align	For aligning horizontal rules	D
noshade	For displaying horizontal rules without shading	D
size	For specifying height of horizontal rule	D
width	For specifying width of horizontal rule	D
html	For identifying a text document as an HTML document (p. 60)	
i	For displaying text in italics (p. 74)	

Page numbers are omitted for those attributes discussed on the same page as the tag to which they belong.

(X)HTML Elements and Attributes

TAG/ATTRIBUTE(S)	DESCRIPTION	VERS.
iframe	For creating floating frames (p. 248)	D*
align	For aligning floating frames	D*
frameborder	For displaying or hiding frame borders (p. 253)	D*
height	For specifying the height of an iframe	D*
name	For specifying the name of the floating frame, to be used as a target	D*
width, height	For specifying size of floating frame	D*
scrolling	For displaying or hiding scrollbars (p. 250)	D*
src	For specifying the URL of the initial page	D*
img	For inserting images on a page (p. 104)	
align	For aligning images (p. 114) and for wrapping text around images (pp. 110, 111)	D
alt	For offering alternate text that is displayed if image is not (p. 105)	
border	For specifying the thickness of the border, if any (pp. 104, 128)	D
hspace, vspace	For specifying amount of space above and below, and to the sides of an image (p. 113)	D
src	For specifying URL of image (p. 104)	
usemap	For specifying the image map that should be used with the referenced image (p. 130)	
width, height	For specifying size of image so that page is loaded more quickly, or for scaling (pp. 106, 108)	
input	For creating form elements (pp. 272, 273, 274, 275, 279, 281, 282, 284)	
accesskey	For adding a keyboard shortcut to a form element (p. 290)	
align	For aligning form elements	D
checked	For marking a radio button or check box by default (pp. 274, 275)	
disabled	For graying out form elements until some other event occurs (p. 291)	
event	For triggering a script with an event like ONFOCUS, ONBLUR, etc.	
maxlength	For determining maximum amount of characters that can be entered in form element (pp. 272, 273)	
name	For identifying data collected by this element	
size	For specifying width of text or password box (pp. 272, 273)	
src	For specifying URL of active image (p. 286)	
readonly	For keeping visitors from changing certain form elements (p. 292)	
tabindex	For specifying the order in which the Tab key should take a visitor through the links and form elements (p. 289)	
type	For determining type of form element	
value	For specifying initial value of form element	

Page numbers are omitted for those attributes discussed on the same page as the tag to which they belong.

*Although not formally described as deprecated, the iframe element (and its associated attributes) are not part of (X)HTML strict. Call it what you will, but use them only in transitional flavor (X)HTML.

TAG/ATTRIBUTE(S)	DESCRIPTION	VERS.
ins	For marking inserted text with an underline (p. 81)	
kbd	For marking keyboard text (p. 76)	
label	For labeling form elements (p. 288)	
for	For specifying which form element the label belongs to	
layer	For positioning elements (p. 366)	N
legend	For labeling fieldsets (p. 287)	
align	For aligning legends	D
li	For creating a list item (p. 204)	
type	For determining which symbols should begin the list item	D
value	For determining the initial value of the first list item	D
link	For linking to an external style sheet (p. 149)	
href	For specifying the URL of the style sheet	
media	For noting a style sheet's purpose (p. 198)	
title	For labeling alternate style sheets (p. 150)	
type	For noting a style sheet's MIME type	
rel	For indicating that a style sheet is primary or alternate (pp. 149, 150)	
map	For creating a client-side image map (p. 130)	
name	For naming map so it can be referenced later	
marquee	For creating moving text (p. 310)	IE
behavior	For controlling how the text should move (scroll, slide, alternate)	IE
direction	For controlling if the text moves from left to right or right to left	IE
loop	For specifying repetitions	IE
scrollamount	For specifying amount of space between each marquee repetition	IE
scrolldelay	For specifying amount of time between each marquee repetition	IE
meta		
content	For adding extra information about the Web page itself (pp. 309, 322, 338, 417, 418, 419, 420)	
http-equiv	For creating automatic jumps to other pages (p. 309), setting the default scripting language (p. 322), and declaring the character encoding (p. 338)	
name	For identifying extra information to the Web page (pp. 417, 418, 419, 420)	
nobr	For keeping all the enclosed elements on one line (p. 358)	N+IE
noframes	For providing alternatives to frames (p. 259)	F
noscript	For providing alternatives to scripts (p. 319)	

Page numbers are omitted for those attributes discussed on the same page as the tag to which they belong.

TAG/ATTRIBUTE(S)	DESCRIPTION	VERS.
object	For embedding objects in Web pages (pp. 260, 298, 304, 306, 307)	
align	For aligning objects	D
border	For creating (or hiding) a border around an object	D
classid	For identifying the kind of object being embedded	
codebase	For defining the base URL of the source object	
data	For identifying the source of the multimedia file to be embedded	
hspace, vspace	For specifying amount of space around an object	D
name	For identifying the object	
standby	For displaying a message as the object is loading	
type	For noting the an object's MIME type	
width, height	For specifying the dimensions of the object's box	
ol	For creating ordered lists (p. 204)	
type	For specifying the symbols that should begin each list item	D
start	For specifying the initial value of the first list item	D
optgroup	For dividing a menu into submenus (p. 277)	
disabled	For graying out menu options until some other event occurs	
label	For specifying how the option should appear in the menu	
option	For creating the individual options in a form menu (p. 276)	
disabled	For graying out menu options until some other event occurs	
label	For specifying how the option should appear in the menu	
selected	For making a menu option be selected by default in a blank form	
value	For specifying the initial value of a menu option	
p	For creating new paragraphs (p. 66)	
align	For aligning paragraphs	D
param	For setting properties of an object (pp. 298, 304, 306)	
name	For identifying the kind of property	
value	For setting the value of the named property	
pre	For displaying text exactly as it appears in HTML document (p. 77)	
q	For quoting short passages of text (p. 78)	
cite	For giving the URL of the source of the quote	
s	(Same as strike) For displaying text with a line through it (p. 350)	D
samp	For displaying sample text—in a monospaced font (p. 76)	

Page numbers are omitted for those attributes discussed on the same page as the tag to which they belong.

TAG/ATTRIBUTE(S)	DESCRIPTION	VERS.
script	For adding "automatic" scripts to a page (p. 314)	
charset	For specifying the character set an external script is written in (p. 315)	
language	For specifying the scripting language the script is written in	D
src	For referencing an external script (p. 315)	
type	For specifying the scripting language the script is written in	
select	For creating menus in forms (p. 276)	
disabled	For graying out menu options until some other event occurs	
name	For identifying the data collected by the menu	
multiple	For allowing users to choose more than one option in the menu	
size	For specifying the number of items initially visible in the menu	
small	For decreasing the size of text (p. 75)	
span	For creating custom character styles (p. 69)	
class	For naming individual custom character styles	
id	For identifying particular HTML elements	
strike	(Same as s) For displaying text with a line through it (p. 350)	D
strong	For emphasizing text logically, usually in boldface (p. 74)	
style	For adding style sheet information to a page (p. 151)	
media	For indicating a style sheet's purpose	
type	For indicating a style sheet's MIME type	
sub	For creating subscripts (p. 80)	
sup	For creating superscripts (p. 80)	
table	For creating tables (p. 217)	
align	For aligning an entire table with respect to the window (p. 222)	D
background	For specifying a background image for the table (p. 228)	N+IE
bgcolor	For specifying the background color of the table (p. 228)	D
border	For specifying the thickness, if any, of the border (p. 218)	
bordercolor	For specifying a solid color for the border (p. 218)	IE
bordercolordark	For specifying the darker (shaded) color of the border (p. 218)	IE
bordercolorlight	For specifying the lighter (highlighted) color of the border (p. 218)	IE
cellpadding	For setting the space between a cell's contents and its borders (p. 230)	
cellspacing	For setting the amount of space between cells (p. 230)	
frame	For displaying external borders (p. 237)	
height	For specifying the height of the table (p. 220)	N+IE
rules	For displaying internal borders (p. 238)	
width	For specifying the size of the table (p. 220)	

Page numbers are omitted for those attributes discussed on the same page as the tag to which they belong.

(X)HTML Elements and Attributes

(X)HTML Elements and Attributes

TAG/ATTRIBUTE(S)	DESCRIPTION	VERS.
tbody	For identifying the body of the table (p. 236)	
align, valign	For aligning the contents of the body of the table	
td; th	For creating regular and header cells, respectively, in a table (p. 217)	
align, valign	For aligning a cell's contents horizontally or vertically (p. 226)	
bgcolor	For changing the background color of a cell (p. 228)	D
char	For aligning the contents of a cell with respect to a character (p. 227)	
colspan	For spanning a cell across more than one column (p. 232)	
nowrap	For keeping a cell's contents on one line (p. 239)	D
rowspan	For spanning a cell across more than one row (p. 233)	
width, height	For specifying the size of the cell (p. 220)	D
textarea	For creating text block entry areas in a form (p. 278)	
accesskey	For adding a keyboard shortcut to a text area	
disabled	For graying out a text block until some other event occurs	
name	For identifying the data that is gathered with the text block	
readonly	For protecting a text area's contents (p. 292)	
rows, cols	For specifying the number of rows and columns in the text block	
tfoot, thead	For identifying the footer and header area of a table (p. 236)	
align, valign	For aligning the footer or header cells (p. 226)	
title	Required. For creating the title of the page in title bar area (p. 64)	
tr	For creating rows in a table (p. 217)	
align, valign	For aligning contents of row horizontally or vertically (p. 226)	
bgcolor	For changing color of entire row (p. 228)	D
tt	For displaying text in monospaced font (p. 76)	
u	For displaying text with line underneath it (p. 350)	D
ul	For creating unordered lists (p. 204)	
type	For specifying the markers that should precede each list item	D
wbr	For creating discretional line breaks (p. 359)	N+IE

Page numbers are omitted for those attributes discussed on the same page as the tag to which they belong.

CSS PROPERTIES AND VALUES

This book does not cover every single property defined in the Cascading Style Sheets Level 1 and Level 2 specifications. Instead, I focus on those properties that are supported by at least one browser.

I have included the table on the next page to give you a quick reference to each of the properties and its allowed values. I have also indicated each property's default or initial value, the elements to which it may be applied, whether or not the property is inherited, and what percentages refer to if they may be used. Finally, I have referenced the page number in the book where the property or value is discussed.

The table is derived from the more complete specifications at *http://www.w3.org/TR/REC-CSS2/propidx.html* and is copyright © World Wide Web Consortium, (Massachusetts Institute of Technology, Institut National de Recherche en Informatique et en Automatique, Keio University). All Rights Reserved.

Many of the properties accept a length, percentage, or color for values. For more details on entering values, consult *A Property's Value* on page 44.

I hope you will find it useful.

CSS Properties and Values

PROPERTY/VALUES	DESCRIPTION AND NOTES
background any combination of the values for *background-attachment, background-color, background-image, background-repeat,* and/or *background-position,* or `inherit`	for changing the background color and image of elements (p. 182) initial value depends on individual properties; not inherited; percentages allowed for *background-position*
background-attachment either `scroll`, `fixed`, or `inherit`	for determining if and how background images should scroll (p. 182) initial value: `scroll`; not inherited
background-color either a color, `transparent`, or `inherit`	for setting just the background color of an element (p. 182) initial value: `transparent`; not inherited
background-image either a URL, `none`, or `inherit`	for setting just the background image of an element (p. 182) initial value: `none`; not inherited
background-position either one or two percentages or lengths (or one percentage and one length) or one of `top`, `center`, or `bottom` and/or one of `left`, `center`, or `right`. Or use `inherit`.	for setting the physical position of a specified background image (p. 182) initial value: `0% 0%`, if a single percentage is set, it is used for the horizontal position and the initial value of the vertical is set to 50%, if only one keyword is used, the initial value of the other is `center`; applies to block-level and replaced elements: not inherited; percentages refer to the size of the box itself
background-repeat one of `repeat`, `repeat-x`, `repeat-y`, `no-repeat`, or `inherit`	for determining how and if background images should be tiled (p. 182) initial value: `repeat`; not inherited
border any combination of the values of *border-width, border-style,* and/or a color, or `inherit`	for defining all aspects of a border on all sides of an element (p. 186) initial value depends on individual properties; not inherited
border-color from one to four colors, `transparent`, or `inherit`	for setting only the color of the border on one or more sides of an element (p. 186) initial value: the element's `color` property; not inherited
border-spacing either one or two lengths or `inherit`	for specifying the amount of space between borders in a table (p. 230) initial value: 0; may be applied only to table elements; inherited

CSS Properties and Values

PROPERTY/VALUES	DESCRIPTION AND NOTES

border-style
one to four of the following values:
`none, dotted, dashed, solid,`
`double, groove, ridge, inset,`
`outset, inherit`
	for setting only the style of a border on one or more sides of an element (p. 186)
	
	initial value: `none`; not inherited

border-top, border-right, **border-bottom, border-left** any combination of a single value each for *border-width*, *border-style*, and/or a color, or use `inherit`.	for defining all three border properties at once on only one side of an element (p. 186) initial value depends on individual values; not inherited
border-top-color, border-right-color, **border-bottom-color, border-left-color** one color or `inherit`	for defining just the border's color on only one side of an element (p. 186) initial value: the value of the *color* property; not inherited

border-top-style, border-right-style,
border-bottom-style, border-left-style
one of `none, dotted, dashed, solid,`
`double, groove, ridge, inset,`
`outset, or inherit`
	for defining just the border's style on only one side of an element (p. 186)
	
	initial value: `none`; not inherited

border-top-width, border-right-width, **border-bottom-width, border-left-width** one of `thin, medium, thick` or a length	for defining just the border's width on only one side of an element (p. 186) initial value: `medium`; not inherited
border-width one to four of the following values: `thin, medium, thick` or a length	for defining the border's width on one or more sides of an element (p. 186) initial value: `medium`; not inherited
clear one of `none, left, right, both,` or `inherit`	for keeping elements from floating on one or both sides of an element (p. 195) initial value: `none`; may only be applied to block-level elements; not inherited
bottom either a percentage, length, `auto`, or `inherit`	for setting the distance that an element should be offset from its parent element's bottom edge (pp. 179, 180, 181) initial value: `auto`; not inherited; percentages refer to height of containing block
color a color or `inherit`	for setting the foreground color of an element (p. 184) initial value: parent's color, some colors are set by browser; inherited

CSS Properties and Values

CSS Properties and Values

PROPERTY/VALUES	DESCRIPTION AND NOTES
cursor one of `auto`, `crosshair`, `default`, `pointer`, `move`, `e-resize`, `ne-resize`, `nw-resize`, `n-resize`, `se-resize`, `sw-resize`, `s-resize`, `w-resize`, `text`, `wait`, `help`, a URL, or `inherit`	for setting the cursor's shape (p. 185) initial value: `auto`; inherited
display one of `inline`, `block`, `list-item`, `none`, `inherit`	for determining how and if an element should be displayed (p. 178) initial value: `inline`; not inherited
float one of `left`, `right`, `none`, `inherit`	for determining on which side of an element other elements are permitted to float (p. 194) initial value: `none`; may not be applied to positioned elements or generated content; not inherited
font if desired, any combination of the values for *font-style*, *font-variant* and *font-weight* followed by the required *font-size*, an optional value for *line-height* and the also required *font-family*, or use `inherit`	for setting at least the font family and size, and optionally the style, variant, weight, and line-height of text *(p. 165)* initial value depends on individual properties; inherited; percentages allowed for values of *font-size* and *line-height*
font-family one or more quotation mark-enclosed font names followed by an optional generic font name, or use `inherit`	for choosing the font family for text (p. 158) initial value: depends on browser; inherited
font-size an absolute size, a relative size, a length, a percentage, or `inherit`	for setting the size of text (p. 162) initial value: `medium`; the computed value is inherited; percentages refer to parent element's font size
font-style either `normal`, `italic`, `oblique`, or `inherit`	for making text italic (p. 160) initial value: `normal`; inherited
font-variant either `normal`, `small-caps`, or `inherit`	for setting text in small caps (p. 173) initial value: `normal`; inherited
font-weight either `normal`, `bold`, `bolder`, `lighter`, `100`, `200`, `300`, `400`, `500`, `600`, `700`, `800`, `900`, or `inherit`	for applying, removing, and adjusting bold formatting (p. 161) initial value: `normal`; the numeric values are considered keywords and not integers (you can't choose 150, for example); inherited

CSS Properties and Values

CSS Properties and Values

PROPERTY/VALUES	DESCRIPTION AND NOTES
height either a length, percentage, `auto`, or `inherit`	for setting the height of an element (p. 190) initial value: `auto`; may be applied to all elements except non-replaced inline elements, table columns, and column groups; not inherited
left either a length, percentage, `auto`, or `inherit`	for setting the distance that an element should be offset from its parent element's left edge (pp. 179, 180, 181) initial value: `auto`; may only be applied to positioned elements; not inherited; percentages refer to width of containing block
letter-spacing either `normal`, a length, or `inherit`	for setting the amount of space between letters (p. 168) initial value: `normal`; inherited
line-height either `normal`, a number, a length, a percentage, or `inherit`	for setting the amount of space between lines of text (p. 164) initial value: `normal`; inherited; percentages refer to the font size of the element itself
list-style any combination of the values for *list-style-type, list-style-position* and/or *list-style-image*, or use `inherit`	for setting a list's marker (regular or custom) and its position (p. 210) initial value depends on initial values of individual elements; may only be applied to list elements; inherited
list-style-image either a URL, none, or `inherit`	for designating a custom marker for a list (p. 208) initial value: none; may only be applied to list elements; overrides `list-style-type`; inherited
list-style-position either `inside`, `outside`, or `inherit`	for determining the position of a list's marker (p. 209) initial value: `outside`; may only be applied to list elements; inherited
list-style-type either `disc`, `circle`, `square`, `decimal`, `lower-roman`, `upper-roman`, `lower-alpha`, `upper-alpha`, `none`, or `inherit`	for setting a list's marker (p. 206) initial value: `disc`; may only be applied to list elements; not used if `list-style-type` is valid; inherited
margin one to four of the following: `length`, percentage, or `auto`, or `inherit`	for setting the amount of space between one or more sides of an element's border and its parent element (pp. 189, 201) initial value depends on browser and on value of `width`; not inherited; percentages refer to width of containing block

CSS Properties and Values

PROPERTY/VALUES	DESCRIPTION AND NOTES
margin-top, margin-right, margin-bottom, margin-left either a length, percentage, `auto`, or `inherit`	for setting the amount of space between only one side of an element's border and its parent element (p. 189) initial value: `0`; not inherited; percentages refer to width of containing block; the values for `margin-right` and `margin-left` may be overridden if sum of `width`, `margin-right`, and `margin-left` are larger than parent element's containing block
marks either `crop`, `cross` or both, or use `none` or `inherit`	for printing crop marks and/or cross marks (p. 201) initial value: none; can only be applied in a `@page` rule
max-height, max-width either a length, percentage, `none`, or `inherit`	for setting the maximum height and/or width of an element, respectively (p. 190) initial value: `none`; may not be applied to non-replaced inline elements or table elements; not inherited; percentages refer to height/width of containing block
min-height, min-width either a length, percentage, or `inherit`	for setting the minimum height and/or width of an element, respectively (p. 190) initial value: `0`; may not be applied to non-replaced inline elements or table elements; not inherited; percentages refer to height/width of containing block
orphans either an integer or `inherit`	for specifying how many lines of an element may appear alone at the bottom of a page (p. 202) initial value: 2; may only be applied to block-level elements; inherited
overflow either `visible`, `hidden`, `scroll`, `auto`, or `inherit`	for determining where extra content should go if it does not fit in the element's content area (p. 193) initial value: `visible`; may only be applied to block-level and replaced elements; not inherited
padding one to four lengths or percentages, or `inherit`	for specifying the distance between one or more sides of an element's content area and its border (p. 188) initial value depends on browser: not inherited; percentages refer to width of containing block
padding-top, padding-right, padding-bottom, padding-left either a length, percentage, or `inherit`	for specifying the distance between one side of an element's content area and its border (p. 188) initial value: `0`; not inherited; percentages refer to width of containing block
page either a page area's name or `auto`	for specifying on which kind of page an element should be printed (p. 202) initial value: `auto`; may only be applied to block-level elements; inherited; names are defined with `@page` rule

CSS Properties and Values

PROPERTY/VALUES	DESCRIPTION AND NOTES
page-break-after, page-break-before either `always`, `avoid`, `auto`, `right`, `left`, or `inherit`	for specifying when page breaks should or should not occur (p. 200) initial value: `auto`; may only be applied to block-level elements; not inherited
page-break-inside either `avoid`, `auto`, or `inherit`	for keeping page breaks from dividing an element across pages (p. 200) initial value: `auto`; may only be applied to block-level elements; inherited
position either `static`, `relative`, `absolute`, `fixed`, or `inherit`	for determining how an element should be positioned with respect to the document's flow (pp. 179, 180, 181) initial value: `static`; may not be applied to generated content; not inherited
right either a length, percentage, `auto`, or `inherit`	for setting the distance that an element should be offset from its parent element's right edge (pp. 179, 180, 181) initial value: `auto`; may only be applied to positioned elements; not inherited; percentages refer to width of containing block
size either individual lengths for width and height, a single value for both width and height, `landscape`, `portrait`, `auto`, or `inherit`.	for determining the size of the printing area in a defined page (p. 201) initial value: `auto`; may only be used within an `@page` rule
table-display one of `fixed`, `auto`, or `inherit`	for choosing the algorithm that should be used to determine the widths of cells (p. 240) initial value: auto; not inherited
text-align one of `left`, `right`, `center`, `justify`, a string, or `inherit`	for aligning text (p. 171) initial value depends on browser and writing direction; may only be applied to block-level elements; inherited
text-decoration any combination of `underline`, `overline`, `line-through`, and `blink`, or `none` or `inherit`	for decorating text (mostly with lines) (p. 174) initial value: `none`; not inherited
text-indent either a length, percentage, or `inherit`	for setting the amount of space the first line of a paragraph should be indented (p. 169) initial value: `0`; may only be applied to block-level elements; inherited; percentages refer to width of containing block
text-transform either `capitalize`, `uppercase`, `lowercase`, `none`, or `inherit`	for setting the capitalization of an element's text (p. 172) initial value: `none`; inherited

CSS Properties and Values

CSS Properties and Values

PROPERTY/VALUES	DESCRIPTION AND NOTES
top either a length, percentage, `auto`, or `inherit`	for setting the distance that an element should be offset from its parent element's top edge (pp. 179, 180, 181) initial value: `auto`; may only be applied to positioned elements; not inherited; percentages refer to height of containing block
vertical-align either `baseline`, `sub`, `super`, `top`, `text-top`, `middle`, `bottom`, `text-bottom`, a percentage, a length, or `inherit`	for aligning elements vertically (pp. 196, 226) initial value: `baseline`; may only be applied to inline-level and table cell elements; not inherited; percentages refer to the element's *line-height* property
visibility either `visible`, `hidden`, `collapse`, or `inherit`	for hiding elements without taking them out of the document's flow (p. 178) initial value: `inherit`, which rather makes the fact that it's not inherited a moot point
white-space either `normal`, `pre`, `nowrap`, or `inherit`	for specifying how white space should be treated (p. 170) initial value: `normal`; may only be applied to block-level elements; inherited
widows either an integer or `inherit`	for specifying how many lines of an element may appear alone at the top of a page (p. 202) initial value: 2; may only be applied to block-level elements; inherited
width either a length, percentage, `auto`, or `inherit`	for setting the width of an element (p. 190) initial value: `auto`; may not be applied to non-replaced inline elements, table rows, or row groups; not inherited; percentages refer to width of containing block
word-spacing either `normal`, a length, or `inherit`	for setting the distance between words (p. 168) initial value: `normal`; inherited
z-index either `auto`, an integer, or `inherit`	for setting the depth of an element with respect to overlapping elements (p. 192) initial value: `auto`; may only be applied to positioned elements; not inherited

INTRINSIC EVENTS

An intrinsic event determines when an associated script will run. However, not every intrinsic event works with every (X)HTML element. This table illustrates which events and tags work together. For more information on associating a script with an intrinsic event, consult *Triggering a Script* on page 316.

Intrinsic Events

EVENT	WORKS WITH	WHEN
onblur	`a, area, button, input , label, select, textarea`	the visitor leaves an element that was previously in focus (see `onfocus` below)
onchange	`input, select, textarea`	the visitor modifies the value or contents of the element
onclick	All elements *except* `applet, base, basefont, br, font, frame, frameset, head, html, iframe, meta, param, script, style, title`	the visitor clicks on the specified area
ondblclick	Same as for `onclick`	the visitor double clicks the specified area
onfocus	`a, area, button, input , label, select, textarea`	the visitor selects, clicks, or tabs to the specified element
onkeydown	`input` (of type name or password), `textarea`	the visitor types something in the specified element
onkeypress	`input` (of type name or password), `textarea`	the visitor types something in the specified element
onkeyup	`input` (of type name or password), `textarea`	the visitor lets go of the key after typing in the specified element
onload	`body, frameset`	the page is loaded in the browser
onmousedown	Same as for `onclick`	the visitor presses the mouse button down over the element
onmousemove	Same as for `onclick`	the visitor moves the mouse over the specified element after having pointed at it
onmouseout	Same as for `onclick`	the visitor moves the mouse away from the specified element after having been over it
onmouseover	Same as for `onclick`	the visitor points the mouse at the element
onmouseup	Same as for `onclick`	the visitor lets the mouse button go after having clicked on the element
onreset	`form` (*not* input of type reset)	the visitor clicks the form's reset button
onselect	`input` (of type name or password), `textarea`	the visitor selects one or more characters or words in the element
onsubmit	`form` (*not* input of type submit)	the visitor clicks the form's submit button
onunload	`body, frameset`	the browser loads a different page after the specified page had been loaded

(X)HTML Symbols and Characters

As we discussed in Chapter 20, *Symbols and Non-English Characters*, you can add symbols and characters that don't belong to your page's encoding by inserting a *character reference*, that is, the symbol's associated number, hexadecimal number, or name in the Unicode character set.

Since there are more than 65,000 characters in Unicode, printing out each one's numeric or hexadecimal reference would require a book of its own, and be rather unwieldy to boot. Instead, you can consult Unicode's site, *(www.unicode.org)* where the characters are neatly divided by language and theme.

I can, however, provide you with a list of the 252 named references (officially called *character entity references*, but also known as *entity references* or *named entity references*) that can be used in (X)HTML. You'll find the complete tables in this appendix, as well as on my Web site: *www.cookwood.com/entities/*. I have included the equivalent numeric codes for your reference. They are divided into categories that I hope will help make them easier to find. (Perhaps the easiest way to find the desired symbol is to go to the Web page cited above and use the Find command.)

Instructions for inserting these symbols and characters on your Web pages can be found in *Adding Characters from Outside the Encoding* on page 340.

Note that the tables were generated with a browser, for authenticity's sake, and thus appear slightly more pixelated than regular text in this book.

Characters with special meaning in HTML and XHTML

To get this...	Type this	Or this	Description
&	&amp;	&#38;	ampersand
>	&gt;	&#62;	greater-than sign
<	&lt;	&#60;	less-than sign
"	&quot;	&#34;	quotation mark = APL quote

Accented characters, accents, and other diacritics from Western European Languages

To get this...	Type this	Or this	Description
´	&acute;	&#180;	acute accent = spacing acute
¸	&cedil;	&#184;	cedilla = spacing cedilla
ˆ	&circ;	&#710;	modifier letter circumflex accent
¯	&macr;	&#175;	macron = spacing macron = overline = APL overbar
·	&middot;	&#183;	middle dot = Georgian comma = Greek middle dot
˜	&tilde;	&#732;	small tilde
¨	&uml;	&#168;	diaeresis = spacing diaeresis
Á	&Aacute;	&#193;	latin capital letter A with acute
á	&aacute;	&#225;	latin small letter a with acute
Â	&Acirc;	&#194;	latin capital letter A with circumflex
â	&acirc;	&#226;	latin small letter a with circumflex
Æ	&AElig;	&#198;	latin capital letter AE = latin capital ligature AE
æ	&aelig;	&#230;	latin small letter ae = latin small ligature ae
À	&Agrave;	&#192;	latin capital letter A with grave = latin capital letter A grave
à	&agrave;	&#224;	latin small letter a with grave = latin small letter a grave
Å	&Aring;	&#197;	latin capital letter A with ring above = latin capital letter A ring
å	&aring;	&#229;	latin small letter a with ring above = latin small letter a ring
Ã	&Atilde;	&#195;	latin capital letter A with tilde
ã	&atilde;	&#227;	latin small letter a with tilde
Ä	&Auml;	&#196;	latin capital letter A with diaeresis
ä	&auml;	&#228;	latin small letter a with diaeresis
Ç	&Ccedil;	&#199;	latin capital letter C with cedilla
ç	&ccedil;	&#231;	latin small letter c with cedilla
É	&Eacute;	&#201;	latin capital letter E with acute
é	&eacute;	&#233;	latin small letter e with acute
Ê	&Ecirc;	&#202;	latin capital letter E with circumflex
ê	&ecirc;	&#234;	latin small letter e with circumflex
È	&Egrave;	&#200;	latin capital letter E with grave

(X)HTML Symbols and Characters

Accented characters, accents, and other diacritics from Western European Languages (continued)

To get this...	Type this	Or this	Description
è	&egrave;	&#232;	latin small letter e with grave
Ð	&ETH;	&#208;	latin capital letter ETH
ð	&eth;	&#240;	latin small letter eth
Ë	&Euml;	&#203;	latin capital letter E with diaeresis
ë	&euml;	&#235;	latin small letter e with diaeresis
Í	&Iacute;	&#205;	latin capital letter I with acute
í	&iacute;	&#237;	latin small letter i with acute
Î	&Icirc;	&#206;	latin capital letter I with circumflex
î	&icirc;	&#238;	latin small letter i with circumflex
Ì	&Igrave;	&#204;	latin capital letter I with grave
ì	&igrave;	&#236;	latin small letter i with grave
Ï	&Iuml;	&#207;	latin capital letter I with diaeresis
ï	&iuml;	&#239;	latin small letter i with diaeresis
Ñ	&Ntilde;	&#209;	latin capital letter N with tilde
ñ	&ntilde;	&#241;	latin small letter n with tilde
Ó	&Oacute;	&#211;	latin capital letter O with acute
ó	&oacute;	&#243;	latin small letter o with acute
Ô	&Ocirc;	&#212;	latin capital letter O with circumflex
ô	&ocirc;	&#244;	latin small letter o with circumflex
Œ	&OElig;	&#338;	latin capital ligature OE
œ	&oelig;	&#339;	latin small ligature oe (see notes)
Ò	&Ograve;	&#210;	latin capital letter O with grave
ò	&ograve;	&#242;	latin small letter o with grave
Ø	&Oslash;	&#216;	latin capital letter O with stroke = latin capital letter O slash
ø	&oslash;	&#248;	latin small letter o with stroke, = latin small letter o slash
Õ	&Otilde;	&#213;	latin capital letter O with tilde
õ	&otilde;	&#245;	latin small letter o with tilde
Ö	&Ouml;	&#214;	latin capital letter O with diaeresis
ö	&ouml;	&#246;	latin small letter o with diaeresis
Š	&Scaron;	&#352;	latin capital letter S with caron
š	&scaron;	&#353;	latin small letter s with caron
ß	&szlig;	&#223;	latin small letter sharp s = ess-zed
Þ	&THORN;	&#222;	latin capital letter THORN
þ	&thorn;	&#254;	latin small letter thorn
Ú	&Uacute;	&#218;	latin capital letter U with acute
ú	&uacute;	&#250;	latin small letter u with acute

Accented characters, accents, and other diacritics from Western European Languages (continued)

To get this...	Type this	Or this	Description
Û	&Ucirc;	&#219;	latin capital letter U with circumflex
û	&ucirc;	&#251;	latin small letter u with circumflex
Ù	&Ugrave;	&#217;	latin capital letter U with grave
ù	&ugrave;	&#249;	latin small letter u with grave
Ü	&Uuml;	&#220;	latin capital letter U with diaeresis
ü	&uuml;	&#252;	latin small letter u with diaeresis
Ý	&Yacute;	&#221;	latin capital letter Y with acute
ý	&yacute;	&#253;	latin small letter y with acute
ÿ	&yuml;	&#255;	latin small letter y with diaeresis
Ÿ	&Yuml;	&#376;	latin capital letter Y with diaeresis

Punctuation characters

To get this...	Type this	Or this	Description
¢	&cent;	&#162;	cent sign
¤	&curren;	&#164;	currency sign
€	&euro;	&#8364;	euro sign
£	&pound;	&#163;	pound sign
¥	&yen;	&#165;	yen sign = yuan sign
¦	&brvbar;	&#166;	broken bar = broken vertical bar
•	&bull;	&#8226;	bullet = black small circle (see notes)
©	&copy;	&#169;	copyright sign
†	&dagger;	&#8224;	dagger
‡	&Dagger;	&#8225;	double dagger
⁄	&frasl;	&#8260;	fraction slash
…	&hellip;	&#8230;	horizontal ellipsis = three dot leader
¡	&iexcl;	&#161;	inverted exclamation mark
ℑ	&image;	&#8465;	blackletter capital I = imaginary part
¿	&iquest;	&#191;	inverted question mark = turned question mark
	&lrm;	&#8206;	left-to-right mark (for formatting only)
—	&mdash;	&#8212;	em dash
–	&ndash;	&#8211;	en dash
¬	&not;	&#172;	not sign
‾	&oline;	&#8254;	overline = spacing overscore
ª	&ordf;	&#170;	feminine ordinal indicator
º	&ordm;	&#186;	masculine ordinal indicator

(X)HTML Symbols and Characters

Punctuation characters (continued)

To get this...	Type this	Or this	Description
¶	&para;	&#182;	pilcrow sign = paragraph sign
‰	&permil;	&#8240;	per mille sign
′	&prime;	&#8242;	prime = minutes = feet
″	&Prime;	&#8243;	double prime = seconds = inches
ℜ	&real;	&#8476;	blackletter capital R = real part symbol
®	&reg;	&#174;	registered sign = registered trade mark sign
	&rlm;	&#8207;	right-to-left mark (for formatting only)
§	&sect;	&#167;	section sign
	&shy;	&#173;	soft hyphen = discretionary hyphen
¹	&sup1;	&#185;	superscript one = superscript digit one
™	&trade;	&#8482;	trade mark sign
℘	&weierp;	&#8472;	script capital P = power set = Weierstrass p
„	&bdquo;	&#8222;	double low-9 quotation mark
«	&laquo;	&#171;	left-pointing double angle quotation mark = left pointing guillemet
"	&ldquo;	&#8220;	left double quotation mark
‹	&lsaquo;	&#8249;	single left-pointing angle quotation mark (see notes)
'	&lsquo;	&#8216;	left single quotation mark
»	&raquo;	&#187;	right-pointing double angle quotation mark = right pointing guillemet
"	&rdquo;	&#8221;	right double quotation mark
›	&rsaquo;	&#8250;	single right-pointing angle quotation mark (see notes)
'	&rsquo;	&#8217;	right single quotation mark
‚	&sbquo;	&#8218;	single low-9 quotation mark
			em space
			en space
			no-break space = non-breaking space
			thin space
	&zwj;	&#8205;	zero width joiner
	&zwnj;	&#8204;	zero width non-joiner

Mathematical and technical characters, (including Greek)

To get this...	Type this	Or this	Description
°	&deg;	&#176;	degree sign
÷	&divide;	&#247;	division sign
½	&frac12;	&#189;	vulgar fraction one half = fraction one half
¼	&frac14;	&#188;	vulgar fraction one quarter = fraction one quarter
¾	&frac34;	&#190;	vulgar fraction three quarters = fraction three quarters
≥	&ge;	&#8805;	greater-than or equal to
≤	&le;	&#8804;	less-than or equal to
−	&minus;	&#8722;	minus sign
²	&sup2;	&#178;	superscript two = superscript digit two = squared
³	&sup3;	&#179;	superscript three = superscript digit three = cubed
×	&times;	&#215;	multiplication sign
ℵ	&alefsym;	&#8501;	alef symbol = first transfinite cardinal (see notes)
∧	&and;	&#8743;	logical and = wedge
∠	&ang;	&#8736;	angle
≈	&asymp;	&#8776;	almost equal to = asymptotic to
∩	&cap;	&#8745;	intersection = cap
≅	&cong;	&#8773;	approximately equal to
∪	&cup;	&#8746;	union = cup
∅	&empty;	&#8709;	empty set = null set = diameter
≡	&equiv;	&#8801;	identical to
∃	&exist;	&#8707;	there exists
ƒ	&fnof;	&#402;	latin small f with hook = function = florin
∀	&forall;	&#8704;	for all
∞	&infin;	&#8734;	infinity
∫	&int;	&#8747;	integral
∈	&isin;	&#8712;	element of
⟨	&lang;	&#9001;	left-pointing angle bracket = bra (see notes)
⌈	&lceil;	&#8968;	left ceiling = apl upstile
⌊	&lfloor;	&#8970;	left floor = apl downstile
∗	&lowast;	&#8727;	asterisk operator
µ	&micro;	&#181;	micro sign
∇	&nabla;	&#8711;	nabla = backward difference
≠	&ne;	&#8800;	not equal to
∋	&ni;	&#8715;	contains as member (see notes)
∉	&notin;	&#8713;	not an element of
⊄	&nsub;	&#8836;	not a subset of
⊕	&oplus;	&#8853;	circled plus = direct sum

(X)HTML Symbols and Characters

Mathematical and technical characters, (including Greek), cont.

To get this...	Type this	Or this	Description
∨	&or;	&#8744;	logical or = vee
⊗	&otimes;	&#8855;	circled times = vector product
∂	&part;	&#8706;	partial differential
⊥	&perp;	&#8869;	up tack = orthogonal to = perpendicular
±	&plusmn;	&#177;	plus-minus sign = plus-or-minus sign
∏	&prod;	&#8719;	n-ary product = product sign (see notes)
∝	&prop;	&#8733;	proportional to
√	&radic;	&#8730;	square root = radical sign
〉	&rang;	&#9002;	right-pointing angle bracket = ket (see notes)
⌉	&rceil;	&#8969;	right ceiling
⌋	&rfloor;	&#8971;	right floor
·	&sdot;	&#8901;	dot operator (see notes)
~	&sim;	&#8764;	tilde operator = varies with = similar to (see notes)
⊂	&sub;	&#8834;	subset of
⊆	&sube;	&#8838;	subset of or equal to
∑	&sum;	&#8721;	n-ary sumation (see notes)
⊃	&sup;	&#8835;	superset of (see notes)
⊇	&supe;	&#8839;	superset of or equal to
∴	&there4;	&#8756;	therefore
A	&Alpha;	&#913;	greek capital letter alpha
α	&alpha;	&#945;	greek small letter alpha
B	&Beta;	&#914;	greek capital letter beta
β	&beta;	&#946;	greek small letter beta
X	&Chi;	&#935;	greek capital letter chi
χ	&chi;	&#967;	greek small letter chi
Δ	&Delta;	&#916;	greek capital letter delta
δ	&delta;	&#948;	greek small letter delta
E	&Epsilon;	&#917;	greek capital letter epsilon
ε	&epsilon;	&#949;	greek small letter epsilon
H	&Eta;	&#919;	greek capital letter eta
η	&eta;	&#951;	greek small letter eta
Γ	&Gamma;	&#915;	greek capital letter gamma
γ	&gamma;	&#947;	greek small letter gamma
I	&Iota;	&#921;	greek capital letter iota
ι	&iota;	&#953;	greek small letter iota
K	&Kappa;	&#922;	greek capital letter kappa

Mathematical and technical characters (including Greek), cont.

To get this...	Type this	Or this	Description
κ	&kappa;	&#954;	greek small letter kappa
Λ	&Lambda;	&#923;	greek capital letter lambda
λ	&lambda;	&#955;	greek small letter lambda
Μ	&Mu;	&#924;	greek capital letter mu
μ	&mu;	&#956;	greek small letter mu
Ν	&Nu;	&#925;	greek capital letter nu
ν	&nu;	&#957;	greek small letter nu
Ω	&Omega;	&#937;	greek capital letter omega
ω	&omega;	&#969;	greek small letter omega
Ο	&Omicron;	&#927;	greek capital letter omicron
ο	&omicron;	&#959;	greek small letter omicron
Φ	&Phi;	&#934;	greek capital letter phi
φ	&phi;	&#966;	greek small letter phi
Π	&Pi;	&#928;	greek capital letter pi
π	&pi;	&#960;	greek small letter pi
ϖ	&piv;	&#982;	greek pi symbol
Ψ	&Psi;	&#936;	greek capital letter psi
ψ	&psi;	&#968;	greek small letter psi
Ρ	&Rho;	&#929;	greek capital letter rho
ρ	&rho;	&#961;	greek small letter rho
Σ	&Sigma;	&#931;	greek capital letter sigma
σ	&sigma;	&#963;	greek small letter sigma
ς	&sigmaf;	&#962;	greek small letter final sigma (see notes)
Τ	&Tau;	&#932;	greek capital letter tau
τ	&tau;	&#964;	greek small letter tau
Θ	&Theta;	&#920;	greek capital letter theta
θ	&theta;	&#952;	greek small letter theta
ϑ	&thetasym;	&#977;	greek small letter theta symbol
ϒ	&upsih;	&#978;	greek upsilon with hook symbol
Υ	&Upsilon;	&#933;	greek capital letter upsilon
υ	&upsilon;	&#965;	greek small letter upsilon
Ξ	&Xi;	&#926;	greek capital letter xi
ξ	&xi;	&#958;	greek small letter xi
Ζ	&Zeta;	&#918;	greek capital letter zeta
ζ	&zeta;	&#950;	greek small letter zeta

Shapes and Arrows

To get this...	Type this	Or this	Description
↵	&crarr;	&#8629;	downwards arrow with corner leftwards = carriage return
↓	&darr;	&#8595;	downwards arrow
⇓	&dArr;	&#8659;	downwards double arrow
↔	&harr;	&#8596;	left right arrow
⇔	&hArr;	&#8660;	left right double arrow
←	&larr;	&#8592;	leftwards arrow
⇐	&lArr;	&#8656;	leftwards double arrow (see notes)
→	&rarr;	&#8594;	rightwards arrow
⇒	&rArr;	&#8658;	rightwards double arrow (see notes)
↑	&uarr;	&#8593;	upwards arrow
⇑	&uArr;	&#8657;	upwards double arrow
♣	&clubs;	&#9827;	black club suit = shamrock
♦	&diams;	&#9830;	black diamond suit
♥	&hearts;	&#9829;	black heart suit = valentine
♠	&spades;	&#9824;	black spade suit (see notes)
◊	&loz;	&#9674;	lozenge

Notes: **Rho:** there is no `Sigmaf`, and no U+03A2 character either; **bull:** `bullet` is *not* the same as `bullet operator`; **alefsym:** `alef` symbol is *not* the same as Hebrew letter `alef`, U+05D0 although the same glyph could be used to depict both characters; **prod:** `prod` is *not* the same character as U+03A0, `greek capital letter pi`, though the same glyph might be used for both; **sum:** `sum` is *not* the same character as U+03A3, `greek capital letter sigma` though the same glyph might be used for both; **sim:** `tilde` operator is *not* the same character as the `tilde`, U+007E, although the same glyph might be used to represent both; **sup:** note that `nsup`, (not a superset of), U+2283, is not covered by the Symbol font encoding and is not included. **sdot:** `dot` operator is *not* the same character as U+00B7, `middle dot`; **lang:** `lang` is *not* the same character as U+003C, `less than`, or U+2039, (single left-pointing angle quotation mark); **rang:** `rang` is *not* the same character as U+003E (greater than) or U+203A (single right-pointing angle quotation mark); **spades:** black here seems to mean filled as opposed to hollow; **oelig:** ligature is a misnomer, this is a separate character in some languages; **lsaquo:** `lsaquo` is proposed but not yet ISO standardized; **rsaquo:** `rsaquo` is proposed but not yet ISO standardized

The information in these tables is Copyright © 1994-2002 W3C ® (Massachusetts Institute of Technology, Institut National de Recherche en Informatique et en Automatique, Keio University), All Rights Reserved. *http://www.w3.org/Consortium/Legal/*

Hexadecimals

Hundreds $1 \times 100 = 100$
Tens $2 \times 10 = 20$
Ones $\underline{7 \times 1 = 7}$
    Total = 127

127

256's $0 \times 256 = 0$
Sixteens $7 \times 16 = 112$
Ones $\underline{F (15) \times 1 = 15}$
    Total = 127

7F

Figure E.1 *Hexadecimal numbers are base 16, that is the first digit (starting on the right) represents the ones, the second digit represents the 16's, the third digit represents the 256's, and so on.*

"Regular" numbers are based on the base 10 system, that is, there are ten symbols (what we call "numbers"): 0, 1, 2, 3, 4, 5, 6, 7, 8, and 9. To represent numbers greater than 9, we use a combination of these symbols where the first digit specifies how many *ones,* the second digit (to the left) specifies how many *tens,* and so on.

In the hexadecimal system, which is base 16, there are sixteen symbols: 0, 1, 2, 3, 4, 5, 6, 7, 8, 9, a, b, c, d, e, and f. To represent numbers greater than *f* (which in base 10 we understand as *15*), we again use a combination of symbols. This time the first digit specifies how many ones, but the second digit (again, to the left) specifies how many sixteens. Thus, 10 in the hexadecimal system means one *sixteen* and no *ones*. In the base 10 system, it'd be *16.*

In (X)HTML and CSS, hexadecimal numbers are used to define colors *(see page 46)* and to insert symbols *(see page 340).* While you can convert hexadecimal numbers by hand, I've also included a table to help you quickly look up a number's hexadecimal equivalent.

Hexadecimal Equivalents

#	Hex.	#	Hex.	#	Hex.	#	Hex.	#	Hex.	#	Hex.	#	Hex.	#	Hex.
0	00	32	20	64	40	96	60	128	80	160	A0	192	C0	224	E0
1	01	33	21	65	41	97	61	129	81	161	A1	193	C1	225	E1
2	02	34	22	66	42	98	62	130	82	162	A2	194	C2	226	E2
3	03	35	23	67	43	99	63	131	83	163	A3	195	C3	227	E3
4	04	36	24	68	44	100	64	132	84	164	A4	196	C4	228	E4
5	05	37	25	69	45	101	65	133	85	165	A5	197	C5	229	E5
6	06	38	26	70	46	102	66	134	86	166	A6	198	C6	230	E6
7	07	39	27	71	47	103	67	135	87	167	A7	199	C7	231	E7
8	08	40	28	72	48	104	68	136	88	168	A8	200	C8	232	E8
9	09	41	29	73	49	105	69	137	89	169	A9	201	C9	233	E9
10	0A	42	2A	74	4A	106	6A	138	8A	170	AA	202	CA	234	EA
11	0B	43	2B	75	4B	107	6B	139	8B	171	AB	203	CB	235	EB
12	0C	44	2C	76	4C	108	6C	140	8C	172	AC	204	CC	236	EC
13	0D	45	2D	77	4D	109	6D	141	8D	173	AD	205	CD	237	ED
14	0E	46	2E	78	4E	110	6E	142	8E	174	AE	206	CE	238	EE
15	0F	47	2F	79	4F	111	6F	143	8F	175	AF	207	CF	239	EF
16	10	48	30	80	50	112	70	144	90	176	B0	208	D0	240	F0
17	11	49	31	81	51	113	71	145	91	177	B1	209	D1	241	F1
18	12	50	32	82	52	114	72	146	92	178	B2	210	D2	242	F2
19	13	51	33	83	53	115	73	147	93	179	B3	211	D3	243	F3
20	14	52	34	84	54	116	74	148	94	180	B4	212	D4	244	F4
21	15	53	35	85	55	117	75	149	95	181	B5	213	D5	245	F5
22	16	54	36	86	56	118	76	150	96	182	B6	214	D6	246	F6
23	17	55	37	87	57	119	77	151	97	183	B7	215	D7	247	F7
24	18	56	38	88	58	120	78	152	98	184	B8	216	D8	248	F8
25	19	57	39	89	59	121	79	153	99	185	B9	217	D9	249	F9
26	1A	58	3A	90	5A	122	7A	154	9A	186	BA	218	DA	250	FA
27	1B	59	3B	91	5B	123	7B	155	9B	187	BB	219	DB	251	FB
28	1C	60	3C	92	5C	124	7C	156	9C	188	BC	220	DC	252	FC
29	1D	61	3D	93	5D	125	7D	157	9D	189	BD	221	DD	253	FD
30	1E	62	3E	94	5E	126	7E	158	9E	190	BE	222	DE	254	FE
31	1F	63	3F	95	5F	127	7F	159	9F	191	BF	223	DF	255	FF

So, to use this chart, imagine you want to find the hex value for a color with 35% red, 0% green, and 50% blue. The percentages are relative to 255, so 35% x 255 = 89. Now, find the hexadecimal equivalent of 89, near the bottom of the third column above. So for red, we have 59. Green is easy; 0 = 00. For blue, we again have to multiply the percentage by 255 to get the numerical value. 50% x 255 is 127 (more or less). Then find the hex value for 127, at the very bottom of the fourth column. So, the blue is 7F. The final step is to write it all together: #59007F, which will get us a fine dark purple, precisely 35% red, 0% green, and 50% blue.

(X)HTML Tools

The lists on the following pages are by no means exhaustive. There are literally hundreds of programs, some commercial, some shareware, and some freeware, of varying quality, that you can use as you design and create your Web pages. If you don't find what you're looking for on these pages, jump to any search service on the Web (e.g., *www.google.com*) and look for *Web tools*, *Web graphics*, or whatever it is you need.

(X)HTML Editors

You can use *any* text editor to write (X)HTML, including SimpleText or TeachText on the Macintosh, WordPad for Windows, or vi in Unix systems. The (X)HTML code produced with these simpler programs is no different from the (X)HTML produced by more complex (X)HTML editors.

A simple text editor is like the most basic SLR 35 mm camera. You have to set your f-stop and aperture manually, and then focus before shooting. The dedicated (X)HTML editors are point-and-shoot cameras: just aim and fire, for a price. They are more expensive, and generally less flexible.

What (X)HTML editors offer	Disadvantages of (X)HTML editors
Dedicated (X)HTML editors offer the following advantages over simple text editors (of course, not every (X)HTML editor has every feature): • they insert opening and closing tags with a single click • they check and verify syntax in your (X)HTML and CSS • they allow you to add attributes by clicking buttons instead of typing words in a certain order in a certain place in the document • they offer varying degrees of WYSIWYG display of your Web page • they correct mistakes in existing (X)HTML pages • they make it easy to use special characters • they color code elements, attributes, and values, making them easy to edit	These extra features come at a price, however. Some things that may annoy you about (X)HTML editors is that • they don't all support the full (X)HTML or CSS specs 100% • they are more difficult to learn, and less intuitive than they promise • they cost money (all simple text editors are included free with their respective system software) • they use up more space on disk and more memory • some add proprietary information (like *their* name, for example), and tags to the (X)HTML document • some eliminate tags that they don't understand—even if the tags are part of the standard (X)HTML specifications

(X)HTML Editors

WYSIWYG		
Macromedia Dreamweaver (M, W)	$400. Probably the most popular editor among Web professionals.	*http://www.macromedia.com/ software/dreamweaver/* demo available
Adobe GoLive (M,W)	$400. Formerly GoLive Cyber-Studio. Dreamweaver's main competition.	*http://www.adobe.com/ prodindex/golive/main.html* demo available
NetObjects Fusion (M, W)	$150. NetObjects WYSIWYG editor for professional Web masters.	*http://www.netobjects.com/ products/html/nof.html* demo available
Microsoft FrontPage (M, W)	$170. WYSIWYG Editor from Microsoft Corporation.	*http://www.microsoft.com/ frontpage/* (FrontPage Express included with Office; demo also available)
Netscape Composer	Much improved editor included free with Netscape Communicator.	*http://home.netscape.com/*
Corel HoTMetaL (M, W)	$100, WYSIWYG editor that creates standard, universal (X)HTML and XML. Formerly from Softquad.	*http://www.hotmetalpro.com/* demo available
Text Based		
BBEdit (M)	$120. Excellent HTML editor from Bare Bones Software. The most popular non-WYSIWYG HTML editor.	*http://www.barebones.com* demo available
HotDog Professional (W)	$100, Sausage Software. "Express" version also available.	*http://www.sausage.com/*
Macromedia HomeSite (W)	$100. Formerly Allaire HomeSite. Popular text-based HTML editor for Windows, now included free with Dreamweaver.	*http://www.macromedia.com/ software/homesite/*
World Wide Web Weaver (M, W)	$60, Miracle Software.	*http://www.miracleinc.com/ Products/W4*

(X)HTML Editors

Images and Graphics

Name	Description	URL
Yahoo	List of sites with graphics	*http://dir.yahoo.com/Arts/Design_Arts/Graphic_Design/Web_Page_Design_and_Layout/Graphics/*
Lycos Picture Gallery	Searchable database of images and sounds	*http://www.lycos.com/picturethis/*
Google	Site that searches the Web for images that fit your criteria	*http://images.google.com* or go to *http://www.google.com* and click the Images button

Graphics Tools

Name	Description	URL
Adobe Photoshop (M, W)	$600. Excellent, all-purpose image editing program. Version 7 includes Image-Ready, Adobe's Web graphics program	*http://www.adobe.com/prodindex/photoshop/main.html* demo available
Adobe Photoshop Elements (M, W)	$100. A remarkably robust, consumer-end version of the excellent Adobe Photoshop	*http://www.adobe.com/products/photoshopel/main.html*
Macromedia Fireworks	$300. A specialized graphics program for creating Web images	*http://www.macromedia.com/software/fireworks/* demo available
Macromedia Flash	$500. Designed for creating Web animations.	*http://www.macromedia.com/software/flash/* demo available
Paint Shop Pro (W)	$100. Jasc Software. Powerful image editing program for Windows. Commercial and shareware versions available. Supports JPEG, PNG, GIF.	*http://www.jasc.com/products/psp/* demo available
GraphicConverter (M)	$35. Thorsten Lemke's image editor for Macintosh. Reads and writes an incredible array of graphics formats, including Progressive JPEG, GIF89a (Animated), etc.	*http://www.graphicconverter.net/* demo available
LView Pro (W)	$40. Popular shareware graphics program.	*http://www.lview.com*

Images and Graphics

Index

Symbols

Index

file names *32*
  and uppercase letters and symbols *55*
  problems with *401*
  See also file extensions
File scheme, in URLs *33*
files
  compressing *125*
  creating new *49*
  making available for download *125*
  organizing *55*
  transferring to AOL *412–413*
  transferring to server *408–413*
  uploading *279*
  working with *47–57*
Fireworks. *See* Macromedia Fireworks
`:first-child` pseudo-element *140*
`:first-letter` pseudo-element *142–143*
`:first-line` pseudo-element *142–143*
fixed positioning *180*
Flash animations, embedding *307*
Flash. *See* Macromedia Flash
flavors of (X)HTML *38*
`float` property *194–195*
floating elements
  with styles *194–195*
  and width *191*
  with (X)HTML *110*
floating frames. *See* inline frames
flow, and CSS *177*
`:focus` pseudo-class *141*
`font` element *346*
`font-family` property *158, 159*
`font` property *165*
`font-size` property *162*
`font-style` property *160*
`font-variant` property *173*
`font-weight` property *161*
fonts
  choosing *158, 165*
  with (X)HTML *346*
  common *158*
  embedding *159*
  monospaced *76*
  size *162–163*
  with (X)HTML *344, 346*
  small caps *173*
  variants *173*
footnotes *80*
`for` attribute, in `label` element *288*
foreground colors *184*
foreign language Web pages *333–342*
`form` element *269*
form hosting services *271*

formats
  choosing appropriate *90*
  images *84–88*
  Text Document *50*
  Text Only *50*
  Web pages *50*
  See also encodings, character
formatting
  aligning with styles *171*
  background color *167, 354*
  blinking text *174, 351*
  bold *74, 161, 165*
  case *172*
  color *166, 167, 344–349*
  fonts *76, 77, 158, 159, 165, 344–347*
  indents *169*
  italics *74, 160, 165*
  kerning *168*
  line height *164, 165*
  link color *141, 349*
  link labels *119*
  logical *74*
  monospaced fonts *76, 77*
  overlining *174*
  physical *74*
  preformatted text *77*
  size *75, 162–163, 165, 344, 346*
  small caps *173*
  strike out *81, 350*
  subscripts *80*
  superscripts *80*
  testing *398*
  text *73–82, 157–174, 343–351*
  tracking *168*
  underlining *81, 174, 350*
  with (X)HTML *350*
  white space *170*
  See also style sheets
forms *263–292*
  active images *286*
  and CGI scripts *264*
  and tables *269*
  bullets *273*
  buttons *282*
    with image *283*
  centering *356*
  CGI script included with this book *267*
  checkboxes *275*
  default values *284*
  disabling elements *291*
  e-mailing data *270*
  free-form text *272*
  getting scripts *266*
  grouping options *277*
  hidden fields *281*
  keeping elements from being changed *292*
  keyboard shortcuts *290*
  labeling areas *287*
  labeling parts *288*

  menus *276*
  organizing elements *287*
  password boxes *273*
  radio buttons *274*
  reset button *284–285*
  sending data via e-mail *270*
  structure of *269*
  submit buttons *282–283*
  submitting with image *286*
  tab order *289*
  text areas *278*
  text blocks *278*
  text boxes *272*
  uploading files *279*
  using form hosting service *271*
  using script from book *267*
  WML *384–385*
foundation of Web page, creating *62*
`frame` attribute, in `table` element *237*
`frame` element *242*
`frameborder` attribute, in `frameset` or `frame` element *253*
frames *241–262*
  allocating space *243*
  alternatives to *259–261*
  and `body` element *243*
  and search engines *426*
  asterisks *243*
  borders
    colors *251*
    eliminating *252*
    showing/hiding *253*
    thickness *252*
  changing multiple with one link *326*
  control over resizing *254*
  definition *241*
  DOCTYPE declaration for *243*
  escaping from *256*
  floating *248*
  hash mark *254*
  in columns *244*
  inline *248*
  keeping in framesets *327*
  making more accessible *262*
  margins *249*
  naming *242*
  problems in Netscape 4.x *403*
  scroll bars *250*
  special links *256*
  specifying URL *242*
  tabbing to links *127*
  tables of contents *241*
  targeted with links *255–257*
  turning off *256*
  viewing (X)HTML *57*
  width *244*
  with rows and columns *245*
  See also framesets

Index

Index

Colophon:

I wrote and laid out this book entirely in Adobe FrameMaker 5.5. I could never have done any of the cross references, figure numbering, and especially the index without it. If you're curious about Frame (or indexing), drop me a line. I'm geeky enough to like to talk about it.

I viewed the examples on all major browsers on both platforms. I used Virtual PC to run Windows right in my Mac. I took screen captures with Snapz (Macintosh) and then cleaned them up with Adobe Photoshop 7. I used Adobe Illustrator (version 6!) to create the line drawings. The font faces in this book are various weights of Garamond and Futura.

Except for the ones in other people's Web sites (obviously), and the nice illustration in Figure 14.2 on page 216 by Andreu Cabré, the photos and drawings in this book are of my own creation, though I'm sometimes embarrassed to admit it.